Research in Networked Learning

Series Editors:

Vivien Hodgson
David McConnell

For further volumes:
http://www.springer.com/series/11810

Vivien Hodgson • Maarten de Laat
David McConnell • Thomas Ryberg
Editors

The Design, Experience and Practice of Networked Learning

 Springer

Editors

Vivien Hodgson
Department of Management
  Learning and Leadership
Lancaster University
  Management School
Lancaster University
Lancaster, United Kingdom

David McConnell
Port of Menteith
Stirling, United Kingdom

Maarten de Laat
Welten Institute, Research Center
  for Learning, Teaching
  and Technology
Open University
Heerlen, The Netherlands

Thomas Ryberg
Department of Communication
  and Psychology
Aalborg University
Aalborg, Denmark

ISBN 978-3-319-01939-0   ISBN 978-3-319-01940-6 (eBook)
DOI 10.1007/978-3-319-01940-6
Springer Cham Heidelberg New York Dordrecht London

Library of Congress Control Number: 2013956135

Printed on acid-free paper

Springer is part of Springer Science+Business Media (www.springer.com)

Contents

Contributors

Nina Bonderup Dohn Department of Design and Communication, University of Southern Denmark, Kolding, Denmark

Janne Gleerup Roskilde University, Roskilde, Denmark

Mariette de Haan Faculty of Social and Behavioral Sciences, Utrecht University, Utrecht, The Netherlands

John Hannon La Trobe Learning and Teaching, La Trobe University, Melbourne, VIC, Australia

Simon Heilesen Roskilde University, Roskilde, Denmark

Niels Henrik Helms University College Zealand, Sorø, Denmark

Vivien Hodgson Department of Management Learning and Leadership, Lancaster University Management School, Lancaster Univeristy, Lancaster, UK

Brian Holmes European Commission's Executive Agency for Education, Audiovisual and Culture (EACEA), Brussels, Belgium

Juliette Hommes Department of Educational Development and Research, Faculty of Health Medicine and Life Sciences, Maastricht University, Maastricht, The Netherlands

Maarten de Laat Welten Institute, Research Center for Learning, Teaching and Technology, Open University, Heerlen, The Netherlands

Kevin Leander Department of Teaching & Learning, Vanderbilt University, Nashville, TN, USA

David McConnell Independent higher education consultant, Stirling, Scotland, UK

Kevin Mogensen Department of Psychology and Educational Research, Roskilde University, Roskilde, Denmark

Nuria Hernandez Nanclares Faculty of Economics, University of Oviedo, Oviedo, Spain

Hanne Westh Nicolajsen Aalborg University, Copenhagen, Denmark

Gale Parchoma University of Calgary, Calgary, AB, Canada

Linda Perriton The York Management School, University of York, York, UK

Michael Reynolds Lancaster University Management School, Lancaster University, Lancaster, UK

Bart Rienties Department of Higher Education, University of Surrey, Guildford, UK

Thomas Ryberg Department of Communication and Psychology, Aalborg University, Aalborg, Denmark

Bieke Schreurs LOOK, Open Universiteit, Heerlen, The Netherlands

Uzair Shah Department of Management Learning & Leadership, Lancaster University Management School, Lancaster, UK

Julie-Ann Sime Department of Educational Research, Centre for Technology Enhanced Learning, Lancaster University, Lancashire, UK

Asli Ünlüsoy Faculty of Social and Behavioral Sciences, Utrecht University, Utrecht, The Netherlands

Koen Veermans Department of Teacher Education, Centre for Learning Research, University of Turku, Turku, Finland

Richard Walker E-Learning Development Team, University of York, York, UK

Steve Wright Faculty of Health and Medicine, Furness College, Lancaster University, Lancaster, UK

Chapter 1
Researching Design, Experience and Practice of Networked Learning: An Overview

Vivien Hodgson, Maarten de Laat, David McConnell, and Thomas Ryberg

Introduction

The chapters in this book are a selection of reworked and peer-reviewed papers presented at the 2012 Networked Learning Conference held in Maastricht, The Netherlands. Each chapter brings a particular perspective to the themes of "design", "experience" and "practice" of networked learning, which we have chosen as the focus of the book. In this introductory chapter, we explore how networked learning has developed in recent years followed by a summary of the research presented across the book's chapters.

We conclude by discussing four main themes that have emerged from our reading of the chapters and which we believe are important in taking forward the theory of networked learning. They are as follows: practice as epistemology; the coupling of learning contexts (that is, the relationship and connection of learning contexts and spaces); the agency and active role of technology within networked learning; and the messy, often chaotic and always political nature of the design, experience and practice of networked learning.

V. Hodgson (✉)
Department of Management Learning and Leadership, Lancaster University
Management School, Lancaster University, Lancaster, UK
e-mail: v.hodgson@lancaster.ac.uk

M. de Laat
Welten Institute, Research Center for Learning, Teaching and Technology,
Open University, Heerlen, The Netherlands
e-mail: maarten.delaat@ou.nl

D. McConnell
Independent higher education consultant, Stirling, Scotland, UK
e-mail: davidmcconnell01@gmail.com

T. Ryberg
Department of Communication and Psychology, Aalborg University, Aalborg, Denmark
e-mail: ryberg@hum.aau.dk

V. Hodgson et al. (eds.), *The Design, Experience and Practice of Networked Learning*,
Research in Networked Learning, DOI 10.1007/978-3-319-01940-6_1,
© Springer International Publishing Switzerland 2014

Since its inception in 1998, the Networked Learning Conference has placed a high value on research that focuses on both the practice of learning and teaching in networked environments and on theoretical issues that have relevance to our understanding of these practices. Papers presented at the conference have covered a wide spectrum of theoretical and practice issues and concerns and have made a substantive contribution to our understanding of how learning and teaching take place in these environments. In the early conferences, the focus was initially on higher education, with some contributions from the field of continuing education. Today, some 15 years on, the conference embraces a wide field of educational areas including those of informal learning, work-based learning, continuing professional development (CPD), academic staff development, and management learning—as well as higher education (both at the undergraduate and postgraduate levels).

Since the first Networked Learning Conference, we have also seen an exponential growth in the use of information and communication technologies in learning and teaching. The popularisation of Web 2.0 and the plethora of social networking tools and environments have in some ways shaped the face of networked learning, strongly influencing the pedagogical and socio-technical design of learning and teaching practices. Consequently in this book many authors have revisited central tenets, beliefs and pedagogies such as the oft quoted definition of networked learning as being "learning in which information and communication technology (ICT) is used to promote connections: between one learner and other learners; between learners and tutors; between a learning community and its learning resources" (Goodyear, Banks, Hodgson, & McConnell, 2004, p. 1). We are energised by the prospect that Web 2.0 and social networking technologies have the potential to lead to innovative designs in learning and teaching, which in turn leads many of the contributors to this book to reconsider, redefine and broaden their interpretation of networked learning. However, within networked learning learners have always been seen as proactive, engaging agents: they bring agency to what they do, and many chapters in this volume show that they are acknowledged producers rather than consumers of knowledge.

Although the way in which we think about the nature of networked learning and its underpinning pedagogical values and beliefs has broadened in the past years, it is fair to say that there is still a shared view on this, which is that networked learning can be seen to be derived from critical and humanistic traditions (e.g. those of Dewey, 1916; Freire, 1970; Mead, 1934) and that learning is social, takes place in communities and networks, is a shared practice, involves negotiation and requires collaborative dialogue (Hodgson, McConnell, & Dirckinck-Holmfeld, 2012). Many of the chapters in this volume and in the previous volume in the Research in Networked Learning Book Series (Dirckinck Holmfeld, Hodgson, & McConnell, 2012) testify to this shared view. The chapters in this volume explore new and innovative ways of thinking about the nature of networked learning and its pedagogical values and beliefs. They pose a challenge to us to reflect on what we thought networked learning was 15 year ago, where it is today and where it is likely to be headed.

The emergence of social practice theories together with sociomaterial perspectives challenges previously held views of learning and knowledge and how we think about networked learning. In the previous volume of the Networked Learning Book Series, some consideration was given to this in the final chapter (Hodgson et al., 2012) where networked learning was described as striving to transcend the dualism between abstract mind and concrete material social practice. The issue of separating theory from practice was noted. Practice is seen as epistemic—a way of seeing or acting—and it was claimed that networked learning exists within practice.

We return to this theme of epistemology and "practice" in the current volume of the Networked Learning Book Series. The authors of the selection of papers from the 2012 conference discuss the notion and role of practice within their networked learning research. In this introductory chapter we have brought together the papers in three sections, each highlighting a particular aspect of practice. The first of the sections focuses on the relationship between design and its influence on how networked learning practices are implemented. The second section extends this discussion by raising the notion of experiencing networked learning practices. Here the expected and unexpected effects of design and its implementation are scrutinised. These chapters elegantly indicate the lessons we can learn from the discrepancies between the intended and actual practices. The third and final section draws attention to a growing topic of interest within networked learning: that of networked learning in informal practices. It raises the question of how networked learning practices emerge and what we can learn from this for improving design and experience of networked learning. Additionally, we provide a reflection on the theories, methods and settings featured in the networked learning research of the chapters before concluding with a discussion of the four themes that emerged from our reading of the chapters.

Section 1: Networked Learning Spaces and Context: Design and Practice

The four chapters in this section each contribute to, and seek to extend, existing understanding and ideas about networked learning. More specifically they examine and discuss the way we think about, create and design networked learning spaces. The four chapters each add to the question of design, ranging from the perspective of the teacher's experience and prior exposure to the use of learning technology to the role and social materiality of a learning environment and other nonhuman network objects. Also considered is the significance of the learner's primary context and the importance of coupling practice contexts of where they live and work to the learning context of the education institution where they study.

In addition the chapters by both Nina Bonderup Dohn and by Janne Gleerup, Simon Heilesen, Niels Henrik Helms and Kevin Mogensen question the limitations of the existing definition of networked learning. They suggest that, as currently defined, networked learning does not address the importance of connecting learning contexts or, to use the term adopted by Gleerup et al., the coupling of learning contexts. Dohn argues much of the existing literature, while talking about and claiming to take a social practice theory perspective to learning design, rarely offers activities or designs that actually engage with practice as experienced by the learner in their primary (lived) context. More often than not, she suggests, learners are invited to participate in standalone activities that have no direct relation to their everyday practice or primary context. Consequently such activities always have the potential to be experienced at worse as meaningless or at best only of academic relevance.

The separation of study or learning context from the work or practice context that is often experienced by students is addressed directly in the chapter by Gleerup et al. They propose adopting a user-driven innovation model for the design of networked learning spaces to overcome this. They adopt the user-centred design approach developed by Halonen (2010) to demonstrate how involvement of the end users in the design of the spaces of a networked learning environment can enhance the coupling of the two diverse contexts of a vocational college and the organisations in which students do their work placements.

However, no matter how much we reflect on and aim to bring new ideas into the way we design networked learning spaces, other factors are also at play. John Hannon's chapter is a salutary reminder that the implementation of networked learning, particularly within the context of higher education, is often undermined by more dominant and persuasive networks to that of educators and pedagogical practitioners. As Hannon comments in his chapter, arrangements for learning are a central concern for universities and thus often a site of contention and difference.

If networked learning is to become seen as a pedagogy that is central to the arrangements for learning, we clearly need to understand more about how learning environments come to be assembled as well as the everyday and prior experiences and concerns of those who use and occupy them. In their different ways the four chapters in this section each contribute to a process of either opening up or revealing more—in actor-network terms—of the black box effects upon implementing and designing networked learning spaces that support both reflective practice and situated learning in a learner's primary context.

The final chapter in this section, by Uzair Shah, brings the focus back onto the teacher and their lived previous and current experiences of using learning technology. Teachers' qualitative experience of using learning technology in their learning and teaching practice has surprisingly often been overlooked in networked learning research. As Shah points out, quoting Boon and Sinclair (2012), most lecturers and teachers still have one foot in the real and one foot in the virtual and consequently are having to come to terms with both the difference and disquiet this creates for them. Shah's study is all the more interesting in that it is situated in the experience of teachers working in a Southern Asian University in Pakistan and thus giving us insights, not previously available, into the way teachers in that part of the world experience, think about and use learning technology in their everyday teaching and learning practice. Understanding teachers' experiences of learning technology, Shah argues, will help us to better understand the oft-noted resistance from university staff to the greater adoption and use of technology and networked learning spaces specifically in their own teaching and learning practice. Some of the other main points made in each of the four chapters are further described below.

Dohn in her chapter, "Implications for Networked Learning of the 'Practice' Side of Social Practice Theories—a Tacit-knowledge Perspective", makes the point that we should not be putting in place arrangements that offer networked learning as if it is a primary context (and space) for learning unless this is a clear intention of the pedagogical design that is worked with during the course. She argues: "networked learning will in general be most successful if it is designed as 'mediator' activities' to facilitate the resituating of content between the 'primary contexts' of the learners, rather than to act as a 'primary context' itself".

Primary contexts, she explains, are contexts that carry significance for an individual's learning, in which they involve themselves as persons and which they consider important for whom they are. This view of primary contexts aligns with a view of learning that complements that which was discussed in Hodgson et al. (2012), who stated that the ontology of networked learning includes a belief "in the importance of focusing on making sense from one's own personal experiences and view of the world—or indeed one's own practice".

However, as already mentioned, Dohn argues most examples of networked learning found in the literature seldom engage with practice as experienced by the learner in their primary context. Instead, in her view, the "doing" of learning activities in networked learning is biased in the direction of verbal activity or doing and "practice" that favours "linguistic practice" with an over emphasis on reflection on practice. She would prefer to see a greater recognition of the importance of mediator activities where meaning is embedded in activities people undertake in given contexts and are understood in terms of the meaning they embody in those contexts. Meaning, Dohn claims from a social practice theory perspective, is created and negotiated in activity rather than in linguistic practice or through reflecting on practice. The latter two being aspects that she believes currently dominate the design of most networked learning courses and programmes at the expense of a context dependent and embodied material understanding of practice.

Dohn, not unlike Gleerup et al. in their chapter, also talks about the usefulness of coupling of contexts. In their chapter "Designing for Learning in Coupled Contexts", Gleerup et al. give a detailed example of an experiment in designing for net-based vocational learning where the aim was to provide a coupling between the widely different learning contexts that, in their case, electrician apprentices were exposed to during their vocational education. Previously the apprentices had reported disconnect between what they learnt in college and what they had to do and what they learnt during their in-service training during work placements.

Also, similar in some respects to Dohn in the previous chapter, they point out that the existing main definitions of networked learning do not encompass learning across intra and inter-organisational boundaries. Networked learning, they suggest, not only offers the opportunity to connect with resources and others within an institutional framework as part of an educational programme but also with others and resources that are part of other organisations and contexts.

As already mentioned, the design process used in their work is based on a recently developed method for user-driven innovation and the "quadrant model"—design process set up to involve all potential users. In their case it involved the apprentices, teachers, masters and journeymen from companies, all as active and equal cocreators of the new pedagogical designs, the final outcome being three designs for networked learning that facilitated communication between apprentice and apprentice, between college and apprentice and between apprentice and master/journeyman. As the chapter explains, the apprentices reported that the three designs (a) facilitate community building, (b) help bring the college into the practice environment and (c) encourage reflection on one's own practice. The benefit of adopting the proposed user-centred design, the authors claim, is that it assigns learners a more active and responsible role as co-contributors in the design of their own education and learning spaces.

However, Hannon in his chapter, "Making the Right Connections: Implementing the Objects of Practice into a Network for Learning", reminds us that design is a political as well as pedagogical process. He uses the lens and perspective of actor-network theory (ANT) to analyse the implementation of a new virtual learning environment at his institution. His ANT approach allows him to show the subtle way that the processes of implementation can come to omit networked learning ideas and spaces. The interactions of the social material and the actor networks involved in implementing an institutional learning environment lead to the discourse and the everyday objects of the more dominant networks of the information technologists and project managers to dominate the process and decisions made. The various human and nonhuman actors in these dominant networks render incrementally and imperceptibly as marginal or invisible the discourse, objects and wishes of actors in the pedagogical network. Consequently the networked learning pedagogical approach to practice and design of learning environments does not figure as an important feature in what becomes implemented. These pedagogical actors become, as a result, assigned to the role of activists and/or mavericks who usurp and develop ways to circumvent at an individual level the pedagogical constraints inherent in the resultant institutional learning environment, with its absence of networked learning spaces for learning.

This said, as Shah shows us in his chapter "Teachers' Use of Learning Technology in a South-Asian context", most teachers are neither activists nor mavericks when it comes to using learning technology. Indeed his study showed that the way teachers in a University in Pakistan chose to adopt and use technology in their own practice was influenced by their own prior exposure to learning technology. In addition it was influenced by how they perceived the scope of technology for pedagogical purposes. The teachers who were most likely to experience technology as important in their learning and teaching practice tended to be those who adopted a research-led approach to teaching and saw technology key to keeping abreast with the latest research and thinking.

Shah's research could be seen as specific to the experience of the non-western teachers interviewed in his study. However, much of what he found is recognisable in the experience and practices of most university teachers in most contexts. Shah's research also illuminates the same messy contextual realities referred to in other chapters in the book. He found that the contextual realities which teachers encounter influence their use of learning technology and their pedagogical practices—a finding that could as easily apply to any educational setting once it is acknowledged the contextual realities will vary and differ for each individual setting or context. Shah suggests that only the teachers with the most sophisticated and broadest experience and understanding of learning technology can be expected to find the transition to a networked learning environment and spaces easy.

Summary

An overall message that emerges from these four chapters is the importance, when designing networked learning spaces, of considering networked learning as a way to connect with the different contexts of the learner. Various suggestions are made as to how this might be achieved through the use of social learning spaces created for this purpose or by networked learning-mediated activities that connect back to the learner's primary context. Secondly, the chapters remind us of the political nature and messiness of the contextual realities of both teachers and learners. It is important to be mindful and aware of this when designing, introducing and implementing networked learning. This equally applies to university and education managers, policymakers and the like as it does to teaching staff and learners. It is important to remember that implementing pedagogical changes and institutional learning environments is always a political process first and only secondly pedagogical. The research discussed in this section, however, not only alerts us to such issues and their importance to the design of networked learning spaces but also offers some conceptual tools and ideas to assist us to take more account of them when designing and implementing networked learning.

Section 2: Networked Learning in Practice: The Expected and Unexpected

In the previous section we introduced those chapters that discuss and develop issues and concepts related to the way we think about, create and design networked learning spaces. The chapters introduced in this section examine networked learning designs as experienced in practice.

The chapters explore how different networked learning settings were designed and what was expected from those designs. They then proceed to reflect and report on how emergent behaviours, interactions, events and new tools for learning come to shape the learning process and call for continuous renegotiations and realignments between tutors, teachers and students. A major theme in this section is the exploration of the dynamics and discrepancies between intentions and actual practice—or between the expected and unexpected. The chapters thus reflect and extend previous discussions within networked learning on the notion of "indirect design" (Goodyear, Jones, Asensio, Hodgson, & Steeples, 2001; Jones & Dirckinck-Holmfeld, 2009). This concept entails that learning cannot be designed, but only designed for, and that learning occurs as an emergent, dynamic property of the interactions between the expected or designed and then the situated activities and practices of teachers and learners. This point was equally made in the previous section where an emergent theme is the political nature and messiness of the contextual realities of both teachers and learners. The chapters in this section remind us how productive networked learning is rooted in deliberate and reflexive designs, but equally how learning is an organic process occurring in complex socio-technical infrastructures or ecologies where interpersonal relations, new tools and pedagogies need to be interpreted and made sense of by both learners and facilitators. This seems to raise questions about how well our current theories, conceptualisations and frameworks within networked learning are attuned to the "messiness" and "situated improvisations" of actual learning practices.

Secondly, the chapters in this section explore and challenge notions and boundaries of small-group learning. While all the chapters operate with small groups in their designs or conceptualisations as their point of departure, they also challenge and question the exclusiveness of tightly knit, collaborative orchestrations of learning—either by exploring and presenting alternative designs that seek to leverage more fluid, networked interactions among groups or student cohorts or by critically addressing assumptions about "participation", "collaboration" and "community" in groups. Thus, the chapters reflect and extend discussions of groups and networks or weak and strong ties as different, but not mutually exclusive, orchestrations of learning. This has been a theme in a number of publications on networked learning (Dirckinck Holmfeld et al., 2012; Dirckinck-Holmfeld, Jones, & Lindström, 2009; Jones, Ferreday, & Hodgson, 2008; Ryberg, Buus, & Georgsen, 2012; Ryberg & Larsen, 2008) and also of lively debates as part of the Networked Learning Hot Seat Seminars (Haythornthwaite & de Laat, 2010). In these chapters, these different orchestrations are not treated as oppositional or dichotomous, but rather the chapters explore the relations and transitions between various forms of engagement between the learners and between learners and facilitators. In addition, they also further a line of critical enquiry into some of the core values of networked learning such as community, participation and collaboration and how these in practice might also lead to exclusion, alienation and anxiety in groups or cohorts of learners (Ferreday & Hodgson, 2010; Hodgson & Reynolds, 2005).

In their chapter "Here be Dragons: Approaching Difficult Group Issues in Networked Learning", Linda Perriton and Michael Reynolds critically explore issues of facilitation and moderation in group work or learning communities.

They argue how networked learning theorists and practitioners often advocate for "participative designs", "collaborative" approaches or "learning communities". These are approaches that involve complex interpersonal, social, cultural and/or political dimensions of collective endeavours and, as Perriton and Reynolds point out, can be difficult and anxiety inducing for both facilitators and learners. They state that there has been less theoretical work done in relation to such social, cultural and interpersonal dimensions in the facilitation of online groups than in non-virtual education and more so in terms of developing practical guidelines for online group work dynamics. As they put it "even the most experienced facilitators can be surprised by their own emotional and psychological reaction to group dynamics and what is sometimes experienced as the chore of having to facilitate them". They argue that the theoretical models facilitators hold in order to understand group dynamics and to intervene in a thoughtful way is an important, but often unacknowledged point of difference between staff working on the same programme. Therefore, the aim of their chapter is to provide a set of questions or guidelines that are helpful to educators in programmes with group work or participatory pedagogies at their core but who find that guidance on the facilitation of complex social processes is limited. Another important point is the authors' observation of how inherent values reflected in a "participative" networked learning design can themselves be troublesome. They argue that often implicit expectations or values of the "ideal learner", as consensual or collaborative, can be problematic or even oppressive for some participants. The chapter carries us forward by providing a reflexive set of questions, which takes as its point of departure the "complex messiness" and reality of collaborative engagements. Rather than being a prescriptive guide for how to do effective online facilitation, the authors encourage facilitators and learners to reflect on their own values and interpretative frameworks in making sense of group processes.

From interpersonal dynamics in groups, we move to relations and exchanges between groups. In the chapter "Understanding Emerging Knowledge Spillovers in Small-Group Learning Settings: A Networked Learning Perspective" by Bart Rienties, Nuria Hernandez Nanclares, Juliette Hommes and Koen Veermans, the authors explore knowledge spillovers between groups. They suggest that students not only learn from their group members but also from network connections outside their group. This is what they refer to as knowledge spillovers. The authors seek to understand how people learn from others and how these knowledge spillovers emerge in small-group learning settings by combining perspectives of collaborative learning, computer-supported collaborative learning and networked learning as an integrated theory. Through what they term a (dynamic) social network analysis (SNA) of learning networks in two case studies, they trace how collaborative groups developed knowledge spillovers with other groups over time and the strength of interdependency within the group (inter- and intra-group collaboration). They show how these spillovers emerge and strengthen over time and how, in one of the cases, the learning links outside the formal group structures become more pronounced than learning links within the formal groups. However, they also point to very different patterns of knowledge exchange and group cohesion or interdependency (intra- and intergroup) in the two cases. While in both cases "collaboration" and "group work" were part of the learning design, the authors show how, in one of the cases, the learning networks at the group level appear to be absent or relatively weak and to be more dependent on existing friendship relationships among the wider networks of the students. Based on their SNA of the two case studies, they go on to discuss how teachers can create stronger group interdependencies to encourage knowledge spillovers.

Rienties et al. present an analytic framework grounded in SNA that can help us trace and visualise relations, intensity and interdependencies within and between groups in terms of knowledge exchange. More interesting though, is the authors discussions of how the different pedagogical designs, particularly in terms of assessment, might have influenced these patterns, as they highlight that the case with the weakest intra-group interdependencies was based in a design featuring a stronger focus on individual assessment, rather than group assessment. These observations in many ways corroborate existing theory (and empirical studies) of group work. However, such analyses can help us see how different networked learning designs might impact on the forms of collaboration and interdependencies in and between groups (or in networks). Further it can highlight variation at a different level of scale, which could call for more detailed studies of what might be the explanations for this variation.

Much related to knowledge spillovers, we find in the third chapter a conscious effort to design a networked learning experience, where students are expected to function both in smaller groups and as networked collectives that bridge and work across the smaller groups. In the chapter "Changing the Rules of the Game—Using Blogs for Online Discussions in Higher Education", Hanne Westh Nicolajsen explores how Web 2.0 technologies were employed as an interwoven part of an on-campus course with the intent of students becoming more active, self-driven peer-learners and co-teachers. In analysing feedback and interactions from the course, she argues how Web 2.0 tools and practices challenge current norms for both students and teachers with regard to distribution of control and responsibilities, writing styles, authenticity, quality assurance, and the blurring of the border between university and private life. Also Nicolajsen explores how existing student relations seem to influence the interactions among students to a worrying degree, while at the same time opening up to students the possibility of viewing each other's competences differently than before. In the chapter Nicolajsen raises a number of interesting contradictions and tensions, which arise when adopting Web 2.0 technologies and practices into a course. Much in line with Ross (2012), she explores how the adoption of blogs creates tensions around style and form. Students were asked to use self-chosen discussion spaces (they all chose blogs) from where they wanted to contribute to collaborative and theoretical discussions. However, many of the students from the outset mainly understood blogs as a medium for individual and personal reflections. Similarly, there were tensions around whether blogs would imply a more "informal" tone or should be more "academic" and thus in many ways appeared as an "in-between" between more well-known styles. Finally, Nicolajsen raises an interesting point regarding peer commenting and peer valuation of "good" contributions, showing how some student posts received massive attention, while others were neglected, and how the dynamics between these valorisations may be blurry to both teachers and students—possibly, partly depending on existing relationships, popularity or reputation of students and/or partly delegated by the algorithms of Facebook's news feed stream (who sees what content from whom). Nicolajsen, however, also shows how new roles are shaped for students that might not previously have been considered "active" or "knowledgeable". There are, however, some potentially important issues when adopting pedagogies that use peer commenting and transparency between students where, in Nicolajsen's words, some students see the semipublic conversations as a way to show off and others, as a public humiliation. This point speaks back into the chapter by Perriton and Reynolds and pushes us to ask how we might handle and facilitate social interactions within and beyond the smaller group but also how the unbeknownst dynamics and affordances of the many openly available, but commercial, social media tools might affect the interaction.

The final chapter of this section "Blended Problem-Based Learning: Designing Collaboration Opportunities for Unguided Group Research Through the Use of Web 2.0 tools" by Richard Walker explores the challenges of designing a networked approach to problem-based learning (PBL). The approach sought to encourage students to engage in collaborative and interdependent learning online. The chapter reports on a blended design following a PBL curriculum that introduced group wiki and blogging tools for students to use in a series of unguided group research activities. The chapter looks at the reception of the study methods and the effectiveness of the web tools in supporting the unguided group research tasks. It reveals a positive reception for the learning methods along with evidence of higher-order thinking and reflective skills. Walker also found that contributions gradually evolved from "one-shot" postings of solutions to becoming critiques of peer contributions and revision of original posts. However, the study equally highlights the challenges for instructional support to address students' anxiety over their performance and explores the role and responsibilities of the PBL tutor in facilitating unguided group research tasks. This chapter resembles in many ways the previous chapter, as it introduces new tools and pedagogies to an albeit smaller group of students and discusses the reception of these. While the case in this chapter seems less ridden with the contradictions and tensions of the former, it is also clear that introduction of new tools (wikis and blogs) and pedagogies do create unease among students. However, in the chapter Walker also explores and discusses how these difficulties might be ameliorated through conscious design and facilitation. He discusses and shows how students might gradually take increasing ownership of both the learning spaces and learning process but also how this process of progressing from the guided to unguided group research seems to require facilitation and a careful attention to both the individual students and the group as a whole.

Summary

The chapters in this section explore in various ways how not only design but also teaching and learning practices are messy and unpredictable and occur in complex socio-technical infrastructures. Even small groups of learners act in unexpected ways, and below the surface there are complex interpersonal, social, and cultural conflicts and tensions at play, and we see how social or friendship relationships can affect intra- and intergroup dynamics and "knowledge spillovers". These tensions seem to become more pronounced as new tools, spaces and practices are adopted. When we leave the comfort zones of the institutional VLEs and design for more fluid, networked interactions among groups or student cohorts, or adopt new tools for student knowledge production (wikis, blogs, micro-blogging), both learners and facilitators experience a level of uneasiness. While the dynamics of participation, voice and equality are complex in small groups, they seem to become more diffuse and blurred with new spaces, tools and levels of scale. We should in many ways celebrate new patterns of peer participation and production and a destabilisation of the teacher or facilitator as a centre of control or a panopticon. However, we should acknowledge that this can be accompanied by a certain level of unrest among (some) students in need of facilitation and support. We would suggest that we need a much deeper understanding of how power, equality and voice function in these settings, particularly because these new spaces are often rhetorically hailed as nonhierarchical places for participative dialogue and communal knowledge production.

Section 3: The Practice of Informal Networked Learning

The chapters in this third section consider networked learning as it is conducted in informal and CPD contexts. A major theme here is how practice emerges within the processes of informal learning networks. This is in contrast to formal learning where learning starts with the practice of the teacher and with the teachers' or lecturers' design and structure being externally imposed on the learners. Informal learning is characterised by practice being emergent. It is internal, and learners construct the design through their experiences and learning processes and by what they learn through "doing practice". Within CPD there is a "light" touch to the imposition of learning design. Here facilitators may provide some structure or scaffolding in order to bring about participation and exchange of ideas and experiences among those professionals taking part. But the focus is on participants working towards the development of knowledge-in-practice, which emerges through dialogue. It seems to us that practice, as referred to in these chapters, is likely referred to "learning from direct experience on which every professional community is founded" (Corradi, Gherardi, & Verzelloni, 2008, p. 2), and knowledge is about organising as a practical accomplishment (Corradi, Gherardi, & Verzelloni, 2010).

The chapters in this section challenge us to reconsider what we think we know about learning and teaching. They highlight that in informal learning networks, those involved typically do not follow a given curriculum and are not confined to learning in an environment that is structured by a teacher's "design". The chapters build on and extend existing ideas about informal and CPD learning. They show, through the examination of the use of networked technologies in novel contemporary contexts, that informal learners learn by doing, they learn in natural settings and in situated contexts and much of what they do in their learning is incidental (Fox, 2002). Indeed networked learners are often not aware that they are learning. The "curriculum" and the "design" are situated and assembled by the learners as they proceed to shape their learning. However, in saying this we should not assume that formal and informal learning are completely different and that they do not have common and interrelated attributes. Informal and formal learning can take place in many "formal" and "informal" contexts, spaces and places. These chapters throw light on this, helping bridge the oft-perceived binary opposition between formal and informal learning.

Given that informal learners and those participating in CPD in networked learning contexts may not have recourse to the forms of external support that might play an important role in encouraging formal learners, how do informal and CPD learners sustain themselves in the learning process? The chapters in this section help us begin to understand how this happens. Learners in these contexts are often more likely to be self-directed: they often have an intrinsic wish to learn. External criteria (and accreditation) are less important to them, and they can be driven by friendship and the strong personal interest they have in what they are learning which may well exceed local, social and cultural boundaries. Informal and CPD learning often occurs in meaningful learning contexts.

Finally, in reading these chapters, an important question arises concerning knowledge creation in informal and CPD: does informal learning and CPD lead to the creation of new knowledge? The chapters in this section suggest a positive answer, a viewpoint that is supported by previous research into this which suggests that a great deal of knowledge can be created in informal and CPD contexts (De Laat, 2006; Haythornthwaite, 2006).

The chapter by John Holmes and Julie-Ann Sime—"Online Learning Communities for Teachers' Continuous Professional Development: An Action Research Study of eTwinning Learning Events"—investigates how an online learning community can support teachers' continuous professional development within a social network. The authors indicate that much emphasis has been placed on network individualism and the power of the Internet to support independent learning through a multitude of learning resources, opportunities and relationships. They say that even when learning is with others in a community, the focus is still on the individual within a larger social grouping. In their research, the authors applied "The Community of Inquiry" framework which includes elements of learning, social interaction, tutoring and facilitation as being interrelated and mutually dependent (Garrison, Anderson, & Archer, 2001). This was used to investigate three features of the teacher's professional development, which are as follows: the development of teachers' competence in online collaboration, how social aspects contribute to learning and how online tutors influence the development of critical thinking and metacognition. The study was underpinned by an action research approach, which allowed researcher and teachers to collaboratively develop the research through two action research cycles. The study was undertaken within the European Community's eTwinning initiative, where learning events are short duration, non-formal learning opportunities for teachers.

The participants in this study taught a range of subjects at primary and secondary school level in general and vocational education. The research suggests that teachers need to have the opportunity to apply what they have learned in practice and to reflect on that practice with peers in order to develop knowledge-in-practice. As a result they gain belief in the value of the changes being applied and develop knowledge-of-practice, which is seen as essential for long-term change. The research also highlights the essential role of the tutor in designing activities that engender collaboration, encourage critical thinking and foster mutual support among peers. Finally, the research emphasises that social presence is essential for effective collaboration and that sufficient time, space and activities should be included in online learning communities for the community to work together. The research has implications for Community of Inquiry theory and for future learning events. Holmes and Sime conclude their chapter by presenting an emerging model for supporting continuing professional developers and for e-moderating communities that may be useful for designing and moderating networked learning for teachers and other professional groups.

The chapter titled "Analysing Learning Ties to Stimulate Continuous Professional Development in the Workplace" by Bieke Schreurs also looks at networked learning in the context of the CPD of teachers. Schreurs points out that CPD in the workplace is difficult to analyse and evaluate because it is often invisible to others, and even the learners themselves may not be aware of the learning that occurs. The knowledge acquired can be tacit and the learning activities are usually informal. Research, policy and practice recognise the need for tools that can analyse, value and support CPD activities in the workplace. In carrying out the research on professional development networks among teachers reported in this chapter, a methodology to be used as a reflection tool was developed, to give professionals opportunities to gain insights into their own CPD activities and that of others in their organisation. This methodology, aimed at capturing continuous professional development in the workplace, resulted in the development of a Web 2.0 tool, "The Network Awareness Tool" (De Laat & Schreurs, 2011). Schreurs illustrates how the methodology—founded on theories of Networked Learning, Social Network Theory, Social Capital and Communities of Practice—gives insights into the structure of CPD networks, the learning content and the learning context of the workplace. In addition, the methodology provides teachers with concrete artefacts to assist better organisation of the learning environment in the workplace to support their CPD. The author discusses how the methodology holds the potential to be adopted and plugged into the virtual world to detect, connect and investigate networked learning activities. The findings of this research will be important for current research in networked learning about solutions and methodologies for gathering and analysing relational data on learning to create a holistic view of peoples' off- and online CDP in education, work and society.

Chapter 11—"Learning Through Network Interaction: The Potential of Ego-Networks"—by Asli Ünlüsoy, Mariette de Haan and Kevin Leander considers how networking platforms on the Internet constitute a significant place in the lives of young people. The authors point out that networking platforms are not often considered as potential learning environments, yet they facilitate the circulation of a great amount of information and digital artefacts. People share, discuss, encounter ideas, find each other and form communities via these sites. The chapter focuses on how, through these platforms, informal learning networks become available. The authors claim that social networks mediated by networked technologies provide ongoing opportunities to engage in activities and conversations that could potentially lead to learning. The kinds of social relationships and interactions that occur online heavily define the learning potential in networks. They indicate that the principles of networked learning and ego-network analysis, a sub-strand of SNA, guided them in their research. Based on the survey data of 1,227 high-school pupils, the network composition and networked interactions of youth are mapped. The authors present detailed results regarding with whom online interaction happens and if network interactions in young people's personal networks (i.e. ego network) result in discovering new information, artefacts, websites, etc. They focused on "discovery of new information" as a measure of awareness of learning among the young people that they studied. They did this because, to young people, "discovery of new information" seemed like a recognisable concept that could be associated with "learning" for them. But they do not claim that "discovering new information" solely represents learning in all its complexity. The findings show that similarity between the respondents and their network contacts prevailed. Online networks were often a replica of offline social circles. The authors conclude that although one might expect that these homogenous networks would not provide these youths with new discoveries, the participants reported that they encountered novel content frequently.

The final chapter in this section—"Mobile Learning and Immutable Mobiles: Using iPhones to Support Informal Learning in Craft Brewing"—presents two case studies of the use of iPhones in informal learning practices in craft brewing. Steve Wright and Gale Parchoma trace how a smartphone is entangled in practices, and how an informal learning network is assembled. They consider this assemblage through ANT, a theory that does not place any specific emphasis on any particular objects or elements of a learning context or process, but seeks to consider all elements in a symmetrical way. The authors describe the origins, applications and intersection of this approach with educational research and networked learning. In doing this, they do not, for example, assume the prior existence of "community" in the learning process. Rather they seek to show how learning takes place, emerges and is formed as a consequence of the ways in which informal learners interact and where "community" is an emergent networked effect. They argue that ANT allows the researcher to forego any preconceived notions of social structures or bounded institutions and instead assemble descriptions of the learning process, how it is formed and maintained and how it may continue or disintegrate.

In their research, the methodology followed included ethnographies of several sites alongside participant observations which allowed the authors to link what was occurring in home brewery settings to discussions in online forums. Images showing the situated use of iPhones in two home breweries are accompanied by thick descriptions. From this fieldwork the authors draw three implications. Firstly, how formal educational settings can productively learn from the situated use of apps to support calculation, simulation and recording of data in these informal practices. Secondly, how aspects of Marsick and Watkins (2001) model of informal learning as haphazard and unrecognised are less helpful than a more nuanced and context-sensitive theorisation. Finally, Wright and Parchoma consider the challenge of actor-network theory to conceptualisations of the epistemology and ontology of networked learning and question the anthropocentric view of agency and narrow views of mediation advanced therein. In conclusion, they raise implications concerning three areas of their interest: the design of mobile learning apps, theorising informal networked learning and the challenge ANT makes to the epistemology of networked learning.

Summary

The chapters in this section open up to the reader the processes of learning in informal and CPD as they occur in networked learning environments. As we read them, we become aware that learning seems to often have a direction of its own in these contexts. We are also made aware that informal learners often have an intrinsic wish to learn. They are often driven by self-motivation, friendships with other learners and by their personal interest in what they are learning and doing, and this often directs them more than a wish to please a teacher or to follow a curriculum, which is often the case in formal learning settings. We also get a keen sense that the processes of informal learning lead to knowledge production, although those involved do not always credit this as an outcome as they are often unaware of the knowledge that they are producing or do not equate it with the formal definition or meaning of "knowledge" that they are familiar with or have been educated to understand.

These chapters provide important insights into networked learning as it takes place in informal and CPD contexts. On a general level, they help us understand that learning is a natural phenomenon, that it is social in nature and that it takes place in our everyday lives. They also help us understand how informal learning and CPD can be supported by the technology and pedagogy of networked learning, making it possible for learners no matter where they are to cooperate in what they are doing, to build shared understandings and to develop learning repertoires and processes from their practices.

Theories, Methods and Settings Featuring Networked Learning Research

The previous sections provided a focused overview on the issues around design, experience and practice that are being studied and presented at the Networked Learning Conference. The Networked Learning Conference also showed how the field has grown and how it now embraces different research settings ranging from more formal learning such as higher education to informal learning in organisations and society. This growing interest in adopting the underlying Networked Learning principles to understand how people learn collaboratively through the development of networked relationships and the use of technology also came with the use of a richer theoretical and methodological landscape to help explain and study these phenomena. In this section we highlight some of the approaches the authors of the book chapters have used in order to illustrate this as well as to offer some guidance and pointers to specific areas of interest.

Theories

Traditionally there is a strong theoretical interest in social theories of learning where (online) communities and social network perspectives serve as a lens to understand networked learning activities. Holmes and Sime (Chap. 10) use, for example, a community of inquiry framework to examine how an online learning community can support teachers' continuous professional development. In their chapter they focus on teachers' competences in online collaboration, how social aspects contribute to learning and how online tutors influence critical thinking and metacognition. Perriton and Reynolds (Chap. 6) are interested in the dynamics of groups. They take a critical approach and argue that within networked learning research, ideas about group learning have not featured greatly. In their chapter they move away from exclusive virtual frameworks of group learning to use a variation of Potter's (1979) "dilemma's" to construct a framework for understanding group dynamics. Walker (Chap. 9) situates his research on designing a networked approach to PBL in the context of collaborative learning and interdependent learning online. He looks into online interaction to analyse and design-blended PBL using Web 2.0 tools. Similar to Walker, Nicolajsen (Chap. 8) frames her study in the domain of social learning emphasising the role Web 2.0 blogs have on student collaboration. Both are inspired by a networked learning approach to understand learning in which information and communication technologies (ICT) are used to promote connections between one learner and other learners, between learners and tutors and between a learning community and its learning resources (Goodyear et al., 2004).

Rienties et al. (Chap. 7) take a networked perspective on small-group learning. Their interest is on the impact of networked connections outside the group—referred to as knowledge spillovers—and their impact on student learning. In their approach they combine theoretical frameworks from collaborative learning, computer-supported collaborative learning and networked learning in order to understand how these knowledge spillovers emerge in small-group learning settings. Schreurs (Chap. 11) uses theories of networked learning, social network theory, social capital and communities of practice to illustrate a methodology for visualising informal professional development networks. Finally Ünlüsoy, de Haan and Leander (Chap. 12) study how social networks of young people mediated by networked technologies provide ongoing opportunities to engage in activities and conversations that potentially lead to learning. They are interested in the social relationships and interactions that emerge online and the way these social networking sites facilitate the ways in which young people share, discuss, encounter ideas, find each other and form communities.

A different theoretical approach is taken by Hannon (Chap. 4) and Wright and Parchoma (Chap. 13). They use ANT as a theoretical lens to research networked learning. Hannon uses ANT to recognise the role of nonhuman participants in the configurations of a university learning management system. He uses ANT to develop a sociomaterial account in order to challenge notions of separateness and the existence of entities prior to the relations formed with them. He draws on three ANT concepts in order to follow particular nonhuman actors, or objects, in the work of organising the implementation that produces the institutional online learning environment. These concepts are as follows: that objects exist in networks, they are enacted into reality, and they imply absent realities. In a similar way Wright and Parchoma are interested in understanding how both human and nonhuman agencies perform realities. In their study they trace how the smartphone is entangled in practices and how an informal learning network is assembled. They consider this assemblage through ANT describing the origins, applications and intersections of this approach with educational research and networked learning.

Dohn (Chap. 2) takes yet another theoretical perspective and develops a situated learning approach to form a view of knowledge that is tacit, situated, context dependent and embodied. She argues that the context which carries significance for the learner involving themselves as persons and which they consider important for who they are should be the prime focus of networked learning activities rather than being detached from their primary context.

Methods

This wide range of theoretical positions and different aims for conducting Networked Learning research is followed by a set of different methodological approaches. Dohn (Chap. 2), for example, uses a phenomenological informed approach to develop a tacit-knowledge perspective on networked learning. Shah (Chap. 5), in a similar fashion, adopts a phenomenographic approach in order to offer "a direct way in" to unpacking the micro-level social processes that underpin the use of digital technologies in educational settings. Phenomenography aims to identify the qualitative variations within the participants' descriptions of experiences. The epistemological approach of phenomenography is founded on the assumption that there is always variation in the way we perceive or experience the world, and this variation can be described, portrayed and categorised. A somewhat different but slightly related approach is used by Nicolajsen. In her Chap. 8 she follows an interpretative design of the constructivist type developed by Guba and Lincoln (1994) in order to create an understanding about students' and teachers' perceptions of the benefits and challenges in using blogs as tools for learning. Based on 37 written student reflections, she coded emergent themes that were later theoretically informed and analysed against discussions within the field of networked learning and Web 2.0 in higher education. Wright and Parchoma (Chap. 13) use Marcus' (1998) approach of multisite ethnographies where research is designed around chains and paths of locations in which the ethnographer establishes some sort of literal, physical presence following connections (using participant observation) from home breweries to online forums and use of media. These observations are illustrated through thick descriptions and images of the situated use of iPhones in two home breweries. The concept of following connections aligns to an ANT approach of tracing chains and paths through participant observation using focused ethnography (as a form of short-term ethnographies) by which information relevant to the development of change of technological systems are collected in an intensive and rapid way. Similar to Wright and Parchoma, Hannon (Chap. 4) also draws on ethnographic approaches to guide his actor-network studies, including observation of project activity and meetings, interviews, focus groups and documents analysis. Gleerup et al. (Chap. 3) combine ethnographical observation with design-based research. Their ethnographical observations involved 2 days of intense educational field work by three researchers observing teachers at different educational levels. These observations were backed up by interviews with teachers, management and group interviews with apprentices to ensure a valid identification and contextualisation of the specific, localised domain knowledge and practices. Their design-based approach is used to study a design process that is based on a method for user-driven innovation. It presents a four-phase model that enables close dialogue between designer perspective and user perspective, and it generates an understanding of the different roles of user and designer: from the initial phase where the users are being observed, to the lab where participants are constructing together, to the project phase where users and researchers/designers are equal partners and to the final phase where the users are on their own. This final phase is an organisational process where a new practice is constructed and adopted. Holmes and Sime (Chap. 10) take an action research approach to designing and moderating online communities. Their method involves close collaboration between researcher and practitioners, with an emphasis on promoting change during the research process rather than as an afterthought in the research conclusions. Action research was used to follow and influence the development of an online learning event entitled "Exploiting Web 2.0: eTwinning and Collaboration".

Yet another emerging methodology is SNA to explore and understand networked relationships. Rienties et al. (Chap. 7) use a (dynamic) analysis of social networks in order to understand how knowledge spillovers emerge. SNA can be considered as a wide-ranging strategy to explore social structures to uncover the existence of social positions of (sub) groups within the network. Schreurs (Chap. 11) uses an SNA approach combined with the Network Awareness Tool (De Laat & Schreurs, 2011) to develop a method for visualising networks and raising awareness about the impact social networked relationships have on teachers' own CPD activities and that of others within the organisation. Somewhat similar to the approach taken by Schreurs, Ünlüsoy, de Haan and Leander (Chap. 12) use ego-network analysis (a sub-strand of SNA) as the preferred method during their research. They mapped high-school pupils' network composition and interactions. Ego-net research is an SNA method that considers personal social networks from a bottom-up perspective starting with the individual actor and accounting for the individual's direct relationships. This method enables the researcher to see the respondent's social context and relationships.

Research Settings

We started this section by saying that the field of Networked Learning research has branched into different research contexts. Studying networked relationships seem to be helpful in understanding social learning in formal, non-formal and informal settings as well as understanding the (potential) links that might be established between them. Studies in Networked Learning have not only developed a keen interest in understanding learning within those traditional settings of learning but is now actively crossing those boundaries to understand how mixed forms exist and enhance learning.

The first set of chapters presented here all position their research in a formal (higher) educational setting. Hannon (Chap. 4), for example, is working in a formal learning context. He focuses on how learning environments are assembled and what kind of networked learning technologies are put-in-place by universities. Nicolajsen (Chap. 8) focuses on the challenges of using blogs for Networked Learning as experienced by 37 students during their online discussions. These discussions were an assignment part of an undergraduate course aimed at making students active collaborative learners. Perriton and Reynolds (Chap. 6) base their study of group dynamics on a fictionalised context of online learning within UK higher education. Walker (Chap. 9) is interested in a blended design for a postgraduate University Law programme following a PBL curriculum. In his design he combines campus-based and online events. Rienties et al. (Chap. 7) also compare two designs of a blended learning environment in higher education, but within this setting they were interested in the formal and informal learning relations that developed over time. The development of such relations over time is hard to measure since they can be developed within or outside the classroom setting.

Finally Dohn (Chap. 2) uses the tacit-knowledge perspective to argue for networked learning to become an anchor to resituate learning in other contexts, both educational and noneducational.

Already in the formal setting, we see an interest in crossing the boundaries between the formal and the informal. This emerging issue of fading boundaries between traditional approaches to learning is further researched in the chapters presented below. The chapter by Gleerup et al. (Chap. 3), for example, deals with vocational education and addresses the problem of alternating between learning taking place at college and at work. In their chapter they aim to develop a design approach where networked learning couples formal learning and informal learning contexts to facilitate networked learning between apprentice and apprentice, college and apprentice and apprentice and master/journeyman. Holmes and Sime (Chap. 10) focus their study on non-formal learning events of short duration where teachers are involved in CPD activities that offer teachers the opportunity to undertake inquiry-based learning with their peers, in an online learning community and in the context of their everyday practice. Schreurs (Chap. 11) also situates her study in the context of CPD. She argues that CPD in the workplace is difficult to analyse because the emergence of networks is ad hoc, spontaneous and "unplanned" by nature, driven by challenges experienced in everyday practice. The knowledge acquired can be tacit and the learning activities are informally situated in the (small) networks that teachers are part of. Wright and Parchoma (Chap. 13) have taken a similar interest in understanding informal professional development networks. In their two case studies, they focus on the use of iPhones in informal learning practices in craft brewing. They trace how a smartphone is entangled in practices and how an informal learning network among home brewers is assembled. Ünlüsoy, de Haan and Leander (Chap. 12) take informal learning in yet another direction and focus on the significance of social networking platforms for youths and their development of informal learning networks. They discuss how online interactions happen and if networked interactions in young people's networks result in informal learning activities.

Chapter Conclusions

Looking back at what we have learnt in reviewing the various chapters in the book, we believe that a number of interesting themes emerge that are important in taking the theory of networked learning forward. These include returning to the theme and importance of practice as epistemology. Related to this is the relationship and connection of learning contexts and spaces or, as discussed by several authors, the coupling of learning contexts. Then there is increasingly the recognition of the agency and active role of technology within networked learning. How technology acts within the network is one dimension of a fourth theme identified, which is the messy and often chaotic and political nature of the design, experience and practice of networked learning. Each of these themes has implications for how we view networked learning and thus how we think about it in terms of design, experience and practice.

Practice as epistemology, the first theme, as already mentioned is discussed in the first book in the Research in Networked Learning Book Series when examining the epistemology of networked learning. At that time we said that it was important to recognise that practice is always epistemic. From a practice as epistemology perspective, the designs we implement and the way we go about and do network learning is a performative accomplishment of situated, social work and organisation. Gherardi and Strati (2012) explain in the introduction to their book on "Learning and Knowing in Practice Based Studies", "knowledge (therefore) does not reside in people's minds nor is it a commodity; rather it is an activity situated in social, working and organisational practice".

To see learning and knowing as a practical accomplishment is equally relevant to how we do our designs and how we see the doing of learning. Within practice-based studies (PBS) and a practice as epistemology perspective, there is a shift from seeing knowledge as an object to seeing knowing and indeed learning as a situated activity and something people "do" together, collectively and socially.

Many of the chapters in the book implicitly or explicitly work with the notion of learning as the organisation and doing of practice. Some of the chapters raise concerns about the activities we offer in our designs being either removed or disconnected from the situated practice of learners. How and if the designs we offer connect with practice is a long-standing debate within education. Fox (2005) picked up on this issue in relation to networked learning when he wrote about ideas initiated by Illich (1971) and others on Deschooling Society, including the optimism that computerisation was seen to offer for changing the way we organise education and access to knowledge. An optimism that was rather more circumspect a decade later in the writing of Lyotard who, according to Fox, believed computerisation would either "become the 'dream' instrument for controlling and regulating the market system" or it could "give the public free access to the memory and data banks" (Lyotard, 1994, p. 67). It is interesting to reflect on these two scenarios nearly another decade on from Fox's review of the issue.

What is perhaps most interesting in the chapters in this book is that there is a move in the discussions of networked learning away from what might be considered as the decoupling of education and non-institutional learning spaces and contexts, as advocated by the deschooling thesis. Instead there is now recognition of the potential for networked learning through its design, pedagogy and use of technology to provide a more meaningful coupling or connecting of learning spaces and contexts. In particular there is the suggestion that it provides a greater coupling between the learning context of educational institutions and the learning context of, as referred to by Dohn, the primary contexts of the learner or, we would suggest, the "lived context" where learners "do" their practice. It is interesting to see how Web 2.0 or social media, such as social networking sites, seem to live in-between or be consciously designed to serve as crossing points/boundary zones between these contexts. In several chapters we see how these spaces are vehicles for informal or unacknowledged learning and how social networking sites, blogs and wikis can also be meaningfully embedded into educational designs. However, we can equally sense how such a coupling can create tensions between everyday life as an intimate space of social relations and then an "intrusion" of educational practices into these spaces. Further, there seem to be challenges and tensions in aligning the personal, socially oriented practices of social media with scholarly social media practices. For example, when students are asked to adopt blogs for a particular scholarly set of writing practices, which may be distinctly different from the writing practices commonly associated with blogs as a wider cultural phenomenon (Ross, 2012). This reiterates the argument against technological determinism repeatedly made within networked learning, namely, that technologies and tools do not uniformly shape or change practice. Particularly this point is being raised in chapters adopting an ANT or sociomaterial perspective.

A much-debated issue in relation to ANT studies is the notion of "symmetry" and how we should think of technologies and artefacts as having agency, rather than discriminating between human and nonhuman actors. From a sociomaterial or ANT perspective, the frequently referred-to definition of networked learning (Goodyear et al., 2004) might seem heavily anthropocentric, favouring human actors over, for example, resources or technology. We do not intend to enter deeply into this debate. However, we do believe that the studies and chapters drawing on a sociomaterial or ANT approach remind us that it is useful to think of networked learning designs and practices as complex assemblages that cannot be easily reduced to consisting of only a number of human learners connected by neutral technologies. An ANT approach helps us to understand how an "institutional learning space" and its associated learning practices is a complex mixture of policies, technologies and competing discourses that over time (temporarily) crystallises into spaces, tools and practices that come to shape the possibilities for learning.

Linking back to social media and the adoption of commonly available and "free" tools, such as Facebook or Twitter, we are also reminded that these are technologies designed for other purposes than education. For example, Friesen and Lowe (2012) argue how the underlying logic or design of these spaces are to draw the users' "eyeballs" towards advertising and how this is insidiously embedded in designs that favour conviviality, "likes" and growth of one's network over dissent, debate, dislike and careful selection. While being a somewhat gloomy analysis of the educational value of (some) social media, it does remind us that the algorithms selecting what will be presented, for example, in the Facebook newsfeed might be beyond control and inspection, but nevertheless affect interaction. Furthermore, there is a growing interest in recommendation systems, learning analytics and instant visualisations of interactions. In this book we see how network visualisations can help us understand knowledge spillovers and recognise patterns of interaction and knowledge exchange we might not, as facilitators, be immediately aware of. Many of these tools, methods and visualisation techniques are becoming increasingly embedded as more immediate "real-time" or "near-real-time" functionalities in learning management systems, smartphone apps and as part of social media software (metrics, graphs, network visualisations, recommendations, etc.). In this way we may increasingly be experiencing forms of networked learning where interactions, relations, recommendations and so forth are intermediated, affected and represented by algorithmic processes that can shape our understandings and actions in online dialogues or interactions. While these developments hold promises and are interesting avenues to explore within networked learning, they also hold hidden dangers. What is more, they demonstrate how "technology" is increasingly difficult to disentangle and separate from human activity. It is important to carefully examine the rationales and theoretical assumptions underpinning their design.

The final theme that we feel is important and discussed in many of the chapters is how teaching and learning practices are both messy and unpredictable and contain many complex interpersonal, social and cultural conflicts and tensions looming under the surface. In relation to the latter, it seems that interpersonal relations among students come to shape knowledge exchange and patterns. This is a challenge to facilitators who may need to make sense of, and understand, these relations in order to successfully support group interaction and discussions. However, as argued by Enriquez (2008), this might also be a challenge to what we can learn from visualisations and diagrams of interaction based on software mining of only a limited set of online interactions.

The messy and unpredictable nature of networked learning highlights the tension between the expected and unexpected and squarely emphasises "teaching or facilitation" as a practice. While productive networked learning certainly hinges on a carefully crafted and reflexive design, we should equally view it as considerate and careful reflection-in-action (Schön, 1983). While this book provides many insights into understanding the social dynamics of networked learning, the chapters also provoke the question of how well our current theories and conceptualisations within networked learning are attuned to the "messiness" and "situated improvisations" of networked learning practices.

References

Boon, S., & Sinclair, C. (2012). Life behind the screen: Taking the academic online. In L. Dirckinck-Holmfeld, V. Hodgson, & D. McConnell (Eds.), *Exploring the theory, pedagogy and practice of networked learning* (pp. 273–287). New York, NY: Springer. Retrieved from http://link.springer.com/chapter/10.1007/978-1-4614-0496-5_16

Corradi, G., Gherardi, S., & Verzelloni, L. (2008). Ten good reasons for assuming a "practice lens" in organization studies. In *International conference on organizational learning, knowledge and capabilities*. Copenhagen: OLKC. Retrieved from http://www2.warwick.ac.uk/fac/soc/wbs/conf/olkc/archive/olkc3/papers/contribution312.pdf

Corradi, G., Gherardi, S., & Verzelloni, L. (2010). Through the practice lens: Where is the bandwagon of practice-based studies heading? *Management Learning, 41*(3), 265–283. doi:10.1177/1350507609356938.

De Laat, M. (2006). *Networked learning*. PhD thesis, Politie Acedemie, Apeldoorn. Retrieved from http://www.open.ou.nl/rslmlt/Maarten%20De%20Laat_Networked%20Learning_2006.pdf

De Laat, M., & Schreurs, B. (2011). *Network Awareness Tool: Social Learning Browser for visualizing, analysing and managing social networks*. Herleen: Ruud de Moor Centrum—Open Universiteit.

Dewey, J. (1916). *Democracy and education: An introduction to the philosophy of education*. New York, NY: The Macmillan Company.

Dirckinck Holmfeld, L., Hodgson, V., & McConnell, D. (Eds.). (2012). *Exploring the theory, pedagogy and practice of networked learning*. Berlin: Springer.

Dirckinck-Holmfeld, L., Jones, C., & Lindström, B. (Eds.). (2009). *Analysing networked learning practices in higher education and continuing professional development*. Rotterdam: Sense.

Enriquez, J. G. (2008). Translating networked learning: Un-tying relational ties. *Journal of Computer Assisted Learning, 24*(2), 116–127.

Ferreday, D. J., & Hodgson, V. E. (2010). Heterotopia in networked learning: Beyond the shadow side of participation in learning communities. Lancaster: Lancaster University, The Department of Management Learning and Leadership. Retrieved from http://www.research.lancs.ac.uk/portal/services/downloadRegister/615478/Document.pdf

Fox, S. (2002). Studying networked learning: Some implications from socially situated learning theory and actor network theory. In C. Steeples & C. Jones (Eds.), *Networked learning: Perspectives and issues* (pp. 77–91). London: Springer. Retrieved from http://link.springer.com/content/pdf/10.1007/978-1-4471-0181-9_5.pdf

Fox, S. (2005). An actor-network critique of community in higher education: Implications for networked learning. *Studies in Higher Education, 30*(1), 95–110. doi:10.1080/0307507052000307821.

Freire, P. (1970). *Pedagogy of the oppressed*. New York, NY: Continuum.

Friesen, N., & Lowe, S. (2012). The questionable promise of social media for education: Connective learning and the commercial imperative. *Journal of Computer Assisted Learning, 28* (3), 183–194. doi:10.1111/j.1365-2729.2011.00426.x.

Garrison, D. R., Anderson, T., & Archer, W. (2001). Critical thinking, cognitive presence, and computer conferencing in distance education. *American Journal of Distance Education, 15*(1), 7–23. doi:10.1080/08923640109527071.

Gherardi, S., & Strati, A. (2012). *Learning and knowing in practice-based studies*. Cheltenham: Edward Elgar.

Goodyear, P., Banks, S., Hodgson, V., & McConnell, D. (2004). *Advances in research on networked learning*. Dordrecht: Klüwer Academic.

Goodyear, P., Jones, C., Asensio, M., Hodgson, V., & Steeples, C. (2001). *Effective networked learning in higher education: Notes and guidelines*. Lancaster: Centre for Studies in Advanced Learning Technology (CSALT). Retrieved from http://csalt.lancs.ac.uk/JISC/guidelines_final.doc

Guba, E. G., & Lincoln, Y. S. (1994). Competing paradigms in qualitative research. In N. K. Denzin & Y. S. Lincoln (Eds.), *Handbook of qualitative research* (pp. 105–117). Thousand Oaks, CA: SAGE.

Halonen, J. (2010). *Research framework and methods overview for user driven open innovation* (Deliverable). Retrieved from http://www.flexibleservices.fi/files/file/pdf/UDOI_B_deliverable_310410_final.pdf

Haythornthwaite, C. (2006). Learning and knowledge networks in interdisciplinary collaborations. *Journal of the American Society for Information Science and Technology, 57*(8), 1079–1092. doi:10.1002/asi.20371.

Haythornthwaite, C., & de Laat, M. (2010). Social networks and learning networks: Using social network perspectives to understand social learning. In L. Dirckinck-Holmfeld, V. Hodgson, C. Jones, M. de Laat, & T. Ryberg (Eds.), *Proceedings of the 7th international conference on networked learning* (pp. 183–190). Retrieved from http://www.lancaster.ac.uk/fss/organisations/netlc/past/nlc2010/abstracts/PDFs/Haythornwaite.pdf

Hodgson, V., McConnell, D., & Dirckinck-Holmfeld, L. (2012). The theory, practice and pedagogy of networked learning. In L. Dirckinck-Holmfeld, V. Hodgson, & D. McConnell (Eds.), *Exploring the theory, pedagogy and practice of networked learning* (pp. 291–305). New York, NY: Springer. Retrieved from http://link.springer.com/chapter/10.1007/978-1-4614-0496-5_17

Hodgson, V., & Reynolds, M. (2005). Consensus, difference and "multiple communities" in networked learning. *Studies in Higher Education, 30*(1), 11–24.

Illich, I. (1971). *Deschooling society*. London: Calder & Boyars.

Jones, C., & Dirckinck-Holmfeld, L. (2009). Analysing networked learning practices. In L. Dirckinck-Holmfeld, C. Jones, & B. Lindström (Eds.), *Analysing networked learning practices in higher education and continuing professional development* (pp. 10–27). Rotterdam: Sense.

Jones, C., Ferreday, D., & Hodgson, V. (2008). Networked learning a relational approach: Weak and strong ties. *Journal of Computer Assisted Learning, 24*(2), 90–102.

Lyotard, J.-F. (1994). *The postmodern condition*. Manchester: Manchester University Press.

Marcus, G. E. (1998). *Ethnography through thick and thin*. Princeton, NJ: Princeton University Press.

Marsick, V. J., & Watkins, K. E. (2001). Informal and incidental learning. *New Directions for Adult and Continuing Education, 2001*(89), 25–34. doi:10.1002/ace.5.

Mead, G. (1934). *Mind, self & society from the standpoint of a social behaviorist*. Chicago, IL: University of Chicago Press.

Potter, S. G. (1979). *Three dilemmas*. Presented at the group relations training association conference.

Ross, J. (2012). Just what is being reflected in online reflection? New literacies for new media learning practices. In L. Dirckinck-Holmfeld, V. Hodgson, & D. McConnell (Eds.), *Exploring the theory, pedagogy and practice of networked learning* (pp. 191–207). New York, NY: Springer. Retrieved from http://dx.doi.org/10.1007/978-1-4614-0496-5_11

Ryberg, T., Buus, L., & Georgsen, M. (2012). Differences in understandings of networked learning theory: Connectivity or collaboration? In L. Dirckinck-Holmfeld, V. Hodgson, & D. McConnell (Eds.), *Exploring the theory, pedagogy and practice of networked learning* (pp. 43–58). New York, NY: Springer. Retrieved from http://www.springerlink.com/content/l106kr1006u7r770/export-citation/

Ryberg, T., & Larsen, M. C. (2008). Networked identities: Understanding relationships between strong and weak ties in networked environments. *Journal of Computer Assisted Learning, 24*(2), 103–115. doi:10.1111/j.1365-2729.2007.00272.x.

Schön, D. A. (1983). *The reflective practitioner: How professionals think in action*. New York, NY: Basic Books.

Part I
Networked Learning Spaces and Context: Design and Practice

Chapter 2
Implications for Networked Learning of the 'Practice' Side of Social Practice Theories: A Tacit-Knowledge Perspective

Nina Bonderup Dohn

Introduction

In the first book of the present series on the theory, pedagogy, and practice of networked learning, the editors in their final chapter identify the ontology and epistemology of the networked learning approach as, broadly speaking, socio-constructionist and as seeking to transcend the dualism between abstract mind and concrete material social practice (Hodgson, McConnell, & Dirckinck-Holmfeld, 2012). That is, they put forward a view of the world and our human understanding of it as 'socio-culturally influenced and constructed' (p. 292) and of '[p]ractice as epistemic, as a way of seeing or acting' (p. 293). They stress that the approach implies a social theory of learning similar in many respects to the ones expressed in activity theory and the communities of practice approach, respectively. The similarity is, of course, not coincidental—rather it stems from the fact that many researchers within the field of networked learning have taken their point of departure in what might be termed 'social practice' theories, among which some of the most influential are activity theory, expansive learning, and the communities of practice approach, or social learning theory as I prefer to call it, following Wenger (1998).

In this chapter I wish to point out that the 'practice' side of 'social practice' theories has been somewhat neglected by networked learning and that as a consequence too little attention has been paid to the view of knowledge inherent in these theories and to the implications which this view has for the theoretical understanding and practical design of networked learning activities. I argue that networked learning activities in general risk taking on the role of artificial, stand-alone activities detached from the 'primary contexts' (Dohn, 2013) of the participants,

N.B. Dohn (✉)
Department of Design and Communication, University of Southern Denmark,
Kolding, Denmark
e-mail: nina@sdu.dk

V. Hodgson et al. (eds.), *The Design, Experience and Practice of Networked Learning*,
Research in Networked Learning, DOI 10.1007/978-3-319-01940-6_2,
© Springer International Publishing Switzerland 2014

i.e. contexts which carry significance for them, in which they involve themselves as persons and which they consider important for who they are. Networked learning activities which have this role are not experienced as fully meaningful—they appear somewhat 'off' from 'what is really at stake' in actual, full-fledged practical situations. In some cases, especially within distance learning programmes, the networked learning setting may itself become a 'primary context', but this cannot be counted on. The main claim of the chapter as it concerns designs for learning is that networked learning will in general be most successful if designed as 'mediator activities' to facilitate the resituating of content between the 'primary contexts' of the learners, rather than to act as a 'primary context' itself.

The conception of networked learning used in the chapter takes as a starting point the definition provided by Goodyear, Banks, Hodgson, and McConnell (2004) which is concerned with the facilitation of learning through some kind of structured educational activity (in a broad sense) involving information and communication technology. It states that networked learning is:

> learning in which information and communications technology (ICT) is used to promote connections: between one learner and other learners; between learners and tutors; between a learning community and its learning resources. (p. 1)

Here, the 'structured educational activity' of networked learning may be in the form of more traditional educational courses designed to help learners fulfil specific predefined educational goals. A step removed, the term also covers the type of professional development and action learning courses which are designed to facilitate learners' reflection on their practice experiences and their formulation and pursuit of their own more specific learning objectives and practice development goals on this basis (for an example, cf. Smith, 2012). However, it is a consequence of the argument put out in the chapter that the definition needs supplementation in one crucial way: As it stands, it is focused solely on ICT-mediated contexts and on the learning taking place through engaging with resources, tutors, and other learners in such contexts. It therefore seems to miss the possibility of (and need for, I would contend) designing activities which help participants resituate course content in their existing physical and virtual primary contexts. A more apt definition which better highlights the possibility of utilising networked learning as 'mediator activities' between primary contexts would read:

> Networked learning is learning in which information and communications technology (ICT) is used to promote connections: between one learner and other learners; between learners and tutors; between a learning community and its learning resources; between the diverse contexts in which the learners participate.

The chapter thus takes on the question of how best to conceptualise networked learning—including a development of the concept itself—given a view of knowledge which, it is claimed, is inherent but undeveloped and partly unacknowledged, in the way networked learning is made theoretical sense of within the research community. According to this view, knowledge is first and foremost an attunement to the 'gestalt' of the specific situation one is in—an attunement, which is primordial, practical, and embodied and supplies the background upon which linguistic utterances can be made and understood. Only secondarily and derivatively is knowledge expressible in words.

The Neglect of 'Practice' in Networked Learning's Use of 'Social Practice Theories'

'Social practice' theories such as activity theory and social learning theory converge on stressing that the meaning of actions, artefacts, and procedures are bound up with concrete social contexts of activity. More precisely, the basic view is that meaning is embedded in the activities people undertake in given contexts and that conversely these activities can only be understood in terms of the meaning they embody. Meaning is created and negotiated in activity and activity is formed by the meaning it instantiates and perpetuates.

This basic view is put forward with a primary focus on the individual's appropriation of cultural meaning within 'activity systems' in *activity theory* with its roots in the writings of Vygotsky (1978) and Leont'ev (1978) and with Cole (1990), Hedegaard (1995), and Wertsch (1998) as significant Western heirs and theory developers. *Expansive learning theory*, developed by Engeström (1987, 2001), constitutes an important modification to the theory because it moves focus to the collective level and centres on 'expansion' or transgression of existing 'activity systems' and their limitations, rather than on development within an 'activity system'. The significance of this modification warrants treating Engeström's approach as a perspective of its own even though it is a branch of activity theory. Engeström's version of activity theory has influenced research within networked learning as a theory in its own right. *Social learning theory*, with Wenger as its prime representative, is inspired by activity theory and developed out of situated learning (Lave & Wenger, 1991) but articulates the basic view, not in terms of activity systems but of communities of practice, and conceptualises learning not as appropriation or expansion but as participation (Sfard, 1998), in the form of a negotiation of meaning and identity in—and to some extent across—communities of practice (Wenger, 1998).

The significance of these 'social practice' theories within the networked learning field is illustrated by the fact that the only plenary session at the 2010 Networked Learning Conference in Aalborg was devoted to a dialogue with Wenger and Engeström on the contribution of their theoretical perspectives to the understanding of networked learning (http://nlc.ell.aau.dk). Fifteen of the papers presented at the conference included reference to Engeström, 34 referred to Wenger, and nine referred to activity theory as such. Examples of recent articles within the field which draw on one or more of the theoretical approaches are Ryberg and Larsen (2008); Chen, Chang, and Wang (2010); Geithner and Schulz (2010); Cousin and Deepwell (2005); Fulantelli (2009); Booth and Hultén (2004); Vines and Dysthe (2009); Nielsen and Danielsen (2011); Jones, Dirckinck-Holmfeld, and Lindström (2006); Pilkington and Guldberg (2009); and Jones and Dirckinck-Holmfeld (2009). Of these articles, the first two draw on Wenger and Engeström, the next one on Engeström, the fourth and fifth on Wenger, the sixth on activity theory, the next two on activity theory and Wenger, and the last three on all three perspectives.

The social practice theories are influential in large part through the conceptual tools they offer for analysing the communities of learners, the mediation of dialogue, the role of artefacts, and the establishment of meaning as an ongoing social process. Central concepts which have been taken over from such theories are 'activity system', 'zone of proximal development', 'mediation', 'rules', 'community of practice', 'negotiation of meaning', 'identity', 'repertoire', 'participation', and 'reification'. Interestingly, and somewhat ironically, the 'practice' side of the social practice theories has been neglected to a large extent. Or rather, 'practice' and 'activity' tend to be taken as more or less synonymous with 'discourse' and 'verbal activity', respectively; 'participation' as synonymous with 'contributing with online posts' (or, less frequently, 'contributing orally'); and 'reification' as synonymous with 'writing down', 'concluding', or 'filing'. The 'repertoire' of a community of learners tends to be understood as a 'repertoire of concepts, phrases, and verbal communications'. Even in cases where the 'repertoire' is taken to include representations in other modes than writing, such as pictures and videos, these representations are viewed as carrying significance in virtue of the role they have in discourse. 'Mediation' in the context of networked learning of course refers first and foremost to ICT mediation, i.e. to the fact that networked learning takes place in synchronous or asynchronous virtual settings with participants dispersed geographically. However, beneath this obvious meaning of 'mediation', and prerequisite for the establishment of ICT-mediated learning communities, is the presupposition that the mediation most interesting and fruitful to focus on when it comes to learning in general is the mediation of thought provided by language. In sum, the 'doing' in networked learning is biased in the direction of verbal doing and 'practice' in the direction of 'linguistic practice'.

A few examples will serve to illustrate the point. Cousin and Deepwell, in their application of a Wenger perspective to networked learning, say explicitly that 'Translated to the context of network learning, reification can be about shared assessment assignments and/or the generation of learning resources; it can also be about a set of ground rules ... and conventions for shared discussion' (Cousin & Deepwell, 2005, p. 63). That is, reification is a matter of saying or writing, i.e. of linguistic practice. Similarly, Fulantelli (2009) writes of a blended learning course that 'students and teachers became a community of practice, by sharing a common enterprise (the solution of real cases), through a mutual engagement and building a shared repertoire of cases and solutions' (p. 58). The 'real cases' in question, it should be noted, were *linguistic representations* of actual projects, not the projects themselves. That is, the students worked on producing linguistically formulated solutions to the representations of problems in practice, not on actually solving the problems *in* practice. It is, perhaps, symptomatic of the linguistic and representational bias of networked learning's utilisation of social practice theories that no comment is made whatsoever on this point.

To these examples of linguistic bias in the utilisation of social learning theory, the following quote from Booth and Hultén (2004) may be added. It illustrates a corresponding bias in the way activity theoretical concepts are used. They claim that

> One clear point for further investigation is the relation between activity and interactivity, or *in other words* the amount participants contribute to the discussion and the degree to which they listen to, think about, and act on what they find there. Wännman-Toresson's [2002] work indicated convincingly that activity is a prerequisite for interactivity: the greater the activity in a group the proportionally greater the interactivity she measured. (p. 170, emphasis added, NBD)

In the latter part of the quote, 'activity' and 'interactivity' clearly refer exclusively to what goes on in online environments. In the first part of the quote, Booth and Hultén do mention 'acting on' the interaction in the online discussions, but given that they explicate their view in terms of Wännman-Toresson's findings, it seems clear that the acts they have in mind are verbal ones, i.e. the acts of writing new comments to the discussion.

In line with this view, Pilkington and Guldberg, who as indicated draw on all three types of social practice theory, seem not to differentiate significantly between studies of communities of practice and studies of discourse (and therefore, by implication, between 'practice' and 'discourse') when they say that

> Common to both is the suggestion that to be a community, a community should show evidence of mutual engagement, joint enterprise toward shared goals and shared repertoires or mechanisms for inter-communication. (Pilkington & Guldberg, 2009, p. 65)

The last part of the quote bears additional, more concrete, witness to the linguistic bias when 'shared repertoires' are treated as equivalent to 'mechanisms for intercommunication'. In a similar fashion, Pilkington and Guldberg utilise Engeström's model of an activity system in ways which stress linguistic representation and verbal doings. Their use of the model thus depicts Engeström's node 'rules' as 'task instruction and interaction rules' which 'constrain/enable' the learner's 'co-construction' 'through discussion' of 'shared understanding and resources' when she/he 'interacts with' others (p. 66). Audio and visual material is supplied and integrated with assignments in order to facilitate 'pause-for-thought' and 'time-to-talk' activities (p. 72). That is, the material is seen as carrying significance precisely to the extent that it gets to play a role in (linguistically mediated) thought and discourse.

Finally, at a more basic level beneath the distinction between the concepts of different 'social practice theories', the following example is to be found in the final chapter of the first book in the present series on networked learning: The very next sentence after the one quoted above to the effect that the networked learning approach seeks to transcend the dualism between mind and 'concrete material social practice' reads: 'The epistemology of networked learning is in essence that knowledge emerges or is constructed in relational dialogue or collaborative interaction' (Hodgson et al., 2012, p. 293). The material side of practice thus seemingly slips out of focus from one sentence to the next.

Given that networked learning to a large extent takes place in virtual environments structured around reading and writing posts, the bias towards 'verbal doing' and 'linguistic practice'—in theorising about networked learning and, it would seem from the quotes, in the practice of networked learning as well—is perhaps not so surprising. Theoretically, it also finds vindication in the so-called linguistic turn within philosophy and sociology, represented by the (first generation of the) Anglo-American reception of Wittgenstein's writings (e.g. Kenny, 1973; Kripke, 1982; Winch, 1990) in conjunction with post-structuralism exemplified by the works of Butler (1990), Foucault (1970), and Derrida (1997). This 'linguistic turn' argues for the ontological and epistemological significance of language and discourse for the construction of our world and of our understanding of it. However, the neglect of the material side of practice means that the underlying presuppositions and implications of 'social practice theories' as concerns the significance of embodied activity have been somewhat overlooked. This significance, on the other hand, is articulated in the contrasting 'practice turn' which, though inspired by (different) readings of some of the same thinkers (e.g. Wittgenstein and Foucault) (Schatzki, Knorr-Cetina, & von Savigny, 2001), focuses on 'practices as embodied, materially mediated arrays of human activity centrally organized around shared practical understanding' (Schatzki et al., 2001, p. 2) where the practical understanding is constituted in no small degree by non-propositional knowledge (ibid p. 1).

Furthermore, though some thought has been given to the question of how virtual learning environments (VLEs) might facilitate context crossings between work and educational practices (Dirckinck-Holmfeld & Fibiger, 2002; Dirckinck-Holmfeld & Jones, 2009; Dirckinck-Holmfeld, Tolsby, & Nyvang, 2002; Dohn & Kjær, 2009; Smith, 2012), still, the more far-reaching implications have not been addressed of the social practice theories' notion that significance and our understanding are always and fundamentally situated and locally realised.

Specifically, too little attention has been given to the view of knowledge incipient in the social practice theories. For instance, Lave and Wenger say that

> ...[E]ven so-called general knowledge only has power in specific circumstances... What is called general knowledge is not privileged with respect to other 'kinds' of knowledge. It too can be gained only in specific circumstances. And it too must be brought into play in specific circumstances. The generality of any form of knowledge always lies in the power to renegotiate the meaning of the past and future in constructing the meaning of present circumstances. (Lave & Wenger, 1991, p. 33–34)

And Dall'Alba and Sandberg argue on the basis of a number of empirical studies that

> ...an embodied understanding of practice ... forms the basis for professional skill and its development ... [T]he knowledge and skills that professionals use in performing their work depend on their embodied understanding of the practice in question. The professionals' way of understanding their practice forms and organizes their knowledge and skills into a particular form of professional skill. (Dall'Alba & Sandberg, 2006, p. 390)

In what follows I shall present an elaboration of the view of knowledge indicated by statements such as these and discuss the implications it has for how networked learning may be conceptualised.

Knowledge as Tacit, Situated, Context-Dependent, Embodied Doing

The Lave and Wenger statement cited above echoes the hermeneutic point made by Gadamer that a statement (be this a law, a biblical phrase, or a text) only gets its full, concrete meaning in the interpretation (Auslegung) given to it in the specific situation (Gadamer, 1990 p. 338). In turn, it echoes the underlying Hegelian view that 'absolute' knowledge has full existence, not in abstract general idealisations, but in concrete realisation (Hegel, 1952). It further reminds one of the Wittgensteinian dictum that a rule does not itself show how it is to be applied, that any future behaviour might be interpreted as being in agreement with or in contradiction to it, and that for this reason practical examples are necessary in order to know how to apply the rule in any given situation (Wittgenstein, 1984).

These convergences are no coincidence. As argued by Packer and Goicoechea (2000), social practice theories have their roots in the philosophies of Hegel and Marx and have evolved through inspiration from (among others) the phenomenological tradition, especially Heidegger (who in turn inspired Gadamer) and Merleau-Ponty, and post-structuralism, notably Bourdieu (who is inspired by both Merleau-Ponty and Wittgenstein). Schatzki et al. (2001) trace somewhat the same history of ideas, though they do not start as far back as Hegel and Marx nor end up explicitly discussing the learning theories under consideration here. In various ways, the said phenomenological and post-structuralist thinkers have all articulated the ontological point that significance is 'built into' the human world at the outset, that it is holistic, and that it finds concrete realisation in the 'gestalt' of the specific situation. And that, correspondingly, knowledge is primordially an embodied and practical attunement to this gestalt—an attunement upon which linguistic utterances can be made and upon which, secondarily and derivatively, knowledge expressible in words may be had.

I have developed this view of knowledge at length in a recent article, drawing on the Scandinavian interpretation of Wittgenstein (Johannesen, 1988; Josefson, 1998; Molander, 1992), which—in contrast to the first generation of his Anglo-American reception—does not focus on rule-following and linguistic practice, but on the tacit understanding in and of practice which makes rule-following (among other phenomena) possible. As noted by Schatzki et al. (2001), some Anglo-American readers like Hubert Dreyfus and Charles Taylor have read Wittgenstein in a similar way. In addition, I draw on Merleau-Pontian phenomenology and on considerations from distributed cognition and situated learning (Dohn, 2011). To comply with length requirements, I must here restrict myself to recapitulate the basic points of the argument presented there. The argument takes the following line:

1. With Wittgenstein it is argued that since any future behaviour may be interpreted as in accord with/contradictory to a given rule, 'knowing how' to follow the rule is not a question of interpretation at all. Rather, it is a tacit, practical, embodied understanding present in the action itself—a 'feel for' the unique situation and

for what amounts to 'following the rule' here. This is why examples are necessary for learning how to follow a rule—and why it is necessary for learners to work through examples themselves rather than just have them explained by a teacher: Only through doing applications of the rule—examples—can one acquire the practical 'feel for' the situation. This practical 'feel for' is the 'gut feeling' whereby we (in practice, not intellectually) evaluate the rule and sometimes find that an exception to it has to be made. On this view, the hermeneutic point made by Gadamer should be read, not with an intellectualist emphasis on the term 'interpretation', but with a pragmatist underscoring of the significance of concrete realisation.

2. The tacit, practical, embodied understanding is given a more positive character-isation by drawing on Merleau-Pontian phenomenology (Merleau-Ponty, 1962) and the use Dreyfus and Dreyfus make of it (Dreyfus & Dreyfus, 1986). This characterisation determines practical understanding as grounded in immediate (intuitive) recognition of the overall gestalt of the situation and 'holistic pairing of new situations with associated responses produced by successful experiences in similar situations' (Dreyfus & Dreyfus, 1986, p. 35). Gestalt recognition and response pairing are flexible forms of identification, i.e. they accommodate situational variations instead of grouping situations into rigid categories. Inci-dentally, the critique which Dall'Alba and Sandberg (2006) aim at the stage model of skill development proposed by Dreyfus and Dreyfus does not concern their fundamental phenomenological premises, but only their claim that skill develops in definite stages which are the same across diverse professions.

3. Leading on from this, I argue that there is no reason—apart from a Cartesian legacy—to think that knowledge is constituted by mental or linguistic represen-tation. On the contrary, since the primary ontology of knowledge is situated realisation in the action it enables, representation necessarily involves funda-mental ontological reconstruction, i.e. change in ontology. Of course thinking and language play large roles in human practices, but these are roles they have as part of exercising competence. That is, thoughts and linguistic statements are grounded in the tacit situational 'feel for' the situation—and are made as part of enacting this 'feel for'—not the other way around.

4. Fleshing out the tacit understanding, I argue with distributed cognition (Hutch-ins, 1996) and situated learning (Lave, 1988; Lave & Wenger, 1991; Wenger, 1998) that competence is a relationship in action between the agent and the environment, including tools and people present, and that knowledge is always locally realised and negotiated. Knowledge therefore always has aspects of situational specificity which are essential to its realisation and cannot be abstracted away. In consequence, complex processes of transformation and resituating are involved when content from one setting is utilised in another.

5. In conclusion, knowledge is characterised as tacit, situated, context-dependent, embodied doing, grounded in immediate recognition of and response pairing to the situation's gestalt. Thinking and communicating are phenomena of this doing and as such take their meaning in part from the situation in which they arise.

6. The implications of this view for the instantiation of reflective activities such as journal writing or professional dialogue groups are discussed. Basically, such reflective activities are problematic because they build on epistemological premises shown in the argument 1–5 not to hold. More specifically, reflective activities build on the problematic presupposition that one can 'get at' the competence in one kind of setting (the action practice) by representing it mentally or linguistically in another (the reflective setting or practice).

7. In contrast, on the view elaborated in 1–5, there is no easy path from one kind of practice to another. This does not mean that one can never be inspired in one type of settings by ongoings in another. It does mean the following, however: One, educational planners cannot design predictable routes of 'content transfer' or 'content transformation' from educational settings to practice settings. Two, inspiration to alter action practice may come from unforeseen angles quite as much as from planned interventions, just by people traversing borders between practices and reacting to the situations of one on the background of the tacit understanding they have in the other. There need be no representation of the inspiration involved—and often there will not be since that would require a transformation of ontological status twice over (from practical embodied understanding in one setting to representation to practical embodied understanding in the other setting). And three, when insights from one practice is to be made use of in another, it requires resituation, contextualisation, and reactualisation of these insights as well as (and building upon) a change in ontological status from representation to actionable knowledge. That is, it requires hard, non-predictable work, involving a significant renegotiation and transformation of the insights in question.

The considerations in 7 constitute a radicalisation of the point made by Goodyear, Jones, Asensio, Hodgson, and Steeples (2001) and Dirckinck-Holmfeld et al. (2009) that learning can never be directly designed but only designed *for*. My claim is not just that

[t]he activities, spaces and organisations that we design rely on being inhabited by others, the particular teachers and learners who 'enact' our designs. Goodyear et al. [2001] argue that we can design the tasks, the organisation and the space, in which learning may take place, however we can't be sure how the tasks are carried out, organisation becomes community or spaces become places. (Dirckinck-Holmfeld et al., 2009, p. 162)

I fully agree with this claim, but my point is the further one that we a fortiori cannot know, predict, or design what sense—if any—participants will make of whatever they might have learned in the activities and spaces we have designed, once they involve themselves in other practice settings.

This point—and the view of knowledge it builds on—is in line with the well-known situated learning thesis that learning activities within the formal educational system are framed, formed, and given content by the settings they take place in (Lave, 1988; Packer, 2001; Säljö & Wyndhamn, 1996). There is no simple transfer of content between settings; indeed, the very notion of transfer is unclear (cf. Packer, 2001): Given that tasks are concretely realised in the specific situations in which they are encountered and therefore get structure and content from these situations, what constitutes 'the same task' across settings is not a simple, objective matter. It is a complex question of negotiation and resituating.

These claims should not lead one to despair as an educator, though. Rather, they constitute a reason for an increased focus on the necessity of supporting students in developing their sensitivity towards the given situation and towards ways in which their understanding and perspectives from other situations might be resituated and reactualised there. The significance of such a focus is increased by the fact that students in the society we live in today will most probably not spend their full professional life in one job in one organisational context but will traverse different settings and repeatedly have to resituate and transform their knowledge.

By way of contrast and for the sake of clarity, it is worth emphasising that these considerations differ somewhat from recommendations set forth by others noting the challenges posed by today's society—whether characterised as 'network society', 'knowledge society', 'learning society', or the like. Thus, in the last chapter of the first book in this series, Hodgson et al. (2012) summarise and discuss points made throughout the book and elsewhere, stressing critical reflexivity, the ability to judge one's own learning and that of others, and investment of self in the learning process as crucial to participation in today's society. To the extent that 'reflexivity' and 'ability to judge learning' are taken to be inherently dependent on reflection as a process of 'stepping back from' and thinking about/discussing/critically evaluating practice, such recommendations actually run counter to the view presented here: The sensitivity towards the concrete situation which is called for is not primarily one of reflection, but of openness and attunement towards the situation's gestalt in its complexity. Similarly, the resituation and reactualisation necessary for insights from one practice to become relevant to another are not brought about by reflection on differences between the practices, but by a flexible attuning in action of one's embodied expectations of situational gestalts. As for the investment of self in the situation, I do agree that this is an essential aspect—sensitivity and attunement would seem impossible without an investment of self, and conversely, such investment is a defining characteristic of the 'primary contexts' of a person.

Conceptualising Networked Learning Activities

Looking across the literature on cases of networked learning, common concerns are how to get students to participate (Dirckinck-Holmfeld & Fibiger, 2002; Fischer, Kollar, Mandl, & Haake, 2007; Goodyear et al., 2004; Salmon, 2000, 2002; Wasson, Ludvigsen, & Hoppe, 2003); how to ensure relevance of the networked learning activities for the students (Dirckinck-Holmfeld et al., 2002; Farmer, Yue, & Brooks, 2008; McConnell, 1994, 2006; McConnell, Hodgson, & Dirckinck-Holmfeld, 2012); how to facilitate that the 'space' of the VLE becomes a 'place' for the students (Pilkington & Guldberg, 2009; Ryberg & Wentzer, 2011); and how one as teacher or VLE facilitator supports the emergence of 'activity systems' or 'communities of practices' revolving around the networked learning activities (Nielsen & Danielsen, 2011; Pilkington & Guldberg, 2009).

In the literature, there are clear examples of students and teachers having experienced their VLE as a 'place of their own'; as an anchorage point for their learning, where the 'presence' of participants was sensed as prominently as presence in physical encounters—sometimes even more so (Hodgson, 2008; Pilkington & Guldberg, 2009; Rudestam & Schoenholtz-Read, 2002). Stepping outside the educational world, there is no doubt that Facebook and MySpace are significant anchorage points for many young people—a 'place' where they sense their own and other people's 'presence' acutely (Boyd, 2008). To a somewhat lesser extent, some online communities specialised to a certain domain (e.g. open-source programming, reef aquariums, or MMORPGs like World of Warcraft) tend to be experienced as 'places' or anchorage points for some of the participants, too. Such examples prove that it is possible for virtual contexts to become 'primary contexts' for the participants involved. Thus, no claim is being made here to the effect that only physical 'real life' settings can foster belonging and/or constitute a primary context. Quite the contrary, virtual settings may be just as much a part of 'real life' as physical settings, and risk taking, identity negotiation, and insecurity—contrary to what Dreyfus has claimed (Dreyfus, 2001)—can play as significant roles here as in face-to-face encounters, though sometimes in somewhat different ways (Land, 2004).

This said, the general impression one gets from an overview of the literature is that VLEs/groups on VLEs within networked learning settings are not among the virtual settings where its participants most often feel a sense of belonging. Even when tutors focus on facilitating the development of such a feeling, there seem to be a number of learners for whom it doesn't happen (Dohn, 2007; Dohn, Thorsen, & Larsen, 2013; Ryberg & Wentzer, 2011; Salmon, 2000, 2002). In particular, it would seem to be the exception rather than the rule for VLEs to take on the role of 'primary context' for the learners.

In general, as judged from the literature as well as from nearly 15 years of experience with working with networked learning activities (as teacher, researcher, and educational developer), networked learning activities tend for given participants to fall into one of three categories:

• Activities which in practice are 'stand-alone' activities and for which participants feel no great intrinsic motivation (Ryan & Deci, 2000). The instrumental purpose and justification of the activities in terms of educational goals may be quite clear, and they may be thematically quite well integrated with activities taking place in physical contexts (e.g. further course activities or practice experiences from informal everyday learning contexts). However, because they are designed to fulfil educational ends in themselves rather than be integrated practically with other activities, they tend to be experienced as somewhat artificial formalisations which do not quite 'hit the mark' or lack 'common ground' (cf., e.g. Farmer et al., 2008; Ryberg & Wentzer, 2011; Salmon, 2002, p. 20, for student comments to this effect). A typical indicator that one has to do with activities of this kind is teacher worries of 'how to involve the learners and get them to contribute' (cf. Salmon, 2000, 2002). Extreme examples of such activities (bordering on not being 'activities' at all) are learning objects, posited as self-explanatory, stand-alone tools for learning, which the learner is expected to make use of and learn from without any further support on the part of the course (e.g. Open University's OpenLearn platform taken by itself, http://openlearn.open.ac.uk/). That is, learning is supposed to come from the object in itself rather than from course activities which centre on the use which learners should make of the object as a resource (on a par with books and other physical resources) in carrying out the activity. Further, not so extreme, examples are constituted by discussion forum activities where students are to have a stand-alone debate on a text they have read; stand-alone in the sense that course activities are not designed so that this debate is to be directly taken up in future learning activities. I shall term this kind of activity 'stand-alone activities'.

- Activities which succeed in being (part of) a 'primary context' for the participants and which they therefore view as natural and rewarding for expressing and developing their knowledge. References to literature which present examples of such activities are given above. I shall term this kind of activity 'primary context activities'. As indicated, many networked learning activities do not succeed in becoming primary context activities even though they are designed with that aim.

- Activities which do not aim at attaining educational ends in themselves, but which serve as 'mediators' or 'brokers' between primary contexts. They gain what significance they have by being catalysts for participants to remediate and resituate content across settings. The mediation may, for example, be between educational settings and other life contexts, between different study contexts within a course, between courses within an educational programme, or, in some professional development courses, between the participants' diverse action learning contexts in practice. Portfolios in professional education may take on this role (Klenowski, 2002) as may PBL activities which span virtual and physical study settings (Vines & Dysthe, 2009). Web 2.0-mediated learning activities focused on facilitating flow and resituation of content across contexts is another case in question (Farmer et al., 2008) as is the situated curriculum co-constructed by owner-managers of small businesses (SMEs) in the LEAD programme discussed by Smith (2012). In the latter case, action learning in each participant's own primary business context was integrated with physical meetings and discussions in an online space in a way which focused on the participants' need for renegotiation and resituation of content across the different contexts. I shall term this kind of activity 'mediator activities'. Many activities which are intended as mediator activities on the part of the teacher or course planner in point of fact end up being stand-alone activities for the learners. Examples concerning the use of a blog and of a Facebook group, respectively, are reported in Dohn (2009) and Andersen, Dohn, Irminger, and Vestergaard (2012).

The same activity need not fall in the same category for all of the participants involved in it. That is, a given activity may be experienced as a 'stand-alone' activity for some learners and as a 'primary context activity' for others. My own very first experiences with teaching networked learning activities may serve as example: A few students evaluated the activities as essentially 'a home for their learning' whereas a number of students hardly participated at all. Other examples are provided in Salmon (2002) and Dohn et al. (2013). Similarly, an activity may function as a 'mediator activity' for some students whereas others experience it as a 'stand-alone' activity. This was the case with the Facebook activities reported in Andersen et al. (2012).

As indicated in the beginning of the chapter, the concept of networked learning provided by Goodyear et al. (2004) does not really take into account the type of activity here designated as 'mediator activity'. As it stands, their definition seems implicitly to build on a paradigm of networked learning where the activities take place in a VLE or similar virtual setting, i.e. where the connections which the definition highlights are all connections within a relatively well-demarcated virtual context or (smaller) set of contexts. Though the definition does not *preclude* an interpretation where the 'learning resources' connected to are (from the point of view of the course) contingent resources dispersed across the many life contexts which course participants between them participate in, the definition seems focused on 'primary context activities' and 'stand-alone activities'. My suggested addition of the sentence 'connections between the diverse contexts in which the learners participate' on the other hand centres on the type of connections involved in 'mediator activities'. It thus affords thinking about how to design activities which support learners in resituating content across their existing physical and virtual 'primary contexts', educational and otherwise.

In the following I present a philosophical analysis of what is at stake in each of the three kinds of activities, as viewed from the knowledge perspective presented above (henceforth KP). More specifically, I explain why most networked learning activities fall into the first group and argue that the third kind is worth aiming for (though difficult to attain). Towards the end I elaborate a bit on the philosophical question how it is possible at all for networked learning activities to become primary context activities if knowledge is a tacit, embodied doing.

From the KP view, stand-alone activities are activities which are not anchored in the lifeworlds of the participants, i.e. their familiar everyday world with its primary and near-primary, physical and virtual, contexts, the everyday world in which they engage and are absorbed and which constitutes the outset for their sensemaking (Heidegger, 1986; Schutz & Luckmann, 1973). Because of their lack of anchorage in the lifeworld, stand-alone activities do not present natural or regular ways for the participants to enact their knowledge. The dialogue in the stand-alone activities is correspondingly 'detached' from the contexts in which words get their deeper, fully realised meaning for the participants. In turn, the dialogue may phenomenologically be experienced as 'abstract', lacking depth or reality, as 'off the mark' or lacking 'common ground' (Salmon, 2002). The very characteristics which are often proposed as the strength of networked learning—their geographical and temporal flexibility and the 'distance' and 'moment of pause and reflection' they allegedly represent—are their most problematic traits, too: Their 'flexibility', combined with their self-contained stand-alone focus on educational ends not directly integrated as objectives in the primary contexts of the lifeworld, implies their non-essentiality for the participants in the ongoing of these primary contexts.

Indicative, though not conclusive, empirical support for this philosophical point is supplied by studies of e-learning in Swedish industry (Svensson, Ellström, & Åberg, 2004). Similarly, the problems of disconnectedness which academics (and learners) experience in making the transition from familiar face-to-face practices to teaching online (Boon & Sinclair, 2012) find their deeper explanation in the detachedness of the online discourse and the words used there from the primary contexts of the participants. As Boon and Sinclair note:

> In our own experience … the seeming constants of language, identity, engagement, and time were shown to be inconstant and made unfamiliar through this transition or crossing. This inconstancy and unfamiliarity can be a very real barrier for academics and students alike. With one foot in the real and another in the virtual, users must come to terms with both difference and disquiet in order to participate effectively in networked learning environments.' (Boon & Sinclair, 2012, p. 278)

The simple point to be made from the viewpoint of KP is that not all participants can or are willing to 'come to terms with' this inconstancy—and, one might add, initial lack of significance—and that to those that do not 'come to terms' the networked learning activities will never evolve past being 'stand-alone activities' in which they only engage half-heartedly or not at all. Incidentally, Boon and Sinclair seem to imply that *all* virtual contexts show this inconstancy and conse-quently seem less 'real' than physical settings. Given the above mentioned signif-icance which some virtual settings have for some people, I think this hard-drawn distinction between the physical and the virtual distorts the point somewhat. The problem is the detachment of 'stand-alone activities' from the primary contexts (be they physical or virtual) of the participants, not the virtuality per se.

Phenomenologically, the point is that participants, in their situated, embodied recognition of and response to the situational gestalts of their action practice, do not immediately see and feel the relevance of the stand-alone activities and the content presented through them. The networked learning activities do not spring to mind (or rather: spring to action) as compelling elements to be resituated in their actions in practice. Though participants may be convinced at some level of linguistic/mental representation of the relevance of the networked learning activities and the educational ends aimed at through them, this conviction in itself will be of little help given that there is no easy and direct route between mental/linguistic repre-sentations of practice and actions in practice. As indicated above, it requires hard non-predictable work to resituate content and insights across contexts. If this hard work is not supported at all (as it will not be in the case of learning objects presented as self-explanatory tools for learning) or only supported casually (e.g. through a noncommitting invitation to contribute with practice examples to forum discus-sions), but not facilitated actively through anchoring the activities in the action practices of the participants, the risk is correspondingly great that the activities will be experienced as insignificant, only to be carried out 'because we have to'—or that they will simply be neglected.

On the other hand, given that resituating insights across contexts is hard and difficult work, and given that it is important to support students in learning to resituate their tacit, embodied understanding from one context to another (cf. the last section), the significance of the third type of networked learning activities, the mediator activities, is clear. The point here is less to supply a 'place' for activities such as reflecting on practice and more to make possible the coupling between contexts that are already significant for the participants and where their words thus have fully realised meaning. Mediator activities have their anchorage in the settings to be coupled and are centred on transforming meaning between them. As viewed from KP, a design focus on establishing a virtual 'place' where the coupling can be done is misguided because such a 'place' will necessarily be a representational space. That is, activities here will at most constitute *representations* of couplings rather than *be* couplings. For this reason, networked learning activities intended as mediator activities run a clear risk of ending up as stand-alone activities, as in the case described in Dohn (2009) and in some of the Facebook activities reported in Andersen et al. (2012). Conversely, portfolios may get to be mediator activities in teacher education (Klenowski, 2002) precisely when the representation of profes-sional practice in the portfolio is not treated as goal in itself, but is carried on into the classroom with a focus on resituating the tacit understanding of the teaching practice in classroom discussions of learning and teaching. Analogous points may be made for the role of the PBL activities in the case reported by Vines and Dysthe (2009) and of the online discussions in the LEAD case described by Smith (2012).

The question remains how it is at all possible for virtual contexts to succeed in becoming 'primary contexts' for at least some of the participants, i.e. how networked learning activities of the second kind are possible. The answer is that we involve ourselves as embodied beings even in settings where we do not physically meet the others. We engage ourselves as bodily beings placed in physical surroundings (at a desk, with keyboard and screen, with enough light to see etc.) and we enact our tacit understanding of the situation in corresponding virtually with others exactly as we do in other situations. As Land has pointed out, one commits an 'incorporeal fallacy' if one thinks that cyberspace is a space of bodiless minds, just because bodies are not visible 'in' it (Land, 2004). The point is that 'the minds that meet' in cyberspace are not 'in' cyberspace at all, they are the embodied minds of material people. A clear indicator that we are not 'disembodiedly' involved as minds when communicating virtually is the physical discomfort one may feel after reading an unpleasant comment in a virtual setting. One may acquire a 'feel for' the communication in a certain virtual setting with a certain group of people; slip-ups may make one squirm and blush alone in one's office; and one may become so proficient in corresponding virtually that the 'right thing to write' comes naturally and immediately to one. As such, corresponding virtually with others is as much an embodied action as any other action. However, since the physical location of this embodied action is displaced from the physical locations of the other participants but most often identical to the physical location of one or more of our (other) primary contexts (at work or at home), it is easy to be distracted from involving oneself in a virtual setting. As Merleau-Ponty would say, being bodies in a world means an anchoring of our involvement in the world, where our body is 'the unperceived term in the centre of the world towards which all objects turn their face' (Merleau-Ponty, 1962, p. 82) and where 'The word 'here' applied to my body [refers to] the laying down of the first co-ordinates, the anchoring of the active body in an object, the situation of the body in face of its tasks' (ibid, p. 100). By which he meant that 'here' is always first and foremost the 'here' of our bodily being (which thereby sets the 'first co-ordinates', i.e. determines the 'zero' of the co-ordinate system of inhabited space). And, further, that our bodily being is always already engaged in the world and only experiences itself through this lived engagement— actually only experiences itself as 'here' through the 'here' of the objects with which it engages.

Primary context networked learning activities therefore are possible for the same reason as any involvement in practice is possible: We are bodily beings and as such may develop a tacit, embodied understanding of what constitutes adequate action in the given situation, virtual or physical. On the other hand, the reason why most networked learning activities do not succeed in becoming primary context activities is that we as bodily beings are always already engaged in many primary contexts (most of them physical, some perhaps virtual), the significance of which give anchorage to our being. Networked learning activities which do not directly relate to one or more of these primary contexts (as mediator activities) start out as stand-alone activities into which the participants' tacit embodied understandings from their primary contexts are not easily resituated (because they have not as yet developed a practice understanding hereof) and which for their part seem somewhat unrelated to 'what really matters', i.e. their primary context activities. These networked learning activities have yet to prove their worth in themselves for the participants (i.e. become a primary context) and the dialogue to acquire fuller, deeper meaning than the 'abstractions deficit of tacit practice understanding' with which it necessarily starts. And given the participants' already existing involvement in other primary contexts, chances are that despite initial motivation and resolve to engage in virtual activities, stand-alone activities will in practice appear 'off the mark' and be neglected. This is, I would claim, the deeper reason for the fact noted (and lamented) by McConnell et al. (2012) that

> For many present-day networked learning students and tutors, the perception that learning technologies lack social presence and do not match the experience of face-to-face meetings still persists. (p. 6)

As McConnell et al. go on to say, there is much evidence to the contrary. However, from the view of KP, the problem is precisely that networked learning discussions start out lacking the fuller, deeper meaning and that this lack is experienced as a 'social distance' between learners.

In Conclusion: Implications for the Design of Networked Learning

In this chapter I have attempted to flesh out a 'practice' view of knowledge, incipient though seldom fully articulated in the social practice theories which many researchers within networked learning take as their point of departure. I have drawn on prior work which integrates insights from the Scandinavian reception of Wittgenstein, phenomenology, and situated learning to formulate a view of knowledge as tacit, situated, context-dependent, embodied doing. Building on this view of knowledge, I have pointed out that insights and understandings from one context have to be resituated, transformed, and reactualised to be brought into use in other contexts. Educators today should challenge their students to resituate their tacit, practical understandings across the different contexts they participate in—and support them in learning to do so. Networked learning activities may potentially play important roles here because they can be designed as 'mediator activities' which are characterised by catalysing the coupling of primary contexts, whilst not aiming at the attainment of educational ends themselves. Such mediator activities have their anchorage in the settings to be coupled, not in the coupling. On the other hand, networked learning activities designed to be a 'place' for the pursuit of educational goals tend to become stand-alone activities which seem somewhat unrelated to 'what is really at stake' for the participants, i.e. what their tacit practical embodied understanding, anchored in the participants' primary contexts, show them as significant.

In conclusion, the implications of this view for the design of networked learning activities should be briefly mentioned. In most cases it is not advisable to plan networked learning activities as primary context activities. That is, it is not advisable to design activities which presuppose that learners engage in them for their own sake, because they consider the activities significant for who they are, and where the activities will only succeed if the participants develop fully realised tacit knowing and understanding of the virtual settings in which they take place. It is not impossible for networked learning activities to become primary context activities, but their geographical and temporal flexibility and their detachment from the participants' other primary contexts—often hailed as a great advantage and inducive to a 'reflective stance'—may easily lead to the activities being experienced as insignificant or beside the point. Instead, networked learning activities should be designed to facilitate an anchorage in action in the already existing primary contexts of the participants, both educational and noneducational ones. This allows networked learning to bridge contexts and support students in resituating knowledge from their educational settings to their other life contexts—and vice versa. The requirement is that networked learning activities are not expected to be goals in themselves, but are allowed the role as necessary medium for activities crossing contexts. Learning activities designed in this way, all things being equal, stand the best chance of not only succeeding as activities but also of developing significance for the participants.

One last comment, is this chapter not itself a stand-alone activity and if yes, is it not self-defeating to hope anyone might find it interesting? Not quite. Due to length restrictions, I have only pointed to, not elaborated on, specific examples. However, given the context—a book on networked learning aimed at researchers and practitioners within the field—it is perhaps not unreasonable to expect readers to be participants in primary contexts which supply examples such as the ones pointed to. Their resituating of the article's arguments may be helped in this way and hopefully their interest awakened. On the other hand, resituating *will* be necessary. The paper taken by itself is just a resource and as argued above the interesting question concerning resources is what use they will be put to in concrete activities, not what they 'do' themselves. My clear hope is that the chapter may inspire lively discussion in the primary contexts of its readers.

References

Andersen, P., Dohn, N., Irminger, S., & Vestergaard, A. (2012). Eksperimenter med Facebook i undervisningen. *Unge Pædagoger, 4*, 17–27.

Boon, S., & Sinclair, S. (2012). Life behind the screen: Taking the academic online. In L. Dirckinck-Holmfeld, V. Hodgson, & D. McConnell (Eds.), *Exploring the theory, pedagogy and practice of networked learning* (pp. 273–287). Dordrecht, The Netherlands: Springer.

Booth, S., & Hultén, M. (2004). Opening dimensions of variation: An empirical study of learning in a web-based discussion. In P. Goodyear, S. Banks, V. Hodgson, & D. McConnell (Eds.), *Advances in research on networked learning* (pp. 153–174). Dordrecht, The Netherlands: Kluwer.

Boyd, D. (2008). Why youth loves social network sites: The role of networked publics in teenage social life. In D. Buckingham (Ed.), *Youth, identity, and digital media* (pp. 119–142). Cambridge, MA: The MIT Press.

Butler, J. (1990). *Gender trouble*. London, England: Routledge.

Chen, F., Chang, H., & Wang, T. (2010). Collective brokering practice: A constellation of practices perspective. *Proceedings of the 7th International Conference on Networked Learning*, 88–96.

Cole, M. (1990). *Vygotsky and education*. New York: Cambridge University Press.

Cousin, G., & Deepwell, F. (2005). Designs for network learning: A communities of practice perspective. *Studies in Higher Education, 30*(1), 57–66.

Dall'Alba, G., & Sandberg, J. (2006). Unveiling professional development: A critical review of stage models. *Review of Educational Research, 76*(3), 383–412.

Derrida, J. (1997). *Of grammatology*. Baltimore: The Johns Hopkins University Press.

Dirckinck-Holmfeld, L., & Fibiger, B. (Eds.). (2002). *Learning in virtual environments*. Copenhagen, Denmark : Samfundslitteratur.

Dirckinck-Holmfeld, L., & Jones, C. (2009). Issues and concepts in networked learning. Analysis and the future of networked learning. In L. Dirckinck-Holmfeld, C. Jones, & B. Lindström (Eds.), *Analysing networked learning practices in higher education and continuing professional development* (pp. 259–285). Rotterdam, Denmark: Sense.

Dirckinck-Holmfeld, L., Nielsen, J., Fibiger, B., Danielsen, O., Riis, M., Sorensen, E., et al. (2009). Issues and concepts in networked learning. Analysis and the future of networked learning. In L. Dirckinck-Holmfeld, C. Jones, & B. Lindström (Eds.), *Analysing networked learning practices in higher education and continuing professional development* (pp. 259–285). Rotterdam, Denmark: Sense.

Dirckinck-Holmfeld, L., Tolsby, H., & Nyvang, T. (2002). E-læring systemer i arbejdspladsrelateret projektpædagogik. In K. Illeris (Ed.), *Udspil om læring i arbejdslivet* (pp. 123–153). Roskilde, Denmark: Roskilde Universitetsforlag.

Dohn, N. (2007). It-baserede læreprocesser—Nogle muligheder og nogle begrænsninger. *Dansk Universitetspædagogisk Tidsskrift, 4*, 41–49.

Dohn, N. (2009). *Web 2.0 som lærings- og arbejdsredskab.* Jelling, Denmark: UC Lillebælt.

Dohn, N. (2011). On the epistemological presuppositions of reflective activities. *Educational Theory, 61*(6), 671–708.

Dohn, N. (2013). 'Viden i praksis'—implikationer for it-baseret læring, *Res Cogitans 9* (1) (in press).

Dohn, N., & Kjær, C. (2009). Language is not enough—Knowledge perspectives on work-based learning in global organisations. *Hermes—Journal of Language and Communication Studies, 43*, 137–161.

Dohn, N., Thorsen, M., & Larsen, S. (2013). E-læring. In L. Rienecker, P. Stray, J. Dolin, & G. Ingerslev (Eds.), *Universitetspædagogik.* Samfundslitteratur. 299–328.

Dreyfus, H. (2001). *On the internet.* New York: Routledge.

Dreyfus, H., & Dreyfus, S. (1986). *Mind over machine.* New York: The Free Press.

Engeström, Y. (1987). *Learning by expanding.* Helsinki, Finland: Orienta-Konsultit.

Engeström, Y. (2001). Expansive learning at work: Toward an activity theoretical reconceptualization. *Journal of Education and Work, 14*(1), 133–156.

Farmer, B., Yue, A., & Brooks, C. (2008). Using blogging for higher order learning in large cohort university teaching: A case study. *Australasian Journal of Educational Technology, 24*(2), 123–136.

Fischer, F., Kollar, I., Mandl, H., & Haake, J. (Eds.). (2007). *Scripting computer-supported collaborative learning.* Dordrecht, The Netherlands: Springer.

Foucault, M. (1970). *The order of things. An archaeology of the human sciences.* New York: Pantheon Books.

Fulantelli, G. (2009). Blended learning, Systems thinking and communities of practice. A case study. In L. Dirckinck-Holmfeld, C. Jones, & B. Lindström (Eds.), *Analysing networked learning practices in higher education and continuing professional development* (pp. 45–62). Rotterdam, The Netherlands: Sense.

Gadamer, H. G. (1990). *Wahrheit und Methode.* Tübingen, Germany: J.C.B. Mohr.

Geithner, S., & Schulz, K. (2010). Networks as platforms for expansive development—Examples from a school development programme. In *Proceedings of the 7th International Conference on Networked Learning* (pp. 159–167).

Goodyear, P., Banks, S., Hodgson, V., & McConnell, D. (Eds.). (2004). *Advances in research on networked learning.* Dordrecht, The Netherlands: Kluwer.

Goodyear, P., Jones, C., Asensio, M., Hodgson, V., & Steeples, C. (2001). *Effective networked learning in higher education: Notes and guidelines.* Lancaster, England: CSALT, Lancaster University.

Hedegaard, M. (1995). *Tænkning, viden, udvikling.* Aarhus, Denmark: Aarhus Universitetsforlag.

Hegel, G. (1952). *Phänomenologie des Geistes.* Hamburg, Germany: Felix Mainer.

Heidegger, M. (1986). *Sein und Zeit.* Tübingen, Germany: Max Niemeyer.

Hodgson, V. (2008). Learning spaces, context and auto/biography in online learning communities. *International Journal of Web Based Communities, 4*(2), 159–172.

Hodgson, V., McConnell, D., & Dirckinck-Holmfeld, L. (2012). The theory, practice and pedagogy of networked learning. In L. Dirckinck-Holmfeld, V. Hodgson, & D. McConnell (Eds.), *Exploring the theory, pedagogy and practice of networked learning* (pp. 291–305). Dordrecht, The Netherlands: Springer.

Hutchins, E. (1996). Learning to navigate. In S. Chaiklin & J. Lave (Eds.), *Understanding practice* (pp. 35–63). New York: Cambridge University Press.

Johannesen, K. (1988). The concept of practice in Wittgenstein's later philosophy'. *Inquiry, 31*(3), 357–369.

Jones, C., & Dirckinck-Holmfeld, L. (2009). *Analysing networked learning practices. An Introduction. In L. Dirckinck-Holmfeld, C. Jones & B. Lindström, B. (Eds.), Analysing networked learning practices in higher education and continuing professional development. (pp. 1-27).* Rotterdam, Denmark: Sense.

Jones, C., Dirckinck-Holmfeld, L., & Lindström, B. (2006). A relational, indirect, meso-level approach to CSCL design in the next decade. *International Journal of Computer-Supported Collaborative Learning, 1*(1), 35–56.

Josefson, I. (1998). *Läkarens yrkeskunnande.* Lund, Sweden: Studentlitteratur.

Kenny, A. (1973). *Wittgenstein.* London, England: Penguin.

Klenowski, V. (2002). *Developing portfolios for learning and assessment.* London, England: RoutledgeFalmer.

Kripke, S. (1982). *Wittgenstein on rules and private language.* Oxford, England: Blackwell.

Land, R. (2004). Issues of embodiment and risk in online learning. In R. Atkinson, C. McBeath, D. Jonas-Dwyer & R. Phillips (Eds.), *Beyond the comfort zone: Proceedings of the 21st ASCILITE Conference* (pp. 530–538).

Lave, J. (1988). *Cognition in practice.* Cambridge, England: Cambridge University Press.

Lave, J., & Wenger, E. (1991). *Situated learning.* New York: Cambridge University Press.

Leont'ev, A. (1978). *Activity, consciousness, and personality.* Engelwood Cliffs, NJ: Prentice-Hall.

McConnell, D. (1994). *Implementing computer supported cooperative learning.* London, England: Kogan Page.

McConnell, D. (2006). *E-learning groups and communities.* Maidenhead, England: SRHE/OU Press.

McConnell, D., Hodgson, V., & Dirckinck-Holmfeld, L. (2012). Networked learning: A brief history and new trends. In L. Dirckinck-Holmfeld, V. Hodgson, & D. McConnell (Eds.), *Exploring the theory, pedagogy and practice of networked learning* (pp. 3–24). Dordrecht, The Netherlands: Springer.

Merleau-Ponty, M. (1962). *Phenomenology of perception.* London, England: Routledge & Kegan.

Molander, B. (1992). Tacit knowledge and silenced knowledge: Fundamental problems and controversies. In B. Göranzon & M. Florin (Eds.), *Skill and education: Reflection and experience* (pp. 9–31). London, England: Springer.

Nielsen, J., & Danielsen, O. (2011). Problem-oriented project studies—the role of the teacher as supervisor for the study group in its learning processes. In L. Dirckinck-Holmfeld, V. Hodgson, & D. McConnell (Eds.), *Exploring the theory, pedagogy and practice of networked learning* (pp. 257–272). Dordrecht, The Netherlands: Springer.

Packer, M. (2001). The problem of transfer, and the sociocultural critique of schooling. *Journal of the Learning Sciences, 10*(4), 494–514.

Packer, M., & Goicoechea, J. (2000). Sociocultural and constructivist theories of learning: Ontology, not just epistemology. *Educational Psychologist, 35*(4), 227–241.

Pilkington, R., & Guldberg, K. (2009). Conditions for productive networked learning among professionals and carers. In L. Dirckinck-Holmfeld, C. Jones, & B. Lindström (Eds.), *Analysing networked learning practices in higher education and continuing professional development* (pp. 63–83). Rotterdam, Denmark: Sense.

Rudestam, K., & Schoenholtz-Read, J. (2002). *Handbook of online learning.* Thousand Oaks, CA: Sage.

Ryan, R., & Deci, E. (2000). Intrinsic and extrinsic motivations: Classic definitions and new directions. *Contemporary Educational Psychology, 25*, 54–67.

Ryberg, T., & Larsen, M. (2008). Networked identities: Understanding relationships between strong and weak ties in networked environments. *Journal of Computer Assisted Learning, 24* (1), 103–115.

Ryberg, T., & Wentzer, H. (2011). Erfaringer med e-porteføljer og personlige læringsmiljøer. *Dansk Universitetspædagogisk Tidsskrift, 11*, 14–19.

Säljö, R., & Wyndhamn, J. (1996). Solving everyday problems in the formal setting. In S. Chaiklin & J. Lave (Eds.), *Understanding practice* (pp. 327–342). New York: Cambridge University Press.

Salmon, G. (2000). *E-moderating*. London, England: Routledge.

Salmon, G. (2002). *E-tivities*. London, England: Routledge.

Schatzki, T., Knorr-Cetina, K., & von Savigny, E. (Eds.). (2001). *The practice turn in contemporary theory*. London, England: Routledge.

Schutz, A., & Luckmann, T. (1973). *The structures of the life-world*. London, England: Heinemann.

Sfard, A. (1998). On two metaphors of learning and the dangers of choosing just one. *Educational Researcher, 27*(2), 4–13.

Smith, S. (2012). How do small business owner-managers learn leadership through networked learning? In L. Dirckinck-Holmfeld, V. Hodgson, & D. McConnell (Eds.), *Exploring the theory, pedagogy and practice of networked learning* (pp. 221–236). Dordrecht, The Netherlands: Springer.

Svensson, L., Ellström, P., & Åberg, C. (2004). Integrating formal and informal learning at work. *The Journal of Workplace Learning, 16*(8), 479–491.

Vines, A., & Dysthe, O. (2009). Productive learning in the study of law. In L. Dirckinck-Holmfeld, C. Jones, & B. Lindström (Eds.), *Analysing networked learning practices in higher education and continuing professional development* (pp. 175–199). Rotterdam, Denmark: Sense.

Vygotsky, L. (1978). *Mind in society*. Cambridge, MA: Harvard University Press.

Wännman-Toresson, G. (2002). *Kvinnor skapar kunskap på nätet*. Umeå, Norrland: Pedagogiska Institutionen, Umeå University.

Wasson, B., Ludvigsen, S., & Hoppe, U. (Eds.). (2003). *Designing for change in networked learning environments*. Dordrecht, The Netherlands: Kluwer.

Wenger, E. (1998). *Communities of practice*. New York: Cambridge University Press.

Wertsch, J. (1998). *Mind as action*. New York: Oxford University Press.

Winch, P. (1990). *The idea of a social science and its relation to philosophy*. London, England: Routledge.

Wittgenstein, L. (1984). *Philosophische Untersuchungen: Vol. 1. Werkausgabe*. Frankfurt am Main, Germany: Suhrkamp

Chapter 3
Designing for Learning in Coupled Contexts

Janne Gleerup, Simon Heilesen, Niels Henrik Helms, and Kevin Mogensen

Introduction

This chapter deals with vocational education. On the one hand, this kind of training focuses directly on jobs and the labour market, while on the other hand vocational education should ensure that the participants develop general competencies that equalise this education with other educations for young people (upper secondary education). The main characteristic of vocational education in Denmark is the principle of alternation, where the apprentices alternate between periods at college and periods of working in a company. By means of close cooperation between vocational colleges and companies, the practice of alternating training is meant to guarantee the quality and relevance of the curriculum by continually ensuring that competence development at the college matches the needs of the companies and the labour market (Wilbrandt, 2002).

Prominent among the problems relating to the educational practice of alternating training is the fact that the interplay between learning processes taking place at college and at work typically is perceived as being weak. It is challenged by the

J. Gleerup (✉)
Roskilde University, PAES, Building 30C.1, 4000 Roskilde, Denmark
e-mail: gleerup@ruc.dk

S. Heilesen
Roskilde University, PAES, Building 30C.2, 4000 Roskilde, Denmark
e-mail: simonhei@ruc.dk

N.H. Helms
University College Zealand, Slagelsevej 7, 4180 Sorø, Denmark
e-mail: nhhe@ucsj.dk

K. Mogensen
Department of Psychology and Educational Research, Roskilde University,
Building 30C.1, Office No. 15, 4000 Roskilde, Denmark
e-mail: kevin@ruc.dk

V. Hodgson et al. (eds.), *The Design, Experience and Practice of Networked Learning*,
Research in Networked Learning, DOI 10.1007/978-3-319-01940-6_3,
© Springer International Publishing Switzerland 2014

different rationalities of the two widely different learning contexts of the vocational education programmes (Jørgensen, 2004). Recent research indicates that responsibility for creating coherence in and making sense of vocational education is left to the learners who, working as apprentices in companies, have to deal with the challenges of establishing continuity and integration in the learning processes (Nielsen, 2009). Thus, it is the apprentices in cooperation with colleges and companies who have to be provided with tools and structural frameworks that may help support the individual pupil/apprentice in developing professional skills and competencies (Schwencke & Larsen, 2011).

In the case to be discussed in this chapter, the training of Danish electrician apprentices, the curriculum consists of five modules of attending college interspersed with five modules of working as an apprentice in a company. The transition from one module to the next is documented in the so-called "personal education plan", stating what competencies the apprentice had prior to the module, what competencies have been acquired in the course of the module and what the objectives are of the next module. Apart from drawing up a contract, formal communication between company and college may be limited to the documentation in the personal education plan. So, in the understanding of many of the apprentices, college and practice are quite separate worlds (Gleerup, 2010). "What I was taught in college isn't worth a damn out here", is a typical comment indicative of a transfer problem. Dealing with it is not just an organisational issue but also one of creating a meaningful coupling between two widely different learning contexts (Christensen, 2010).

The project reported on in this chapter attempts bridging the gap by means of networked learning. In the present context, the concept of networked learning is understood in the sense of the working definition of networked learning proposed in the networked e-learning manifesto:

> Networked e-learning refers to those learning situations and contexts which, through the use of ICT, allow learners to be connected with other people (for example, learners, teachers/tutors, mentors, librarians, technical assistants) and with shared, information rich resources. Networked e-learning also views learners as contributing to the development of these learning resources and information of various kinds and types. (E-Quality Network, 2002)

The two positions emphasised here, that is, *firstly* the potentials of ICT to interconnect people and resources and *secondly* the contributions of Learners of learning resources, are both essential to the case we are working with. This goes also for the underlying premise which to some extent is elaborated in the manifesto: the move from a transmission mode to a participating mode of learning. However, the very concept of networked learning is rather weak in the manifesto. In our understanding, networked learning means a kind of learning that is mediated through ICT and that emerges across intra- or inter-organisational boundaries. The latter part is important because it suggests that networked learning calls for more than just ICT-mediated training or communication within an institutional framework of an organisation or in a formal educational context.

The design model we present in this chapter rests on two premises. *Firstly*, it should open up for a networked learning solution which should involve all actors in the learning context—that is apprentices, teachers, masters and journeymen in companies. Below, they are referred to as "users" in order to avoid assigning connotative labels to individuals whose role, it will be argued, will always be a construct in a particular setting. However, they are users in an active sense of "participants", as will be argued below. *Secondly*, that developing new pedagogical designs should be based on user-driven innovation.

User-Driven Innovation

For decades, in designing IT systems there has been a tradition of involving the users in cooperative, participatory or contextual design, and there is even an ISO standard for it (International Organisation for Standardisation, 2010). In recent years, users have become increasingly engaged, not only as consultants but as cocreators and innovators in so-called user-driven innovation (Hippel, 2005; Nordic Council of Ministers, 2006). User-driven innovation is a broad field that has developed from several different traditions, one of which is user-centred design (Halonen, 2010). The design model employed in the current project has been inspired by the user-centred design approach (Helms & Heilesen, 2012).

The developed and applied design model accepts that the user has different roles embedded in structures, and the design model aims to elicit these different roles and thereby enable a more beneficial understanding of these different roles. Initially, the users are observed in practice and are acting as informants. In the next phase, they are engaged as co-constructors. Then they are mobilised as project partners, and finally, they become owners of the process.

The method adopted for the electrician apprentice case has been developed for the Danish ELYK-project,[1] the main objective of which has been to develop innovative pedagogical designs to help develop competencies in small- and medium-sized enterprises (Gynther, 2010). The method is visualised in the quadrant model (Fig. 3.1).

The model is circular, and it should be read clockwise starting in the upper left quadrant. The inner circle enumerates four stages in design. The ones on the left (shaded grey) take place in the organisation. The ones on the right take place in the research and development environment. The outer circle provides a label for

---

[1] The research has been carried out as a contribution to the Danish ELYK-project (2009–2012; http://www.elyk.dk) which has been funded by the European Regional Development Fund and the Danish Enterprise and Construction Authority. Overall, the ELYK-project has addressed the problem of developing and retaining competencies in outlying areas—on the premise that net-based learning may help provide the competences needed for the development and growth of small and medium-sized enterprises (SME).

Fig. 3.1 The quadrant
model

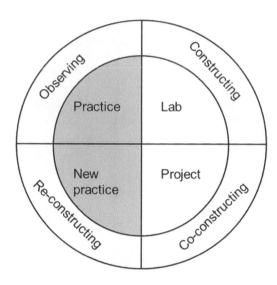

the main activities associated with each stage. The model suggests a chronological progression, but iterations may occur within and across quadrants.

Observing current *practice* (upper left quadrant) is the natural basis for developing designs for new practices or modifying existing ones. Observation is practised in various forms including document reading, interviewing and ethnographical observation. All types of actors involved in the practice should be consulted, and observation includes explicit knowledge (curricula, setting, tools) as well as tacit knowledge (attitudes, general circumstances and actual actions). The main objective at this stage is to provide the researchers and developers with domain knowledge. Hence, the users act only as informants. Based on domain knowledge, the researchers arrive at initial ideas on how to improve or change current practices.

Constructing in the *lab* (upper right quadrant) is the initial stage of innovation where the ideas generated in the first phase are used to lead off discussions with the users on current practice, on how it may be augmented or changed, and on how artefacts should be designed to support such processes. "Lab" is used to signify any space, physical or virtual, where researchers and users meet outside the actual work setting. Reflecting on their own practice, the users are invited to participate actively in proposing and challenging designs or even state tasks in new terms. Outcomes are various sketches and descriptions on the basis of which actual prototypes are developed at the next stage. At this stage, roles begin to converge as researchers and users participate in the design process on equal terms. Researchers as well as users representing all types of actors involved help explore the case from various perspectives and on all levels from simple tool functionality and to relevance in a company or school context.

Co-constructing the *project* (lower right quadrant) involves designing, building, testing and evaluating prototypes. By "co-constructing" we suggest that all users and researchers act as cocreators and indeed partners, irrespective of job-defined roles, contributing their competencies, experience and perspective on the task. At this stage, the outcomes are prototypes and designs that can be tested in a real-world situation.

Reconstructing *new practice* (lower left quadrant), the new designs and artefacts are introduced, implemented, adjusted and integrated in the work environment. All users revert to their conventional roles, but they may act as advocates for changing practices, thus facilitating adoption of the innovation. If successful, the new practice will become routine and eventually may form the point of departure for a new cycle of innovation processes.

The model generates a comprehensive approach through combining different approaches to user-driven innovation. One is the traditional approach of observing users and thereby forecasting needs. Eric von Hippel in particular has been critical of this approach and has suggested that it would be more beneficial to identify lead users, because it is difficult or impossible to foresee the needs of the users in a world with extremely rapid development of products. This means that it is lead users who recognise the importance of products, and they are the ones who develop new practices around products. In the words of von Hippel (1986), they become "... a need-forecasting laboratory". In the initial stage of the quadrant model, however, focus is on observation.

A second approach, the laboratory, is well known from traditional HCI research. In the quadrant model context, however, it should be seen along the lines of "Future Workshops" (Jungk & Müllert, 1987) or the "Change Laboratories" suggested and tried by Engeström, Virkkunen, Helle, Pihlaja, and Poikela (1996). This is a form that enables participation and commitment. It is driven by a mutual interest in developing new practices and observations, and early prototypes can and should be seen as important inputs.

In the third quadrant, the developments and the findings from the lab are used as a set-off for developing new practices mobilising different users and testing the prototypes. This quadrant draws on the approach of the Scandinavian school of participatory or cooperative design (Bødker, Grønbæk, & Kyng, 1993) as well as the tradition for project work and "action learning". The idea is to involve the actual users in the design of the system they will be using. The quadrant model enables a structured process encouraging a phase of project work.

The model enables close dialogue between designer perspective and user perspective, and it generates an understanding of the different roles of user and designer: from the initial phase where the users are being observed to the lab where participants are constructing together. Next comes the project phase, where users and researchers/designers are equal partners. And in the final stage, the users are on their own. In a way, this final phase is an organisational process where a new practice is constructed and adopted.

Empirical Work

Initially, in our case involving electrician apprentices, current practice was observed in a study involving both interviews and ethnographical observation (Gleerup, 2010). The project design involved 2 days of intense educational field-work at the vocational college. The practice of teaching was observed at different educational levels by three researchers. This observation study was backed by interview with teachers, the management and group interview with apprentices to ensure a preliminary identification and contextualisation of the specific, localised domain knowledge and practices (Fig. 3.2).

Next, construction in the "lab" was carried out in the form of two workshops concerned with generating ideas on how to improve the quality of the education. In the first workshop, a class of apprentices, some of their teachers and representatives from local companies employing apprentices all participated in two sessions of group work, first within and next across their job-defined roles. Finally, the outcome of the group work was visualised in posters, presented and discussed. Input from the first workshop was systematised by the researchers into categories defined by (a) relevance to education, (b) user perspective(s) (apprentices, college and company), (c) ranking made by the workshop participants and (d) requirement for involving technology (Fig. 3.3).

As a result, four general themes were identified to be elaborated on further:

1. Employment after graduation, further education and knowledge sharing
2. Dialogue between the different actors in education
3. The problem of insufficient workplace safety
4. Ad hoc teaching and theory practice relations throughout the study programme

Based on this analysis, eight subjects were identified as potentially interesting, and a set of rudimentary prototypes were designed so as to help visualise the design ideas. In the second workshop, involving only apprentices, seven designs involving this type of user were discussed at length, leading to a clarification of needs and objectives and to the reduction of the number prototypes to three viable designs (Fig. 3.4).

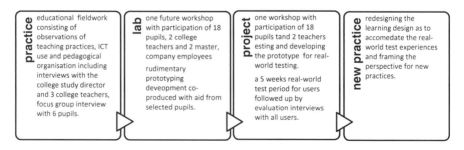

Fig. 3.2 Project design

Group 1	Workshop Ideas for improvement of educational quality	Numbers of votes
	Instructions in Podcast	-
	Smart boards as standard	-
	New books	5
	Dedicated teachers for each class	2
	Better wireless network	9
Group 2	Make the Personal Education Plan digital and central	4
	Make it possible for the companies to follow the apprentices test scores	5
	Easy to use ITC solutions	-
	Make grades electronically accessible	-
Group 3	Always use smart boards	-
	Make the LMS calendar downloadable to mobile phone	-
	The companies need to prioritize the educational aspects of work	4
	Basic questionnaire for pupils to fill out	-
	If the apprentice have to go to the emergency room because of safety disregards they should be fined	5
	Better information service for further education	8
Group 4	Receive on the mobile or PC simple assignments while at work every week or forth night	-
	Organize the education in more segments	7
	Better the dialogue between college, work place and pupil	-
	Make it possible for college and work place to have video meetings	-
	Always at least 1 teacher to attend the class	9

Fig. 3.3 Workshop ideas

The co-construction phase was initiated by producing a new set of learning design prototypes to be tested and further developed in a real context. Co-construction was initiated at a workshop at the college involving a class of pupils and their teachers, and representatives from companies to be involved, when the pupils entered a period of practice. Given the physical framework of two college teachers and 18 apprentices testing designs in about as many companies, the space for cocreation primarily had to be a virtual one, consisting of dialogues and reports in virtual space, using text, images and video. At the end of a 5-week test period, a group of apprentices was gathered for an evaluating qualitative interview carried out as a group discussion. In the interview, the apprentices reflected on their experiences using the digital prototype. Positive and negative aspects as well as unforeseen side effects were pointed out, and new improvement ideas evolved among the participants.

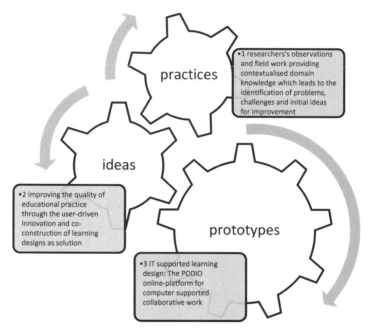

Fig. 3.4 Project process from practices to prototypes

Net-Based Practices and Needs

E-learning at the vocational college is based on SharePoint 2007™. According to our interviews with teachers and pupils at the college, the system functions as an intranet with newsletter and directory and as a learning management system with time tables, class pictures, practical information, assignments and teaching materials. Communication is from college to apprentice, and it is reserved for registered faculty, administrators and students. As noted in the introduction, the curriculum consists of alternating periods of school and apprenticeship, the link between the two being the "personal education plan". The empirical findings from the initial research activities showed that neither the apprentices, nor the company representatives, seem to appreciate these tools greatly. While working in companies away from school, SharePoint intranet has apparently little to offer the apprentices, and contact with school seems to dwindle. Socially and professionally, the apprentices tend to be isolated from their classmates, barring informal private contacts. According to the apprentices themselves, they like to share their successes in terms of images of jobs well done. Outside school, extensive relevant information is available for electricians and apprentices at the website of the Danish Union of Electricians (Dansk El-forbund, http://www.def.dk/).

The design ideas which will be developed into prototypes in cooperation with the apprentices relate to the conditions already described, involving facilitating of communication between:

- College and apprentice. The apprentices wish to remain in contact with the college, and they need affirmation that they are still part of the education. They would like to receive feedback and appreciation from teachers during their in-service training.
- Apprentice and apprentice. The apprentices wish to share experiences in a context not interfered with by either school or the companies they work for. The bright side to this is the sharing of successes. But there is also a desire to communicate critically about work conditions, notably violations of safety measures that allegedly are not infrequent.
- Apprentice and master. The need for this type of communication can be inferred from statements about the "Personal Education Plan". As discussed below, it may also involve communication with the school.

The Prototypes and the Communities

The prototypes developed have both a practical and a cultural dimension. As implemented in Podio they help perform certain tasks better or in new ways. But they are also vehicles for developing and changing the more general practices of interaction between the various actors. During the process the prototypes become a negotiation point for the different perspectives engaged in the process.

The workshops in the project could be seen as temporary settings for a special kind of temporary communities. They are not a community of practice (COP), as conceptualised by Lave and Wenger (1991). COPs are characterised by uniformity and vertical development (from novice to expert), whereas these temporary communities are based on difference and horizontal development (expert to expert). The participants come from different domains. They are stepping outside of these and at the same time representing them, and they come together mobilised by interest in creating better educational practices. This novelty and the idea, which in the different domains will be interpreted in different ways, generate the need for a conceptualisation different from that of communities of practice. Hence, we propose to make use of Fisher's concept of "Communities of Interests" (COIs) (Fischer, 2001). They are what he calls communities of communities. This is indeed the case in this project. From the point of view of innovation, it is essential to bring actors or stakeholders from different domains together to generate new emerging knowledge. Thus, it is also important that these communities are and remain temporal to avoid homogeneity. When actors work together in zones between different domains in a special creative and innovative context, we need materiality or mediating artefacts. Fisher states that:

> ...learning in CoIs requires externalizations ... in the form of boundary objects ... which have meaning across the boundaries of the individual knowledge systems. Boundary objects allow different knowledge systems to interact by providing a shared reference that is meaningful within both systems. ... In this sense, the interaction between multiple knowledge systems is a means to turn the symmetry of ignorance into a resource for learning and social creativity (because innovations come from outside the city wall). (Fischer, 2001)

In a COP, we would also talk about the relationship between reifications (or mediating artefacts) and participation. It is a central point in Lave and Wenger's (1991) theory, that we learn by becoming part of a community and that this becoming is a dual process between reification and participation. Whereas reifications stabilise the process, we do not use reifications as means to tell us what to do, but as ways of understanding. When we move into the more temporal communities of innovation and creativity, they are unstable, and the reifications change and become different both through our changing interpretation of them and through the actual development of the very externalisation.

As to the practical dimension, the task-specific and general learning environment needs and requirements were analysed by means of Bates and Poole's (2003) SECTIONS model, focusing on organisational, technological, pedagogical and communicative factors. On the basis of this analysis, it was decided to develop prototypes on the Podio online platform for computer-supported collaborative work. Podio (established 2009, http://company.podio.com) is extremely versatile in terms of uses, and it provides simple and fast tools for developing apps. Podio runs on computers as well as on tablets and mobile devices, and therefore it can be accessed easily from the work place.

Within a Podio "organisation" framework for the vocational college, a "space" was created for each of the design ideas to be tested. These are described below. Access to the spaces can be regulated so that only relevant users can access them. Each space has an "activity stream" that helps provide awareness of other users and that also allows for a simple dialogue in the form of comments.

- The apprentice—apprentice space is the most restrictive, giving the apprentices a private space for sharing experiences in words, images and videos. Its main app allows for an asynchronous threaded discussion in text, images and videos. A filter mechanism provides facilities for sorting postings in various ways, including by tags, so that the apprentices can develop their own categories of concepts. The space is meant to help maintain social and professional contacts between apprentices during the long periods of working in companies when they are not likely to meet often.
- The college—apprentice space. This space is meant to help maintain ties between college and apprentice during practice periods, to train theoretical competencies, and also, importantly, to help the apprentices maintain an identity as members of an educational community. The space is an interactive system with two apps by means of which every week the college issues an assignment to be completed and submitted online in a forum or by e-mail. Only teachers and apprentices can access the space.

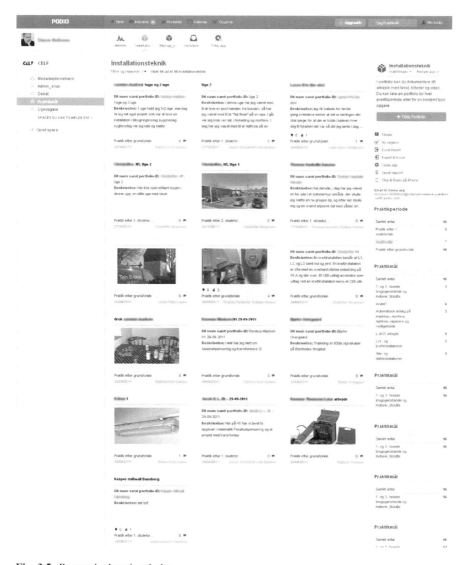

Fig. 3.5 Personal educational plan

- The apprentice—master space is open to all users within the "organisation" framework. Its main application is a mini portfolio based on the personal education plan. Having selected a practice period, the apprentice selects an entry from the list of learning objectives (skills) for the practice period. The portfolio entry may consist of text, photos and video (Fig. 3.5). The space helps document the skills and competences acquired by the apprentices, and by adding narrative and visualisations to the items listed in the practice form, it makes it relevant to the daily life of the apprentices, drawing on their enthusiasm for sharing their achievements.

Changing Practices

Working on new pedagogical designs by means of user-driven innovation is a challenging and rewarding process for all actors involved, inviting them reflect on their own practices and providing them with a chance to test possible futures in education within their particular field. Especially in the evaluating interview with apprentices, it was stressed, that the experiment had opened up opportunities for the emergence of new ideas to improve the interplay between the two contexts of learning. Integrating the innovations into the organisation ("reconstructing" in the terminology of the quadrant model, Fig. 3.1), however, is another matter. The user-driven approach guarantees that within the organisation there will be actors with a profound understanding of the innovations acting as ambassadors for change. But they are unlikely to succeed unless the new designs are understood not only as instrumental solutions to concrete problems but also as "triggers" for broader discussions of educational purpose and pedagogy in relation to the organisation of work to be taken on by the actors.

In the case of the electrician apprentices, where the modularisation of the curriculum has favoured an understanding of college and apprenticeship as being separate worlds, the pedagogical designs are meant to bridge the gap. Thus from the perspective of the apprentices, the designs facilitate community building; bringing the school into the practice environment; and encouraging reflection on one's own practice. The electrician masters/journeymen and the teachers, all partners in the design process, however, also need to reflect on how the coupling of contexts affects relationships. In a sense, the apprentices are empowered when recognised as active and responsible learning subjects, both by input from college that may be tested and reflected upon in a work setting and by being able to document skills and practice-based learning in such a way that it can serve as examples to be drawn upon in classroom teaching. Thus, in a wider perspective, successful bridging depends on allowing the apprentices more actively and responsibly to contribute to their own education.

Project Outcomes

The full account of the electrician case in the ELYK-project has been presented in a report in Danish (Mogensen, Gleerup, & Heilesen, 2012). Below, we summarise the main points in the report on the apprentices as learners in coupled contexts.

Firstly, the apprentices recognise that there are potentials in strengthening the interplay between learning taking place in companies and at college. Furthermore, the apprentices believe that a stronger interplay could facilitate better cooperation between the workplace management and the college environment. On the one hand, such closer cooperation can support a renewal of practice at the workplace, engaging also the journeymen in continuous processes of learning. On the other hand, closer cooperation opens up for using the apprentices' learning experiences from work in the theoretical teaching in the classroom. As we can see from these ideas on how to expand and further develop the prototype for bridging between learning contexts, the apprentices view the process of learning in a social perspective. In their analysis of the potentials of the prototype tested, they reflect on the underlying institutional conditions—that to some extent determine how successfully new technological learning resources may be integrated.

Secondly, it has been demonstrated that by developing tools and structures for networked learning, it is possible to support the learning processes of apprentices working in companies. An online learning platform offers the apprentices opportunities for searching for and communicating informal and formal knowledge.

Thirdly, the apprentices express an interest in having a platform like the Podio prototype introduced as a recognised learning tool at the workplace. There, it could support the apprentices' reflections on the process of learning taking place throughout the practice period. Also, the portfolio could support the interaction between apprentice and more senior colleagues, who may also be able to make use of the knowledge offered to the apprentice through the net-based tool.

Finally, from the perspective of method and theory, the use of the quadrant model has offered a way of structuring processes and choosing methods according to the rationalities of different phases. In addition, this has enabled an understanding of the changing roles of the "user" from informant to constructor and to co-constructor. Thus it has become possible to establish shared but not identical expectations. This means that in the different phases, the participants need to establish a kind of "common ground". Yet at the same time the expected outcome will be different: the participating apprentices want an education that is relevant as well as motivating. The teachers wish to develop their teaching, so that it remains relevant and motivating and, importantly, also in accordance with the legal requirements. The researchers of course are interested in education and learning, but to them the important outcome would also be generating qualified and validated research. This reciprocal process between different rationalities is at the core of innovation, yet it is a complicated process that can be enhanced and scaffolded by a general point of reference such as the quadrant model.

Whereas most e-learning and networked learning research is based largely in researchers observing, analysing and theorising, this project offers a design model that enables a structured process for engagement of different users in the development process of new pedagogical designs for networked learning. The design model thereby offers an operational approach to the development of networked learning, on the one hand using the potentials of new technology and on the other hand working with active participation not only in the learning process but also in the design of the learning process. This also meets the aspiration in the original manifesto:

> Networked e-learning allows for the possibility of new forms of communication, language and discourse. Such new forms of communication have the potential to be more open and supportive of inclusive educational practices. It promotes use of a wider range of resources, both material and human, directly relevant to learners' own intentions and interests.

It offers the potential for dialogue with a broader range of people and in a form which allows different styles and preferences to be supported. (E-Quality Network, 2002)

The project has demonstrated that such visions can be realised and that the realisation is a way of developing the pedagogical designs that are necessary for developing education in the cross field between in-service training in the workplace and teaching at the college. In the project, we have worked with peer to peer designs that have attempted "to foster inclusion and democracy" (as stated in the manifesto) through inclusive designs which created ownership among the participants. This again created space for that very collaboration that the manifesto calls for:

> ... wider collaboration between academics, between academics and professionals, between people across cultures, between learners, and between learning and those who can support their learning. (E-Quality Network, 2002)

Networked learning is an important part of modern education. Further development of the concept calls for design models that enable a structured dynamic process, mobilising different user groups. This paper offers an initial model, which could and should be developed and tested in other settings.

References

Bates, T., & Poole, G. (2003). *Effective teaching with technology in higher education: Foundations for success* (1st ed.). San Francisco, CA: Jossey-Bass.

Bødker, S., Grønbæk, K., & Kyng, M. (1993). Cooperative design: Techniques and experiences from the Scandinavian scene. In D. Schuler & A. Namioka (Eds.), *Participatory design: Principles and practices*. Hillsdale, NJ: Lawrence Erlbaum.

Christensen, O. (2010). Learning in coupled contexts. In T. Cerrato-Pargman, P. Hyvönen, S. Järvelä, & M. Milrad (Eds.), *The first Nordic symposium on technology-enhanced learning* (pp. 34–35). Växjö, Sweden: Linnnæus University.

Engeström, Y., Virkkunen, J., Helle, M., Pihlaja, J., & Poikela, R. (1996). The change laboratory as a tool for transforming work. *Lifelong Learning in Europe, 1*(2), 10–17.

E-Quality Network. (2002). *E-quality in e-learning Manifesto*. Presented at the Networked Learning 2002 conference, Sheffield, England. Retrieved from http://csalt.lancs.ac.uk/esrc/

Fischer, G. (2001). *Communities of interest: Learning through the interaction of multiple knowledge systems*. 24th Annual Information Systems Research Seminar in Scandinavia (IRIS'24), Ulvik, Norway (pp. 1–14).

Gleerup, J. (2010). *Kompetenceudvikling i små og mellemstore virksomheder i regionale yderområder—og potentialer i øget inddragelse af e-læring* (ELYK Rapport 1). Roskilde, Denmark: KnowledgeLab. Retrieved January 1, 2013, from http://elyk.dk/wp-content/uploads/2011/09/ELYK-Rapport-1.pdf

Gynther, K. (2010). *Brugerdreven forskningsbaseret innovation af didaktisk design—transformative metoder i forsknings- og udviklingsprojektet ELYK* (ELYK Working Paper 1). Odense, Denmark: University of Southern Denmark, KnowledgeLab. Retrieved January 1, 2013, from http://elyk.dk/wp-content/uploads/2011/09/ELYK-Working-Paper-2.pdf

Halonen, J. (2010). *Research framework and methods overview for user driven open innovation: FS-UDOI booster*. Retrieved January 1, 2013, from http://www.flexibleservices.fi/files/file/pdf/UDOI_B_deliverable_310410_final.pdf

Helms, N. H., & Heilesen, S. B. (2012). *Structures and processes in didactic design.* Paper presented at the SUMMER 2nd International Symposium on Integrating Research, Education, and Problem Solving: Summer IREPS 2012, Orlando, FL.

Hippel, E. V. (1986). Lead users: A source of novel product concepts. *Management Science, 32*(7), 791–805.

Hippel, E. V. (2005). *Democratizing innovation.* Cambridge, MA: MIT Press.

International Organization for Standardisation. (2010). *ISO 9241-210:2010. Ergonomics of human-system interaction—Part 210: Human-centred design for interactive systems.* Retrieved January 1, 2013, from http://www.iso.org/iso/iso_catalogue/catalogue_ics/catalogue_detail_ics.htm?csnumber=52075

Jørgensen, C. H. (2004). Connecting work and education: Should learning be useful, correct or meaningful? *Journal of Workplace Learning, 16*(8), 455–465.

Jungk, R., & Müllert, N. (1987). *Future workshops: How to create desirable futures.* London, England: Institute for Social Inventions.

Lave, J., & Wenger, E. (1991). *Situated learning: Legitimate peripheral participation.* Cambridge, England: Cambridge University Press.

Mogensen, K., Gleerup, J., & Heilesen, S. B. (2012). *Den digitale læringsbro. Et forsøg med brugerdreven innovation og kompetenceudvikling i vekselvirkende uddannelseskontekster* (ELYK Rapport 11). Roskilde, Denmark: KnowledgeLab. Retrieved January 1, 2013, from http://elyk.dk/wp-content/uploads/2011/09/ELYK-forskningsrapport-11-Den-digitale-l%C3%A6ringsbro-140212.pdf

Nielsen, K. (2009). A collaborative perspective on learning transfer. *Journal of Workplace Learning, 21*(1), 58–70.

Nordic Council of Ministers. (2006). *Understanding user-driven innovation* (TemaNord, 2006:522). Copenhagen, Denmark: Nordic Council of Ministers.

Schwencke, E., & Larsen, A. K. (2011). Spenningsfeltet mellom "nytte" for bedriften og "frirom" for studenten—Et samarbeidsprosjekt mellom skole og arbeidsliv for gjensidig påvirkning og ønske om forandring. *Nordic Journal of Vocational Education and Training, 1*(1), 1–14.

Wilbrandt, J. (2002). *Vekseluddannelse i håndværksuddannelser. Lærlinges oplæring, faglighed og identitet.* København (Copenhagen), Denmark: Undervisningsministeriet, Uddannelsesstyrelsen.

Chapter 4
Making the Right Connections: Implementing the Objects of Practice into a Network for Learning

John Hannon

Introduction

This chapter asks questions about how learning environments are assembled and what kind of networked learning is composed and enabled in the process of implementing institutional learning technologies. Arrangements for learning are a central concern of universities, but what is less clear is how these are put in place, that is, how disparate institutional actors and structures are accommodated and reconciled. The focus in this chapter is on the type of networked learning that is enabled through these arrangements: how a learning environment is assembled in particular ways, and how practices associated with pedagogies and technologies are enacted and negotiated when different parts of the organisation intersect. While the literature on online education and networked learning takes up issues concerning the shaping of learning by institutional technologies (Conole, White, & Oliver, 2007; Hodgson, McConnell, & Dirckinck-Holmfeld, 2012; Nyvang & Bygholm, 2012; Price & Oliver, 2007), what happens during, and prior to, implementation is less examined, despite being critical for the resultant arrangements for networked learning.

A persistent theme from the literature on learning technologies is the troublesome accommodation between technologies and practices in learning environments, captured by Blin and Munro (2008) who commented that despite the investment in virtual learning environments (VLEs) in universities:

> ... there is little evidence of significant impact on teaching practices and current implementations are accused of being focused on improving administration and replicating behaviourist, content-driven models (p. 475).

This comment reflects a vexed issue that can be tracked over the historical development of educational technologies (Cuban, 2003; Feenberg, 1999; Nespor, 2011),

J. Hannon (✉)
La Trobe Learning and Teaching, La Trobe University, Melbourne, VIC, Australia
e-mail: j.hannon@latrobe.edu.au

V. Hodgson et al. (eds.), *The Design, Experience and Practice of Networked Learning*, Research in Networked Learning, DOI 10.1007/978-3-319-01940-6_4, © Springer International Publishing Switzerland 2014

phrased in various terms: the gap between e-learning policy and practice (Conole, 2008; Gunn, 2010); the difficulty of integrating top-down strategies for e-learning with bottom-up initiatives (De Freitas & Oliver, 2005; Gunn, 2010; Marshall, 2010; Price & Oliver, 2007; Russell, 2009; Uys, 2010); and recurring issues about e-learning effectiveness (Goodyear & Ellis, 2008; Stepanyan, Littlejohn, & Margaryan, 2010). The legacy of large-scale investment in learning technologies in universities, their poor return on investment and their history of failure, breakdown and ongoing maintenance raises questions of why their implementation continues to be so troublesome.

Institutional e-learning encounters further trouble with the emergent sociality of participation and collaboration in Web 2.0 spaces (Ryberg, 2008). Learning involving social media makes a poor fit for the tradition of educational research that studies technologies as impact or interventions on a pre-existing state of affairs (Hannon, 2013; Price & Oliver, 2007), since such studies attempt to avoid the complexity of practice and messy reality of actual learning settings. Goodyear and Ellis (2008) refer to the need to shift away from "simplistic comparisons" (p. 41), and Selwyn (2010) calls for a rejection of "means-end" thinking: "thinking that starts from a given end and then strives to find the means of accomplishment" (p. 68). Perhaps the real issue for researching learning technologies concerns the questions that are asked: rather than presupposing the end effects of a learning technology, we can instead enquire into what arrangements are put in place by its implementation, and what type of practices are thereby enabled.

In this study I aim to address a lack of attention in research into learning technologies to the arrangements that accompany the implementation of learning environments. Contributing to this tendency is an emphasis on studying design approaches that focus on the application and practical uses of learning technologies, rather than a critical engagement with them (Bennett & Oliver, 2011; Jones & Kennedy, 2011). In order to bring a broader focus to learning environments and associated institutional practices, I have adopted two starting points. First, organisations are not a given and settled state of affairs, what Alcipani and Hassard (2010) refer to "as a discrete structural entity" (p. 420); rather, they entail continual effort and practices around the activity of organisations. Second, following from this, organisational practices are entangled and inseparable from materials. Orlikowski (2007) describes the activity of "everyday organizing" (p. 1435) as bound up with "material artifacts, bodies, arrangements, and infrastructures" (p. 1436). Instead of researching learning environments as arrangements already in place in an organisation considered as an uncontroversial entity, this study brings into purview the effort of *organising*, considering the organisation as agonistic, its processes contingent and institutional interests in dynamic interplay.

To bring this type of activity into focus, I will foreground the "objects" of a technology implementation that are often taken for granted in their role in a learning environment, that is, the particular artefacts, technologies, materials or documents that become the object of attention during implementation. I argue that objects are embedded in human practices and that in order to develop and enable a form of networked learning that does justice to its sociocultural and critical origins, valuing student learning as "cooperation and collaboration" rather than "competitive and individualistic" (Hodgson et al., 2012, p. 296), it is necessary to extend its constituents to encompass relations with nonhuman participants. Consequently there is a need for networked learning to acknowledge the role of objects in decision-making about pedagogies and the assembly of learning environments.

This case discussed in this chapter concerns the implementation of a new university learning management system (LMS) or VLE. While implementation was completed successfully, the resulting learning environment was inconsistent with the notions of networked learning described above. In order to understand how this learning environment was produced (and by implication, similar ones), I draw attention to the intricate work of organising and assembling during implementation in order to show the role of the LMS in shaping a learning environment, one that is, nonetheless, masked by its presumed role as a technological platform. This study departs from the tradition of educational research that studies strategic or technological change regimes (De Freitas & Oliver, 2005; Goodyear & Ellis, 2008; Marshall, 2010). It aims to shift from studying the *what* of organisation to the *how* of organising and identify the points at which network ties and connections are established and assembled, making visible the objects that put these arrangements into place.

Methods

The transition to a new institutional learning technology system offered an opportunity to observe an organisational change project that aimed to replace a university-wide LMS, to prepare academics for its use, and to renew the university's foundation for online learning. My involvement in the implementation project assumed a double role: as an invited participant with advisory status granted by membership of the Project Reference Group and as a researcher with university ethics approval for an evaluation of the implementation as a change process.

Positioning the participant/researcher as separate from the people and objects of study, however, can become methodologically problematic. In order to research my involvement with the complex organisational processes in this instance of implementation, I aimed to adopt methods that could account for the untidy practices, uncertainties, objects, and everyday realities of a large organisational project in progress. Suchman (2007) described an approach which departs from the tradition of a human-centred focus in researching organisations, as one where:

> The task for critical practice is to resist restaging of stories about autonomous human actors and discrete technical objects in favor of an orientation to capacities for action comprised of specific configurations of persons and things (p. 284).

In my study, for example, as I will elaborate further, a particular object identified by participants as the "enhancements list" expressed such an orientation to capacities for action. During my enquiry I understood Suchman's approach as holding in obeyance received notions of organisational change and institutional technologies and focussing on material activity. My methods for enquiry drew upon the ethnomethodological and ethnographic approaches of actor network (actor-network theory, ANT) studies (Law, 2009), including observation of project activity and meetings, interviews, focus groups, and document analysis. Hence the narrative that follows develops from three interwoven strands: first an account of implementation offered by project data, second the theoretical perspectives and methods that I drew upon to guide the enquiry, and lastly a reflective account of my researcher-participant role. In the next section I start with an account of implementation offered by the project data.

The Implementation Project: Setting Terminology, Boundaries, Practices

An official implementation narrative was provided by project documents: from internal reports, newsletters, and communications to the university community. In this account, the replacement of the university LMS was prompted by the pending withdrawal of corporate support for the then existing LMS, a factor that contributed to framing the implementation project with a short timeline and the framing of functional goals. A timeline was published at the outset of the project that presented its distinct components, its staged progression, and its milestones: it commenced with an evaluation of possible LMS options by an information technology team and closed with the institution-wide deployment in time for Semester 1, as shown in adapted form in Fig. 4.1.

The implementation project commenced with the decision that Moodle offered the best fit and responsiveness for the university's context of multicampus teaching arrangements and large student cohorts. The LMS Replacement Project was established as a 6-month project with the goals of a smooth "migration" of all subjects (units of study) from the old to new LMS and the preparation of staff in

John Hannon

April 2010	Aug	Sept	Oct	Nov–Jan	Feb	Mar 2011
Evaluation of LMS options Decision to change LMS announced	**Project start**	Content migration			LMS goes live	**Project close**
	Train the Trainer	*Moodle Basics* Workshop (3 hours) Development of training resources for workshops and website. Support arrangements			*Moodle Basics* & Advanced Training	
	Project Reference Group meetings (fortnightly)					Final meeting
	Website	Project communication to all staff (periodic)				Semester 1

Fig. 4.1 The LMS replacement project timeline

readiness for Semester 1. Implementation, in this case, can be described as a process of minimal organisational change, or "interoperable change" (Marshall, 2010, p. 180), a process that would be least disruptive of other structures and academic teaching activities, and contrasts with change processes that include curriculum review.

The oversight of implementation occurred through the Project Reference Group (see Fig. 4.1), the advisory group that met every fortnight (for a total of 13 meetings), consisting of representatives across the university from faculties and organisational units. Members included academics, education designers, library staff, and project managers. At these meetings, status reports on the progress of implementation were presented, issues were negotiated, and decisions were endorsed. The implementation project left a record of artefacts: meeting agendas and minutes, technical data and reports, professional development training plans and resources, and communications to university staff. Examples of these artefacts can be grouped according to the project's reporting of its own process, reflecting Fig. 4.1:

- Planning: *LMS Evaluation* (preliminary report on LMS options), *Moodle Project Plan* (by vendor)
- Project communications: Notifications and publicity on a university website for the LMS Replacement Project
- Project reporting and monitoring: (1) Progress: Reference Group meeting minutes comprising agenda items for discussion; regular *Project Status Dashboard* or state of play reports (decisions on LMS configuration, LMS roles and terminology, user statistics, test playpens for staff); a regular *Log of Action Items* listing items for action. (2) Final reports: Closing documents, including arrangements for further development and continuing training
- Training and staff support: Moodle Training reports, training program of workshops, demonstrations, list of staff "Moodle Mentors", *Getting Ready Checklist, QuickGuides*, short videos, reports on workshop participation, and reports on activity from a drop-in centre and help desk for staff and students

The progress of implementation was reported regularly to meetings through the *Dashboard* listing of current issues, with agenda items for discussion with members. Matters were canvassed for immediate decision: functions to be enabled (e.g. the operation of file management; interface arrangements and features (blocks) to be included, excluded, or customised; standard features such as the design of faculty templates; and proposed "enhancements" to be configured (such as plug-ins, rubrics, question banks).

The meetings, therefore, were the venue for negotiation and documentation of the implementation that was progressively being put into place. An instance of this precise configuring and organising process occurred as teaching and learning "roles" in the LMS were decided: the meeting agreed on the roles *Subject, Lecturer, Designer, Tutor, Student, Audit student* in order to reflect the university's terminology (replacing the previous LMS categories Course, Instructor, Assistant) (Ref Group Meeting 5). On completion of the project at the start of Semester 1 in March 2011, the following milestones were recorded (Hannon, Hirst, & Riddle, 2011):

- Migration of subjects to the new system without involvement of teaching staff. An initial total of 1,300 subjects were successfully migrated to the new LMS.
- A training program of workshops for academic staff leading up to Semester 1. Attendance for these workshops indicated that 1,239 (48 %) academic staff completed the *Moodle basics* workshop.
- Support included the production of 26 guides in PDF format, 15 two-minute short videos, demonstrations, student "rovers", and drop-in centres, all for use of staff. For students, support included a help desk, student guides (PDF and HTML), and video guides.

The scale of the subject migration within the Semester 1 deadline (approximately 2,600 subjects, involving over 2,000 academic staff and 30,000 students over 5 campuses) indicated an intensive undertaking with high expectations that drew on substantial institutional resources. The goal of minimal change was achieved, in this instance, with the replacement of an LMS with little disruption to existing technology systems, nor to the continuity of teaching subjects in the LMS.

This result was confirmed in interviews with two project managers after project completion. One, an external consultant, commented:

> ...it's been a success—the system is in and staff and students are using it. In the longer term, I would suggest that [the project sponsor] should evaluate how it went with various stakeholder groups later in the year. (Project Manager A)

The second project manager (located within the university) pointed to the constraints in scope, commenting that the project "was subject to a timeline during implementation" and that the LMS required further development through a series of modifications or "enhancements" that "continue as a monthly update after project completion" (Project Manager B).

These statements reflect the functional achievements of implementation. They also hint at some unfinished business concerning how well the implementation will match its contexts of practice. Despite a successful result, what was evident was the lack of pedagogical language in the minutes and reports that documented the project, even with the mix of representatives on the Reference Group. After project completion, I was left with several questions concerning the kind of learning environment that was put into place. Given the involvement of teaching academics and education designers, precisely how was implementation assembled and connected to potential practices? Were there a number of possible arrangements for the LMS, and if so, how did this one come into effect? How can networked learning be represented in such implementations?

Implementation, according to the project documents, entailed putting a plan into action: a narrative of configuring objects and people, with issues progressively resolved, closed off or blackboxed. In order to investigate the arrangements that were *not* covered in this clean account, I sought to focus on the materialisation of organising, that is, the objects of implementation, through a sociomaterial perspective. In the next section I describe in more detail the theoretical perspectives and methods that I drew upon to guide the enquiry,

Reappraising Objects as Material *and* Social

Latour (1992) noted that the "mundane artefacts" that pervade our work and lives were missing in accounts of practice and everyday life, so that the objects that pervade our daily existence become separated from us, forgotten and unanalysed. In order to highlight the role of the material world as intrinsic to everyday activities, Orlikowski and Scott (2008) proposed a thought experiment in which they challenged the reader to:

> ... consider doing anything in the world (whether at home, on the road, or in organizations) that does not in some way or another entail material means (e.g., bodies, clothes, food, spectacles, buildings, classrooms, devices, water pipes, paper, telephones, email, etc.). (p. 455)

Orlikowski and Scott described this inherent inseparability of the social and material as a relational ontology such that "people and things only exist in relation to each other" (p. 456). Indeed, Law (2009) proposes that "nothing has reality or form outside the enactment of those relations" (p. 141). The notion of objects as actors draws on these sociomaterial perspectives, in particular ANT (Latour, 1987, 2005; Law, 2004), in recognising the role of nonhuman participants in the configurations of everyday life. ANT is a sociomaterial account that challenges notions of separateness and the existence of entities prior to the relations formed with them.

Rethinking Implementation

In studies of organisations, Orlikowski and Scott (2008) found that technology tends to be unaccounted for or absent from the literature, which was mainly concerned with "human, cultural, and economic elements of institutions" (p. 436). Similarly, in higher educational research, technologies tend to be understood as given (Oliver, 2013), and studies largely retain a human-centred focus, either investigating technologies as effects on people and organisations (Price & Oliver, 2007; Selwyn, 2010) or through phenomenological and constructivist accounts of practice (Fenwick, 2010; Goodyear & Ellis, 2008). Both these approaches typically involve evaluating human strategies and their attainment, thus reprising an ontology of separation between the social and material.

Adopting a sociomaterial research perspective enables a shift away from a unified view of an organisational project as a "system" by bringing technological objects into view through their material activity and effects. This view of implementation sees its agency less as residing with plans and managers, but as delegated and assigned to an assemblage of people, technologies, policies, and procedures that are ordered and aligned, with considerable effort and resources, to become a stabilised network. This process of ordering into an "assemblage" has the sense of gathering or joining together heterogeneous elements into "a compositional unity"

(Phillips, 2006, p.109). Objects order practices in time and space and are a contingent part of the network that makes an assemblage durable.

This chapter draws on three ANT concepts in order to follow particular nonhuman actors, or objects, in the work of organising the implementation that produces the institutional online learning environment. In brief, these concepts are that objects exist in networks, they are enacted into reality, and they imply absent realities. Law and Singleton (2005), in their paper "Object Lessons", describe these concepts as *network objects* or "immutable mobiles" (Latour, 1987), that is, objects that circulate in relational networks across contexts; objects that are *enacted* in multiple practices and into reality, rather than different perspectives on a single pre-existing object; and objects as absent presences, in which "the present object implies realities that are *necessarily* absent" (Law & Singleton, 2005, p. 342). These concepts will be used to make visible points of controversy and ambivalence (Fenwick, 2011) that point to possible decisions and trajectories that would have enacted an alternative online learning environment.

Network Objects

Law and Singleton (2005) suggest that an object is not visible except as a network of relations (p. 336). Hence *network objects* are durable and hold their shape, maintaining a network of associations as they move over distances and through time. Described also as "immutable mobiles" (Latour, 1987), they are "objects which have the properties of being *mobile* but also *immutable, presentable, read-able* and *combinable* with one another" (p. 26, emphasis in original)."

In this sense, objects lose their fixity and take a relational shape that Law (2002) describes as "enactments of strategic logics" (p. 92), binding together artefacts, people, technologies, organisations, texts, discourses, ideas and actions. Hence network objects can be physical, discursive and technological, and they generate stable, if precarious, networks. Further examples cited in ANT literature are maps, accountancy, a curriculum guide, textbooks, global enterprises (American Express, McDonalds, Sony), codes, newspapers, and databases. Latour (1999) offers the example of a speed bump, which "is ultimately not made of matter; it is full of engineers and chancellors and lawmakers, commingling their wills and their storylines with those of gravel, concrete, paint, and standard calculations" (p. 190). Such descriptions exemplify the "material-semiotic approaches" (Law, 2009, p. 141) that demonstrate how relations are assembled into material and discursive networks.

A network object is known by its effects and takes the form of a stabilised or "blackboxed" entity in which an arrangement is packaged, routinised and "made invisible by its own success" (Latour, 1999, p. 304). Blackboxing is thus not only technical but also discursive. It can embody a history of decisions and processes and entails a "folding of time and space" (Lee, 2008, p. 241) into an object, policy or process. In my study I was able to identify network objects such as the enhancements list and the LMS itself. These objects were composed as highly influential blackboxes that once sealed, could no longer be reopened. Thus, less tangible network objects active in organisational change processes can be made visible by examining their performative functions.

Enactment of Objects

Objects, therefore, can be understood as networks of relations, taking effect in particular settings, enacted or performed in practices. These performances, Law and Singleton (2000) suggest, "need to be enacted. Performances are material processes, practices, which take place day by day and minute by minute" (p. 775). This perspective contrasts with the traditional Durkheimian sociological view that behind social practices there is a prior or hidden presence of structuring forces. Fenwick (2010) describes this contrast with sociomaterial approaches as "[t]he assumption that entities are anterior to their representation is refuted, to focus on the material and discursive practices through which entities and their interactions are enacted into being" (p. 107).

Applied to the case of the LMS implementation project, an object such as "content migration" can be described in terms of its localised enactments and the particular relations that are performed, rather than a routinised process separate from the practices entangled with that content. Then alternative descriptions of learning technologies that have been marginalised in the circulation of this object become possible.

Later ANT studies, or "after ANT" (Alcipani & Hassard, 2010; Law & Hassard, 1999), were able to bring approaches to the materialities of less concrete actors, including discourses, databases, policies, lectures, organisational projects, and spatial and temporal contingencies, entities that can be identified as objects and investigated through their associations in material practices (Barad, 2003; Suchman, 2007). These can be abstract, elusive, and encompass things that are difficult to get at, but are no less a reality, for example, with objects such as diseases that can be accessed through interview and observation (Law & Singleton, 2005; Mol, 2002). The implications are that objects are contingent on performances in which multiple realities are "enacted into being" (Law & Singleton, 2005, p. 334), in ways that may be different, incongruent or contradictory. In this shift from representation to enactment, sociomaterial approaches are a radical break from the implicit dualism in which objects are viewed as separate from their interpretations of them (Jones, Dirckinck-Holmfield, & Lindstrom, 2006). To oppose an ontological separation between materiality and meaning is to be concerned not with what objects and texts *mean* but what they *do*.

Absent Presences

As network objects become visible through their relations and enactments in a more or less stable network, their observation and reporting raises the following kinds of questions: what remains outside a description of a network object? What becomes deferred, sidelined, postponed or made invisible in such accounts? The necessary routines of everyday work, its countless untidy practices, may escape notice in their connections with visible network objects and lapse into an otherness, or a "manifest absence" (Law, 2004, p. 84).

Early ANT studies readings were criticised for emphasising primary actors, replicating their perspective and determining network boundaries that ignore less prominent or "important" entities. Fenwick (2011) noted the potential for a colonising effect of a network reading that can be problematic in "presuming to offer any single account of events" (p. 10). A consequence of a description of a stable actor-network is the issue of what is not accounted for. Not everything in practice can be brought to presence, and the presence of an object entails realities that may be "othered". Drawing on notions such as Derrida's *différance*, Law and Singleton follow the logic of this argument to conclude that such an object "is a pattern of presences and absences" (2005, p. 342), also characterised as inconstant, discontinuous, "fire objects" (p. 344). Law and Singleton list some absent presences in the object alcoholic liver disease in a general medical practice: poverty, unemployment, and violence (p. 346). A different set of absent presences arise in other locations such as the hospital or the substance abuse centre. Hence, they argue, the difficulty in managing the disease.

Of particular interest in a study of technology implementation are the potential manifest absences that derive from legacies of information technology industries or organisational management, where embedded procedures, discourses, and terminology are brought to projects. Law (2004) describes manifest absence as forms "that are *independent* and *prior* to an observer; definite in shape or form; and also singular (there is only one reality)" (p. 145, italics in original). In most organisational research, technology systems, once implemented, tend to become a closed matter, becoming blackboxed and relegated to infrastructure as a hidden or absent presence (Orlikowski, 2010). In such instances, network objects can embody histories that were established over long periods and across vast distances and entail extensive resources, both financial and discursive. Nespor (2011) takes ANT into "extended time frames" (p. 15) in describing organisational change in education, "to stabilize themselves, actor networks draw on relatively more stabilized (which usually means more extensive or 'global') circuits for materials, money, or discursive resources" (p. 24). Implementations bring networks into effect that reach beyond the institution to national and global structures: these include networks of university funding, software corporations, and networks of practice (teaching and learning, higher education management, information technology). These networks may not act in a coherent manner, and Nespor points out that networks can be antagonistic (2011, p. 25), by introducing strong ties and new categories that exercise control over organisational decisions with consequences for local practices.

The foregrounding of objects that have been hitherto neglected in the tradition of educational research (Sorensen, 2009) poses fresh questions for learning technologies: what are the objects that mediate change; how does an object enact particular relations and effects; and what are the consequences of these effects for networked learning practices? Rethinking implementation and infrastructures for learning challenges the assumption that technologies are underpinning (a platform) and uncontroversial (settled matters). Rather technologies can be viewed as an active participant in a process of assembly that is both contingent and political, in which its objects are continually in negotiation and constituting learning environments. In the following section I describe how a discursive object became a key intermediary in the implemented learning environment.

Connections, Controversies and Ambivalences Across Networks

In carrying out my study of implementation, the first question to consider concerned the substantial and disparate amount of data that includes reports, data logs, artefacts, online content, meeting minutes, and related documents such as observation notes and interview data. Faced with this mass of data, I adopted the sociomaterial focus on the "ambivalences, uncertainties and contradictions" (Fenwick, 2010, p. 114) that emerge as *controversies* (Callon, 1986; Latour, 1987). Controversies arise when connections are materialised in localised practices and efforts are brought to such "matters of concern" (Latour, 2005) in order to resolve them into "matters of fact" (p. 251).

The next question, therefore, was to ask to what extent the project's reported success rendered the enquiry a closed issue and implementation as a matter of fact. At the completion of the project, I was faced with a set of data that was connected by consistencies: in terminology, in scope and in goals. Matters of concern appeared already settled; the corpus of data appeared opaque. Issues of pedagogy concerning how learning occurred, however, appeared only in the form of mechanisms: assigning discussion forums, organising "content", and managing assessment. After two interviews that further reflected this pattern, I paused to review how the processes of implementing a learning environment appeared, in Nespor's terms, "to stabilise themselves".

This raised the question of whether any controversies arose, and if so, how they were resolved. The Reference Group meetings were the formal location where issues were raised to inform the implementation process and where consequential matters for the ensuing learning environment were negotiated and endorsed. One issue that recurred over a series of meetings was tied to a specific object, the "enhancements list". Significantly "enhancements" is a term common in information technology discourse where it refers to minor improvements or modifications to an existing system and is granted less status than an "upgrade" (Project Manager B).

The enhancements list was the means by which project managers invited responses from interested stakeholders: first, requests for enhancements were issued to participants (academics, education designers, and the university community), then the ordered list items was presented at meetings, and finally items were tagged for action. Examples of actual items on the enhancements list took the form of requests for:

- Bug fixes, e.g. to render long list items on the LMS interface collapsible into subheadings.
- Functional improvements, e.g. enable the display of discussion posts in order to log student contributions, label icons consistently across the LMS, and enable a repository for content that is common to two or more subjects.
- External plug-ins, e.g. an external grading application, a connection to an eportfolio application, a customisable blog or wiki space for students.
- A "community" location for student projects and staff development projects.

The enhancements list in this study functioned as a network object—mobile yet stable—as it changed over time while holding its shape and function. It exemplified the productive role of the Reference Group in mediating consultation, with the list an object that circulated between stakeholders. This mobile effect prompts a description of the implementation project that is different to the grouping of artefacts in Fig. 4.1. Following the sense of Law's (2002) materialities as "enactments of strategic logics", implementation emerges as enactments of distinct institutional actor-networks. The implementation project brought together a number of networks or assemblages that can each be distinguished by their own discursive practices and resources:

- Network of institutional information technology (IT): servers, installations, testing, fixes, modules (plug-ins), fixes, enhancements, migration of content comprising online subjects, staff "playpens", "interim environment", "production environment"
- Network of project management: project goals and milestones (staged deadlines), project communications, documentation, Reference Group meetings (Dashboard report, "Log of action items")
- Network of training and support: LMS training guides (*Moodle Basics, Quizzes, Gradebook, Assignments*), online videos, workshop program, Moodle mentors, help desk, drop-in centre
- Network of pedagogy: academic teaching and learning practices, educational designer practices

Each network of implementation can be identified by artefacts that reflected a legacy of practice and globally circulating discourses. The conduct of the Reference Group meetings, coordinated by the project management team, drew on a repertoire of well-established project management terminology to bring other institutional networks together in pursuit of organisational change goals. A cycle of consultation between networks was facilitated by the enhancements list, as shown in Fig. 4.2.

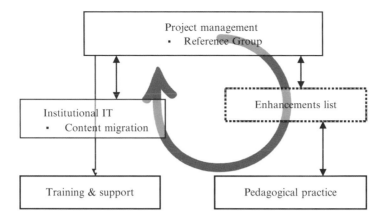

Fig. 4.2 The enhancements list circulates between networks

The enhancements list circulated across stakeholder groups and passed as a token between each network of implementation: list items were discussed at meetings and then conveyed to the institutional IT team, who returned a modified list to the project manager, who presented it again to the Reference Group. During this cycle, the enhancements list was the point at which pedagogical and technological interests intersected during implementation and enacted the discussion and resolution of matters that spanned networks.

The enhancements list embodied Suchman's (2007) approach in which objects entail a "capacity for action". The role of the list as a network object can be illustrated with the following vignette:

After a series of Reference Group meetings, a query arose concerning the stalled progress of particular requests for enhancement by academics and education designers. Two items were raised: plug-ins for Web 2.0 capabilities in the form of blogs and wikis and a community location or customisable online space for projects by students and staff (listed above). A meeting participant (from the network of pedagogy) remarked that these items had been placed on the list several meetings earlier, yet had not progressed in rank order and no action had been taken. The meeting was informed that while all items were listed as scheduled for attention, other "core" items had been added that may be assigned greater priority. This distinction between types of enhancements was recorded in meeting minutes as an action item to "ensure all core activities are fully covered before the 'nice to haves' are worked on" (Project Reference Group meeting 7). The minutes indicated that enhancements that were noncore (or "nice to haves") may be postponed until project completion.

The list thus functioned as a project management object that ordered items for action by the IT team. Instances of core items included file management, interface configuration, faculty templates, migrating quizzes, and interoperability issues concerning recorded lectures and plug-ins. List items that were noncore included flexible modes of presenting discussion forum posts, a "community" location for online projects, and open source plug-ins for blogs, wikis, and Web 2.0 capabilities. These noncore items remained, but generally did not advance in list order to receive attention if "core" items were subsequently added. As indicated in the minutes, the noncore enhancements were scheduled for action at an unspecified date. This state of affairs remained unchanged two years later, with the two items still remaining as scheduled for enhancement

The list materialised the tensions and ambivalences that arose when pedagogical matters were considered against with the contingencies of technology work and project management. In ANT terms, project managers designated the enhancements list as the "obligatory passage point" (Callon, 1986, p. 206) between institutional networks: issues needed to be on the "list" in order to be included in the implementation process. In this way, pedagogical interests could draw on its own extensive network in order to place issues on the agenda and become a stabilised presence. However, the owner of the enhancements list was the spokesperson, to use Callon's term, for the network of project management, and hence for implementation.

Ramifications of Success

With the completion of the implementation project, the goal of re-establishing the LMS as the presence for the university's supported learning environment had been achieved: migrated subjects were ready for Semester 1, with a program of staff training workshops and support in place. What was less visible was a pedagogical presence for the assembled learning environment. In this section I will draw on the sociomaterial concepts introduced previously to attempt to identify the arrangements that were overlooked when this learning environments was put into place.

Implementation established the LMS as "a key intermediary" (Fenwick, 2011, p. 7) for online learning for the university, with the LMS becoming "an actor that can translate thinking and behaviour in the form of an 'immutable mobile'" (p. 7). That is, it became a *network object* that was assigned a primary role in assembling the relations of online learning and maintaining these relations across locations and settings. These arrangements were accomplished by making meticulous social and technological connections that configured the LMS with a standard set of functions, interface and language. The Reference Group was the site where institutional stakeholders *composed* the LMS as *the* environment for online learning. The LMS as a network object, in effect, defined a terminology for online learning and set its boundaries of use and the range of potential activities.

The relatively smooth resolution of implementation accomplished more than content migration and training. The LMS was an object that was performed or was *enacted* in two distinct forms: first as an information technology system requiring configuration, ongoing maintenance and monitoring; second as a vehicle for managed organisational change for staff adoption of the new online learning environment. Despite the representation of the LMS as unified entity, its implementation reflected distinct practices that can be identified from the networks of implementation described earlier. These two enactments worked in concert, as technological efforts were tailored to fit organisational goals and the project management constraints of scope, time and resources.

A third enactment of the LMS can be found in the teaching and learning practices that reflect disparate, local, situated activities. During the implementation project, however, pedagogical approaches were not organised into a unified voice, despite the presence of teaching academics in the Reference Group meetings. The *absent presence* of pedagogical practice is apparent in the enhancements list: issues of pedagogy were first framed as a supplementary matter, an "enhancement" of arrangements already in place; then they were translated into the functional discourse of IT applications, or else assigned the status of noncore items. As a result, issues that were presented in non-functional forms, or warranted a deliberative response, were unable to be articulated or recognised through the enhancements list and remained outside the cycle of negotiation in Fig. 4.2. The enhancement list performed as an obligatory passage point, becoming a necessary spokesperson for the requested online pedagogies that appeared as list items.

A lack of coherence between these enactments arose through the enhancement list as it circulated across the networks of implementation. As a network object, the enhancements list enacted a strategic logic in a literal ordering of list items. Nespor (2011) and Law (2009) describe how a network draws on established connections and extensive material and discursive resources to become stabilised. At the same time, competing or alternative networks become problematic, unstable, and, are displaced. Hence pedagogical issues, despite an extensive literature of theory and practice, were unable to be represented with their own discourse in the negotiation space of the enhancements list. The pedagogies of Web 2.0 collaboration or of participation in online community spaces were evident as unstable presences, or "fire objects" flickering between presence and absence during the Reference Group meetings.

The absent presence of pedagogical practices for networked learning arose at the outset of this project. As with other information technology implementations, this project drew on established networks already legitimised through global circulation: the planned approaches of project management and the ready to hand discourse of technology as a functional tool. The objects of implementation, exemplified by the enhancement list, enacted these prior networks as a manifest absence that was independent and prior to the project, that is, as a normalised procedure that passed unremarked. It was therefore difficult to establish links between the new LMS and potential networked learning practices or commence conversations about innovative practices. Consequently, local practices in online teaching were likely to follow the functional modes of ordering prescribed by the LMS, or else assume the status of "maverick" innovations (Bigum & Rowan, 2004) that are weakly aligned to the LMS and therefore unsupported, unscalable and unsustainable.

Studies of learning technologies rarely extend to the global and historical dimensions of technology (exceptions are Cuban, 2003; Nespor, 2011). In this instance, the prevailing enactments of the LMS reprised the legacy of online learning by emphasising a "centralisation" process (Selwyn, 2007, p. 90), viewing learning as conduct that was standard and measurable, rather than complex and situated, the former a process Law (2002) referred to as "a politics dressed up as functionality" (p. 102). Not learning from this legacy of learning technologies means implementing troublesome effects and elusive outcomes, in addition to an LMS.

Conclusion

This chapter studies an organisational change process that recurs in the ubiquitous deployment of learning technology systems in universities, in which an institutional learning environment is composed as a unified object with a single narrative, yet does not account for the multiple and distributed practices of learning. In this case study of learning technology implementation, I investigated the processes that make visible or make absent particular arrangements for online learning. To do this I examined particular connections that were established during the implementation project that drew on prior networks to organise the LMS as a stabilised sociomaterial assemblage. I also posited enactments during implementation that were outside of the composed unity of the assemblage: the absent presences of local networked learning practices that were displaced or deferred as the LMS was stabilised into an overarching, institutional online learning environment.

Arguing for a reappraisal of the objects of university learning, therefore, does not replay the tradition of technology-centred studies of effects of interventions in static organisational settings, where technologies are treated as separate from organisational and cultural domains (Orlikowski, 2010). Rather, objects are embedded with the social world, and "meanings and materialities are enacted together in everyday practices" (p. 135). In this case study, a particular material object, in the form of the list of potential enhancements for implementation, was the point for negotiation as it was passed between participating stakeholder networks, with the result that the network with the most extensive resources commanded the implementation agenda.

Networked learning is originally understood in terms of the connections enabled by information and communication technologies (ICTs): "between one learner and other learners, between learners and tutors; between a learning community and its learning resources" (Goodyear, Banks, Hodgson, & McConnell, 2004, p. 1). But how do these connections occur? A sociomaterial perspective can address the question of how these connections are materialised in practice, how, in Latour's terms, the artefacts and objects we observe in situ are in fact "programs of action" (1992, p. 174) that are both social and material and that can constrain or enable networked learning.

An orientation to social and material relations and their effects fits with the notion of networked learning described by Hodgson et al. (2012) as a "relational model" (p. 303), which integrates pedagogies with technological and organisational dimensions and develops new arrangements that are not constrained by traditional modes of formal learning. Objects, therefore, are a key actor in the enactment of a particular network of learning: institutional objects enacted as policy and procedures that order and organise learning environments and technological objects that enact ready to use configurations for learning.

Jones (2008) noted reasons why universities are "reluctant to take down the walls around institutional provision of the learning infrastructure" (p. 673), with particular reference to negotiation between institutional interests. As practice-oriented approaches such as networked learning build their own networks that extend and circulate, they are beginning to challenge the colonisation of teaching and learning by centralised LMS enactments. This case study prompts a reappraisal of the term "implementation" that challenges its historical framing as functionality and challenges the institutional separation between organising learning technologies and organising pedagogical practices. This challenge requires early intervention in learning technology implementation that insists on extending its scope to encompass practices that themselves draw on prior networks of networked learning and Web 2.0 pedagogies, including social networking, learner knowledge generation, experiential learning, and open education resources.

References

Alcipani, R., & Hassard, J. (2010). Actor-Network Theory, organizations and critique: towards a politics of organizing. *Organization, 17*(4), 419–435.

Barad, K. (2003). Posthumanist performativity: toward an understanding of how matter comes to matter. *Journal of Women in Culture and Society, 28*(3), 801–831.

Bennett, S., & Oliver, M. (2011). Talking back to theory: the missed opportunities in learning technology research. *Research in Learning Technology, 19*(3), 179–189.

Bigum, C., & Rowan, L. (2004). Flexible learning in teacher education: Myths, muddles and models. *Asia Pacific Journal of Teacher Education, 32*(3), 213–226.

Blin, F., & Munro, M. (2008). Why hasn't technology disrupted academics' teaching practices? Understanding resistance to change through the lens of activity theory. *Computers & Education, 50*, 475–490.

Callon, M. (1986). Some elements in a sociology of translation: domestication of the scallops and fishermen of St. Brieuc Bay. In J. Law (Ed.), *Power, action and belief: A new sociology of knowledge?* (pp. 196–233). London, England: Routledge.

Conole, G. (2008). New schemas for mapping pedagogies and technologies. *Ariadne, 56.*

Conole, G., White, S., & Oliver, M. (2007). The impact of e-learning on organisational roles and structures. In G. Conole & M. Oliver (Eds.), *Contemporary perspectives in e-learning research: Themes, methods and impact on practice* (pp. 69–97). London; New York: Routledge.

Cuban, L. (2003). *Oversold and underused: Computers in the classroom.* Cambridge, MA: Harvard University Press.

De Freitas, S., & Oliver, M. (2005). Does E-learning policy drive change in higher education?: A case study relating models of organisational change to e-learning implementation. *Journal of Higher Education Policy and Management, 27*(1), 81–95.

Feenberg, A. (1999). Whither Educational Technology? *Peer Review, 1*(4).

Fenwick, T. (2010). Re-thinking the "thing": Sociomaterial approaches to understanding and researching learning in work. *Journal of Workplace Learning, 22*(1/2), 104–116.

Fenwick, T. (2011). Reading educational reform with actor network theory: Fluid spaces, otherings, and ambivalences. *Educational Philosophy and Theory, 43*(s1), 114–134.

Goodyear, P., Banks, S., Hodgson, V., & McConnell, D. (2004). Research on networked learning: An overview. In P. Goodyear, S. Banks, V. Hodgson, & D. McConnell (Eds.), *Advances in research on networked learning* (pp. 1–11). Dordrecht, The Netherlands: Kluwer Academic.

Goodyear, P., & Ellis, R. (2008). University students' approaches to learning: Rethinking the place of technology. *Distance Education, 29*(2), 141–152.

Gunn, C. (2010). Sustainability factors for e-learning initiatives, *ALT-J. Research in Learning Technology, 18*(2), 89–103.

Hannon, J. (2013). Incommensurate practices: Sociomaterial entanglements of learning technology implementation. *Journal of Computer Assisted Learning, 29*(2), 168–178.

Hannon, J., Hirst, D. & Riddle, M. (2011). Implementing e-learning: A migration story. In G. Williams, P. Statham, N. Brown, & B. Cleland (Eds.), *Changing demands, changing directions. Proceedings ascilite Hobart* (pp.557–561). Retrieved 5 November 2012, from: http://www.ascilite.org.au/conferences/hobart11/procs/hannon-concise.pdf

Hodgson, V., McConnell, D., & Dirckinck-Holmfeld, L. (2012). The theory, practice and pedagogy of networked learning. In L. Dirckinck-Holmfeld, V. Hodgson, & D. McConnell (Eds.), *Exploring the theory, pedagogy and practice of networked learning* (pp. 291–305). Berlin, Germany: Springer Science+Business Media.

Jones, C. (2008). Infrastructures, institutions and networked learning. *Proceedings of the 6th International Conference on Networked Learning* (pp. 666–674), Halkidiki, Greece. Retrieved 1 April 2013 from http://www.networkedlearningconference.org.uk/past/nlc2008/abstracts/PDFs/Jones_666-674.pdf

Jones, C., Dirckinck-Holmfield, L., & Lindstrom, B. (2006). A relational, indirect, meso-level approach to CSCL design in the next decade. *Journal of Computer-Supported Collaborative Learning, 1*(1), 35–56.

Jones, C., & Kennedy, G. (2011). Stepping beyond the paradigm wars: pluralist methods for research in learning technology. *ALTC 2011 Proceedings of the 18th international conference of the association for learning technology* (pp. 18–28). University of Leeds, Leeds, England, 6–8 September.

Latour, B. (1987). *Science in Action.* Cambridge, MA: Harvard University Press.

Latour, B. (1992). Where are the missing masses? The sociology of a few mundane artifacts. In W. Bijker & J. Law (Eds.), *Shaping technology/building society: studies in sociotechnical change* (pp. 225–258). Cambridge, MA: MIT Press.

Latour, B. (1999). *Pandora's hope: Essays on the reality of science studies.* Cambridge, MA: Harvard University Press.

Latour, B. (2005). *Reassembling the social: An introduction to actor-network-theory.* Oxford, England: Oxford University Press.

Law, J. (2002). Objects and spaces. *Theory, Culture and Society, 19*(5/6), 91–105.

Law, J. (2004). *After method: Mess in social science research.* London, England: Routledge.

Law, J. (2009). Actor network theory and material semiotics. In B. Turner (Ed.), *The new Blackwell companion to social theory* (pp. 141–158). Chichester, England: Blackwell.

Law, J., & Hassard, J. (Eds.). (1999). *Actor network theory and after.* Oxford, England: Blackwell.

Law, J., & Singleton, V. (2000). Performing technology's stories: On social constructivism, performance, and performativity. *Technology and Culture, 41*(4), 765–775.

Law, J., & Singleton, V. (2005). Object lessons. *Organization, 12*(3), 331–355.

Lee, F. (2008). Technopedagogies of mass-individualization: Correspondence education in the mid twentieth century. *History and Technology, 24*(3), 239–253.

Marshall, S. (2010). Change, technology and higher education: are universities capable of organisational change? *ALT-J, Research in Learning Technology, 18*(3), 179–192.

Mol, A. (2002). *The body multiple: ontology in medical practice*. Durham, England: Duke University Press.

Nespor, J. (2011). Devices and educational change. *Educational Philosophy and Theory, 43*(s1), 15–37.

Nyvang, T., & Bygholm, A. (2012). Implementation of an Infrastructure for networked learning. In L. Dirckinck-Holmfeld, V. Hodgson, & D. McConnell (Eds.), *Exploring the theory, pedagogy and practice of networked learning* (pp. 141–156). New York: Springer Science+Business Media.

Oliver, M. (2013). Learning technology: Theorising the tools we study. *British Journal of Educational Technology, 44*(1), 31–43.

Orlikowski, W. (2007). Sociomaterial practices: Exploring technology at work. *Organization Studies, 29*(2), 1435–1448.

Orlikowski, W. (2010). The sociomateriality of organisational life: considering technology in management research. *Cambridge Journal of Economics, 34*(1), 125–141.

Orlikowski, W., & Scott, S. (2008). Sociomateriality: Challenging the separation of technology, work and organisation. *The Academy of Management Annals, 2*(1), 433–474.

Phillips, J. (2006). Agencement/assemblage. *Theory Culture Society, 23*, 108.

Price, S., & Oliver, M. (2007). A framework for conceptualising the impact of technology on teaching and learning. *Educational Technology & Society, 10*, 16–27.

Russell, C. (2009). A systemic framework for managing e-learning adoption in campus universities: Individual strategies in context. *ALT-J, Research in Learning Technology, 17*(1), 3–19.

Ryberg, T. (2008). Challenges and potentials for institutional and technological infrastructures in adopting social media. *Proceedings of the 6th International Conference on Networked Learning* (pp. 658–665), Halkidiki, Greece. Retrieved 1 April 2013 from http://www.networkedlearningconference.org.uk/past/nlc2008/abstracts/PDFs/Ryberg_658-665.pdf

Selwyn, N. (2007). The use of computer technology in university teaching and learning: a critical perspective. *Journal of Computer Assisted Learning, 23*, 83–94.

Selwyn, N. (2010). Looking beyond learning: Notes towards the critical study of educational technology. *Journal of Computer Assisted Learning, 26*, 65–73.

Sorensen, E. (2009). *The materiality of learning: Technology and knowledge in educational practice*. Cambridge, MA: Cambridge University Press.

Stepanyan, K., Littlejohn, A., & Margaryan, A. (2010). *Sustainable eLearning in a changing landscape: A scoping study (SeLScope)*. York, England: UK Higher Education Academy.

Suchman, L. A. (2007). *Human–machine reconfigurations: Plans and situated actions*. Cambridge, England: Cambridge University Press.

Uys, P. (2010). Implementing an open source learning management system: A critical analysis of change strategies. *Australasian Journal of Educational Technology, 26*(7), 980–999.

Chapter 5
Teachers' Use of Learning Technology in a South Asian Context

Uzair Shah

Introduction

Education technologists are exploiting the benefits of information and communications technology (ICT) to transform the teaching methods in universities. There has been a significant increase in the use of e-mail, Internet and computer conferencing especially within technologically advanced countries, allowing interactions and collaboration for supporting networked learning which is defined as 'learning in which information and communications technology is used to promote connections: between one learner and other learners; between learners and tutors; between a learning community and its learning resources' (Goodyear, Banks, Hodgson, & McConnell, 2004).

Hodgson and Watland (2004) suggest that there is much to understand about networked learning in terms of the teaching and learning methods and approaches for students and lecturers, and according to Brower (2003) more attention is required to understand effective utilization of ICT within online pedagogical practices. The transition from the face-to-face 'conventional' teaching settings to online environments can introduce unfamiliarity and uncertainty, which may challenge our perceptions of the world around us as Boon and Sinclair (2012) state:

> With one foot in the real and another in the virtual, users must come to terms with both difference and disquiet in order to participate effectively in networked learning environments (Boon & Sinclair, 2012).

This raises questions around the teachers' experiences of using learning technology within the pedagogical practices generally and in networked learning settings specifically. Considering the metaphor 'one foot in the virtual and another in the real', I wondered if this transition could be made smoother through better

U. Shah (✉)
Department of Management Learning & Leadership, Lancaster University
Management School, Lancaster, UK
e-mail: s.shah2@lancaster.ac.uk

V. Hodgson et al. (eds.), *The Design, Experience and Practice of Networked Learning*,   87
Research in Networked Learning, DOI 10.1007/978-3-319-01940-6_5,
© Springer International Publishing Switzerland 2014

understanding of the teachers' experiences of using learning technology within the conventional pedagogical practices.

There is a growing body of literature available that investigates the phenomenon of using learning technology in education (see for example Hu, Clark, & Ma, 2003; Jimoyiannis & Komis, 2007; Rienties et al., 2012; Rienties, Brouwer, & Lygo-Baker, 2013). However, only a few studies have explored this phenomenon from a *relational*, phenomenographic perspective (González, 2010). Gonzalez called for more research as the 'field is only at the beginning of understanding the complexities of what university teachers think eLearning is good for in their 'established' face-to-face university teaching ... with important implications for academic development'. As Amin and Thrift (2005) stated that 'no particular theoretical approach, even in combination with others, can be used to gain a total grip on what's going on'. This study aims to further enrich our understanding of the teachers' conceptions of using learning technology from a phenomenographic perspective. This is important as according to Lawless and Pellegrino (2007), there is 'absence of empirically grounded knowledge about how to best integrate technology, instruction, and learning into a coherent whole'. Also, Jimoyiannis and Komis (2007) called for a 'thorough analysis of teachers' conceptions of ICT in education (to) provide insights into the prerequisites for their successful preparation'. Furthermore, using the phenomenographic perspective can contribute to our understanding of 'how the gap between contents of the mind and professional practice is bridged' (Dall'Alba & Sandberg, 2006).

While the extant phenomenographic literature has contributed to our understandings of the teachers' practices of using learning technology, these studies are primarily based within western contexts (see 2010; Ellis, Steed, & Applebee, 2006; Gonzalez, 2009; Lameras, Levy, Paraskakis, & Webber, 2012; McConnell & Zhao, 2006; Roberts, 2003). Unfortunately, there is little evidence available on the users' perceptions of e-learning in the context of less developed countries (Bataineh & Baniabdelrahman, 2006) even though one-fifth of the worldwide enrolment in higher education is from within the less developed countries (Schofer & Meyer, 2005). Furthermore, Taylor (2005 cited by Shaikh, 2009) stated that the World Bank expects the 'number of HE students will more than double from 70 million to 160 million by 2025'. These statistics raise some interesting questions around the potential value and contributions of networked learning within the higher education. How should we engage with partners from different contexts where there could be variations in the perceptions, infrastructure and circumstances that are likely to affect the use of learning technology (Czerniewicz & Brown, 2012; Fahmy, Bygholm, & Jaeger, 2012)? Also how could the concept and community of networked learning accommodate these variations in the understandings and exposure of using learning technology in these different contexts?

Considering this, it will be useful to explore the teachers' use of learning technology within their 'conventional' pedagogical practices in a different non-western context. Marton, Dall'Alba, and Beaty (1993) stated that research in a different setting and with a different group could reveal 'new' conceptions that may improve our understanding of phenomena. Such a research focus could contribute to our understandings of using learning technology in different contexts and may facilitate in dealing with the challenges of interculturality considering the growing attention given to internationalization of higher education (see Fahmy et al., 2012).

While the South Asian countries like India, Pakistan, Bangladesh and Sri Lanka are amongst the most populated, these are 'undergoing an uneven modernisation in which large numbers remain undernourished, unhealthy and illiterate. Participation in tertiary education is relatively low … and in most South Asia nations the growing middle class is becoming more interested in cross-border education' (Marginson, 2004, p. 79). While in most western contexts, access to education and availability of quality technological infrastructure are often assumed, locating this study in such contexts makes it more interesting as countries like Pakistan continue to deal with challenges of 'uneven modernisation' where there is relatively limited access to quality education and a low per capita income to discourage wider population to buy computers and afford Internet services (Shafique & Mahmood, 2008). Keogh (2001) warns that 'unless the issue of access is addressed, the ICTs will increase divisions within societies'. Considering these aspects, this study explores the *qualitatively different ways teachers understand use of learning technology in a public university of Pakistan.*

Research Context

Pakistan has a growing population of approximately 180 million. Realizing the importance of using ICT, the government continues to invest in the country's telecommunication infrastructure after its first IT Policy in 2000 (Shafique & Mahmood, 2008). According to Malik and Shabbir (2008), Pakistan's Higher Education sector has been transformed with the adoption of technological advancements to support teaching and student learning. Digital libraries are available to many universities, and the Pakistan Education & Research Network (PERN) pushes for better utilization of learning technology for personal development of teachers (Malik & Shabbir, 2008). Having said this, there is research available suggesting that while some university teachers realize the significance of using learning technology, the majority perceived the use of technology within their pedagogical practices as 'intimidating' and expected administrative support Nawaz and Kundi (2010); Ali et al (2010). According to Shaikh (2009), limited availability of ICT facilities to the wider population remains a barrier in its integration within the higher education.

Also, with greater emphasis on memorization and acquisition of information and less on students' deep thinking, passive rote learning and instructional teaching approach appear dominant within the Pakistani schools. Such a learning and teaching approach could be problematic especially when expecting the students to take ownership and responsibility for their individual learning and for the teachers to assume the role of facilitators of the learning process. Considering that these are important aspects within networked learning, it becomes further worrying as networked learning is seen with the potential to contribute towards the transformation of higher education which is deemed necessary for the 'global economy that is based on information and social networks' (Hodgson, McConnell, & Dirckinck-Holmfeld, 2012).

With the prevailing instructional teaching approach and the growing digitalization of pedagogical practice, such challenges and opportunities make Pakistan an interesting country to locate this research. Influenced by these thoughts and realizing that our own understanding of this phenomenon in this context is limited, this empirical study explores the qualitative variations in the teachers' understandings and perceptions of using learning technology within their 'conventional' pedagogical practices in the context of a South Asian Pakistani public university of Hazara University (HU).

HU was formed in 2002 with the initiative of the Higher Education Commission (HEC) of Pakistan. Since then, it has grown in size and disciplines with three campuses which host Faculties of Science, Arts, Health Sciences, Law and Administrative Science and also a School of Cultural Heritage and Creative Technologies (www.hu.edu.pk). There are around 20 departments that offer undergraduate and postgraduate courses. HU is striving for and developing into a research university. One of its initiatives is the National Centre for Collaborative Research and Training at the main campus. This centre aims to provide opportunities and a platform to the researchers from across the country to contribute and share their knowledge and expertise. Also, as an initiative of HEC to ensure improved and similar quality of education across the universities, Quality Enhancement Cell has been established recently.

Research Methodology

Selwyn (2012) calls for more studies that offer 'a direct 'way in' to unpacking the micro-level social processes that underpin the use of digital technologies in educational settings'. The research methodology of phenomenography presents such an opportunity. It takes a second-order research perspective to focus on the participants' descriptions of their lived experiences of the phenomenon. Phenomenography aims to identify the qualitative variations within the participants' descriptions of experiences (Marton & Booth, 1997).

Adopting an interpretive paradigm, phenomenography takes a non-dualistic, *relational* ontological stance, which implies that the person (subject) and the object of experience are fused or interrelated to one another through experience Sjöström & Dahlgren 2002. This suggests that individuals when describing their experiences are telling something about themselves and the phenomenon (Marton et al., 1997). The associated epistemological assumption of phenomenography is the way we perceive or experience our world would differ from others, and these different worlds can be understood, portrayed and communicated to others.

Marton (1981) states that there are limited number of ways in which a phenomenon can be viewed or experienced. Within phenomenographic studies, the process of data collection and analysis is closely associated to each other (Bruce & Gerber, 1995) as the intention is always to highlight the variations within the descriptions of experiences. This informs the way data is collected and analysed. When deciding on the participants and the number of interviews, one of the major considerations is the requirement to capture and exhaust the different ways a phenomenon is experienced. Booth (2001) explains that:

> Data is collected from a sample of people, deliberately chosen to cover the population of interest in important dimensions, the aim being to exhaust the variations in experience; collection of data can be extended if the variation is felt to be under-represented, or cut short if no new material is forthcoming (Booth, 2001).

Trigwell (2000) recommended a sample of between 15 and 20 participants. However, this number could increase or decrease depending upon the quality of data gathered and/or if the interview discussions repeatedly followed similar theme(s) (Booth, 2001). Ashworth and Lucas (2000) commented that:

> The selection of participants should avoid presuppositions about the nature of the phenomenon or the nature of conceptions held by particular 'type' of individuals, while observing common-sense precautions about maintaining 'variety' of experiences. (Ashworth & Lucas, 2000)

For research within higher education, Bowden (2000) further suggested interviewing participants from different disciplines, academic positions, teaching experience and genders. Keeping these suggestions in mind, I conducted 29 semi-structured interviews of academics belonging to the different Faculties at HU. The participants were from both the genders and taught either at undergraduate and/or postgraduate level. Some of these participants had extensive teaching experience, while others were newly appointed. I also interviewed teachers who were part of higher management that included Head of Departments, Deans, Registrar and also the Vice Chancellor of the HU. This selection of the participants was with the objective of maximizing the range of perspectives on the use of learning technology within their teaching practices at HU.

The focus of a phenomenographic interview is to capture how the participant experiences and understands the phenomenon under exploration. To do so, the interview questions are designed to be open ended to allow the participants to describe their experiences of the phenomenon. Rather than directing conversations, the researcher invites them to describe fully their lived experiences. In this study, the participants were asked few predetermined interview questions (mentioned below), and the follow-up questions depended on the participants' responses.

- Can you please describe your experience using learning technology in your teaching?
- How do you think the use of learning technology affected you as a teacher?
- Would you like to summarize and/or provide any other details regarding your use of learning technology?

During the interviews, the participants used English and the native language of Urdu. These interviews lasted for 40 min on average, which were audio recorded and later translated and transcribed. In this research, I used the theoretical framework of intentionality or *what/how* framework (Marton et al., 1997) to analyse the participants' descriptions of experiences. This framework assumes that any action undertaken has an underpinning intention(s).

While recognizing that an individual is capable of experiencing a phenomenon in different ways, phenomenography aims to categorize and group the participants' descriptions of experiences. As is the norm in phenomenographic analysis, the statements from the transcripts which did not relate with the phenomenon of using learning technology were firstly filtered out. The remaining statements were then arranged according to the different ways the participants responded to the interview questions. This resulted in an initial group of categories. These initial categories contained certain characteristics or 'utterances' (Hasselgren & Beach, 1997) that emerged from the grouping of the similarities and differences within the participants' described experiences of using learning technology. These 'utterances' provided a unique and distinctive aspect of their use of learning technology and laid the foundations for 'categories of descriptions' which is an important outcome of phenomenographic research (Marton et al., 1997). For example, in this study one of the identified categories of descriptions was professional skills development. The utterances that defined and distinguished this use of learning technology were 'student employment and skills' and 'performance at work'. Similarly, other categories had their respective utterance(s) which gave distinct meanings to the way the teachers used learning technology within their practices. Once these utterances were identified, attention was given to understand the relationships between them. Hasselgren and Beach (1997) state 'Phenomenography should be a process of analytic juxtaposition'. To explore the relationships between the utterances, questions such as 'how one category of descriptions is different from another, and what dimensions make these categories different' were considered when analysing the statements. These questions helped to achieve another important aspect of phenomenographic analysis which is to identify the dimensions of variations, or *how* aspects of the categories of description.

According to Marton and Booth (1997), a category of descriptions constitutes of the *what* aspects that highlight its meanings and the *how* aspects which illuminate the structure of the category. The *what* aspect is further linked with *direct object* which represents the primary goal or purpose of the category of descriptions. In this research, the *direct object* is reflected in the meanings associated with the categories of descriptions. Using the example of professional skills development category of description, the meaning associated (or the *what* aspects) with this use learning technology is to provide the necessary skills to their students to be better practitioners and for relevant employment after graduation. This also reflects the primary goal or *direct object* of this use of learning technology within the pedagogical practices. The *how* aspect comprises of two interrelated parts, *act* and *indirect object* (Marton et al., 1997). In this study, the *act* would refer to the action

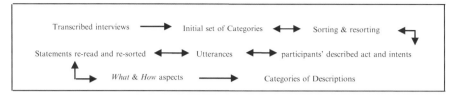

Fig. 5.1 Data analysis process

undertaken by the teachers in using learning technology, whereas the *indirect object* describes the intent(s) behind the *act* of using learning technology. I shall illustrate these aspects later in this chapter. Regarding the use of *what/how* framework, Harris (2011) stated:

> The what/how framework encourages researchers to analyse data in light of not just what is being understood, but to also consider the process, actions, and motives behind this understanding ... (t)his framework allows the conception to be analysed separately from the actions and intentions related to it. (Harris, 2011)

As illustrated in the diagram below, using this framework informed the data analysis and consequently the categories of descriptions (Fig. 5.1).

Reliability and Validity

The issue of reliability and validity is a complex and contentious one within phenomenographic literature with no obvious resolution (see Åkerlind, 2004; Marton et al., 1997; Sandberg, 2005). Within qualitative studies, reliability is concerned with how the researcher deals with his/her 'biased subjectivity' (Kvale, 1994) to be honest and truthful to the participants' descriptions. While acknowledging that the 'researchers cannot escape their interpretation' (Sandberg, 2005), in this study I made conscious efforts to bracket my biases, knowledge and subjectivity using the guidelines provided by Ashworth and Lucas (2000). The research validity is concerned with 'how we, as researchers, can justify that our interpretations are truthful to lived experience within the theoretical and method-ological perspective taken' (Sandberg, 2005). For this, Sandberg suggested ensuring that the participants' descriptions are embedded in their lived experiences. This was achieved through the interview and follow-up questions which encouraged and facilitated the participants to describe fully their lived experiences of using learning technology. Also, when required, I requested them to further contextualize their descriptions by providing concrete examples and situations of their use of learning technology within their practices. In addition, I referred to the guidelines provided by Cope (2002), Lamb, Sandberg, and Liesch (2011) to ensure the validity of the research findings.

Categories of Descriptions

Based on the earlier described analysis process, five qualitatively different ways of understanding the use of learning technology were identified. These are listed below in increasing order of complexity, with omnipotential category of description as the relatively most complex:

- Retaining attention
- Professional skills development
- Information enrichment
- Connectivity
- Omnipotential

Retaining attention category of descriptions represents the least complex category where the teachers described using learning technology to present lecture content in ways to retain students' attention and involvement during the lecture. One of the participants described this use to state:

> You see when you take children to a park or to a colourful area, they are happy and involved. Similar is the case with multimedia—there are many ways of presenting—with different colours, words flying into their place—so when I have used the multimedia I have found students to be more involved and attentive. (Faculty of Health Sciences, 2)

Professional skills development category of descriptions highlights the teachers' use of learning technology to provide the necessary skills to their students for better employment, to meet the expectations and requirements of organizations today and to be better practitioners in their respective fields. One participant described that 'you cannot produce professionals without giving them knowledge or without using technology during the (education) process'.

Information enrichment category of descriptions relates with the teachers' experiences of using learning technology to access multiple-sourced information. They described using learning technology to update their teaching material with recently published research papers and other sources of information related to the lecture topic. This has been described to add value in their preparation of the teaching material as well as their individual research as one of them stated that:

> Usually in my case, since I have 16 years of experience so I am aware of what things need to be done for the lectures and how much time would be designed on the paper and how much on the board. Still, I use Google scholar, amazon, e-journals. (Faculty of Arts, 10)

Connectivity category of descriptions highlights the communicational aspect of learning technology where the teachers experienced using it to connect and collaborate with other academics, universities, research organizations or the government's education departments. In such experiences, the teachers described using learning technology as the platform to share academic material and information, discuss and connect with other academics. One participant described such experience:

Then there is a person in an IT institution in Rajasthan in India. Through the internet, he became my friend with whom I interact about such things (technology applications). That is a great help to us. Suppose there is a new book and we cannot access it here. They would download the book and send it to me. (Faculty of Law & Administrative Sciences, 2)

Omnipotential is relatively the most complex category of description where the teachers described using learning technology as means and tool for numerous possibilities and opportunities that may be difficult otherwise. The teachers described using it in multiple ways ranging from its real-time use in classrooms to information collection and research activities to collaboration with the academics and institutions outside HU. Furthermore, these teachers described themselves as participants of a global academic community and understood the use of learning technology as important to contribute and compete within this global community. Also such use is associated to promote social equality and to mitigate the divisions within the society.

As mentioned earlier that a category of descriptions constitutes of the *what* aspects (i.e. meanings associated as elaborated above) and *how* aspects, or dimensions of variations (Marton et al., 1997). The *how* aspects identified in this study were *prior exposure of technology, research-informed teaching* and *perceived scope of technological use*. 'Prior exposure of technology' highlights the teachers' previous experiences of technology as a student or at earlier employment. The descriptions of experiences suggest that the teachers' prior exposure of technology (ranging from less sophisticated to sophisticated exposure) influenced their use of learning technology.

'Research-informed teaching' dimension of variation relates to the consideration given to include and refer to the research aspects/literature when preparing the teaching material. The relatively 'less' research-informed teaching material comprises largely of existing teaching notes which are modified through a 'peripheral' literature review. However, within the 'more' research-informed teaching material, research aspect/literature review becomes an integral aspect of their pedagogical practices.

The third dimension of variation of 'perceived scope of technological use' describes how the teachers saw the role and use of technology within pedagogical practices in the coming future. When the described perceived scope of use was 'limited', they viewed the use of learning technology to be confined to particular aspects of the pedagogical practices. However, when the teachers described the perceived scope as 'broad', the teachers understood the use of learning technology to have implications not only within their practices but also on a broader, societal level. These dimensions of variations are seen to influence the teachers' use of learning technology. Their relationships with the categories of descriptions of using learning technology are presented in the table below (Table 5.1).

As mentioned earlier, the omnipotential category of descriptions is the most sophisticated and inclusive of other categories. Aspects considered important within networked learning surfaced strongly within the omnipotential descriptions of using learning technology. In this chapter, I will focus on the analysis of the omnipotential category of description in further depth. This is to elaborate on its

Table 5.1 *What* and *How* aspects of teachers' experiences of using learning technology

Category of descriptions	*What* aspects	*How* aspects		
		Prior exposure of technology	Research-informed teaching	Perceived scope of technological use
Retaining attention	To retain attention of students during lectures	Less sophisticated	Less	Limited
Professional skills development	To allow students to be better practitioners and improve employability			
Information enrichment	To efficiently access multiple sourced information to enrich teaching notes and research			
Connectivity	To connect and communicate with other academics			
Omnipotential	As means and tool for numerous possibilities and opportunities	Sophisticated	More	Broad

usefulness and complexity that may assist academics in making the transition from the conventional settings into online learning environments. I will discuss the *what* and *how* aspects using quotations from the transcripts to highlight the meanings and structural aspects of this category of description. The transcripts are labelled with the participants' respective Faculty and a random number for confidentiality purpose.

Omnipotential: What Aspects

In this category of description, the teachers described using learning technology as means and tool for numerous possibilities and opportunities which would have been difficult otherwise. In these descriptions, the role and involvement of learning technology were perceived as important to affect their pedagogical practices on many levels, varying from the preparation of teaching material to individual research to career progression, as described below:

> Technology is the need of the day and has to be tightly linked with teaching. At this time, you cannot go without technology, cannot prosper, succeed or be fruitful or efficient in your teaching without technology. (Faculty of Arts, 1)

The above description elaborates the influence of using learning technology as its use is related with prosperity, success and efficiency within the pedagogical practices. Within the omnipotential descriptions of experiences, the increasing rate of change within academic literature, innovations and global market scenario was highlighted. The teachers also described the importance of understanding and referring to these changes within their teaching as suggested below:

> If you are studying or teaching management or business related things, in that there are almost innovations on daily basis; new innovations, inventions, new marketing tools, new customer complaints and reactions and others; these keep on being updated. Technology is the sole means that keeps us updated with these innovations or developments . . . also you know, make international contacts with people . . . if you keep aside books, latest situations on markets and products, technology can provide us with these situations easily. (Faculty of Law & Administrative Sciences, 3)

As described above, within omnipotential descriptions of experiences, the learning technology is seen as a primary source to keep updated with recent developments. The teacher above mentions using learning technology to establish connections and interact with people/academics in different countries. This aspect of omnipotential experience of using learning technology relates to the conception of 'connectivity', where the teachers experience use of learning technology to purposefully connect and collaborate with other academics, aspects which are considered important within networked learning. In addition, he is able to benefit from such use of learning technology on multiple levels to affect his teaching content to include recent developments of the field to provide exposure to his students and himself. Another teacher views the inclusion of learning technology to have revolutionized the practices to introduce various possibilities and opportunities for individuals as highlighted below:

> The revolution brought by the internet is amazing—I think it has the whole world squeezed—squeezed in one hand, the world is in my hand in my mobile phone which has internet. With this, I can talk to anyone in any corner of this world but I can use it in a wrong way. It depends on me—if my consciousness is not awake, I would use it negatively. (Faculty of Arts, 13)

The above extract elaborates the teacher's meanings of using learning technology as means or tool for opportunities and possibilities. It also highlights aspects of networked learning where learning technology is used to connect and interact with people and to share and discuss ideas and information. While appreciating the various possibilities, the ethical use of technology and self-accountability is considered important. This resonates with the notion of digital tools as 'neither innocent nor culturally neutral' and responsible use of learning technology (Ross, 2012). Furthermore, another teacher elaborates the omnipotential use of learning technology by relating to the success of the institution as mentioned below:

> You should know that our university is ranked 25th nationally from among the 95 degree awarding institutes. If the technology wasn't here, it would not be this soon—would have taken much time. (Faculty of Science, 9)

The above statements illuminate the omnipotential understanding of using learning technology to influence the ranking of the university. This implies that within omnipotential understandings of using learning technology, the teachers described its use with the potential to affect not only at an individual but also on a community level. In order to better understand the structure of omnipotential category of description, I will discuss the *how* aspects separately which will further illuminate the teachers' *acts* and the interrelated *indirect object(s)* of using learning technology.

How Aspect of Prior Exposure of Technology

As mentioned earlier that omnipotential conception is relatively most complex and is inclusive of other conceptions. This implies that while describing their omnipotential experiences of using learning technology, the teacher may illuminate aspects relating to other conceptions, as is described below:

> The role of technology from now onwards would increase tremendously. There are reasons behind it—if you remember things in the last 10 years, if a professor wanted a paper—first there was no option of subscribing and so would continue to search for places from where he could get a volume of a journal and request or write to others for the volume ... now the technology does it! (Use of learning technology) starts from browsing, sifting, analyzing, and bringing to the multimedia—in all these you need to use technology. (Faculty of Law & Administrative Sciences, 2)

The above excerpt illuminates the teacher's prior exposure to technology in describing the difficulties faced in accessing academic journal. This is further related and reflected against the role and use of learning technology within his current pedagogical practices. Such reflections facilitate to foresee the influence of learning technology, as he states that the 'role of technology from now onwards would increase tremendously'. This further describes his intention, or *indirect object* which is related to three different *acts* mentioned in the passage; firstly, the manner in which academic literature was searched in the earlier decade(s), the teacher's existing approach towards searching and analysing literature and, lastly, presentation of the teaching material. Collectively, these *acts* and intent interplay to complement 'sophisticated' prior exposure of technology. This description of experience also reflects his willingness to engage with academic material/learning resources which further influences his use of learning technology within the teaching practices. It also includes aspects of 'information enrichment' category of description when the teacher states that the '(use of learning technology) starts from browsing, sifting, analyzing', suggesting that learning technology is used to gather information from various sources and to analyse the collected data. However, the complex meanings associated to use of learning technology distinguish this description of experiences from other descriptions.

How Aspect of Research-Informed Teaching

The relatively more 'research-informed' teaching reflects upon the pedagogical practices within which the research aspect and/or literature review is considered important. Such teaching practices surfaced prominently within the omnipotential use of learning technology, as is described below:

> If we teach students about what was done 100 years, then the students wouldn't get the latest knowledge. But if we are using computer and internet, we can get latest information. I will give you an example...(of) our own research where we determined three pairing in chromosomes—if a teacher hasn't downloaded this journal, he would still be teaching the old concepts i.e. there is only one pairing. So this is very important to use learning technologies as then we can give latest information to students, about what is happening in the world, about the different methods of detecting diseases, about finding cure for cancer but through authentic sources. (Faculty of Science, 6)

The teacher above provides his omnipotential understandings of using learning technology. He describes the *acts* of using the Internet for literature review and his individual research. This is with the interrelated *indirect object* of providing his students with latest developments in the field, which may lead to the possibility to detect different diseases and finding their cures. He further speaks of finding possible cures for cancer. This interrelation of *act* and *indirect object* influences his meanings to his omnipotential understanding of the use of learning technology as the means for opportunities and possibilities.

How Aspect of Perceived Scope of Technological Use

Omnipotential descriptions of experiences highlight the teachers' perceived 'broad' scope of technological use in the coming future. The teachers described the use of learning technology to not only influence on the individual but also on collective, societal level, as described below:

> If we look from the research point of view, the gap in science between west and east is almost finished. Things that are done in US, Canada or Japan are exactly the same in the lab of HU. The same machine which is used abroad is used here in our lab. See, the books I had with me which I thought were an asset, today they may not be assets anymore and are part of the archives. This is because the knowledge is upgraded on daily basis. This is why the young people and the new universities are moving forward with good pace because people in those universities are accustomed to the new technologies and are benefitting from them ... The lecture which you have to prepare on today's development, if your energy systems are not supporting you then you would speak about yesterday as your knowledge would not be updated ... so it affects the quality of learning of students and the quality of the (research) product. (Faculty of Science, 9)

In this described experience, the described *acts* are using PCR machine in the laboratory of HU, and the other is use of books in his personal library. These *acts* are associated with several *indirect objects*. First is to keep updated with recent research developments; second is to stay tuned with sophisticated research instruments and benefit from them; third is the development and progress of universities at good pace; and last, on a larger scale, is to further reduce the 'gap in science between west and east'. Such complexity of intents is associated the 'broad' perceived scope of technological use. It can also be implied from the above description that he sees the awareness of technological development and comfort/ ease in the use of learning technology to be an asset. The above-described *acts* relate with 'information enrichment' category; however, sophisticated *indirect objects* provide a different, richer meaning of his experiences of using learning technology. This further illuminates the complex nature of omnipotential category of description that is most elaborate and is inclusive of other categories. Having said so, he also highlights contextual challenges faced at HU. There are issues around irregular availability of electricity which affect use of learning technology and negatively influence teaching and research. Also, the limited access to information and published research affected the pedagogical practices, as they are unable to refer to contemporary research within their teaching notes and consequently 'speak about yesterday (research) as your knowledge would not be updated'. This affects not only student learning but also the research conducted at HU. The following figure illustrates the relationship of omnipotential *what* and *how* aspects.

Discussion

The findings of this research have certain similarities with the extant phenomenographic literature. Based in the context of a Scottish university, Roberts's (2003) research identified conceptions of using Web within teaching practices which were to 'provide information' and for 'individual and independent self-paced learning'. González's (2010) study of conceptions of teaching using e-learning in the context of two campus-based research-intensive Australian universities identified conceptions that varied from 'e-learning as a medium to provide information' to 'e-learning as a medium for engaging in communication–collaboration–knowledge building' (González (2010)), while McConnell and Zhao (2006) research findings from interviews of Chinese university teachers suggested they preferred face-to-face lectures and viewed e-learning as a source mainly to upload learning material for students' individual learning.

This study illuminates the ubiquitous nature of learning technology as the teachers attempt to digitalize various aspects of their pedagogical practices in more or less complex ways. It provides additional ways of looking at the use of learning technology to those mentioned in the literature as 'retaining attention' or 'omnipotential' conceptions have not been reported before. Retaining attention conception was the least complex conception that highlights the use of learning technology to retain the students' attention while teaching. Such use of learning technology was underpinned by an 'information–transmission' teaching approach as was highlighted by one of the participants that the 'students have to learn from

Omnipotential conception of use of learning technology

What aspects – means and tool for numerous possibilities and opportunities

How aspect – Prior exposure of learning technology		*How aspect – Research-informed teaching*		*How aspect – Perceived scope of technological use*	
Act – earlier use learning technology as a student or at previous employments	*Indirect objects – reflections from these previous experiences are brought forward to shape and affect current and possible future use of learning technology*	*Act – use of internet and/or research equipment for teaching and research*	*Indirect objects – access to academic material in ways to save time and update on latest developments for possible future research contributions*	*Act – use of technology for pedagogical purposes*	*Indirect objects – to remain competitive in the global academic race, for social equality and to affect collective mindset*

Fig. 5.2 Relationships of omnipotential *what* and *how* aspects

the teacher' (Faculty of Science, 9). These teachers described positioning themselves as the 'sage on stage' and used learning technology accordingly in a classroom setting.

On the other hand, omnipotential conception is the relatively most complex, elaborate and is inclusive of other conceptions. The teachers with omnipotential understanding used learning technology to contribute to their pedagogical practices on different fronts. Such use of learning technology was underpinned by the teachers' rich pedagogical understandings where they perceived the teaching role as the facilitators rather than the drivers of the learning process. They understood the use of learning technology to access and engage with the learning resources and also for students' online discussions and dialogue to develop deeper understandings. One of the participants described that 'I use internet for communication - I use my Facebook account and share it with the students and we get connected to each other and exchange knowledge' (Faculty of Arts, 10). Also, as highlighted in Fig. 5.2, these teachers saw themselves as participants of their respective global academic communities and used learning technology to interact, collaborate and contribute to their respective community.

Aspects considered important within networked learning such as connecting and collaborating, sharing and discussing information/learning resources, learning communities, surfaced prominently in the omnipotential descriptions of experiences. Within such descriptions, the teachers also highlighted the importance of 'online social literacy as well as digital and information literacy' (Hodgson et al., 2012). It is argued that such relatively complex and sophisticated understandings may facilitate a smoother transition from conventional to online learning environments.

Fahmy et al. (2012) and Lameras et al. (2012) in their study highlighted the importance of considering the contextual circumstances when exploring the use of learning technology. The findings of this study also reiterate this consideration. When describing their use of learning technology, the teachers highlighted the contextual issues such as access to information and limited technological support and infrastructure. Their teaching and research suffered due to limited and disproportionate availability of information and access to published research, as one of the teachers mentioned 'at times, we have to rely on only abstracts of the journal'. Although all the participants highlighted the contextual limitations to affect their pedagogical practices, some teachers described using learning technology omnipotentially while attempting to circumvent and/or mitigate the effects of these limitations.

Due to the government regulations, the Pakistani public universities like HU charge subsidized fees. Such universities are much dependent on the government funding to support their practices and infrastructure. This further implies that the quality of exposure and use of learning technology and consequently the learning experiences partly depended on the type of university (whether public or private university) and its financial standing. Czerniewicz and Brown (2012) stated this 'becomes yet another factor which can advantage or disadvantage individual students'.

Selwyn (2012) highlighted the need for further research to 'develop a more socially grounded understanding of the "messy" realities of educational technology 'as it happens' '. Using the phenomenographic framework of intentionality allowed illuminating not only the variations in the teachers' intentions and understandings of using learning technology but also the 'messy' realities and contextual aspects that influence their daily, mundane teaching practices.

Concluding Comments

Based in the context of a South Asian Pakistani public university, this study offers additional ways of looking at the use of learning technology within face-to-face pedagogical practices. Considering the metaphor 'one foot in the virtual and another in the real', this research contributes to our awareness and understanding of the issues around using learning technology within the pedagogical practices. It is argued that the complex use of learning technology and sophisticated underpinning pedagogical understandings associated with omnipotential conception may contribute to the academics' better preparation to 'overcome the alienation and otherness of online spaces' (Boon & Sinclair, 2012) and possibly a smoother transition into networked learning environments. This is potentially an area for future research.

Creanor and Walker (2012) suggest a better understanding of the 'relationship of people, technology and pedagogy in learning technology environments'. The analytical framework of intentionality contributed to our comprehension of this relationship and allowed us to 'consider the process, actions, and motives' (Harris, 2011) behind the teachers' use of learning technology. It highlighted the social context of using learning technology which is essential to examine the role technology plays in learning (Hodgson et al., 2012).

This study also highlights one of the potential challenges of the variations in the pedagogical understandings which may surface when engaging with international members within networked learning environments. The journey from a passive learner to a 'self-directed learner' within a networked learning environment could be problematic and would require encouragement and facilitation in developing different, deeper approaches to learning.

McConnell, Hodgson, and Dirckinck-Holmfeld (2012) stated that 'Web 2.0 technologies have given unprecedented access to information and the world and ways of being and interaction'. However, the contextual limitations at HU affected the participants' access to information, interaction with the world and ways of being. These limitations also hindered developing 'engaged connections and collaborations'. As internationalization of higher education continues, how do we involve and engage with the international partners and members of networked learning community within such contexts for 'greater levels of mutual engagement and dedication, critical reflection, emancipatory formation and empowerments' (Hodgson et al., 2012) is another area for future research.

References

Åkerlind, G. S. (2004). A new dimension to understanding university teaching. *Teaching in Higher Education, 9*(3), 363–375.

Ali, R., Khan, M. S., Ghazi, S. R., Shahzad, S., & Khan, I. (2010). Teachers' training-a grey area in higher education. *Asian Social Science, 6*(7), P43.

Amin, A., & Thrift, N. (2005). What's left? Just the future. *Antipode, 37*(2), 220–238.

Ashworth, P., & Lucas, U. (2000). Achieving empathy and engagement: A practical approach to the design, conduct and reporting of phenomenographic research. *Studies in Higher Education, 25*(3), 295–308.

Bataineh, R., & Baniabdelrahman, A. (2006). Jordanian EFL students' perceptions of their computer literacy. *International Journal of Education and Development Using ICT, 2*(2).

Boon, S., & Sinclair, C. (2012). Life behind the screen: Taking the academic online. In L. Dirckinck-Holmfeld, V. Hodgson, & D. McConnell (Eds.), *Exploring the theory, pedagogy and practice of networked learning* (pp. 273–287). New York: Springer.

Booth, S. (2001). Learning computer science and engineering in context. *Computer Science Education, 11*(3), 169–188.

Bowden, J. (2000). The nature of phenomenographic research. In J. Bowden & E. Walsh (Eds.), *Phenomenography* (pp. 1–18). Melbourne, VIC: RMIT University Press.

Brower, H. H. (2003). On emulating classroom discussion in a distance-delivered OBHR course: Creating an on-line learning community. *Academy of Management Learning & Education, 2*(1), 22–36.

Bruce, C., & Gerber, R. (1995). Towards university lectures' conceptions of student learning. *Higher Education, 29*(4), 443–458.

Cope, C. (2004). Ensuring validity and reliability in phenomenographic research using the analytical framework of a structure of awareness. *Qualitative Research Journal, 4*(2), 5–18.

Creanor, L., & Walker, S. (2012). Learning technology in context: A case for the sociotechnical interaction framework as an analytical lens for networked learning research.

In L. Dirckinck-Holmfeld, V. Hodgson, & D. McConnell (Eds.), *Exploring the theory, pedagogy and practice of networked learning* (pp. 173–187). New York: Springer.

Czerniewicz, L., & Brown, C. (2012). Objectified cultural capital and the tale of two students. In L. Dirckinck-Holmfeld, V. Hodgson, & D. McConnell (Eds.), *Exploring the theory, pedagogy and practice of networked learning* (pp. 209–219). New York: Springer.

Dall'Alba, G., & Sandberg, J. (2006). Unveiling professional development: A critical review of stage models. *Review of Educational Research, 76*(3), 383–412.

Ellis, R. A., Steed, A. F., & Applebee, A. C. (2006). Teacher conceptions of blended learning, blended teaching and associations with approaches to design. *Australasian Journal of Educational Technology, 22*(3), 312.

Fahmy, S. S., Bygholm, A., & Jaeger, K. (2012). Issues in internationalization of education: The case of a Danish Business School exporting a blended learning MBA program to developing countries. In V. Hodgson, C. Jones, M. de Laat, D. McConnell, T. Ryberg, & P. Sloep (Eds.), *Proceedings of the Eighth International Conference on Networked Learning 2012* (pp. 276–283). http://www.networkedlearningconference.org.uk/abstracts/safwat.html

Gonzalez, C. (2009). Conceptions of, and approaches to, teaching online: A study of lecturers teaching postgraduate distance courses. *Higher Education, 57*(3), 299–314.

González, C. (2010). What do university teachers think eLearning is good for in their teaching? *Studies in Higher Education, 35*(1), 61–78.

Goodyear, P., Banks, S., Hodgson, V., & McConnell, D. (2004). Research on networked learning: An overview. In P. Goodyear, S. Banks, V. Hodgson, & D. McConnell (Eds.), *Advances in research on networked learning* (pp. 1–11). Dordrecht, The Netherlands: Kluwer Academic.

Harris, L. R. (2011). Phenomenographic perspectives on the structure of conceptions: The origins, purposes, strengths, and limitations of the what/how and referential/structural frameworks. *Educational Research Review, 6*(2), 109–124.

Hasselgren, B., & Beach, D. (1997). Phenomenography—A "good-for-nothing brother" of phenomenology? Outline of an analysis. *Higher Education Research & Development, 16*(2), 191–202.

Hodgson, V., McConnell, D., & Dirckinck-Holmfeld, L. (2012). The Theory, Practice and Pedagogy of Networked Learning. In L. Dirckinck-Holmfeld, V. Hodgson, & D. McConnell (Eds.), *Exploring the theory, pedagogy and practice of networked learning* (pp. 219–315). New York: Springer.

Hodgson, V., & Watland, P. (2004). Researching networked management learning. *Management Learning, 35*(2), 99–116.

Hu, P., Clark, T., & Ma, W. (2003). Examining technology acceptance by school teachers: A longitudinal study. *Information Management, 41*(2), 227–241.

Jimoyiannis, A., & Komis, V. (2007). Examining teachers' beliefs about ICT in education: Implications of a teacher preparation programme. *Teacher Development, 11*(2), 149–173.

Keogh, K. M. (2001). National strategies for the promotion of on-line learning in higher education. *European Journal of Education, 36*(2), 223–236.

Kvale, S. (1994). Ten standard objections to qualitative research interviews. *Journal of Phenomenological Psychology, 25*(2), 147–173.

Lamb, P., Sandberg, J., & Liesch, P. W. (2011). Small firm internationalisation unveiled through phenomenography. *Journal of International Business Studies, 42*(5), 672–693.

Lameras, P., Levy, P., Paraskakis, I., & Webber, S. (2012). Blended university teaching using virtual learning environments: Conceptions and approaches. *Instructional Science, 40*(1), 141–157.

Lawless, K. A., & Pellegrino, J. W. (2007). Professional development in integrating technology into teaching and learning: Knowns, unknowns, and ways to pursue better questions and answers. *Review of Educational Research, 77*(4), 575–614.

Malik, S., & Shabbir, M. S. (2008). Perception of university students on self-directed learning through learning technology. *European Journal of Scientific Research, 24*(4), 567–574.

Marginson, S. (2004). Don't leave me hanging on the Anglophone: The potential for online distance higher education in the Asia-Pacific region. *Higher Education Quarterly, 58*(2–3), 74–113.

Marton, F. (1981). Phenomenography—Describing conceptions of the world around us. *Instructional science, 10*(2), 177–200.

Marton, F., Booth, S., & Booth, S. A. (1997). *Learning and Awareness Pr.* Mahwah, NJ: Routledge.

Marton, F., Dall'Alba, G., & Beaty, E. (1993). Conceptions of learning. *International Journal of Educational Research, 19*, 277–300.

McConnell, D., Hodgson, V., & Dirckinck-Holmfeld, L. (2012). Life behind the screen: Taking the academic online. In L. Dirckinck-Holmfeld, V. Hodgson, & D. McConnell (Eds.), *Exploring the theory, pedagogy and practice of networked learning* (pp. 3–24). New York: Springer.

McConnell, D., Zhao, J. (2006, December). Chinese higher education teachers' conceptions of e-Learning: Preliminary outcomes. In *Proceedings of the 23rd Annual Ascilite Conference: Who's Learning? Whose technology?* (pp. 513–523). The University of Sydney.

Nawaz, A., & Kundi, G. M. (2010). Predictor of e-learning development and use practices in higher education institutions (HEIs) of NWFP, Pakistan. *Journal of Science and Technology Education Research, 1*(3), 44–54.

Rienties, B., Brouwer, N., & Lygo-Baker, S. (2013). The effects of online professional development on higher education teachers' beliefs and intentions towards learning facilitation and technology. *Teaching and Teacher Education, 29*, 122–131.

Rienties, B., Kaper, W., Struyven, K., Tempelaar, D. T., Van Gastel, L., Vrancken, S., et al. (2012). A review of the role of Information Communication Technology and course design in transitional education practices. *Interactive Learning Environments, 20*(6), 563–581.

Roberts, G. (2003). Teaching using the web: Conceptions and approaches from a phenomenographic perspective. *Instructional Science, 31*(1–2), 127–150.

Ross, J. (2012). Just what is being reflected in online reflection? New literacies for new media learning practices. In L. Dirckinck-Holmfeld, V. Hodgson, & D. McConnell (Eds.), *Exploring the theory, pedagogy and practice of networked learning* (pp. 191–207). New York: Springer.

Sandberg, J. (2005). How do we justify knowledge produced within interpretive approaches? *Organizational Research Methods, 8*(1), 41–68.

Schofer, E., & Meyer, J. W. (2005). The worldwide expansion of higher education in the twentieth century. *American sociological review, 70*, 898–920.

Selwyn, N. (2012). Making sense of young people, education and digital technology: The role of sociological theory. *Oxford Review of Education, 38*(1), 81–96.

Shafique, F., & Mahmood, K. (2008). Indicators of the emerging information society in Pakistan. *Information Development-London, 24*(1), 66.

Shaikh, Z. A. (2009). Usage, acceptance, adoption, and diffusion of information & communication technologies in higher education: A measurement of critical factors. *Journal of Information Technology Impact, 9*(2), 63–80.

Sjöström, B., & Dahlgren, L. O. (2002). Applying phenomenography in nursing research. *Journal of Advanced Nursing, 40*(3), 339–345.

Trigwell, K. (2000). A phenomenographic interview on phenomenography. In J. A. Bowden & E. Walsh (Eds.), *Phenomenography* (Qualitative research methods series, pp. 43–57). Melbourne, VIC: RMIT University Press.

Part II
Networked Learning in Practice:
The Expected and Unexpected

Chapter 6
'Here Be Dragons': Approaching Difficult Group Issues in Networked Learning*

Linda Perriton and Michael Reynolds

Introduction

Participative designs for learning are commonly advocated in networked learning. Whether these designs are presented as 'collaborative' approaches to learning or as more specific models such as the 'learning community' they involve students and teachers in the complex interpersonal, social, cultural and/or political dimensions of collective endeavour. However, despite there being a rich tradition of theorisation of group interaction in non-virtual education there has been less theoretical work done in relation to social, cultural and political dimension of the facilitation undertaken in virtual learning environments (VLEs). What research has been carried out into the social and political aspects of groupwork within VLEs has not been aligned with a particular interpretive frame nor has there been a concern with translating the findings of such studies into practical guidelines for working with (virtual) group dynamics. The parallel research into groupwork in traditionally delivered education has included, amongst its outputs, guides to application. It is as if the tradition of participative pedagogy has found a home within the domain of networked learning, but ideas that could be useful in understanding the dynamics generated within such pedagogies have been left behind.

The aim of this chapter therefore is to address this gap in the VLE groupwork literature and provide a set of questions that are helpful to educators involved with

---

*The phrase 'Here be dragons' is associated with warnings written, or mythical creatures presented in pictorial form, on mediaeval maps where the cartographer wanted to denote unexplored or dangerous territories. Group dynamics are often experienced as unexplored or dangerous territory.

L. Perriton (✉)
The York Management School, University of York, Freboys Lane,York YO10 5GD, UK
e-mail: linda.perriton@york.ac.uk

M. Reynolds
Lancaster University Management School, Lancaster University, Lancaster LA1 4YX, UK
e-mail: m.reynolds@lancaster.ac.uk

V. Hodgson et al. (eds.), *The Design, Experience and Practice of Networked Learning*, 109
Research in Networked Learning, DOI 10.1007/978-3-319-01940-6_6,
© Springer International Publishing Switzerland 2014

programmes with groupwork at their core, but who find that guidance on the social processes that are often unleashed in such approaches is limited. We hope our work complements other, traditional sources that have offered guidelines on facilitating or moderating practices (e.g. Goodyear, Salmon, Spector, Steeples, & Tickner, 2001; McConnell, 2000; Salmon, 2000) within networked learning. Given the wealth of literature that deals with groupwork in face-to-face settings, we have not restricted our sources to online contexts only. Our position is that the differences between the two contexts are mainly structural, rather than fundamentally altering the social dynamics of the two forms of educational groups. And whilst we also recognise that not all programmes that make use of a VLE include dealing with social dynamics as part of their learning outcomes, we believe that it is important that tutors are as practically prepared for the presence of, and occasionally the disruption caused by, social dynamics as possible. Our own experience of networked learning environments, which has been reinforced by the conversations we have had with contributors to this chapter, is that even the most experienced tutors can be surprised by their own emotional and psychological reaction to group dynamics AND what is sometimes experienced as the chore of having to facilitate them. The theoretical models that tutors hold in order to make sense of dynamics and to intervene in a thoughtful way in them is an important, but often unacknowledged, point of difference between staff working on the same programme. Our working definition of networked learning would reflect that of McConnell, Hodgson, and Dirckinck-Holmfeld (2012) in ideally having as its characteristic features: learning and teaching largely via the Internet/Web: an emphasis on participative pedagogy; learning through dialogue; collaborative work in groups; and the application of a critical perspective. It is perhaps the last two of these that forms the particular focus of this chapter.

In writing the chapter we wanted to take advantage of a more flexible format than offered by publishing in journals and draw in other voices to challenge our own interpretive framework and the idea that there is a facilitative consensus about how to approach group dynamics—especially when working with participative pedagogies favoured by many working within the networked learning domain. We have included three virtual discussions in this chapter. The first is a fictionalised online group discussion by students that is based on groupwork discussions we have been involved with in the past. The two tutor discussions which follow on from this have been constructed from the individual email correspondence with experienced tutors of online, and face-to-face groups and presented as if the contributors were present and involved in a synchronous discussion.[1] Our illustrative discussions are included

---

[1] The authors are grateful for the generosity of the colleagues who agreed to take part in this project as 'virtual tutors' and responded with such aplomb. Our special thanks go to Sian Baynes, Tara Fenwick, Vivien Hodgson, David McConnell and Russ Vince, for their thoughtful comments and insights. In order to make the virtual tutor discussion sound as if it is a conversation in real time, we have conflated some individual responses and given them to a single tutor to voice. As a result we took the decision not to attribute the comments of our tutors to named individuals; any inadvertent misrepresentations of the responses given to us are the responsibility of the authors and, we hope, are forgiven.

in order to focus on the difficulties that could arise if tutors working together on a programme did not have access to a structured way of surfacing, and processing, their own interpretive differences.

The chapter is organised in the following way. We first review a range of studies that deal with experiences of working in online learning groups, focusing mainly on a selection of theoretical papers that outline alternative approaches to understanding the social dynamics of networked learning. We then briefly outline our position on the differences and similarities between virtual and non-virtual groups before presenting the fictionalised student discussion and the unstructured form of the tutor discussion about 'what should be done'. Following the first tutor group discussion, we develop a set of possible foundational questions that an individual tutor, or tutor group could use to interrogate their understanding of the group and their own habitual frames of reference.

What's Out There? Alternative Approaches to Understanding Networked Learning

A review of the literature that addresses group processes involved in learning online reveals substantial differences of intention and perspective. Using a rough classification system, we think that it is meaningful to talk of three main clusters of literature. One cluster is primarily theoretical, the other is also research-based but interested in the implications for practice that includes the practice of facilitation and the third is concerned with developing and applying a coherent pedagogy overall.

Authors that we have identified as belonging to the theoretical literature concern themselves with developing an understanding of the complex dynamics of living and learning in VLE-supported groups or networks, and of developing theoretical frameworks which might inform the *design* of technology-enhanced learning programmes and our understanding of what happens personally, socially and politically within them. De Laat and Lally's (2003) chapter is a good example of this type of approach. Their interest was in understanding the learning and tutoring process as experienced by professionals undertaking an online postgraduate programme, drawing on social-constructivist and socio-cultural theory in order to take account of the complexities of individual and group processes in networked learning. De Laat and Lally found that participants' learning was developed through both their interactions with tutors and with each other. Of particular relevance to our focus in this chapter was their observation that tutors reflected about their role and interventions into the discussion more than could be seen in the transcripts of their work with students online.

Drawing on a very different perspective Bayne (2004) applies to the VLE Deleuze and Guattari's (1988) idea of cultural 'spaces' as either smooth (open, as in collaborative pedagogy) or 'striated' (as with the e-learning system, more stable and constrained) and the way these interact. Bayne draws on ideas developed in a different domain and then applies them to illuminate the tensions and complexities of the intersection of pedagogies and the infrastructures intended to support them. The implications for practice have not yet been fully explored to date, but as Bayne observes, the ideas 'offer the promise of a textual, subjective and epistemological openness which presents new possibilities for teaching and learning' (p. 315).

Then there is a group of studies that is research-based and concerns itself with the question 'so what does this mean for my programme?' These authors generate proposals for practice from their research and there is a similarly wide range of underlying theoretical frameworks in use. Some, as does Conrad (2002), develop a set of guidelines for students based on what seems to work for them. Staggers, Garcia, and Nagelhout (2008) introduce students to Tuckman's (1965) theory of phases in group development as a way of helping them 'overcome' (p. 479) conflict in the interest of constructive and productive collaborative teamwork. Then there is a group of researchers who are working from a psychodynamic framework, one which allows for unconscious group process as well as the dynamics which group members are aware of even if they lack a set of interpretative ideas with which to make sense of them. Examples from this group are Allan and Vince whose focus is the emotional dynamics of virtual groups and the way these can consciously and unconsciously affect learning, emphasising tensions such as 'the real and imagined relationship between the learner and the teacher/facilitator' (Allan & Vince 2006, p. 5). Smith (2005), also drawing on a psychodynamic perspective (Bion, 1961), highlights unconscious tensions between a person's desire to belong and their fear that they will subjugate their identity within the group. Echoing our own experiences of working with groups off-line or online, especially in the context of collaborative pedagogies, Smith alerts us to the dynamics of group development and the stresses associated with consensus which can undermine a student's experience of working with online groups. Her chapter underlines the point that to be aware of these processes and to understand them is a first step to being able to support participants in understanding and working with them too.

Our third and perhaps most familiar group of authors are those who are primarily concerned with understanding and developing approaches to online education and learning. Their focus is on course structures, virtual infrastructures, teaching and learning methods, approaches to assessment, roles and relationships. The aim is to provide practical help to tutors working within VLEs. The dominant discourse is—as we outlined in our introduction—based on the concept of 'collaborative' learning, with the now standard reference to the idea of the 'learning community' and more recently, with growing interest in the concept of the 'community of practice'. Although, as with many aspects of the discourse, the reasoning behind the application of this latter construct to Higher Education activities is not always made clear nor is it easy to reconstruct.

As the 'collaborative' narrative is well established within the network learning movement and familiar to its members we will not expand on this perspective. The values, beliefs and procedures are clearly described elsewhere (see for example Dirckinck Holmfeld, Hodgson, & McConnell, 2012; Goodyear, Banks, Hodgson, &

McConnell, 2004) and as we noted earlier in the chapter, these accounts are complemented by others that offer guidelines on facilitating or moderating practices within such pedagogies (e.g. Goodyear et al., 2001; McConnell, 2000; Salmon, 2000). Furthermore, within the NL community there are contributions to a constructive debate of these principles, some of which challenge the dominant narrative (see for example Hodgson & Reynolds, 2005; or Jones, 2004).

In this section we have identified three main areas of the research confronting the online tutor in search of insight into group processes. The pedagogical cluster, whilst significant in the way that it creates a dominant discourse and interpretative frame that justifies the use of networked learning is arguably over-reliant on the idea of positive collaboration. We believe the most helpful literature—paradoxically—may prove to be in the papers that do not initially seek to make a contribution to practice, i.e. De Laat and Lally (2003), Bayne (2004). The papers in this research cluster, although primarily concerned with theory-building, are useful in suggesting new mental models for design and—potentially—facilitation.

In the sections that follow however, we find value in frameworks for making sense of group dynamics that were originally generated in the context of face-to-face groups. So before we discuss possible ways of making sense of the online dynamics in our fictional illustration, it seems appropriate to ask whether or not we should take account of the differences between working online or face-to-face in our analysis and suggested way of working. That there are differences is clear, as in the way time is experienced in virtual learning communities (Allan, 2007), in the fragmented nature of working through digital networks (Jones, Ferreday, & Hodgson, 2008) and the opportunity that working online affords for tutors to craft their feedback to students before sending it out (Crossouard, Pryor, & Torrance, 2004). However, as McKenna and Green (2002) point out, although some differences will be important, the various forms that 'virtual' groups take on are not dissimilar to groups in non-virtual contexts. Our observation would be that in making sense of the personal, social and political processes involved in a VLE, aspects of group work such as group norms, the emergence of leaders and the balance of the social and task activities, might take shape differently in a VLE but are equally relevant aspects to look out for and understand as in a face-to-face environment.

We are not discounting therefore the differences between working online and working face-to-face but see these differences—as mentioned in the Introduction—as primarily structural and procedural, affecting the student's experience of a course without fundamentally changing the social dynamics involved. If we move away from an exclusively virtual framework through which to examine social dynamics, we can exploit a richer seam of material for developing frameworks for making sense of group dynamics. These include the Interaction Process Analysis developed by Bales (1950), Bion's (1961) psychodynamic theory as drawn on by some of the contributors to our tutor conversation, and a framework developed from Potter's idea of the 'dilemmas' likely to be experienced by members of learning groups (Potter, 1979). We will return to this framework in later sections of the chapter.

Group Processes. A Fictionalised Illustration

The fictionalised context of our example online conversation is a pedagogical model in use in UK higher education. Our imagined programme is a 2-year, part-time Masters level course designed for Human Resource Development practitioners. The programme has a mixed mode of delivery and is marketed as 'participative' and run on the lines of a 'learning community' in which responsibility for choosing content and method is shared between students and tutors. At the outset of each module there is a discussion between tutors and students as to the topics of interest to be included and suggestions for who might take a lead with each of them. As the student group comprises people with significant professional experience (managers, teachers, HR specialists, organisational consultants), the aim is that both tutors and students will take responsibility for online discussions.

The programme, an example of blended learning, is divided into six discrete modules that look at a different theme with each module having a summative assessment in the form of an academic report or essay on an aspect of the theme that the student identifies that they wish to work on. In residential workshops of 2–3 days duration students and tutors gather in a single location for a concentrated period of instruction, discussion and whole-group work. These workshops are scheduled every 4 months, forming the end points to learning modules. Groups are formed and work together online in asynchronous discussion fora for the duration of the learning module and then disband, forming again (normally with different membership) at the next residential workshop that introduces the next module theme. Typically groups contain six members + tutor.

This fictional conversation takes place shortly after the residential, when one of the groups is beginning to work together online.

Eleni	I'm sorry that I had to rush away from the residential. I don't feel that we had time as a group to talk about what we would want to get out of working together, and whether there is anything from our experience of working in previous groups that we would (or wouldn't) like to bring to this group.
	Shall I kick off the discussion? From my own perspective, I'd welcome more guidance on the assessment. I understand that we have to choose our own topic, which is ok but then there isn't much guidance as to how to go about it. Louis is great in terms of interacting online, but I think other tutors give out many more leads.
Johanna	Or different leads—which can be confusing.
Thomas	I'm with Eleni on this. We asked for some pointers at the end of the residential as to what this module's theme could cover but got very vague answers. It isn't easy to know what to do.
Robert	It isn't meant to be easy. I think a lot of it they want us to work out for ourselves. What I'd like to be different this time round is to learn from ALL of the members of the group. I feel that, for example, Denise has a

great deal to offer me in terms of her experience in the public sector but my experience from other groups is that she's hardly online. We all signed up to this course knowing what it meant and if we don't all make ourselves available all our learning suffers.

Johanna   I'm sure Denise has her reasons. And can speak for herself. Did any of us *really* know what it was we were signing up for? ☺

Eleni   No! Lol.

Robert   They didn't hide the philosophy of the programme. It was what attracted me to this course in the first place. There are plenty of 'ordinary' Masters courses out there. You have to work quite hard to find courses like this so it's unlikely anyone joins without knowing the score.

By the way, we have to decide whether we want our online conversations to be 'open' to the rest of the cohort. I told Hans I didn't think that anyone would object. It's been the norm in the other groups I've been in.

Eleni   I'm fine with that.

Johanna   I'm not sure I am. After what happened with my last group I think I'd prefer a closed group.

Thomas   I've obviously missed something. What happened?

Eleni   A couple of guys from another group 'contributed' their view that psychometrics were a tool of racism to Ruth's discussion about her project on the use of psychometrics in learning. Ruth felt that the comments were more like heckling from the audience rather than the sort of behaviour that should be tolerated in this programme, in addition to it being personally offensive given her background.

Johanna   She was deep in discussion with the tutor group when I left the residential. She told me she was thinking of leaving.

Sattick   To be honest that doesn't sound much like how a learning community should be behaving.

Robert   I agree. You need to be open to challenge if the whole idea of a learning community is going to work. You can't tiptoe around everyone's sensitivities if you are going to create learning opportunities.

Sattick   That's not really what I meant. . . Does anyone else feel the same way as Johanna about not allowing others access to our discussion space?

Thomas   Learning community or learning dictatorship, what does it matter? I'm still naffed off about the suggestion from Louis that we should read these four chapters and prepare summaries for an online discussion to kick off the learning in this stage. Have you seen them? The titles seem relevant to the module but they're mostly unintelligible. I think we should say we aren't going to do it.

Robert   Steady on.

Eleni   I think it would help if Louis summarised the arguments in the chapters for us—maybe half a side of A4 and then asked us to discuss those.

It's too much work otherwise and I am coming up to a really busy period
at work. It's budget preparation time . . .

Johanna   Louis. . ..?

Whatever individual interpretive frameworks might be in play when this
conversation is being viewed by a tutor there is little doubt that a basic, and
repetitive, set of questions will help the tutor whether they are working from a
position of 'guide on the side' or as a co-participant. These questions are variations
on the themes of: What is happening? What might it mean? Do I (or they) need to do
anything about it at this point? However, the answers to those questions can vary
tremendously depending on the experience level of the tutor group and the ideas
they hold in relation to group dynamics. The two most common reactions we
notice—regardless on the experience level of the tutor group—is a particular
concern with task compliance and also with actual or perceived under-participation
of group members, especially when the design of the programme stresses collaborative learning. When a group is positioned as, or felt to be deviant in terms of task
participation or acceptance we are alerted to the common working 'mis-definition'
of collaborative groupwork, i.e. where collaborative behaviour is equated with
enthusiastic agreeableness to design decisions made by tutors. The other issue
that is most likely to be quickly classified as problematic by both tutors and students
is the non-participation or under-participation (more subjectively defined) of some
of the members of the groups. We see this in tutor groups where there is a persistent
sense of dissatisfaction with groups where a minority of members generate the
majority of the posts. It is commonplace to expect a 'good' tutor to monitor
participation and to work hard to draw the partially engaged participant fully into
the community.

Our response to these (very common) instances where task completion and
non-participation are perceived to be the priority issues to 'fix' in a group is a
frustrated one. Although it is better to have a framework than no framework at all
we believe that many individual tutors, and even more tutor teams, miss the
opportunity to challenge their own assumptions about legitimate forms of participation and presence online by asking more challenging questions of the group
behaviour they see. Even the experienced group of tutors who responded to our
email invitation to comment on the fictionalised conversation were attuned to
'notice', and be troubled by, the issues of task non-completion and the absent
voices from the conversation—as is obvious in their discussion below.

The tutors involved in the programme (Louis and Kara and Chris) have returned
to campus a day after the residential session. In the staff room they are discussing
their experience of the residential, and their response to the online conversations
that have started since the residential ended, with colleagues not involved in the
module in the staff room.

Kara   Have you heard back from Ruth yet?
Louis   Yes, she emailed early this morning and agreed to our suggestion of a
           mediated conversation with the guys. She said that she'd already invested

a lot of energy and money into the programme and didn't want to walk away with nothing because of a couple of idiots who didn't think before they put fingers to keyboard.

Kara   Ah! Sounds like we should give it a few days for things to calm down before getting them all together in the same room.

Louis   That's my plan. And, in the meantime, whilst I was off talking to Ruth my learning set appears to be off and running—although in what direction I have no idea. Have a look at the online activity over the last 24 hours . . . *(Hands a printout of the conversation to Kara. Harry reads it over her shoulder)*

Harry   I wouldn't get too distracted by the talk about assessment. They should accept there will be some variations in the guidance we give. They're worried about assessment. They always are. It's just that it is being expressed as criticism of your role.

Kara   I see Robert has chosen to play the dominant male role. Again. I'm glad you've got him this time Louis. I have to admit to finding his *certainty* about everything very challenging, especially his views on learning. I'm not surprised Denise is choosing to stay quiet at this point. The more present Robert is in the group, the more absent Denise is likely to be.

Louis   I see what you mean. I worry about the pressure he is putting on the others. I wonder if we aren't a bit naive when we tell them we are trying to work as a community. There's quite a coercive edge to how they respond to each other at present.

Harry   I agree, but that's not incompatible with the possibility that the dynamics of the groups reflect varying degrees of anxiety.

Kara   Communities are anxious places. If we can help them see what's going on, there's a lot they can learn from all this. Especially from the way the gender politics of the community is developing. When women or ethnic minority students try to clarify or renegotiate how things work they tend to be branded as resistant, or anti-learning.

Louis   I agree with Harry's point about anxiety—any sort of assessment seems to bring out the anxious adolescent in adult learners—but I think we create anxiety in the context of the learning too by giving contradictory messages about community. I don't think we are ever very clear about what aspects they have some control over and what they don't. Are we clear about rights and responsibilities or about what's open to negotiation and what isn't?

Chris   These are really important issues and they affect all the groups, it's probably just Louis's group that are articulating them at this time.

Louis   I just feel so frustrated. Why do we have to keep on reminding students that the point is not to 'know' something? Rather the point is to put it to work in opening new questions and reopen the controversies as matters of concern.

Chris   I suggest we start a cohort-wide discussion to surface some of these worries and we can restate what's important to us—and not be shy of showing how there are some differences in how we interpret our role, but being clear about the values we do share in how we design and run the programme.

Harry   That sounds a good next step. It won't solve everything. There's a lot at stake for the participants in taking this on and assessment heightens this in ways they aren't necessarily aware of.

Commentary

In the staff room discussion we have intentionally brought together different ideas or perspectives which tutors might use to make sense of the group's online discussion. The first of these different perspectives we would characterise as **participative** (i.e. Chris), emphasising the logic of the way the course structure, roles and relationships are put together, the social and educational values they are based on, and the belief that tutors' responses to events should aim for transparency and consistency with those values. As we commented at the beginning of the chapter, this perspective has a long tradition in adult education and, more recently, networked learning. Variously characterised as 'collaborative', 'cooperative' or 'participative' such pedagogies owe much to the democratic values expressed in the work of Dewey, Friere, Knowles and others. Other tutors see it from a **discourse** perspective (i.e. Louis and Kara), being conscious of how structures and people's responses to them express different values from the social context(s) including notions of 'community', participation, gender, responses to difference—the course as society writ small. Yet others see group behaviour from a **psychodynamic** perspective (i.e. Harry), taking into account the ways in which uncertainty and consequential anxiety can result in characteristic behaviours in groups (including tutor groups), which people are not at the time fully conscious of.

What we haven't shown—but is present in the reactions of our contributing tutors to the excerpt we sent them, was the emotional labour expended in thinking about the group dynamics. Contributors mentioned in their covering emails, or as part of their commentary on how they would make sense of the issues intellectually, how wearily familiar they were with the student voices and their complaints and how surprised they were to notice their own impatience.

The honesty of our contributors regarding their emotional responses (the impatience, occasional condescension and dismissal) also alerted us to the frequency with which tutor intervention was recommended, justified on pedagogical grounds. Some of our contributors confessed to an immediate defensive response before recognising the need to step back and then consciously engage with the material in a more inquisitive, and less value laden, mode of engagement. We believe that it is likely that tutor groups need help not only in sliding back into habitual intellectual, frameworks, which may or may not be informative but also to keep the (occasionally dismissive) 'pedagogical self'[2] in check before it seeks recourse in prescriptions and definitions.

In the next section we use the notion of 'dilemma' as a possible bridge between these perspectives and in a way that translates into questions that tutors and students can ask so as to make sense of their emotional and intellectual experience of the complexities of life in learning groups.

Discussion: Theory into Practice

The thesis of our chapter is (following Potter, 1979) that it is useful for tutors to frame the behaviour of the groups in terms of common dilemmas rather than common interpretations. Our choice of Potter's framework of familiar dilemmas is based on its accessibility and compatibility with alternative interpretative frameworks (e.g. Discourse Analysis, psychodynamic approaches, Actor Network Theory). The discussions that arise as a result of a consideration of common dilemmas can be kept within the tutor group or—where the educational design of the programme is relevant—with the student group. We believe that most group behaviours can be approached, and discussed in fruitful ways, by using the following framework. Adapting Potter's framework, there would seem to be dilemmas that groups are very likely to have to deal with, even though how they deal with them and with what outcome will differ—depending on the individual members of the group and its organisational or educational context.

The three common dilemmas are:

1. Establishing and maintaining oneself in the group
2. Establishing and maintaining the primary task
3. Establishing and maintaining management of the group

A quick, and accessible, way for tutors to explore the group's discourse is to work through a set of questions relevant to each type of common dilemma, which in turn can suggest a useful working perspective to apply to the situation.

The first dilemma—although it is not inevitably the first behaviour that manifests itself in the group—is that of establishing a place within it and finding the best personal balance in terms of openness/closure, intimacy/distance, security/insecurity and role/person. It is important to note that this dilemma is not a stage, as is understood by Tuckman, but a process that may be revisited continually by some members in reaction to changes in the behaviour of other participants or to developments in the task. Nonetheless these individual struggles around position and membership are often the first behaviours noticed by tutors and other group

---

[2] Fenwick (2013) noticed, with some surprise, the appearance of 'a rather alarming pedagogical self that strode forth to define and prescribe' when she first read the fictionalised student discussion. The 'pedagogical self' struck a chord with us and we have retained the label.

members, even if they are not recognised as issues of openness and closure, etc. These issues are often experienced as one of control, and affect the manner in which relationships develop within the group. The individual negotiations around position are however, not just the visible signs of psychodynamics. As we have made clear above we believe that to date our ways of understanding these group membership issues have over-emphasised the personal and interpersonal at the expense of the social and political. Instead we need to also consider that the way that relationships develop are products of context and the history of the group, including the discourses that create its legitimacy internally and externally and the structures that surround the group. By asking questions of our own, and of our colleagues understanding of group membership, we do not presume that the interpersonal should take precedence over the social and political, or vice versa.

Questions the tutor group *could*[3] consider in relation to individual members of the learning group, or of the group as a whole:

- What is the online discussion (tone, content, frequency, type of interaction) telling us about what it is like to be a member of this group?
- What have participants, individually or collectively, had to give up in order to become a member?
- Is the position they have assumed within the, or as a, group being supported (internally and externally)? Is that support conditional? If so, on what?
- Is the individual, or the group, right to privacy being respected and how has this been decided?

The second dilemma addresses an area that, as we have mentioned above, many tutors find difficult because it strikes at the heart of their professional role and competence and that is the relationship of the group to the task. Tasks are the outward expression of the power inherent in the structure surrounding the group and the power of the tutor to direct the group towards a desired performance level and outcome. Most educational groupwork takes place within programmes that are undertaken for certificated achievement, e.g. university degrees or professional qualifications. Whilst traditional academic assessments are often the focus of group activity, deeper learning 'tasks' within a group are often presented implicitly rather than explicitly as part of the expectations of the group with regards to assessment or other activities. These implicit learning tasks often arise from the design of the programme, or pedagogical assumptions underpinning the programme, and are therefore often ideologically connected to it. The implicit (more often than explicit) expectations expressed by tutors regarding what participants 'should' be doing at particular points in the module and the criteria for judging this learning to have been successful are often at the root of the feelings of

---

[3] There might well be other questions that would be as useful to ask. The questions we have provided are those that seemed common sense ones to us in looking at the dilemma. The utility of this approach is in keeping the *questions* tied to the dilemma, rather than generating them from a particular interpretive framework. The answers to those questions, as offered by different members of the tutor team (or students) will, of course, be informed by a particular theory in use.

tutor dissatisfaction with group members. So it is often the tutors, as opposed to the group members, that benefit from being challenged about task behaviours.

The questions we believe are useful in challenging what is being experienced in terms of member-group relations to (all forms of) task are:

- What do the group members understand to be the primary learning task for this group? What is its purpose?
- What do the tutor group identify as the primary learning task for the student group? What is its purpose? Is this the same task as identified by the students?
- Where did the task originate?
- What choice did members have in adopting the task?

The third dilemma is one that covers the more sensitive areas of group behaviour as it examines the way that the group reacts to the management, leadership and politics of the group. One of the implicit expectations of groups in educational contexts is that they should establish 'consensus', 'participation' and model 'collaborative' behaviour. All of these things are expectations that, however unintentionally, may result in some members becoming marginalised or silenced and then, inadvertently, caught by the common tutor impulse to draw quieter members into the centre of the group whilst ignoring the issues that may have resulted in the silence. We think it is important to recognise that it is the *political* processes of the group activity, often shared or established by the tutor group or programme design, that underpin expectations of involvement. The term politics in this sense relates to how issues of authority and control are expressed, or direct, the work and experience of the group.

The questions for tutors and/or students below are designed to uncover differences in theoretical perspective, working practices or demography that might have become salient and require challenge when the normal processes of positioning of the self in relation to the group is distorted by its political processes.

- How are decisions and choices being made in this group? Who is involved in this process?
- What appears to be the basis of power or influence in the group?
- How are differences of preference, opinion or background worked with?
- How do these processes reflect values and beliefs in relevant social or cultural contexts?

In the illustrative discussion that follows we imagine the tutors addressing the same situation as before. But this time round we intend to show how a discussion based on the type of questions we have just presented might, as a result, be a way of making sense of the tutorial group's online exchange which is more complementary rather than, as seemed to be the case in the previous illustration, a disparate set of interpretations. Here, in the interest of simplicity the tutors' focus is around the kind of questions we presented as the first dilemma: establishing and maintaining oneself in the group. Their responses are still informed by the theoretical perspectives they favour (discourse, psychodynamics and so forth) but approaching the analysis of the exchanges as a dilemma allows a common focus, and for the tutor group to move away from the knee-jerk responses to task avoidance and/or under-participation.

Louis	My learning set appears to be off and running—although in what direction I have no idea. Kara, would you mind having a look at this printout of the activity in the last 24 hours and letting me know what you think about how the group is establishing itself. Harry, do you have a moment as well? Chris?
Kara	Sure.
Chris and Harry	Of course.
	(All read through the online discussion)
Louis	What are our first impressions of the way this group operates?
Kara	It seems to be setting some high expectations in terms of being online and contributing. The residential finished yesterday afternoon and yet there is the clear implication that if you haven't yet made your first post you are already late for school, and about to be in trouble.
Chris	I notice that it seems to be a series of statements. No one is speaking in such a way as to make a connection with another member, for example there are no mentions of each other's names. In fact I think they only mention a person's name if they are not visible or present—Ruth, who isn't a member, or Denise who is missing. No one is developing the points that someone else is making. My impression is that people are expressing their own needs and wants without listening to those of other members.
Harry	I think there is a definite sense of being inside the group or being vulnerable to attack—the tutor has been criticised, an absent member named and all the focus is outside of the group where all the bad things are.
Louis	What do we know of any sacrifices that have been made to be a member of this group?
Chris	Robert had to wait a year for his company to release the funds to get on this course, so he has always felt he could have been further through the degree than he currently is. I only know bits and pieces apart from that—Sattick would have preferred to have worked with Harry because he wanted to do his project on psychodynamics, Eleni was at the residential and away from home for her wedding anniversary.
Kara	Johanna thinks that, as Ruth's friend, she should have been more assertive about being in her group again this time round to give support. She thinks it would have made Ruth feel more secure about continuing on the programme.
Harry	I can't add anything to that.

Louis	Does the way the membership is being negotiated feel like it has support, even unconsciously, from us as a tutor group or the other learning sets?
Kara	I think Harry's point about the external focus of the group is right. It is as if the idea of 'outside the group' is being used to justify the positions being taken inside of it—Ruth's experience, the thoughtlessness of the guys in commenting on the posts of another group last time round, the missing member, the mean tutor, the unfair assessment.
Louis	So something about the boundaries of this group being defined by the sense of what is 'out there'?
Kara	Maybe.
Louis	And how is the privacy issue being handled?
Chris	Not all that well! Denise has already been positioned as needing to do better, when she might have very good reasons for not being as present in the group as others want her to be and, at the moment, there is no real space for her to come into the discussion now without having to respond to the implication she is not A Good Member that has been left hanging.
Kara	Louis's absence has also been challenged. Again, there is obviously some sort of expectation of an apology or an acknowledgement of the wrong.
Harry	The assumption seems to be from some members that good learning requires everyone to give all of themselves to the process, without trying to articulate what the process is.
Louis	So what to do? Something? Nothing?
Chris	Hmm, my vote would be for *something*. I have this mental image of the group creating a very small and cramped space for itself to operate in because it is collectively building a straw man out of all these negative thoughts about the size of the problems 'out there' and their potential for threat.
Kara	I think the speed at which they are trying to make decisions is making the discussion feel aggressive and more negative than it probably is intended to be. How about finding a way to slow everything down?
Harry	You think some of them are reaching too high, too far, too soon? Is it an anxiety thing?
Kara	Yep, something like that. It could be worth thinking about Louis. Declare a moratorium on decision making, the reading, the assessment, or the access to the group, or whatever else some of them are in such a rush to pin down.

Final Thoughts

Our aim in this chapter has been to propose an approach to making sense of the complex dynamics which can be generated by participative pedagogies which involve group work, learning 'communities' and the like as an essential/inevitable element of working and learning collaboratively. Why? Because otherwise it seems there is a disparity between the general acceptance that collaborative pedagogies *should* be at the heart of networked learning, and the attention, or rather the lack of attention, given to the ways of making sense of the dynamics that are likely to be generated by them. Our premise is that if we make use of collaborative pedagogies we have a responsibility for contributing some way of making sense of these dynamics and for making this available to the students involved where appropriate and practical to do so—not forgetting that on professional programmes students may be at least as well versed as the tutors.

As mentioned above, we chose Potter's framework of familiar dilemmas because of its accessibility and compatibility with alternative interpretative frameworks (e.g. Discourse Analysis, psychodynamic approaches, Actor Network Theory). But their distinctive function is to ground the analysis in the experience of group members—whether students or tutors. In other words, a framework of this kind gives more opportunity for a constructive and complementary process of sense making—even though individuals might favour particular interpretative frameworks. We hope this point has been illustrated by the second version of the staff room discussion we constructed in contrast to the first. In the second run, the tutor group has more of a constructive, less defensive discussion. Potter's framework is not sacrosanct but we chose it in the knowledge that he developed his 'dilemmas' on the basis of considerable experience of working in multi-perspective tutor teams facilitating group work conferences with social work, management, community work students and professionals—collectively working with ideas from the psychological to the political.

We end on a reflexive, if cautionary note. We were unsurprised that the tutors' responses mirrored their wider academic research and identity. Our instinctive interpretive field is the one we are more intellectually familiar with and from which we draw confidence and comfort. However, our confidence in the utility of our own interpretive frameworks does not help us reflect collectively on what is going on because to a large extent we are talking past each other (much like our fictional programme participants) in the attempt to order the world along the lines we are confident in negotiating with some degree of authority. The clear danger is that in the absence of a dominant, or majority, theoretical framework being present in a group the 'pedagogical self' will appear to overrule individual interpretations with an appeal to pedagogical design as supposedly neutral arbiter. As tutors we often hear the invocation of the idea of the 'ideal learner' (task compliant, collaborative, fully signed up to the principles of the programme) in tutor discussions and the push to place responsibility back on the learners to conform to that ideal. It is important that we separate the voice of the weary, judgemental 'pedagogical self' from the thoughtful consideration of *learning*.

Learning is about openings and closings, new possibilities and unbounded exploration in play beside standards, rules and assessments; controversy and uncertainty in tension with stabilisation and disciplinary regimes (Fenwick, 2013). We hope that our proposed approach allows those important tensions and possibilities to remain as well as providing a new opening for exploration.

References

Allan, B. (2007). Time to learn? E-learners experiences of time in virtual learning communities. *Management Learning, 38*(5), 557–572.

Allan, B., & Vince, R. (2006, March 20–22). *Emotions shared/emotions hidden: Reflections on emotional dynamics in virtual learning communities.* Paper presented at the Organizational Learning, Knowledge and Capabilities Conference at the University of Warwick, Coventry, England.

Bales, R. (1950). *Interaction process analysis: A method for the study of small groups.* Chicago, IL: University of Chicago Press.

Bayne, S. (2004). Smoothness and striation in digital learning spaces. *E-Learning, 1*(2), 302–316.

Bion, W. (1961). *Experiences in groups and other papers.* New York, NY: Basic Books.

Conrad, D. L. (2002). Engagement, excitement, anxiety, and fear: Learners' experiences of starting an online course. *The American Journal of Distance Education, 16*(4), 205–226.

Crossouard, B., Pryor, J., & Torrance, H. (2004, September). *Creating an alternative assessment regime with online formative assessment: Developing a researcher identity.* Paper presented to the European Conference on Education Research, Crete, Greece.

De Laat, M., & Lally, V. (2003). Complexity, theory and praxis: Researching collaborative learning and tutoring processes in a networked learning community. *Instructional Science, 31*, 7–39.

Deleuze, G., & Guattari, F. (1988). *A thousand plateaus: Capitalism and schizophrenia.* London, England: Continuum.

Dirckinck Holmfeld, L., Hodgson, V., & McConnell, D. (Eds.). (2012). *Exploring the theory, pedagogy and practice of networked learning.* New York, NY: Springer.

Fenwick, T. (2013). *Here be dragons response* [email] (Personal communication, January 15 2013)

Goodyear, P., Banks, S., Hodgson, V., & McConnell, D. (Eds.). (2004). *Advances in research on networked learning.* Dordrecht, Netherlands: Kluwer Academic.

Goodyear, P., Salmon, G., Spector, J. M., Steeples, C., & Tickner, S. (2001). Competences for online teaching: A special report. *ETR&D, 49*(1), 65–72.

Hodgson, V., & Reynolds, M. (2005). Consensus, difference and 'multiple communities' in networked learning. *Studies in Higher Education, 30*(1), 1–24.

Jones, C. (2004). Networks and learning: Communities, practices and the metaphor of networks. *ALT-J: Research in Learning Technology, 12*(1), 81–93.

Jones, C. R., Ferreday, D., & Hodgson, V. (2008). Networked learning a relational approach: Weak and strong ties. *Journal of Computer Assisted Learning, 24*, 90–102.

McConnell, D. (2000). *Implementing computer supported cooperative learning* (2nd ed.). London, England: Kogan Page.

McConnell, D., Hodgson, V., & Dirckinck-Holmfeld, L. (2012). Networked learning: A brief history and new trends. In L. Dirckinck Holmfeld, V. Hodgson, & D. McConnell (Eds.), *Exploring the theory, pedagogy and practice of networked learning.* New York, NY: Springer.

McKenna, K. Y. A., & Green, A. S. (2002). Virtual group dynamics. *Group Dynamics: Theory, Research and Practice, 6*(1), 116–127.

Potter, S. G. (1979, September). *Three dilemmas*. Paper presented to Group Relations Training Association Conference.

Salmon, G. (2000). *E-moderating: The key to teaching and learning online*. London, England: Kogan Page.

Smith, R. O. (2005). Working with difference in online collaborative groups. *Adult Education Quarterly, 55*(3), 182–199.

Staggers, J., Garcia, S., & Nagelhout, E. (2008). Teamwork through team building: Face-to-face to online. *Business Communication Quarterly, 71*(4), 472–487.

Tuckman, B. W. (1965). Developmental sequences in small groups. *Psychological Bulletin, 54*, 229–249.

Chapter 7
Understanding Emerging Knowledge Spillovers in Small-Group Learning Settings: A Networked Learning Perspective

Bart Rienties, Nuria Hernandez Nanclares, Juliette Hommes, and Koen Veermans

Introduction

There has been a rapid growth in the use of small groups in teaching and technology-supported networked learning environments to engage students in active learning (Decuyper, Dochy, & Van den Bossche, 2010; Hurme, Palonen, & Järvelä, 2007; Lindblom-Ylänne, Pihlajamäki, & Kotkas, 2003; Michaelsen, Knight, & Fink, 2002). By implementing a group-based structure, teachers aim to convert their classroom in a learning environment where students learn from and together with other students (Hernandez Nanclares, Rienties, & Van den Bossche, 2012; Hurme et al., 2007; Katz, Lazer, Arrow, & Contractor, 2004; Lindblom-Ylänne et al., 2003). One approach to understand how learners interact with other learners in a collaborative and cooperative learning context is networked learning (Hodgson, McConnell, & Dirckinck-Holmfeld, 2012). Goodyear, Banks, Hodgson, and McConnell (2004) define networked learning as 'learning in which information

B. Rienties (✉)
Department of Higher Education, University of Surrey, Guildford, UK
e-mail: b.rienties@surrey.ac.uk

N.H. Nanclares
Faculty of Economics, University of Oviedo, Oviedo, Spain
e-mail: nhernan@uniovi.es

J. Hommes
Department of Educational Development and Research, Faculty of Health Medicine and Life Sciences, Maastricht University, Maastricht, The Netherlands
e-mail: Juliette.Hommes@maastrichtuniversity.nl

K. Veermans
Department of Teacher Education, Centre for Learning Research,
University of Turku, Turku, Finland
e-mail: koen.veermans@utu.fi

V. Hodgson et al. (eds.), *The Design, Experience and Practice of Networked Learning*,
Research in Networked Learning, DOI 10.1007/978-3-319-01940-6_7,
© Springer International Publishing Switzerland 2014

and communication technology is used to promote connections: between one learner and other learners, between learners and tutors; between a learning community and its learning resources'.

According to Hodgson et al. (2012, p. 293), 'the epistemology of networked learning is in essence that knowledge emerges or is constructed in relational dialogue or collaborative interaction—knowledge is not a property but a social construction/way of knowing from our experiences of the world'. Furthermore, Hodgson et al. (2012) highlight the pedagogy of networked learning is in part related to insights from computer-supported collaborative learning (e.g. Rienties et al., 2012; Stahl, 2004; Strijbos & De Laat, 2010) and in part related to principles of problem- and project-based learning (e.g. Dochy, Segers, Van den Bossche, & Gijbels, 2003; Lindblom-Ylänne et al., 2003; Rienties, Willis, Alcott, & Medland, 2013; Springer, Stanne, & Donovan, 1999). Therefore, Hodgson et al. (2012) argue that networked learning provides a theory, practice and pedagogy to understand how people learn from other people and from learning resources.

Cooperation and collaboration in learning processes, working in groups and in communities, discussion and dialogue between learners and openness in the educational process are key elements of networked learning (McConnell, Hodgson, & Dirckinck-Holmfeld, 2012). In particular, the openness in administrative (e.g. location, timing, costs of study) and education constraints (intended learning outcomes, methods of study, assessments) can be considered to be part of the 'radical' (pedagogical) roots of networked learning. While more traditional educational theories look either to learning processes from an individual, cognitive, constructivist or behaviourist perspective or to learning processes from a group perspective. Similar to the socioconstructivist perspective, networked learning takes a wider community perspective to understand how learners work within and outside their formal learning settings.

In a slightly more 'constrained' (from a networked learning perspective) setting of a classroom, Hernandez Nanclares et al. (2012) argue that the introduction of groups as basic learning units redefines the classroom as learning space, a space in which the different agents in the learning process—teachers, groups and students—are together. They are complementary in their goals and can be and are quite often combined. These learning activities resemble the sharing model of cross-boundary spanning (Akkerman & Bakker, 2011). The main premise of this understanding of boundary spanning activity is that knowledge is transferred, translated and transformed between (groups of) people working in different spheres of activities (Hernandez Nanclares et al., 2012; Hsiao, Tsai, & Lee, 2011). Hernandez Nanclares et al. (2012) refer to cross-boundary activities between learners and groups as knowledge spillovers, which are defined as the positive influence that groups receive in terms of knowledge from other groups in the classroom. Conceptually, the notions of knowledge spillovers between learners and groups are visually illustrated in Fig. 7.1.

Although the idea of knowledge spillovers in small-group settings makes intuitive sense and has been verified in organisational science contexts (e.g. Bohle Carbonell, Rienties, & Van den Bossche, 2011; Borgatti & Cross, 2003; Héliot &

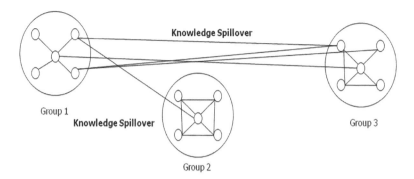

Fig. 7.1 Illustration of knowledge spillovers. *Source*: Hernandez Nanclares et al. (2012)

Riley, 2010; Krackhardt & Stern, 1988), sharing knowledge and expertise with other learners is an implicit cost to an individual learner (e.g. spending time and energy to explain another learner/group, sharing a creative solution that other groups can 'steal'), while the expected returns of receiving relevant new knowledge and expertise from others are unknown. As a result, some individuals may be less willing to share knowledge than others. In research in computer-supported collaborative learning, a similar trend has been found whereby not only the willingness but also the actual behaviour of learners to share knowledge is substantially skewed and not a given artefact when courses are designed based upon collaborative learning (e.g. De Laat, Lally, Lipponen, & Simons, 2007; Rienties et al., 2012; Rienties, Tempelaar, Van den Bossche, Gijselaers, & Segers, 2009). Finally, in a recent meta-review on group dynamics, Decuyper et al. (2010) conclude that the importance of time and development in group literature has mostly been ignored, as well as the notions of nonlinear relationships between learners.

Therefore, in this chapter, we will use two case studies in a blended learning context of economics and medical education to highlight how the notion of knowledge spillovers can be captured and understood by using (dynamic) social network analysis (SNA). SNA can be considered as a wide-ranging strategy to explore social structures to uncover the existence of social positions of (sub)groups within the network (Hommes et al., 2012; Katz et al., 2004; Rienties, Hernandez Nanclares, Jindal-Snape, & Alcott, 2013). We will address the following three questions:

1. How do knowledge spillovers between learners and groups develop (over time)?
2. How do prior friendships affect knowledge spillovers in networks?
3. How can the perspective of networked learning aid the conceptual interpretation of dynamic social networks and knowledge spillovers?

Answering these questions will create a better theoretical foundation for the design of (group-based) networked learning environments. This is expected to result in more exchange of information between learners in groups and knowledge spillovers between groups (not just between individual learners). Analysis of the relation between social and academic network relationships and knowledge spillovers can provide new insights into the boundary conditions under which these knowledge spillovers occur and the channels through which they occur (e.g. academic or social). These insights can subsequently be utilised in the design of learning environments and implementing structures that help to install these boundary conditions in the learning environments within educational institutions. Please note that it is not our intention to compare these two case studies explicitly, as the contexts of the studies (assessment methods, country, disciplines, language, team structure, tasks, etc.) are completely different. However, we are interested in understanding whether and how these two contexts might have played a part in the development of friendship and learning networks.

Knowledge Spillovers and Networked Learning

The concept of knowledge spillovers originated from regional economic development literature, whereby researchers found innovation to be fostered when firms are in close proximity to and interact with one another—and this effect is especially pronounced for smaller firms (Capello, 1999; Capello & Faggian, 2005). In effect, this proximity of and interaction amongst firms creates a learning space for these firms and fosters processes that promote learning and innovation. Naturally, one wonders if this demonstrated phenomenon in regional economic development can provide a metaphor for helping to understand the impact of proximity and interaction of learners in a classroom, community or virtual network.

Within networked learning, for example, Jones, Ferreday, and Hodgson (2008) compared an online closed and open network of principals and school teachers and found that some participants were willing to share their knowledge with their peers from different institutions. In an online master programme of education, using a mixed method study with content analyses, social network analyses (SNA) and critical event recall, De Laat et al. (2007) found that participants' roles emerged over time, whereby some participants became active contributors to discourse, while others took a more passive or reflective role in the network. In a longitudinal study of a Linux global open-source community of 2,000+ programmers, Toral, Martínez-Torres, and Barrero (2010) found that a group of 5–12 key brokers provided the bulk of the contributions in this community, but over time some of these brokers changed.

Within educational psychology, limited research has been conducted in order to assess whether groups also learn from the experiences of other groups in their class and what the underlying mechanisms are for creating such a learning space (Hernandez Nanclares et al., 2012; Hommes et al., 2012). Group literature has recently pointed out that in addition to engaging in internal learning activities, groups or networked learners must engage in external learning activities (Bresman, 2010; Decuyper et al., 2010; Rienties, Hernandez Nanclares et al., 2013). Some educational scientists have adopted concepts from social network theory (Katz et al., 2004; Wassermann & Faust, 1994), whereby several possible explanations (as provided below) are provided why some learners or groups are actively looking to extend their internal and external group network, while others are primarily focussed on their own group.

Typically, people with lots of links to different networks are referred to as brokers, emphasising individuals, or sometimes as structural holes, emphasising the network (Katz et al., 2004; Krackhardt & Stern, 1988; Rienties, Tempelaar, Pinckaers, Giesbers, & Lichel, 2010; Wassermann & Faust, 1994). Brokers often have some positive psychological trait or characteristic that enables them to connect to others in the social network to be beneficial, such as friendships or similar cultural background as members of other groups (Hendrickson, Rosen, & Aune, 2011; Rienties, Hernandez Nanclares et al., 2013).

Using a dynamic SNA method, preliminary findings in a blended economics context by Hernandez Nanclares et al. (2012) indicate that students not only developed learning links with their own group members but in an 'organic' manner also developed links across different groups over time. A follow-up study amongst 69 postgraduate hospitality students by Rienties, Heliot, and Jindal-Snape (2013) indicated that students in an international classroom did not only develop strong relations within their group but also developed substantial knowledge spillovers with students outside their group over time, primarily based upon prior friendships and similarities of cultural backgrounds.

However, using the same dynamic social network approach in a large cohort of 215 postgraduate business students, Rienties et al. (2013) found that students did not develop strong intragroup relations in a blended programme and primarily interacted with peers with whom they already developed friendships. Rienties et al. (2013) concluded that in the absence of formative and summative assessment of group products, the learning environment failed to create dependencies within and across the groups, even though focus group interviews indicated that most students in principle supported the notion of networked learning. Therefore, the main goal of this chapter is to explore whether and how learning networks within and knowledge spillovers across groups emerged and developed over time and how researchers, practitioners and conceptual thinkers can use (dynamic) SNA to produce (different) insights from the complex formal and informal interaction patterns and how the framework of networked learning can help in their interpretation.

Method

In this chapter, we will compare two designs of a blended learning environment whereby groups were working on authentic and complex group assignments. In economics case study 1, groups were dependent on the outcomes of other groups (for a detailed description of the module design, we refer to Hernandez Nanclares et al., 2012), while in medical case study 2, each group could work independently to solve a range of PBL tasks (Hommes et al., 2012). Learners interacted in both a face-to-face context and an educational technology context with Campus Virtual or Blackboard, using collaborative learning tools such as wikis or discussion forums. Small working groups constructed (shared) knowledge and tried to reach successful collaboration in their social learning space. Although in networked learning there is an explicit focus on technology (McConnell et al., 2012), in this study we were primarily interested in the formal and informal learning relations that developed over time, which are difficult to measure using log-data from technology tools (e.g. Engel, Coll, & Bustos, 2013; Martinez, Dimitriadis, Rubia, Gomez, & De la Fuente, 2003; Rienties, Hernandez Nanclares et al., 2013; Toral et al., 2010). These relations could be developed in the virtual learning environment (VLE), in the classroom, or outside the classroom setting. At the same time, the two case studies were situated (to use the language of networked learning) in a 'constrained' environment whereby formal classrooms, group structures and formal assessment of individual and/or group processes and products were put into place.

Economics Case Study 1 Small-Group Learning

In an elective third-year course of business administration in the economics faculty at University of Oviedo, the aim was to introduce students to the ideas, concepts and theories in international economic relations (Hernandez Nanclares et al., 2012). As students were enrolled from a range of specialisations, at the start of the module, most students were unfamiliar with each other. The students met twice a week during a 2-h class session in a 14-week period. 57 (26 males, 31 females) students were divided into 11 groups, which consisted of 4–7 members per group, who self-selected their members. During the 14 weeks, the 11 groups had to solve five authentic highly interrelated international economics tasks. These activities included the creation of a conceptual map of globalisation, writing a comment from an economic blog by a famous economist or organisation and preparing and participating in a final conference about globalisation. The assignments were designed in such a way that they required a broad range of concepts, abilities and skills from groups. In this way, groups and students had to establish a profound understanding of the complex relationships between prior personal and group knowledge and international economic relations concepts. One important thing to remember for case study 1 is that the instructional design offered groups several opportunities to share knowledge both within and across groups.

Medical Case Study 2: Problem-Based Learning

The study took place amongst 303 first-year students at a medical school at Maastricht University in the Netherlands. Using principles of problem-based learning (Hommes et al., 2012; Schmidt, Van Der Molen, Te Winkel, & Wijnen, 2009),

Table 7.1 Instructional design differences between case study 1 and case study 2

	Economics case study 1	Medical case study 2
Familiarity of students	Limited	Medium (most students knew some students in their group as they have studied together for 9 months, even when cohort is 300+)
Group selection	Self-selected (with remainder of students who were not selected enrolled by the teacher)	Randomised
Intergroup dependency	Medium–high (group products followed upon previous group products)	Formally none
Assessment focus	Group	Individual
Technology support	Both within and across groups (and actively encouraged by teacher)	Only within groups and across the entire cohort (but with limited active encouragement)

students worked in small tutorial groups under supervision of a tutor on authentic tasks related to 'unconsciousness'. These groups consisted of 8–11 students, which in contrast to case study 1 were randomly created, leading to 34 groups. Lectures, skill trainings and anatomy sessions complemented the tutorial groups. The measurements were implemented after 36 weeks during the final module of the first year, when students had collaborated in five (different) group compositions before. As reported in Hommes et al. (2012), 63.4 % of students were female, with a mean age of 20.0 years (SD 1.21). In contrast to case study 1, no formal group assessments were conducted, and the formal assessment was completely individual (Hommes et al., 2012). Furthermore, no formal arrangements were made in the VLE to allow groups to learn from other groups, although each group had its own private forum. In Table 7.1, the main instructional design differences between the two case studies are illustrated.

Measuring Knowledge Spillovers Using SNA Questionnaires

For ascertaining whether intragroup learning and knowledge spillovers occurred during the course, we employed a questionnaire survey method developed within the field of SNA. First, friendship relations representing passive information diffusion within or outside the group were measured using SNA techniques. The students in the Spanish and Dutch context answered the social network question stem 'I am friends with...' in Spanish and Dutch, respectively. A list with all 57 and 303 names of the students, respectively, was provided as is commonly done in SNA (e.g. Bohle Carbonell et al., 2011; Hernandez Nanclares et al., 2012; Hommes et al., 2012). In case study 1, students marked on a Likert response scale of 1 (totally disagree)–5 (totally agree) whether they were friends with each respective student or not; an N/A option was also provided. In case study 2, students first indicated with whom they were friends. Next, students indicated the intensity of the friendship on a 5-item Likert scale, ranging from 1 (not intense) to 5 (very intense).

Second, the (possible) knowledge sharing was measured in two ways. In case study 1, in line with De Laat et al. (2007), we measured the social learning network at three phases (week 4, week 7 and week 14) during the course in order to analyse the dynamics of inter- and intragroup learning. In case study 2, two communication networks (e.g. asking explicitly for help on a certain topic) were assessed at one time point: 'giving' and 'getting' medical- and study-related information. Getting information was assessed since this directly represents information acquisition, while giving information to students with information was regarded as an active process of elaboration, which has been shown to induce learning (Hommes et al., 2012). Again, students first indicated with whom they shared information. Next, students valued the information they had received or provided on a 5-item Likert scale ranging from 1 (not valuable) to 5 (very valuable).

As we focus on positive (learning) relations between students and groups, the valued social network matrices that resulted from the questionnaires were dichotomised by recoding values 4 and 5 to 1 (indicating that student learned from a respective student), while values 1–3 were recoded as 0 (indicating that a student did not learn from a respective student). For all three measurements, a 100 % response rate was established in case study 1, while in case study 2 a response rate of 85.7 % was established.

Data Analysis

First, graphical analyses of the learning networks at week 4 and week 14 of case study 1 and the three SNA networks of case study 2 after 4 weeks were conducted in order to identify the overall social network structures and identify patterns of subgroup development, as recommended by Wassermann and Faust (1994). Second, in order to determine knowledge spillovers, we calculated the position of each student within their group (intra) relative to other students (inter) in the (dichotomised) social learning network using the external–internal (E–I) index developed by Krackhardt and Stern (1988). Basically, the E–I index takes the number of ties of members of the group to students outside the group, subtracts the number of ties to members with the group and divided by the total number of ties. The resulting index ranges from -1 (all ties are only with own group members) to $+1$ (all ties are to students outside the group).

Third, multiple regression quadratic assignment procedures (MRQAP) were used to test whether pre-existing friendship and group divisions predicted social learning networks using 2,000 random permutations. Basically, MRQAP tests are permutation tests ($2,000\times$) for multiple linear regression model coefficients for data organised in square matrices of relatedness of friendship and learning, and the interpretation of the standardised betas is similar to OLS regression analyses

(Rienties, Hernandez Nanclares et al., 2013). Data were analysed on a network level using UCINET version 6.414. Although SNA data can be transformed and exported to 'classical' statistical programmes, such as STATA or SPSS as done by Hendrickson et al. (2011), analysis in UCINET is superior given that the specific internal and external learning relations in groups (i.e. our primary research interest) remain intact (Hernandez Nanclares et al., 2012; Rienties, Hernandez Nanclares et al., 2013).

Results

Development of Learning Networks Using Graphical Analysis: Economics Case Study 1

In order to illustrate the power of SNA in understanding the knowledge spillovers within and between groups for case study 1, the social networks of learning at week 4 (Fig. 7.2) and week 14 (Fig. 7.3) are presented, whereby the colours refer to the students' respective groups. Four aspects can be distinguished from these figures. First of all, the social networks illustrate from whom students learned a lot and the direction of learning. For example, as indicated by the grey arrow in Fig. 7.2, one female economics student of group 3 (black, diamond) indicated that she learned a lot from one student of group 2 (blue, box), positioned in the top of Fig. 7.2, which was indicated by the direction of the arrow (Wassermann & Faust, 1994). Second, the respective student from group 2 had four so-called reciprocal links with the other four members of group 2. In other words, all five members of group 2 indicated to have learned a lot from each other's contribution, and the arrows went to each of the five members, as illustrated by the grey circle. However, there was no reciprocal link between the student from group 2 and group 3, indicating that knowledge spillovers were primarily from group 2 to group 3. In other words, SNA graphs can be used to determine how knowledge spillovers occur within groups as well as across groups.

Third, the social network graphs show the respective positions of individual students as well as of groups. As students were allowed to self-select their members, relatively clear group structures are visible in Fig. 7.2. At the same time, some learners and groups were on the outer fringe of the network and were not well connected to other members or groups. For example, only one member of group 2 (blue, box, positioned on top of Fig. 7.2) and group 5 (pink, up triangle, positioned on left of Fig. 7.2) was connected to a student from another group. As a result, these groups were situated on the outer fringe of the network, while some students and groups were more central in the learning network. Group 3 was an interesting exception to the other groups, who mainly were situated closely with their own group members, as members of group 3 were more in contact with other students than with their own group members. Finally, when comparing Fig. 7.2 with Fig. 7.3,

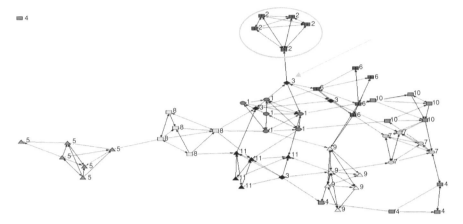

Fig. 7.2 Social learning network after 4 weeks

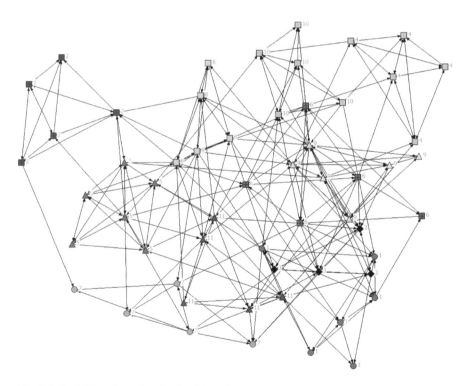

Fig. 7.3 Social learning network after 14 weeks

Fig. 7.4 Getting study-related information (based upon group membership)

the number of learning links between students and groups alike increased substantially over time. More importantly, after 14 weeks, the 'natural borders' of groups became blurred. That is, while after 4 weeks in Fig. 7.2 students were primarily interacting within their group, after 14 weeks in Fig. 7.3 the position of the members of each group was increasingly mixed and intertwined with other groups.

Development of Learning Networks Using Graphical Analysis: Medical Case Study 2

In Fig. 7.4, the graphical representation and the knowledge spillovers between the 32 tutorial groups of case study 2 are illustrated. In comparison to the figures from case study 1, the sheer amount of medical students and number of groups makes it more complex to visually identify which knowledge spillovers occurred between which groups. Even when it is difficult to visually identify the exact trial of knowledge spillovers between group X and group Y, the social network graph does illustrate some important concepts. First of all, if one would look at the nodes on the outer fringe of the network, most students were connected to students with a different colour (i.e. group). Secondly, in contrast to case study 1, no clear group structures can be visually identified, as most students were closely connected to students from different groups. Finally, some students were not at all connected to the main learning network, and quite a few others were only connected to one of the other students. In other words, the students who were connected in the 'main' network hardly received information from these students.

Quantifying Knowledge Spillovers: Case Study 1

Although the social network graphs seem to indicate that groups (over time) developed more links and knowledge spillovers to other groups in case study 1, distilling the actual number of intra- and intergroup learning relations per group is difficult to quantify based upon visual inspection, in particular for case study 2. Therefore, the E–I index was used to measure the intra- and intergroup learning network relations in Table 7.2. On average, in case study 1, economics students had 3.0 (SD = 1.2) friends within their group and 2.6 (SD = 2.2) friends outside their group, whereby standard deviations are in brackets. After 4 weeks, all groups except group 3 had more internal links to their group members than to students from other groups. On average, a group had 17.8 (SD = 7.0) ties within their group, while 6.5 (SD = 4.0) ties were made outside the group after 4 weeks. As a result, the E–I index for most groups was negative and the average E–I index for all 11 groups was −0.53, implying that most learning took place within the respective group. In other words, in the first month of the course, students learned most from their group members, rather than from students from other groups, in line with 'classical' group learning literature (Decuyper et al., 2010; Dochy et al., 2003; Lindblom-Ylänne et al., 2003; Springer et al., 1999). This was already visually illustrated by Fig. 7.2, whereby most connections amongst learners were with other group members. Furthermore, with the exception of group 3, groups were visually distinctly positioned and clearly identifiable.

After 7 weeks, the average number of external links increased to 20.0 (SD = 9.3), whereby the E–I index increased to −0.12, implying that in comparison to the beginning of the course learning occurred both within groups and outside groups but relatively more within their group. Finally, after 14 weeks, the average number of links decreased slightly to 18.4 (SD = 7.6), whereby the E–I index dropped to −0.17, implying that students continued to learn both within and outside their formal group structure, in line with network learning concepts and recent findings in external and internal group literature (Bresman, 2010; Michaelsen et al., 2002). In sum, while at the beginning of the course students were primarily interacting with their group members, over time substantial learning occurred within and across groups in line with Figs. 7.2 and 7.3. At the same time, not all groups became externally focussed over time.

Quantifying Knowledge Spillovers: Case Study 2

As was already visually represented in Fig. 7.4, in case study 2, most medical students had both internal and external relations with other groups. On average, students indicated that they gave medical- and study-related information to 2.1 (SD = 2.2) group members, while they also gave information to 7.6 (SD = 4.5) students outside their formal PBL group. In other words, even though students

Table 7.2 Intra- and intergroup knowledge spillovers after 4, 7 and 14 weeks

Group (members)	Measurement after 4 weeks			Measurement after 7 weeks			Measurement after 14 weeks		
	Internal	External	E–I	Internal	External	E–I	Internal	External	E–I
Group 1 (7)	30	7	−0.62	28	13	−0.37	24	16	−0.20
Group 2 (5)	20	1	−0.91	20	8	−0.43	20	7	−0.48
Group 3 (4)	6	15	0.43	6	20	0.54	12	20	0.25
Group 4 (6)	8	3	−0.46	20	14	−0.18	20	8	−0.43
Group 5 (6)	24	1	−0.92	30	40	0.14	30	17	−0.28
Group 6 (5)	16	7	−0.39	14	29	0.35	18	26	0.18
Group 7 (5)	20	8	−0.43	18	13	−0.16	14	12	−0.08
Group 8 (5)	18	5	−0.57	20	24	0.09	20	25	0.11
Group 9 (6)	24	7	−0.55	24	27	0.06	28	30	0.03
Group 10 (5)	16	8	−0.33	16	13	−0.10	18	16	−0.06
Group11 (5)	14	10	−0.17	18	19	0.03	20	25	0.11
Average	17.82	6.55	−0.53	19.45	20.00	−0.12	20.36	18.36	−0.17

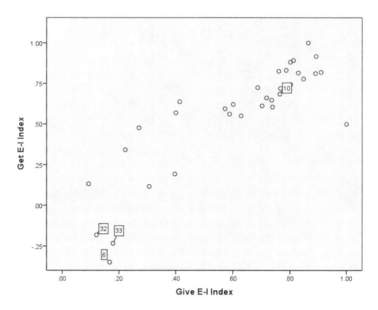

Fig. 7.5 E–I index of giving and getting information (per group)

worked on average with 8.4 students together in a group, with only 24 % did students indicate to give information, which is probably less than advocates of PBL like Schmidt et al. (2009) would expect. Similarly, students indicated that they got information from 1.4 (SD = 1.8) group members, while they received information from 4.0 (SD = 2.6) students outside their formal PBL group. As a result, the overall E–I index for the tutorial groups in the module was +0.60 (SD = 0.36) for the network giving others information, indicating that students were 60 % more likely to give information outside their tutorial group. In the getting information network, the E–I index was +0.55 (SD = 0.49), while the friendship network had the highest E–I index of +0.81 (SD = 0.20).

As is illustrated in Fig. 7.5, most groups (e.g. group 10) had a strong positive E–I index for both giving and getting information, which was strongly positively correlated (rho = 0.85, $p < 0.00$). Three groups labelled in Fig. 7.5 (6, 32, 33) were an exception to this trend, as in these groups relatively more information was obtained within a group, but at the same time again relatively more information was given outside the group. In comparison to case study 1, whereby the E–I index was negative, in case study 2 students on average shared relatively more information outside their formal group setting. Even when students in case study 2 were not formally encouraged to share information with other students (like in case study 1 where the teacher created intergroup wikis and groups were building on each others' work in the presentation sessions), 81.2 % of students primarily learned more with and from students outside their formal group configuration. As already highlighted by Hommes et al. (2012), most research of PBL focusses on knowledge construction and social interaction patterns within formal group settings (e.g. Dochy et al., 2003; Lindblom-Ylänne et al., 2003; Schmidt et al., 2009). In line with networked learning principles, these results indicate that most learning occurred outside the formal group settings, that is, with students who followed the same medical programme but who were enrolled into different PBL groups.

Multiple Regression Quadratic Assignment Procedures

Finally, in order to identify the magnitude of initial friendships and group divisions on learning networks, we used MRQAP, as illustrated in Table 7.3. In Model 1, learning networks after 4 weeks were primarily predicted by group division ($\beta = 0.70$; $p < 0.01$). In Model 2, learning networks after 14 weeks for case study 1 were positively predicted by initial friendships ($\beta = 0.24$; $p < 0.01$). In Model 3, group divisions and learning networks after 4 weeks were added, whereby primarily group divisions followed by learning networks after 4 weeks and initial friendships predicted learning networks after 14 weeks. The amount of variance explained by these three factors was 42 %, indicating (for social science disciplines) a relatively powerful fit. At the same time, 58 % of the learning links that took place outside the group and friendship relations were not explained, indicating the complexities of how networked learning relations over time are developed and maintained.

For case study 2, we conducted MRQAPs for both give-and-get networks, given the slightly different findings reported earlier. As illustrated in Table 7.2, initial friendships were a primary predictor for both give-and-get networks in Models 4–7. Adding the group division matrix in Models 5 and 7 further improved the fit of the model; however, the betas of group divisions ($\beta_{Give} = 0.13$, $\beta_{Get} = 0.11$) were substantially lower than those in case study 1 ($\beta = 0.54$). In other words, in contrast to what one would probably expect based upon the case study descriptions, in the more formal case study 2, more knowledge spillovers were developed than in the more 'intergroup networked' case study 1. As students in the medical programme had already worked with other students in five previous modules, the need to develop strong learning links with new group members seemed to be prevalent than in the economics context.

Discussion

In this chapter, we explored three research questions: how learning networks and knowledge spillovers between learners and groups emerge (over time), how prior friendship relations affect these learning networks and knowledge spillovers and how the perspective of networked learning can aid the conceptual interpretation of knowledge spillovers in these two cases. Using a (dynamic) analysis of social

Table 7.3 Regression analyses of social friendship and social learning networks and cultural differences (standardised beta coefficients)

	Case study 1			Case study 2			
	Model 1	Model 2	Model 3	Model 4	Model 5	Model 6	Model 7
	Learning after 4 weeks	Learning after 14 weeks	Learning after 14 weeks	Give information	Give information	Get information	Get information
1. Initial friendship	0.088***	0.235***	0.073***	0.498***	0.490***	0.480***	0.441***
2. Group division	0.699***		0.535***		0.127***		0.108***
3. Learning network after 4 weeks			0.126***				
R-squared adjusted	0.49	0.06	0.42	0.25	0.27	0.20	0.21

*** $p < 0.001$

learning networks in our two case studies, in a blended economics and medical science context, we found evidence for knowledge spillovers between groups in two different settings. In case study 1, these knowledge spillovers were not yet omnipresent after 4 weeks but developed over time and started appearing after 7 weeks and continued to be present after 14 weeks. In case study 2, the knowledge spillovers were strongly present in the network in the end of the first academic year.

These findings also show that different network structures emerged in the two cases. In case study 1, the network was primarily organised around the groups that were installed in the course as part of the learning context, with prior friendships playing a limited role in relation to the connections in the network (see Table 7.3). As knowledge exchange within their own group (17.8 links internal, 6.5 links external) shows, the structures and boundaries of the groups (research question 1) were clearly defined in the social network graph after 4 weeks. However, over time the network structures and boundaries became more mixed or blurred with other groups, which illustrates that groups were actively learning from other groups' knowledge and experience. This is also reflected in the findings that after 14 weeks the number of knowledge spillovers to other groups almost tripled (20.4 links internal, 18.4 links external). Thus, one could argue that at the beginning of the course students learned mainly from the members of its own group, but as time passed, most students also learned beyond the borders of their own group and developed substantial knowledge spillovers between groups. It is important to note that prior friendship relations (research question 2) did not predict these knowledge spillovers that developed during the duration of the course in this case. In other words, in case study 1, the knowledge spillovers followed an academic rather than a social path.

This in sharp contrast with the network that had emerged in case study 2 after studying together for 36 weeks in a large medical cohort. The networks show more interconnected students, primarily organised around friendship ties (research question 2). In this medical programme, the group composition (research question 1) played a less substantial role in relation to the communication network connections. In comparison to case study 1, in case study 2, the interaction between medical students was primarily predicted by friendships, which were formed outside the 'formal' group composition in the final module of the first year.

In order to interpret these contrasting findings, it might help to view these networks from a networked learning perspective. As described by Jones et al. (2008), friendship ties or 'social relations' are not the core of a learning network, positing that networked learning ties do not necessarily need to be strong since the function of the network learning is to exchange information rather than being friends. This perspective is in line with the goals of blended or collaborative learning context, when groups are created to engage students in collaborative learning exchange over the group tasks. One of the ideas behind the concept of knowledge spillovers is that groups can also learn from (members of) other groups. As such, the ideal in such learning context would be that learning networks are established both inside and between groups.

Interpreting the results from the two cases from this perspective, one could argue that in case study 1 information exchange occurred initially inside groups, gradually changing to exchange between groups, as already found in recent team literature (Decuyper et al., 2010; Michaelsen et al., 2002). This exchange between groups was not guided by prior friendship relations, as was also shown by MRQAP, indicating that group membership was a stronger predictor for learning networks at the end of the course. This is an indication that the network had an academic rather than social origin. In our opinion, this setting resembled a community of learners (Rehm, 2009), who were dependent on each others' input to further develop and solve subsequent group tasks. In case study 2, learning networks at the group level appear to be absent or relatively weak, whereby the network that has emerged seemed to be based upon social and academic relations established previously in the first year of the medical programme. One important distinction between the two case studies is that students in case study 1 were not randomised into groups but were able to select their group members, which in part may explain how learning interactions were initially focussed on internal group members.

Another explanation for the differences between the networks after 4 weeks and the development of the network in case study 1 might be provided by dependencies between learners (McConnell et al., 2012). With its focus on individual rather than group assessment, the learning setting in case study 2 did not create group interdependencies, 'needs' or reasons for students to learn with and from each other in the groups. As students had already established formal and informal friendships and learning networks with other students who followed the same programme for 9 months, several learners were primarily relying on previous developed network relations. The lack of dependency in the groups and pre-existing network relations also might have created fewer learning opportunities within the groups. As such, group learning and knowledge spillovers could be seen as a two-level process, in which learning on the first level (group) acts as a facilitator for learning on the second level (knowledge spillovers) in a productive learning community.

Going beyond the two case studies and comparing them to networks in more informal settings, one important distinction between the networks described here and networks described by, for instance, Jones et al. (2008) was the absence of really central active members of the learning community. It could be that this kind of pattern is more likely to occur in more informal learning communities than in 'institutionalised' communities like the ones studied in the two cases. The fact that in the end all students in the network are assessed on the course may explain the absence of these central figures that are often prominent in voluntary networks (Toral et al., 2010).

The findings reported in this chapter might have some implications for the design of the learning environments. The first relates to the finding that the network in case study 2 did not resemble an optimal networked learning community (Hodgson et al., 2012; Jones et al., 2008). As we suggested previously, the reason can be found in the lack of dependency between group members and readily available network connections from friendships emerged beforehand. The implication for practice is that creating groups is not enough for a functional networked community to emerge. Group work may need to be combined with a design that creates dependency within groups (and between groups) before both strong intra- and intergroup learning can emerge.

Another implication related to the two-level process of learning in groups within a larger context is the method of compiling groups in a learning context. Part of the explanation for the findings of case study 1 could be that being more familiar with each other (self-selection) 'speeds' up the process of within-group exchange, explaining 'better' communication within groups, which in turn creates between-group dependency (better group learning processes create more learning opportunities between groups). Therefore, educational designers might have valuable tools to optimise learning when compiling groups in the formal context.

Future research needs to address whether the explanations and implications that were derived from viewing the network analyses from a networked learning perspective can indeed help to create learning environments in which productive networks of learning emerge. This would be necessary in order to determine if (inter- & intragroup) dependency can be designed more explicitly into course modules and whether this can stimulate groups to develop more knowledge spillovers over time. The contradictory findings from case study 1 and case study 2 highlight that learning inside groups and knowledge spillovers between groups are not an automatic artefact of group learning and that more clarity on the impact of design and assessment on the learning networks that emerge is needed.

References

Akkerman, S. F., & Bakker, A. (2011). Boundary crossing and boundary objects. *Review of Educational Research, 81*(2), 132–169. doi:10.3102/0034654311404435.

Bohle Carbonell, K., Rienties, B., & Van den Bossche, P. (2011). Transactive memory profiles and their influence on advice seeking. In P. Van den Bossche, W. H. Gijselaers, & R. G. Milter (Eds.), *Building learning experiences in a changing world* (Vol. 3, pp. 267–283). Dordrecht, The Netherlands: Springer.

Borgatti, S. P., & Cross, R. (2003). A relational view of information seeking and learning in social networks. *Management Science, 49*(4), 432–445. doi:10.1287/mnsc.49.4.432.14428.

Bresman, H. (2010). External learning activities and team performance: a multimethod field study. *Organization Science, 21*(1), 81–96. doi:10.1287/orsc.1080.0413.

Capello, R. (1999). Spatial transfer of knowledge in high technological milieu: learning vs. collective learning process. *Regional Studies, 33*(4), 353–365. doi:10.1080/00343409950081211.

Capello, R., & Faggian, A. (2005). Collective learning and relational capital in local innovation processes. *Regional Studies, 39*(1), 75–87. doi:10.1080/0034340052000320851.

De Laat, M., Lally, V., Lipponen, L., & Simons, R.-J. (2007). Online teaching in networked learning communities: a multi-method approach to studying the role of the teacher. *Instructional Science, 35*(3), 257–286. doi:10.1007/s11251-006-9007-0.

Decuyper, S., Dochy, F., & Van den Bossche, P. (2010). Grasping the dynamic complexity of team learning: An integrative model for effective team learning in organisations. *Educational Research Review, 5*(2), 111–133. doi:10.1016/j.edurev.2010.02.002.

Dochy, F., Segers, M., Van den Bossche, P., & Gijbels, D. (2003). Effects of problem-based learning: a meta-analysis. *Learning and Instruction, 13*(5), 533–568. doi:10.1016/S0959-4752 (02)00025-7.

Engel, A., Coll, C., & Bustos, A. (2013). Distributed teaching presence and communicative patterns in asynchronous learning: name versus reply networks. *Computers & Education, 60*(1), 184–196. doi:10.1016/j.compedu.2012.06.011.

Goodyear, P., Banks, S., Hodgson, V., & McConnell, D. (2004). Research on networked learning: An overview. In P. Dillenbourg, M. Baker, C. Bereiter, Y. Engeström, G. Fischer, H. Ulrich Hoppe, T. Koschmann, N. Miyake, C. O'Malley, R. Pea, C. Pontecorovo, J. Roschelle, D. Suthers, P. Goodyear, S. Banks, V. Hodgson, & D. McConnell (Eds.), *Advances in research on networked learning* (Vol. 4, pp. 1–9). Dordrecht, The Netherlands: Springer.

Héliot, Y., & Riley, M. (2010). A study of indicators of willingness in the knowledge transfer process. *Journal of Management & Organization, 16*(3), 399–410. doi:10.5172/jmo.16.3.399.

Hendrickson, B., Rosen, D., & Aune, R. K. (2011). An analysis of friendship networks, social connectedness, homesickness, and satisfaction levels of international students. *International Journal of Intercultural Relations, 35*(3), 281–295. doi:10.1016/j.ijintrel.2010.08.001.

Hernandez Nanclares, N., Rienties, B., & Van den Bossche, P. (2012). Longitudinal analysis of knowledge spillovers in the classroom. In P. Van den Bossche, W. H. Gijselaers, & R. G. Milter (Eds.), *Learning at the crossroads of theory and practice* (Vol. 4, pp. 157–175). Dordrecht, The Netherlands: Springer.

Hodgson, V., McConnell, D., & Dirckinck-Holmfeld, L. (2012). The theory, practice and pedagogy of networked learning. In L. Dirckinck-Holmfeld, V. Hodgson, & D. McConnell (Eds.), *Exploring the theory, pedagogy and practice of networked learning* (pp. 291–304). London, England: Springer.

Hommes, J., Rienties, B., de Grave, W., Bos, G., Schuwirth, L., & Scherpbier, A. (2012). Visualising the invisible: A network approach to reveal the informal social side of student learning. *Advances in Health Sciences Education, 17*(5), 743–757. doi:10.1007/s10459-012-9349-0.

Hsiao, R.-L., Tsai, D.-H., & Lee, C.-F. (2011). Collaborative knowing: The adaptive nature of cross-boundary spanning. *Journal of Management Studies, 49*(3), 463–491. doi:10.1111/j.1467-6486.2011.01024.x.

Hurme, T., Palonen, T., & Järvelä, S. (2007). Metacognition in joint discussions: An analysis of the patterns of interaction and the metacognitive content of the networked discussions in mathematics. *Metacognition and Learning, 1*(2), 181–200. doi:10.1007/s11409-006-9792-5.

Jones, C. R., Ferreday, D., & Hodgson, V. (2008). Networked learning a relational approach: Weak and strong ties. *Journal of Computer Assisted Learning, 24*(2), 90–102. doi:10.1111/j.1365-2729.2007.00271.x.

Katz, N., Lazer, D., Arrow, H., & Contractor, N. (2004). Network theory and small groups. *Small Group Research, 35*(3), 307–332. doi:10.1177/1046496404264941.

Krackhardt, D., & Stern, R. N. (1988). Informal networks and organizational crises: An experimental simulation. *Social Psychology Quarterly, 51*(2), 123–140.

Lindblom-Ylänne, S., Pihlajamäki, H., & Kotkas, T. (2003). What makes a student group successful? Student-student and student-teacher interaction in a problem-based learning environment. *Learning Environments Research, 6*(1), 59–76. doi:10.1023/A:1022963826128.

Martinez, A., Dimitriadis, Y., Rubia, B., Gomez, E., & De la Fuente, P. (2003). Combining qualitative evaluation and social network analysis for the study of classroom social interactions. *Computers & Education, 41*(4), 353–368. doi:10.1016/j.compedu.2003.06.001.

McConnell, D., Hodgson, V., & Dirckinck-Holmfeld, L. (2012). Networked learning: a brief history and new trends. In L. Dirckinck-Holmfeld, V. Hodgson, & D. McConnell (Eds.), *Exploring the theory, pedagogy and practice of networked learning* (pp. 3–24). New York, NY: Springer.

Michaelsen, L. K., Knight, A. B., & Fink, L. D. E. (Eds.). (2002). *Team-based learning. A transformative use of small groups in college teaching*. Sterling, VA: Stylus.

Rehm, M. (2009). Unified in learning—Separated by space: Case study on a global learning programme. *Industry and Higher Education, 23*(4), 331–342. doi:10.5367/000000009789346158.

Rienties, B., Giesbers, B., Tempelaar, D. T., Lygo-Baker, S., Segers, M., & Gijselaers, W. H. (2012). The role of scaffolding and motivation in CSCL. *Computers & Education, 59*(3), 893–906. doi:10.1016/j.compedu.2012.04.010.

Rienties, B., Heliot, Y., & Jindal-Snape, D. (2013). Understanding social learning relations of international students in a large classroom using social network analysis. *Higher Education, 66*(4), 489–504. doi:10.1007/s10734-013-9617-9.

Rienties, B., Hernandez Nanclares, N., Jindal-Snape, D., & Alcott, P. (2013). The role of cultural background and team divisions in developing social learning relations in the classroom. *Journal of Studies in International Education, 17*(4), 322–353.

Rienties, B., Tempelaar, D. T., Pinckaers, M., Giesbers, B., & Lichel, L. (2010). The diverging effects of social network sites on receiving job information for students and professionals. *International Journal of Sociotechnology and Knowledge Development, 2*(4), 39–53. doi:10.4018/jskd.2010100103.

Rienties, B., Tempelaar, D. T., Van den Bossche, P., Gijselaers, W. H., & Segers, M. (2009). The role of academic motivation in computer-supported collaborative learning. *Computers in Human Behavior, 25*(6), 1195–1206. doi:10.1016/j.chb.2009.05.012.

Rienties, B., Willis, A., Alcott, P., & Medland, E. (2013). Student experiences of self-reflection and peer assessment in providing authentic project based learning to large class sizes. In P. Van den Bossche, W. H. Gijselaers, & R. G. Milter (Eds.), *Facilitating learning in the 21st century: leading through technology, diversity and authenticity* (Vol. 5, pp. 117–136). Dordrecht, The Netherlands: Springer.

Schmidt, H. G., Van Der Molen, H. T., Te Winkel, W. W. R., & Wijnen, W. H. F. W. (2009). Constructivist, problem-based learning does work: A meta-analysis of curricular comparisons involving a single medical school. *Educational Psychologist, 44*(4), 227–249. doi:10.1080/00461520903213592.

Springer, L., Stanne, M. E., & Donovan, S. S. (1999). Effects of small-group learning on undergraduates in science, mathematics, engineering, and technology: A meta-analysis. *Review of Educational Research, 69*(1), 21–51. doi:10.3102/00346543069001021.

Stahl, G. (2004). *Building collaborative knowing: Elements of a social theory of CSCL*. Boston, MA: Kluwer Academic.

Strijbos, J.-W., & De Laat, M. F. (2010). Developing the role concept for computer-supported collaborative learning: An explorative synthesis. *Computers in Human Behavior, 26*(4), 495–505. doi:10.1016/j.chb.2009.08.014.

Toral, S. L., Martínez-Torres, M. R., & Barrero, F. (2010). Analysis of virtual communities supporting OSS projects using social network analysis. *Information and Software Technology, 52*(3), 296–303. doi:10.1016/j.infsof.2009.10.007.

Wassermann, S., & Faust, K. (1994). *Social network analysis: Methods and applications*. Cambridge, UK: Cambridge University Press.

Chapter 8
Changing the Rules of the Game: Using Blogs for Online Discussions in Higher Education

Hanne Westh Nicolajsen

Introduction

The use of Web 2.0 in educational settings presents a number of new possibilities as well as challenges as regards a number of issues, one of them being active student participation. The use of, e.g. blogs, as an individual reflection tool is one way to make students participate (e.g. Ross, 2010). However, in this chapter, the focus is on Web 2.0 and more precisely blogs used for collaboration and thus social learning. The experiment reported in this chapter investigates a learning design requiring student participation in online blog discussions. The understanding of social learning is inspired by a networked learning approach understood as

> ... the learning in which information and communications technology (ICT) is used to promote connections: between one learner and other learners, between learners and tutors; between a learning community and its learning resources. (Goodyear et al., 2004)

Hodgson et al. (2012) are a bit more specific, arguing that networked learning celebrates the use of technology to connect and mediate cooperation and collaboration as well as discussion and dialogue, working in groups and communities. Deeper values are those of reflexivity and acknowledgement of differences among learners and their perspectives, as well as ambiguity and pluralities. According to Dohn (2009), Web 2.0 learning (which may be argued to follow the line of networked learning) happens when learning processes profit from Web 2.0 characteristics regarding content and processes being open, collaborative and bottom-up (Dohn, 2009).

As already mentioned, this chapter investigates an experiment using blogs for online student discussions. The experiment was part of a course on E-learning. The pedagogical intention of the experiment was to use Web 2.0 technologies as a vehicle to involve students beyond traditional course activities by encouraging them to interact on a set assignment. The students were asked to find and bring

H.W. Nicolajsen (✉)
Aalborg University, Copenhagen, Denmark
e-mail: westh@hum.aau.dk

V. Hodgson et al. (eds.), *The Design, Experience and Practice of Networked Learning*,
Research in Networked Learning, DOI 10.1007/978-3-319-01940-6_8,
© Springer International Publishing Switzerland 2014

in relevant theoretical material and empirical examples regarding self-chosen
E-learning topics and discuss these collaboratively on a Web 2.0 platform. The
experiment challenged the students in a number of different ways. This was
investigated by asking *which challenges and tensions of networked learning* were
identified based on the *experiences* of students *participating in student discussions,
using blogs.*

In the following, existing insights in the use of Web 2.0 technologies to support
learning in higher education are presented. Subsequently, the learning experiment is
described, followed by methodological considerations. This leads on to a presentation of the students' reflections regarding a number of selected elements, which is
followed by a discussion on the complexity and contradictory insights identified.
Lastly, conclusions are drawn.

Networked Learning, Using Web 2.0 Technologies

Using Web 2.0 technologies to facilitate participation and social learning is a
complex matter, not least due to the relationships and dependencies that are created.
Ryberg, Dirckinck-Holmfeld, and Jones (2010) argue that the approaches to learning found in networked learning and Web 2.0 learning present a "disturbance" of
the traditional ways of thinking about technologies for sharing, collaborating,
participating and learning, which raises new challenges and opportunities in education. Taking seriously the Web 2.0 characteristics of collaboration, distributed
authorship, active open access, etc., implies a radical move towards a networked
learning approach where the students gain more control of their learning space
(Dohn, 2009; E-QualityNetwork (2002); Ferreday and Hodgson (2008)).

Glud, Buus, Ryberg, Georgsen, and Davidsen (2010) reflect upon learner-driven
learning and the tensions emerging when Web 2.0 provides for shifts in control
between teachers and students. They argue that control should be seen as the four-
dimensional delegation of control on a continuum between teacher and student
control. The first dimension is the *learning process*, addressing who decides on
what to be learned and how, as well as who performs the activities. *Motivation*
concerns whether extrinsic or intrinsic motivation is used and if students are self-
motivated. The *infrastructure* is about who provides and organises the tools being
used. The fourth dimension is *resources*, addressing who decides on the kind of
material to use and create, who are seen as experts, etc. Glud et al. (2010) argue that
shifts in control from teacher to students are only recommendable if students are
ready to take the responsibility. It is also argued that fully learner-managed
programmes are out of fit with the existing education programmes but that single
courses might to a high extent be learner driven. Regarding learner-driven activities, Ferreday and Hodgson (2008) go much further and argue that online environments should seek for "heterotopia"—spaces where it is possible to act differently
and to imagine and desire what they see as the real drivers of the learning wanted.
They argue in favour of spaces that are free of the tyranny of dominance, oppression

and control, which they see as the dark side of participation. Ferreday and Hodgson (2008) thus leverage a critical approach to participation. Referring to Cooke and Kothari (2001), they refer to the tyranny of decision making and control, tyranny of the group and tyranny of method, which may be acted out by teachers or peer students. Hodgson and Reynolds (2005) see all participation as taking place in communities, and they argue in favour of participation in multiple and shifting communities as a natural part of our lives. Communities often celebrate consensus, and oppress individual differences due to pressure for conformity. Hodgson and Reynolds recommend communities that celebrate differences in views and understanding rather than consensus. According to them, online work provides a good structure for actually supporting multiple communities that recognise and support differences and learning from differences.

Another stream within the studies of Web 2.0 technologies for learning deals with the IT literacy and readiness of students to engage further. Much hype surrounds the IT literacy of young generations known as "digital natives" (Prensky, 2001). According to Jones and Healing (2010), the "digital natives" concept is misleading as it provides a very limited account, overseeing differences in technology adaptation. They argue that students' understanding of technologies should be seen as responses to local infrastructures and the use of technology as designed for courses, for instance. A related argument is made by Clark, Logan, Luckin, Mee, and Oliver (2009) who claim that there is a lack in understanding as to how these technologies may support critical and creative use and assist learning, which has led Clark et al. to define a gap, "digital dissonance", between qualifications for informal and formal use of Web 2.0. New practices of Web 2.0 influence negotiations of identity, authenticity, ownership, privacy and performativity as in the case of online writing (Ross, 2010). Quite a challenge relates to the students being cocreators and commentators rather than knowledge receivers (Clark et al., 2009; Conole & Alevizou, 2010; Glud et al., 2010). These changes are not just challenging the students' behaviour; teachers need to leave behind the role of being experts in control, which may collide with the expectations of authority of teachers and students (Collins & Halverson, 2010). The new roles of teachers and students often demand a number of implicit competences to perform the requested tasks (Dohn, 2009; Ross, 2010). Dohn (2009) has found that some teachers feel insecure about their roles, and Ross (2010) has reported that online reflective student practices lead to anxiety (Ross, 2010). The anxiety relates to difficulties in writing online as this mixes genres and breaks with the current conventions, and at the same time it may lead to personal disclosure and risk online as well as produce new power relations and subject positions. This argument is further supported by the fact that participation, in any community, is about building and negotiating relationships and impacts on the relational positioning (Jones, Ferreday, & Hodgson, 2008) as well as the construction of identity (Wenger, 1998).

The move towards Web 2.0 learning or networked learning thus seems complicated. Ryberg et al. (2010) argue that we cannot expect students to have advanced and creative capabilities in using Web 2.0 for learning or academic purposes; these need to be practised.

Unfolding the Experiment

The experiment on students' use of Web 2.0 technologies for networked learning was part of the course "interaction, learning and collaboration in virtual environments", which is an elective course at the fourth semester at Humanistic Informatics at Aalborg University. The course is passed through "active participation", meaning that the students need to sit in on all lectures and complete the assignments set. In the spring semester 2011, 37 students attended the course at our campus in Copenhagen. The students enrolled included a fairly equal number of males and females in their twenties. The students were well acquainted as they follow the same bachelor programme (along with another 14 students who chose the second course option available). For the last three semesters, the students have met regularly and collaborated in a number of different group constellations. They are familiar with Facebook and Moodle. On Facebook they have their own group for informal communication about study issues, parties, etc. Moodle is used primarily for course communication primarily from the teachers. Some of the students use Google Docs for collaborative writing in their semester projects and Dropbox for sharing material. However, the students have limited experience in using Web 2.0 technologies as part of the learning design in courses.

The course aims at providing an insight into the theoretical and practical discussions in the field of E-learning, and learning by doing is also thought of, becoming acquainted with a broad range of Web 2.0 technologies and more familiar with a few. Only 12 h for lecturing was allocated to the five ECTS courses (equals 135 student working hours), meaning limited time was available for sessions at the university to support the student activities in the course. The 12-h lectures were given as four 3-h lectures spread over a month to provide sufficient time for activities in-between lectures. The four lectures were designed as a mix of lecturing by the teacher (the author), student demonstrations and group work. In addition, homework such as reading and trying out different E-learning tools was accounted for through three assignments. As already explained, the students had to sit in on all lectures and solve all assignments to pass the course; alternatively, they had to write up a ten-page report to pass. For an overview see Table 8.1.

Before coming to class, the students were asked to set up a Twitter and Facebook account for use in the course. The idea was to use Twitter as a back channel for students to make announcements and raise issues during and between lectures. Few students had a Twitter account before the course and only a number of students had used it regularly. At the first lecture, it turned out that many students had experienced problems or had forgotten to create an account; time was given in class to set up Twitter accounts, and students were asked to help one another. A first round of comments—mainly funny ones—was posted; no questions ever appeared.

At the end of the first lecture, the first assignment was given. The students (in groups of six) were asked to look into a Web 2.0 tool of their own choice (e.g. Delicious, Tumblr, Mahara). They were asked to play around with their tool and look into the possibilities of the tool to support interaction. At the second

Table 8.1 The revised course design

Course session	On-site student Web 2.0-related activities	Web 2.0 activities between lectures
1) Lecture on learning paradigms	Grouping the students making them choose a Web 2.0 tool to present	Groups trying out their Web 2.0 tool—getting familiar with functionalities and interaction potentials (assignment 1)
2) Lecture on E-learning	Group presentations of Web 2.0 tools Introducing the online discussion experiment	Online student discussions to begin (assignment 2—nothing happened)
3) Lecture on organisational use of Web 2.0 technologies	Group presentation of Web 2.0 tools (continued) Re-energising the understanding of the online discussions	Online student discussions (took of) Individual reflections on potentials of E-learning in higher education (assignment 3)
4) Discussing the experiment	a) Discussing the online discussions on class b) Feedback on the individual assignments	

lecture, the groups each made a demonstration/presentation on their Web 2.0 technology to their fellow students (and their teacher).

The second assignment (the experiment) was to engage in a number of online discussions, using Web 2.0 tools. The intention of the online discussions was to enable the students to learn together, by building knowledge on a number of topics through short interrelated and reflected posts, providing different angles and understandings. Moving to an online media rather than in-class discussion or on-site group work was thought of as an opportunity to try out and become accustomed with Web 2.0 tools. In addition, it was seen as a way to provide alternative and open spaces for networking, giving the students time to prepare for discussion and hopefully challenge the social patterns, e.g. groupings, dominance of strong/extrovert students. The set-up allows for many different discussions, thus motivating students with different interests to start their own discussion and then engage in discussions of others that they find interesting. In this assignment, all students were asked to make at least three contributions (no distinction was made between posts or comments). Two contributions had to include theoretical material, whereas one could provide case material such as examples found in magazines/newspapers. One of the contributions could initiate a discussion; the others should respond to entries by others. These requirements were made to ensure collaboration and some level of quality in the discussions. The students were encouraged to work either alone or in groups, deciding on a topic to discuss. The group opportunity was given to limit feelings of insecurity. At the same time, the students were asked to contribute to other discussions. All discussions had to be announced. In the beginning, Twitter was used for announcements of new discussions; however, this did not work as new entries made the old ones disappear. Due to time pressure and the familiarity of Facebook, a closed Facebook group was formed for discussion announcements.

The "online student discussions" were thus seen as an experiment providing an alternative way to unfold a topic or phenomena. The intention was to expand the learning design beyond the set course hours and, even more important, to involve the students and turn them into active learners. This approach understands learning design as the pedagogical considerations regarding how the design of the course is intended to support students in learning. The students could choose any Web 2.0 technology they found suitable (e.g. discussion boards, wikis and blogs). However, all students chose blogs. The themes discussed should be E-learning related, resulting in topics such as crowdsourcing, podcast lectures and Web 2.0 for support of the semester project. The students had to introduce different understandings and angles and draw on theoretical material and practical examples. This method of working was intended to provide for multiple perspectives, forcing critical thinking as well as making the students more active and confident in finding, presenting and reading material in a critical way.

In the third and last assignment in the course, the students were asked for their individual reflection on Web 2.0 technologies for supporting learning. The reflection had to be theoretically based, using course literature introducing learning (Illeris, 2007) or E-learning (Dohn & Johnsen, 2009) or self-chosen theory. The two pages of reflection had to be submitted to the teacher by e-mail shortly before the last lecture. This assignment was thus more conventional, ensuring an individual contribution.

In the last course session, general and interesting findings from the individual reflections were summed up and presented by the teacher. The experiment and issues raised in the reflections were discussed on class to generate a common and nuanced account of how the experiment could be understood.

The evaluation of the students was a pass/non-pass, based on a combination of participation and content meeting the set requirements.

Methodology

The experiment reported was not designed as a research project. However, the insights obtained from the student reflections revealed interesting tensions and challenges as regards the use of Web 2.0 for networked learning. Thirty-seven reflections were received, each of two pages, equal to approximately 1,000 words. The data material used is primarily the written reflections but combined with the design of the course and the intentions of the teacher/researcher. The combined role of teacher/researcher might be problematic, due to the involvement of the teacher and therefore a lack of distance or a wish to appear successful. As the focus is the tensions and challenges (and a wish to improve the learning design) rather than documenting or discussing if the experiment was a success or not, this is not seen as problematic. Apart from the student reflections, the online discussions and the entries on Facebook are also used to understand the online discussions, but only to a limited extent regarding topics, number of contributions, timely patterns of contributions, etc.

The study follows an interpretative design of the constructivist type (Guba & Lincoln, 1994), creating an understanding about the students' and the teacher's perceptions and understandings of the benefits and challenges in using blogs as tools for learning. The reflections were read several times to pinpoint and categorise the student-raised themes, using open coding (Neuman, 2000), e.g. motivation to partic-ipate, the role of learners, the benefits and problems encountered were broken into issues such as overview and information overload. In a second round, the material was reread to see if more data would fit the emerging categories (selective coding, ibid). Later on, analysis using theory to categorise and discuss the insights was done (Kvale, 1990) informed by discussions and insights within the field of networked learning and Web 2.0 in higher education, e.g. by using the categories of Glud et al. (2010). The chapter presents major challenges and tensions rather than an exhaustive account.

The student reflections are taken at face value. This might be problematic as the reflections are means for passing the course, which may have caused some students try to please the teacher and write the "right" reflections rather than what they experienced and how they really felt. There was no request to discuss the experi-ment; however, the majority of students include personal thoughts on their experi-ences of using Web 2.0 for learning. The reflections seem credible; some of the reflections are overly positive, some are more critical towards the experiment; however, most of them provide considerations concerning the experiment by discussing the experienced outcome as well as the joy and frustrations felt during the course. A few of the reflections take a less personal stand to the experiment and discuss the use of Web 2.0 for learning in general; these are of cause of less interest to this study. Another potential bias with regard to the type of challenges identified is the potential limitation of issues addressed arising from the recommendation to use theoretical material by Illeris (2007) (learning theory) or Dohn and Johnsen (2009) (E-learning theory). However, most students also draw on other materials, resulting in quite a number of issues dealt with, and in addition, students also provide important experiences without theoretical analysis. The many different issues raised give a nuanced picture of the challenges encountered, but it also means that it makes no sense to talk about frequencies. The outcome of the study should be seen as an investigation of both issues often mentioned and the "extreme examples" (Flyvbjerg, 2006; Miles & Huberman, 1994), pinpointing any issue that may help understand a new phenomenon—in this case using blogs for online discussions.

In the following, interesting and contradicting statements from the students' reflections are presented to pinpoint potentials, tensions and challenges in the process of making sense and building a practice of using blogs for online student discussion. The students have given consent for the material being used for research. Fictive names are used.

Reflections on the Learning Design Based on Student Input

The findings from the experiment are presented and discussed, following the four dimensions of control of Glud et al. (2010): the *motivation* for students to engage in networked learning using Web 2.0 technologies; the *resources* used and produced; the *infrastructure*, i.e. the tools and media used; and the *learning process* going on. As appears in the analysis, the dimensions are highly related and sometimes condition each other.

Motivation

A number of the students argue that the extrinsic motivation in the form of the formal request to participate to pass the course was found to be determining for the online discussions to get started. Barriers to engaging are argued to relate to confusion regarding the way to use the technologies as well as to unfamiliar learning tasks resulting in students experiencing a need for "activation" through explicit instructions. However, as the statement below indicates, there is also a need for some framing of the activity, which is difficult for the students to provide by themselves:

> It has in general been exiting trying out this form of teaching and I hope it is something that we will meet again later on. I'm afraid that there isn't momentum to continue using blogs this way, without involving the lecturers, who needs to place demands like what happened here. I think the reason being that we are not used to this type of educational approach and we therefore need to be activated to a higher degree than normally. This might also be spurred in the initial confusion around the tasks. (Ian)

The enforced participation ensures critical mass of content. Whether this could in fact have happened without the demands set is unclear. It seems that the requested participation was important, particularly in the beginning, when the experiment made little sense to most students. However, when the discussions started to take shape, some students became curious about following the discussions. It may be argued that an inner motivation arose for some, which is also indicated by the fact that a few students provided more of the requested contributions than required. A student wanted to make a statement on a given discussion without backing it up theoretically as otherwise required. This may be seen as an extension of the given design:

> I've read all blogs with great interest and have on the way posed a number of questions to the different discussions mainly for myself. I posed an open question on the blog where I asked, if it was possible to imagine discussing a problem definition entirely on a blog, meaning all perspectives and important inputs would be kept. Comments like these did not count, as you had to find relevant articles and theories which made it a longer and more time demanding process, however also an educational process. (Sarah)

Apart from the request and the interest in the discussions, some of the students argue that social issues are at stake. Some argue that the motivation to participate increases due to a mirroring effect, meaning when friends or student peers write, this motivates others to follow:

> Your own motivation to write is likely to raise when your friends or student peers write. We compare ourselves with others in our circles, if they update a site with links, new then we want to do the same. (Carl)

Relating to the socialising issue is the possibility to show off. It is argued that the "Web 2.0 is like a showroom where you get the opportunity to show the rest of the world what you know". While some students find this motivating, others find it demotivating, as the following quote shows:

> I did not have the mental surplus to meet the task with the positive energy and perfectionism that I normally demonstrate and I was primarily driven by the necessity to pass the course.

> When you find yourself in such a situation it is incredible difficult to motivate one self to
> write in public. (Clara)

There are other implications from this way of connecting and communicating as member of a community. A student suggests that the choice regarding topics to discuss provides knowledge on the interest of peers and thus an opportunity to make connections based on interest.

Another consequence of the experiment and the transparency of everybody's contributions is the insight into the resources of peers and thus additional information to the students' existing picture of peer students:

> Socially it had a significant effect. In a class with more than 50 students, it cannot be
> avoided that impressions, meanings and prejudices are made about certain persons. I found
> that the collective knowledge sharing influenced these impressions. Some persons surprised
> me positively through really worked through and interesting posts. This will without doubt
> affect e.g. group formation. The opposite also happened and in this instance the blogs had
> negative influence socially. (Janet)

The online discussions thus have consequences beyond the course. They influence the possibility to form connections due to common interests, and they are yet another source of gaining an insight about the qualifications and motivation, of peer students, with consequences regarding future collaboration partners in, e.g. semester projects.

Resources/Content

The instructions regarding the resources to be used as well as the student-produced content were quite open. Attempts were made to ensure quality by demanding input based on theory, but some empirical material was also accepted. This of course provided some overall guidelines with respect to the form of the writing and the types of resources accepted. The students were encouraged to find material on their own; however, hints were given to material that could be used if the students felt unsure. The students were thus given quite an amount of control over the resources to be used and the input to be made.

The content created received a certain personal touch, both because the choice of topic and resources to be used was open and because most students included their personal perspectives and opinions regarding the topics discussed:

> The blogs become academic in a way, where it is still possible to include your own
> experiences and positions. Which probably makes the topics even more interesting. (Eva)

The contrary is also argued for that due to the theoretical demands the content is found less interesting because it becomes artificial. The student below argues that a conflict is found between what is required and the existing well-known blog genre as personal accounts:

> Blogs are primarily used to write personally and meaningfully, but instead we see in the
> results, that the tone from our side somehow is forced to have an academic language with
> content based on sources of academic content and finally stripped for personal opinions. I
> don't argue that blogs cannot or should not be used in academic dissemination or exchange

of views, but I find the results of our debates fulfilling the task at times appears animated and impersonal. (Greg)

Another concern raised is the quality of the student-generated content. Quite a number of the students raise concerns about quality assurance of the discussions, despite the fact that they find the quality of the debates to be quite good and despite acknowledging that part of the task is for them to act more critically:

I have to a much larger extent considered what my co-students have written, than what I would have if I had been presented to the same material in a traditional teaching session. (Ian)

The concerns regarding quality assurance indicate that the students do not accept themselves or each other as accountable or competent. Some of the students suggest that the teacher acts as a moderator securing focus and quality of content.

Contradicting statements pertaining to the production process were also made. Some students argue that the written and asynchronous form of the posts and comments allow for reflection and carefully prepared contributions. Others find that the immediacy of the media allows for here-and-now contributions that seem more natural like everyday-life communication in everyday language, making the participation less demanding:

I believe for sure that it creates new limits regarding who says what. You may take your time and adjust your posts in a forum, to make you reach 100 % satisfaction with your utterances. (Carl)

You communicate in a more relaxed way, where there are no real expectations to your achievements. This makes it possible to control your own learning pace and it works more like a nice downwind than an obstacle. Here we have the possibility to search around, reflect and discuss the different cases that are presented. This strengthens ones independence and creativity. (Frederic)

The students describe two rather different approaches to writing the blogs—the first feels much more in control of what is contributed, whereas the second feels less burdened from the process and form. Other students argue for a better overview of the discussions.

Infrastructure

The choice of tool (control) rested between the students and the teacher. The teacher decided the Web 2.0 class of tools, whereas each student could decide which Web 2.0 technologies to use when initiating an online discussion. Everybody's choice of blogs was surprising as, e.g. wikis or discussion forums might be more suitable.

The Learning Process

Using Facebook for the announcement of new blogs and posts meant a constant alertness to changes for most students, resulting in many students reporting blurring of the borders between university and private life. Some celebrate this as learning becomes more flexible in time and space; the here-and-now debate is found appealing and more involving than in-class discussion:

> The use of Web 2.0 has made it possible for all of us to participate in one another's discussions and made us independent of time and place. We have had time to do research continuously and thereby build on each other's contributions, something that is not possible if the discussion was taken during a lecture. (Siri)

However, others found this blurring of borders disturbing, especially as the number of posts rose exponentially with few in the beginning and a lot in the last few days. Some students felt it was hard to follow the pace and keep updated on all developments, and many of the students report lost overview of the different discussions. As a consequence, some decided to focus on a few topics, or they followed the more popular discussions, popular students or friends:

> More and more blogs appeared and the information became massive, I experienced that I— with the purpose of writing a post—ended up surfing around the internet here and there, because I was looking at all blogs and topics. I had to change my strategy. (. . .) I decided to focus on three of the discussions. (Janet)

This student was not the only one who developed a strategy to handle the numerous inputs. How and which blogs she decided to follow is unknown; however, other students reported that they used social information (likes and author) on Facebook or topics to select which discussions to follow:

> I have to say that I have been motivated to look into several of the blog posts according to whom liked the post and the number of comments on them. (Ian)

The feedback in terms of comments and likes was also seen as acknowledgement of what the students had written. For example, one of the students felt unsupported as no one commented on her first two posts, which made her insecure about whether she did it "right".

Another interesting aspect about the experiment is the changed roles of students and teacher. The students are well aware of their changed roles with extended responsibilities regarding the content created in the online discussions. One of the students argues that students become sort of "experts", very much like the lecturer, when they (the students) contribute with new angles and nuances on the different themes:

> We take part in creating the teaching and the learning, as we are the ones forming the content of the discussions. (Susan)

The changed role of the students is argued to place a number of demands on the students, which many of the students acknowledge as fruitful, as exemplified in the following quote that includes words such as meaningful, evaluate and critical, words which are often associated with a deep learning approach:

> It has giving me much more to initiate discussion, read others texts with critical eyes, evaluate the material, comment and provide meaningful responses. (Julie)

Another student complements the above statement by arguing that it is the collaborative element, the accumulation of different angles constituting a more nuanced understanding, which provides for good learning:

> You see several sides of the case and this I believe is an optimal way to learn. This would not be possible in individual reflections. (Frederic)

Not all students agree that the responsibility of the learning process and the choices given constitute a good learning experience. One of the students argues that all these requirements resulted in her finding the task overwhelming, and Marvin explains that it was time consuming and difficult to find material:

> We had to find information relating different concepts and theories. In the beginning I found this demotivating as it was difficult to find quality assured material on our subject. (Marvin)

In addition, some of the students reported that they felt insecure about the demands, e.g. the type of theory to be used, the amount of theory and the length of posts. The insecurity about the demands was raised in many of the reflections. However, some students only experienced this in the beginning, whereas others kept feeling a bit lost due to unfamiliar working methods or genre confusion:

> It works really well making the teaching more dynamic, as there is a significant greater level of interaction in this form of teaching. I do however still find it hard to get the full outcome of Web 2.0 technologies for learning, probably because it is still rather awkward to use them in a professional context. (John)

Challenges in Using Web 2.0 Technologies for Networked Learning

Looking into the students' experiences and perceptions of the Web 2.0 experiment, we find rather different understandings among the students regarding whether it was easy, interesting, authentic, etc. These insights may help us understand what is at stake in this type of networked learning. In the following, the major challenges and tensions identified are discussed. These may be either general challenges emerging from the changed demands, but may also arise from contradicting understandings and needs between students.

Literacy, Genres and Norms

Generally, the students report that they felt challenged by the design of the online student discussions. They felt unsure about the requirements and demands with regard to the responsibility given, the type and form of content and how the discussions would flow. Part of the problem arises from the blog genre used.

The students were asked to contribute to collaborative and theoretical discussions, but many of the students (due to their prevailing experience) understand blogs as a medium for individual and personal reflections. The discussions did not have the content or form as found in the blogs they were reading, nor were they as long or academic as their written assignments, but something in-between. Well-known genres and norms were thus challenged and broken, and a quite different type of mixed genre and behaviour appeared, as documented in the study of Ross (2010). For most students, this created some reluctance to participate; they did not exactly know what to do or what to expect, despite the examples and instructions given. For some, this reluctance never disappeared, whereas others made sense of it as they gained experience. These findings support Ryberg et al.'s (2010) argument that Web 2.0 for learning "disturbs" the current way of thinking about technologies for sharing, collaborating, participating and learning, and therefore it needs to be developed. This is in line with Jones' (2010) argument that technology understanding is closely related to the activities in which the technology is used and learned. It may therefore be argued that the students (as well as the teacher) had to learn and develop a practice on how to use blogs for online discussions. The instructions and requests given condition the development, but there is more to it, e.g. the selection of discussions to follow.

The contradictions of norms are also seen in relation to the changed roles in the experiment. The students argue that they become sort of experts and teachers of one another. This shift is argued by some of the students to be a significant driver in what makes the experiment rewarding. The responsibility is reported to make students act more critically towards their own content production as well as that of their peers. This, along with the many perspectives created, is argued to provide for a more nuanced understanding, thus meeting primary values in networked learning such as allowing for heterogeneity—according to, e.g. Hodgson and Reynolds (2005). Despite this new role being celebrated, the students generally argue in favour of the teacher exercising quality assurance. This seems contradictory, as it would undermine the need for the students to be critical. Rather than appreciating the openness and uncompleted understanding developed, the students are searching for final and right answers or at least more "right" answers; this does not adhere to the networked learning or Web 2.0 learning characteristics, which argue for multiple perspectives, open-endedness, etc.

Interaction Within Communities

There are quite a number of indications that the online student discussions are not context-free and that the activities become framed within a broader structure as the students all belong to the same well-defined group during their bachelor studies, meaning that they have a past and a future as a group.

The transparency of the contributions as well as choice to decide which discussions to follow and engage in had consequences for the student community beyond the course. The material created new insight and thus paved the way for new relations between students who became aware of unknown common interests. Although the choice of discussions to follow was found appealing, it also had a less positive side. Some of the discussions did not flow, as there were no responses to the blog posts. Having no answers was found both confusing and demotivating, probably because it was difficult to interpret what this meant and why. It gave some of the students an impression that they were not good enough or not liked. This interpretation is probably too simple but might hold part of the truth; indications on some of the reasons are found when students argue for strategies to cope with the many discussions appearing. Some of the students decided to follow a few discussions. Selection seems to be based on either popularity of the discussion, the author (a friend or clever students) or interesting topics. The social element identified is thus highly influenced by social status and not by the contributions alone, meaning that existing relational positioning is important. On the other hand, the transparency did not only affect the interaction taking place on the basis of existing social reputation and relations, it also created an opportunity to gain new and additional knowledge about fellow students challenging the current images of others, meaning the existing relational positioning or power relations were challenged as argued for by a number of scholars (e.g. Jones et al., 2008; Ross, 2010; Wenger, 1998). Here we see that this is influenced by the content created but also the existing social pattern, which seems to guide part of the interaction. This insight probably explains why some see the request to write "in public" as a way to "show off", while others see it as "public humiliation". It is thus found that the interaction is influenced by existing relationships and knowledge of the others but at the same time that the interaction holds potential to develop this knowledge. The findings suggest that networked learning using Web 2.0 technologies creates a different type of learning activity for students compared to, e.g. discussions in class. The findings also suggest that it helps students in need of time to reflect and prepare to get better conditions to participate as compared to lectures and group work. On the other hand, the visibility might reveal and worsen the situation for students experiencing difficulties in participating in general, combined with a weak positioning and thus no support in the group. These findings produce yet another input to a critical view on communities and participation in addition to the argument of coerciveness made by Hodgson and Reynolds (2005). The social implication of the experiment also means that talking about student versus teacher control as discussed by Glud et al. (2010) is too simple. Giving the students an open choice regarding which discussions to contribute to and thereby whom to interact with, as in our case of networked learning using Web 2.0, results in distributed input and control of the many (all the students), meaning there is little opportunity to actually manage or control the community implications.

Conclusion

Using Web 2.0 technologies to create learning communities for students poses possibilities, challenges and tensions. Unknown genres are likely to appear, requiring new practices with changed mindsets and behaviour of students and teachers. This is a demanding process. Instructions may help, but the activities demanded are more complicated than that and need not only to be learned but also to be developed. These findings are well in line with the existing literature within the field of networked learning. The role of the student as a valuable resource and the valuation of multiple insights on a topic by students without teacher quality assurance of what is right and wrong were reported to work well and create a critical learning environment, but at the same time it was questioned and found to be a weakness. Contradicting needs and values seem at issue.

Another contribution to the networked learning community is found within the insight regarding community issues. The study reveals that the transparency of the communities and the interactions following from high student control have both positive and negative social implications, not least when the activities are not context-free. Learner-driven designs, with more choices and control exercised by students, result in distributed control and consequently little control. The student-driven learning community develops a life on its own. Any activity before, after or here and now affects or will affect the relational positioning of the participants, with important implications regarding patterns of interaction and inclusion/exclusion. Some students may stand out as academically poor, whereas, for others, this online arena with different conditions for interaction (e.g. time to prepare) may help students with certain qualities and learning needs find an arena that fits them and helps them participate.

The findings presented here are based on an analysis of an activity in one course and were provided primarily from students' experiences reported in an assignment. The study pinpoints interesting issues, which may inform future considerations regarding learning design for online student communities. However, the findings need to be backed up by other studies.

References

Clark, W., Logan, K., Luckin, R., Mee, A., & Oliver, M. (2009). Beyond Web 2.0: Mapping the technology landscapes of young learners. *Journal of Computer Assisted Learning, 25*, 56–69.

Collins, A., & Halverson, R. (2010). The second educational revolution: Rethinking education in the age of technology. *Journal of Computer Assisted Learning, 26*, 18–27.

Cooke, B., & Kothari, U. (2001). *Participation: The new tyranny?* London: Zed Books.

Conole, G. C., & Alevizou, P. (2010). *A literature review of the use of Web 2.0 tools in higher education.* The Open University, Walton Hall, Milton Keynes, UK. A report commissioned by the Higher Education Academy. Accessed April 2011. www.heacademy.ac.uk/assets/ EvidenceNet/Conole_Alevizou_2010.pdf

Dohn, N. B. (2009). Web 2.0: Inherent tensions and evident challenges for education. *Computer-Supported Collaborative Learning, 4*, 343–363.

Dohn, N. B., & Johnsen, L. (2009). *E-læring på Web 2.0*. Frederiksberg: Samfundslitteratur.

E-QualityNetwork (2002). E-quality in e-learning Manifesto presented at the Networked Learning 2002 conference, Sheffield. Retrieved November 26, 2012 from http://csalt.lancs.ac.uk/esrc/

Ferreday, D., & Hodgson, V. (2008). The tyranny of participation and collaboration in networked learning. *Proceedings of the 6th International Conference on Networked Learning.*

Flyvbjerg, B. (2006). Five misunderstandings of case-study research. *Qualitative Inquiry, 12*(2), 219–245.

Glud, L. N., Buus, L., Ryberg, T., Georgsen, M., & Davidsen, J. (2010). Contributing to a learning methodology for Web 2.0 learning—Identifying central tensions in educational use of Web 2.0 technologies. In Dirckinck-Holmfeld, L., Hodgson, V., Jones, C., De Laat, M., McConnell, D, & Ryberg, T. (Eds.). Proceedings of the 7th International Conference of Networked Learning, Aalborg.

Goodyear, P., Banks, S., Hodgson, V., & McConnell, D. (2004). Research on networked learning: An overview. In P. Goodyear, S. Banks, V. Hodgson, & D. McConnell (Eds.), *Advances in research on networked learning*. Dordrecht, The Netherlands: Kluwer.

Guba, E. G., & Lincoln, Y. S. (1994). Competing paradigms in qualitative research. In N. K. Denzin & Y. S. Lincoln (Eds.), *Handbook of qualitative research* (pp. 105–117). Thousand Oaks, CA: Sage.

Hodgson, V., McDonnell, D., & Dirckinck-Holmfeld, L. (2012). The theory, practice and pedagogy of networked learning (Chapter 17). In L. Dirckinck-Holmfeld et al. (Eds.), *Exploring the theory, pedagogy and practice of networked learning*. New York: Springer Science+Business Media.

Hodgson, V., & Reynolds, M. (2005). Consensus, difference and 'multiple communities' in networked learning. *Studies in Higher Education, 30*(1), 11–24.

Illeris, K. (2007). *Læring*. Frederiksberg, Denmark: Roskilde Universitetsforlag.

Jones, C. (2010). A new generation of learners? The net generation and digital natives. *Learning, Media and Technology, 35*(4), 365–368.

Jones, C., Ferreday, D., & Hodgson, V. (2008). Networked learning a relational approach: weak and strong ties. *Journal of Computer Assisted Learning, 24*, 90–102.

Jones, C., & Healing, G. (2010). Net generation students: Agency and choice and the new technologies. *Journal of Computer Assisted Learning, 26*, 344–356.

Kvale, S. (1990). Det kvalitative interview i. In I. Andersen (Ed.), *Valg af organisationssociologiske metoder—et kombinationsperspektiv* (pp. 215–240). Copenhagen, Denmark: Samfundslitteratur.

Miles, M. B., & Huberman, A. M. (1994). *Qualitative data analysis* (2nd ed.). Thousand Oaks, CA: Sage.

Neuman, W. L. (2000). *Social research methods. Qualitative and quantitative approaches*. Needham Heights, MA: Allyn & Bacon.

Prensky, M. (2001). On the horizon. *MCB University Press, 9*(5), 1–6.

Ross, J. (2010). Just what is being reflected in online reflection?: new literacies for new media practices. In L. Dirckinck-Holmfeld, V. Hodgson, C. Jones, M. de Laat, D. McConnell, & T. Ryberg (Eds.). *Proceedings of the 7th International conference on networked learning* (pp. 353–360).

Ryberg, T., Dirckinck-Holmfeld, L., & Jones, C. (2010). Catering to the needs of the "digital natives" or educating the "Net Generation". In W. Lee & C. McLoughlin (Eds.), *Web 2.0-based E-learning: Applying social informatics for tertiary teaching*. Hershey, PA: IGI Global.

Wenger, E. (1998). *Communities of practice: Learning, meaning, and identity*. New York: Cambridge University Press.

Chapter 9
Blended Problem-Based Learning: Designing Collaboration Opportunities for Unguided Group Research Through the Use of Web 2.0 Tools

Richard Walker

Introduction

There is an emerging evidence base for using technology to support problem-based learning (PBL), although until recently most studies had focused on technology as an alternative method of delivering the content and resources supporting the problem scenario (as noted by Savin-Baden and Wilkie 2006; Donnelly, 2006, 2010), as opposed to a way of supporting collaborative and dialogical learning in problem solving. New research points to a shift in instructional design from using technology for content delivery towards supporting interaction and the active engagement of students in learning activities. Wheeler, Kelly, and Gale (2005) have described how online learning may support active problem solving and the immersion of students within situated learning tasks which address real-life problems. Studies on blended PBL have indeed begun to address student-centred learning designs and their impact on learning behaviour (Savin-Baden, & Wilkie, 2006). There are indications that students prefer to have web support for PBL (Cunningham, Deal, Neville, Rimas, & Lohfeld, 2006), and that a blended format can have a transformational impact on their learning, encouraging learners to engage in critical thinking (Donnelly, 2009), although in the majority of studies to date, the positive reception of technology by students relates more to the ease of online access to resources, provision of tools for enhancing face-to-face discussions (de Leng, Dolmans, Muijtjens, & van der Vleuten, 2006) or basic tutor–student question and answer interactions (Dalsgaard & Godsk, 2007).

Identifying and enabling peer (learner–learner) collaboration in the online environment in a way that demonstrably supports student-directed learning outcomes remains a challenge and may involve a variety of instructional roles in managing the learning process (Danielsen & Nielsen, 2010), although some studies have

R. Walker (✉)
E-Learning Development Team, University of York, Heslington, York, UK
e-mail: richard.walker@york.ac.uk

V. Hodgson et al. (eds.), *The Design, Experience and Practice of Networked Learning*,
Research in Networked Learning, DOI 10.1007/978-3-319-01940-6_9,
© Springer International Publishing Switzerland 2014

reported positive responses from students in qualitative surveys and focus groups in relation to their learning experience (McCall, 2010; Woltering, Herrler, & Spitzer, 2009). Studies applying the pedagogy of online interaction to analysis of collaboration in the context of PBL are beginning to emerge (Bromby, 2009; Danielsen & Nielsen, 2010; Donnelly, 2006, 2010; Ryberg, Koottatep, Pengchai, & Dirckinck-Holmfeld, 2006), and it is within this context that this chapter is placed.

Defining PBL and Its Relationship to Networked Learning Theory

In recent years a close association has been asserted between PBL design and networked learning theory, based on their shared critical and humanistic traditions of learning (Hodgson, McConnell, & Dirckinck-Holmfeld, 2012). PBL has been commonly described as a student-centred pedagogy which engages learners in problem solving as a way of developing their knowledge and understanding (Costello, Brunner, & Hasty, 2002; Hmelo-Silver, 2004): learning is derived as an outcome of the work involved in tackling and resolving the problem (Barrows & Tamblyn, 1980), involving an act of cognitive construction by the learner (Schmidt, 1994). Networked learning may be viewed through the prism of ICT-enabled human interactions in cooperative and collaborative tasks, emphasising interdependent relationships between participants in the conduct of inquiry-based learning. It has been defined by Goodyear, Banks, Hodgson, and McConnell (2004) as

> learning in which information and communications technology is used to promote connections: between one learner and other learners; between learners and tutors; between a learning community and its learning resources. (p. 1)

The Danish tradition of problem-oriented project pedagogy (POPP) has highlighted the overlap between PBL and networked learning in pedagogic design, informing the way in which learning environments may be created to support inquiry and action-based learning. The POPP approach employs ICT as part of an integrated design, supporting a networked approach to problem-oriented study, which is based on socio-constructivist and sociocultural approaches to the understanding of ICT and learning (McConnell, Hodgson, & Dirckinck-Holmfeld, 2012). Central to this approach are the concerns of problem orientation and participant control, which distinguish problem-based networked learning from more traditional PBL design approaches (Ryberg et al., 2006). In a departure from a teacher-controlled or guided PBL, students exercise greater control over the problem definition, formulation of learning outcomes and the process of inquiry for the problem in hand, developing a sense of ownership and responsibility for the whole educational process, rather than a controlled component of it.

Danielsen and Nielsen (2010) in particular have focused on the cooperative and collaborative properties of student-centred rather than teacher-directed activity in problem-based networked learning, highlighting the changing role of the tutor in facilitating the learning process. Knowledge acquisition can be seen as the result of cooperative and collaborative actions led by the students:

> In the problem-oriented project work the students themselves are responsible to identify the problem, to work with, and the very act of formulating a problem actually to work on is a large part of the learning process. (Danielsen & Nielsen, 2010, p. 529)

In this chapter we consider how the pedagogic values associated with problem-based networked learning may be applied to a blended course design. The chapter explores how Web 2.0 technologies may be employed to support the processes of knowledge sharing, negotiation and resolution in unguided PBL group research activities, where the focus is placed on student-directed learning. An underlying issue for consideration in this chapter is the degree to which we can design for collaborative and interdependent problem solving to take place online. How far can curriculum design take us in creating the conditions for student-centred self-directed learning, and what should the role and responsibilities of the tutor be in fostering the targeted learning behaviour?

York's Approach

This chapter reports on a blended design approach for a new postgraduate LLM International Corporate and Commercial Law programme at the University of York, which was first delivered to students in October 2009 using a combination of lectures, discursive seminars and problem-based learning activities. The LLM programme is taught over one year, during which students study for 180 credits through a mixture of compulsory and optional taught modules (worth 10/20 credits each) followed by a dissertation. The use of problem-based learning is presented to students as a core element of their study programme, enabling them to focus on aspects of law which have been introduced in the seminars and lectures. The emphasis on PBL is indeed common to all taught programmes delivered by York Law School and aims to

> facilitate the delivery of an integrated curriculum: theory and skills can be taught and learnt together and socio- legal aspects of law can be considered alongside practical problems and the basic law underpinning them. (York Law School Guide to Problem-Based Learning, 2009, pp. 9–10)

However, a defining characteristic of the postgraduate curriculum design relates to the level of student autonomy in the performance of PBL tasks. Whereas the University's LLB teaching to undergraduates is based on a guided discovery model for PBL activities with learning outcomes for problems prescribed by the teaching staff to ensure consistency in what is studied across a cohort, the LLM model follows a more open discovery model, more closely associated with andragogical self-directed learning (Walton & Matthews, 1989). A dedicated PBL tutor, rather

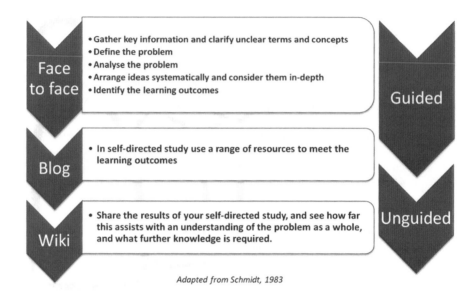

Adapted from Schmidt, 1983

Fig. 9.1 Blended design for the LLM programme

than a member of the teaching staff, oversees the learning process with students given a freer hand to determine their learning objectives, how to address them and to evaluate what they have learned. Figure 9.1 above captures the essence of the blended design approach for the LLM programme, outlining the range of activities that LLM students perform and the balance between guided and unguided learning.

Following this approach the PBL tutor's role is more akin to that of a learning facilitator, ensuring that students are on the right track in their definition of the learning outcomes and suitably prepared to tackle the problems in the performance of unguided research activities. Another defining characteristic of the LLM approach is the integrated use of ICT tools to support the performance of the unguided group research tasks—an essential part of the blend in course delivery and study methods. The selection of collaborative tools and a virtual space for student-managed activity aligns with the philosophy of the teaching programme to foster self- and group-management skills expected of students at this level. Web 2.0 tools assist with this process, with a group blog used to support information sharing and discussion of the problem and a wiki tool for the presentation of a group's combined solution. The emphasis on virtual collaboration is also intended to be enabling for postgraduate students, who are geographically dispersed and unable to collaborate face-to-face during the period of unguided group work, given that there is no requirement to be resident on campus during the period of self-study.

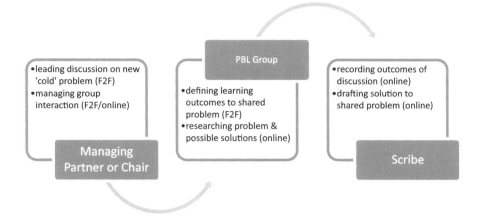

Fig. 9.2 PBL cycle: roles and responsibilities

The PBL Cycle Within the 2009–2010 LLM Programme

The 2009–2010 LLM programme was designed to include an assessed PBL activity in each module, worth 30 % of the total marks on offer to students in the module assessment. The PBL activity followed on after the delivery of introductory lectures and seminars by the teaching staff, which provided students with a theoretical overview of the key themes of the module. The PBL cycle ran over 1 week, from the introduction of the problem to the submission of a group solution by students: once initiated, it was designed to run as a 'stand-alone' activity, exploring a practical aspect of law which not been dealt with in detail in the seminar, with a dedicated tutor overseeing the cycle as depicted in Fig. 9.2 above.

At the start of each cycle, a new problem was introduced 'cold' to students in a face-to-face session, with the PBL tutor acting as facilitator and providing feedback on the performance of the group. The problem took the form of a case history, which students were invited to analyse and then respond to questions, addressing principles of law and citing relevant cases in their solution. For example, one problem in the Law and Commercial Transactions (LCT) module was presented as a summary of contract negotiations between two parties, with students invited to analyse the terms and conditions for the commercial transaction under negotiation, determining whether an agreement had been reached.

For each problem, a student acting as managing partner or chair assumed responsibility for leading the discussion and managing the interaction of the group, and another student acted as scribe, recording the details and outcomes of the discussion. These roles were rotated amongst the group to ensure that all students had the opportunity to participate. In these sessions the students identified their prior knowledge as well as the learning outcomes and priorities for the group research task, which were elicited through a brainstorming exercise facilitated by the PBL tutor. The learning then moved to the self-managed collaborative space on the University's virtual learning environment (VLE), where students were presented with the group wiki and blog tools (Learning Objects Campus Pack 3 tools hosted within the Blackboard VLE) to manage their own research activity to address the learning outcomes and seek an agreed solution to the problem.

At this stage of the PBL cycle, it was anticipated that students would engage in self-directed learning, researching solutions to all of the targeted learning outcomes for the problem under review. They were encouraged to post their ideas to a group blog area, with no prescription as to the form in which they made their submissions. The choice of a group blog tool was intentional, with the aim of supporting an open and free-flowing discussion, rather than a predefined or structured discussion mediated through a discussion forum. Reflections on all the learning outcomes were to be captured in holistic posts, with students setting out their individual perspectives on the problem. The collaborative process was intended to follow on from this, when students were in a position to share their findings and engage in the problem-solving process as a group, negotiating and constructing new knowledge online (Hmelo-Silver, 2004; Schmidt, 1983). Discussion was conducted through the blog, with a commenting facility also made available for students who wanted to attach responses to specific blog posts from their peers.

The group wiki was reserved as the space for the presentation of the group's finalised solution, drawing on the blog postings and combined research effort. Students were encouraged to reach an agreed group solution to the problem, although the scribe could record differing interpretations to aspects of the problem in the final wiki report if disagreements existed within the group.

The research and negotiation of the finalised solution were intended to be unguided, with no input from the PBL tutor, although an interim face-to-face meeting was convened midway through each exercise to check that students were on the right track. Individual contributions to the group work were assessed as 30 % of the coursework mark for the module, acting as an incentive for engagement, group participation and adoption of the targeted learning methods.

Research Focus and Evaluation Methods

The PBL sessions were delivered in the first term of the new programme in October 2009 across two compulsory modules (20 credits each) and two optional modules (10 credits each) for a small cohort of 7 international postgraduate students, drawn from a mixture of countries including China, South Korea, Pakistan, Germany and the United Kingdom.

Evaluation focused on the nature of group interaction within the virtual space that had been set up for the unguided research task—in particular how students responded to this medium in their approach to the weekly problems. This involved a study of the full range of learning that was being supported online, from evidence collection and reporting of findings relevant to the problem under discussion to deeper levels of learning involving the critiquing of conclusions and delivery of constructive feedback to others.

By drawing on multiple data collection methods, the research aimed to build up a rich picture of student learning across a selected range of PBL activities. Weekly blog sites were randomly selected from the compulsory LCT and the optional Corporate Finance and Corporate Insolvency (CFCI) modules of the LLM programme to serve as a focus for the research activity, which investigated PBL activities over a period from October to November 2009. Wiki sites were of less interest and not a feature of the research, as they were used exclusively by the PBL scribe to post the group's finalised solution and were not intended to be used in an interactive way by other members of the group to record their perspectives on the problem.

The unit of analysis for the online blog contributions was a blog post or comment associated with a post, which could contain multiple 'units of meaning' within each post. To evaluate the posts for each selected weekly problem, Fox and MacKeogh's 16 categories of cognitive thinking (Fox & MacKeogh, 2003) were employed, which are in turn adapted from Salmon's original framework for interpreting online contributions (Salmon, 1998). This framework maps closely to the stated objectives for the unguided research in addressing evidence of self-directed research (reading/ citation of resources) and of skills ranging from opinion forming (declarative statements) to higher-order cognitive skills (articulating and explaining, critiquing and challenging ideas of others).

Quantitative research methods were also used to track students' visits to the VLE module sites and to the weekly blogs where research findings were posted. In addition to this, a number of blog posts and comments that were made were recorded as a means to measure individual contributions to the PBL group research activity. Finally, focus group interviews were conducted with the course instructor, PBL tutor and students to probe their accounts of the learning that had taken place online.

Evaluation Findings

Profile of the LLM Cohort

The cohort had little prior familiarity with the PBL approach and use of online tools at the outset of the LLM programme. One of the students had encountered a seminar-based discussion of law in her undergraduate studies, although this was focused on the theory rather than the practice of law. For the others, the discursive and research-based components of PBL were entirely new. Some of the students were familiar with VLE platforms and module sites as repositories for course resources and test questions, but not as spaces for collaborative research and the elaboration of knowledge. As a way of introduction to prepare students for

Table 9.1 Frequency of individual contributions to PBL blogs

| | Frequency of blog posts and comments | | | |
| | LCT | CFCI | CFCI | LCT |
Students	Week 3	Week 2	Week 4	Week 6
Student 1	1	2	4	2
Student 2	1	2	1	2
Student 3	2	6	2	1
Student 4	1	3	1	1
Student 5	3	–	–	5
Student 6	2	–	–	1
Student 7	1	–	–	2

these new learning methods, the cohort observed a face-to-face undergraduate PBL session and followed a dedicated training session on how to post messages to a blog site within the VLE.

Outline of Key Findings

Activity logs for the CFCI and LCT modules reveal a regular pattern of logins for the weekly PBL tasks, with students accessing the VLE on a daily basis. However, the pattern of posts reflects a concentrated period of activity at the end of the weekly study cycle during which students delivered their responses to the targeted learning outcomes. Table 9.1 above reveals the frequency of individual contributions, with individuals contributing a mean average of two posts per problem. Whilst the number of posts may seem low, it is worth noting that students were expected to address all of the learning outcomes in their posts, which led to long and considered responses to the PBL problem under investigation. Interaction between students was limited, but some responses acknowledged previous blog posts—for example, an elected scribe provided an aggregate response at the end of each weekly research cycle, summarising the group solution to the problem, drawing out differences in interpretations of the problem, where they existed within the group.

The next level of analysis focused on the content of the blog messages that were posted to the blog, with each message coded against Fox and MacKeogh's adapted framework (2003, pp. 129–131) to record instances of cognitive skills. Following the assessment guidelines, students tackled all of the learning outcomes in their contributions, rather than focusing on a subset as part of a cooperative learning strategy. The lengthy nature of blog posts enabled multiple categories of cognitive skills to be recorded in one contribution, ranging from surface level examples (e.g. offering resources) to deeper levels of learning (e.g. critiquing and challenging ideas of others). Table 9.2 below captures some excerpts from the blog messages, mapping them against a selected range of the cognitive skills that were observed.

Table 9.2 Categories of cognitive skills and examples from the weekly blogs

Characteristic of cognitive skill	Example from blog posts
Offering resources	This case relates to cases of master and servant, these principles apply equally to directors serving the company under express or implied contracts of service, and who are therefore also employees (Dranez Anstalt v. Zamir Hayek)
Adding examples	The offence of insider dealing can be committed in 3 ways. If an insider: deals in price-affected securities, when in possession of inside information, s.52(1) CJA 1993 encourages another to deal in price-affected securities, when in possession of inside information, s.52(2)(a) CJA 1993, or discloses inside information other than in the proper performance of his employment or profession, s.52(2)(b) CJA 1993
Supporting positions on issues	Once Ackerman heard from the inside information from his father in law, he would be as insider under s. 118B (e) of FSMA because he has information "which he has obtained by other means which he could be reasonable expected to know is inside information". Therefore his action to sell his share of SAH would be dealt with as insider dealing
Critiquing and challenging ideas of others	I am open to being corrected on this, so this is just a question: regarding the paragraph wherein you say "In this case, there may have been a counter offer by N by stamping the performance certificate but there was no acceptance as it was never communicated further to M"—the better approach here may be to take the 'first shot' approach as advocated by Lord Denning in Butler v Machine Tools . . .

The coded frequencies were then totalled up for each week for the PBL exercise under observation, with percentage scores for each cognitive skill derived from that total. Table 9.3 (below) reveals the categories of messages that students posted to the blog sites.

Matching the results against the targeted objectives for the unguided research, we can observe a close fit in terms of the evidence of wider reading and citations (examples/offering resources categories) that were included in blog posts. Evidence of higher-order thinking is also revealed in the results, with the leading categories reflecting skills in articulating and explaining positions, as well as negotiating and interpreting issues. This reflects developed lines of argumentation, moving beyond opinion-based conclusions to reasoned discussion on the issues at stake, as illustrated in the following excerpt from a blog post for the LCT research task:

> I am open to being corrected on this, so this is just a question: Regarding the paragraph wherein you say "In this case, there may have been a counter offer by N by stamping the performance certificate but there was no acceptance as it was never communicated further to M". The better approach here may be to take the 'first shot' approach as advocated by Lord Denning in Butler v Machine Tools so as to see whether the first offer communicated,

Table 9.3 Content analysis of PBL blog posts

	% of posts exhibiting characteristic			
	LCT	CFCI	CFCI	LCT
Characteristic of cognitive skill	Week 3	Week 2	Week 4	Week 6
Offering resources	16	14	16	13
Making declarative statements	0	5	0	2
Supporting positions on issues	11	8	14	6
Adding examples	8	8	8	19
Articulating and explaining	18	16	14	17
Asking questions	8	5	0	4
Inviting critique	3	0	5	0
Reflecting personal experience	0	0	0	2
Re-evaluating personal positions	3	0	0	2
Agreeing with ideas of others	3	5	3	8
Expanding ideas of others	11	5	5	2
Critiquing and challenging ideas of others	3	3	3	10
Negotiating and interpreting	13	19	16	6
Defining	0	5	14	6
Summarising previous contributions	3	0	0	4
Proposing actions based on developed ideas	3	5	3	0

that of M to N was accepted by N. It seems it was, so according to this approach the fact that N had their own standard terms and conditions stamped on top of M's is irrelevant as it was never communicated to M. (Law & Commercial Transactions, week 6 blog post)

Interestingly, an increased frequency of messages acknowledging other contributions is apparent in the week 6 LCT blog, either by agreeing with or critiquing the ideas of others. This may suggest that students acquired a greater confidence in the virtual space as a location to test out ideas, rather than publish answers to the learning outcomes under research as the LLM course progressed. This extended to disagreements and questions, with group members perceiving the virtual space as a place to log issues that they were struggling with, thereby making their working process transparent to the course instructor, as evidenced in the excerpt below:

Reply to [X]: You are absolutely right that the party to the contract, which should be taken into consideration is M, not LC. I got it wrong for some reason. Nevertheless, neither of the contractors is a consumer! They are both dealing in the course of their businesses. Please have a look at this definition of consumer in UCTA. (Law & Commercial Transactions, week 6 blog post)

In order to gain a clear insight into what was happening during the online unguided learning phase, a focus group was convened with participants to review their learning experiences across both modules. Students were invited to comment on their study approach in the performance of the group tasks. Focus group responses revealed that students conducted all communication for the problems online, without recourse to face-to-face meetings or telephone discussions to resolve problems. Indeed, they viewed this approach as a strength in supporting the flow of the research tasks:

> It's quite helpful because you are actually seeing someone's argument written out, so you can actually follow it, which is useful. Sometimes when people are speaking, you get lost with what they are saying, whereas when you're reading it you can think—you can read back—and it's quite good to see two views. If you're not involved in the argument, you can see which side you agree with, so it's useful. (UK female student)

Given the assessment criteria governing individual contributions to the PBL work—accounting for 30 % of the coursework mark for a module—this was an important consideration to take into account. However, the emphasis on communication through blog posts also appeared to help students to engage in reflective learning and the application of theory to practice, obliging them to take a position on all the learning outcomes in a transparent way to demonstrate their learning to their peers. This fostered a process of self-reflection amongst group members, as outlined in the following comment recorded in the focus group:

> . . . when you are forced to write something and put it on the blog you have to reflect your own thoughts more, and I think that's quite helpful. Because sometimes if you just read a book, you read it and take it and maybe you learn it or maybe not and that's it. But you have really to think about it and make some research and find different information and put it all together and think about it, and then . . . you are more involved into this legal material and sometimes . . . . you can see new problems. (German male student)

Disagreements led in some cases to the revision of original arguments, with individuals posting corrections to their original posts, acknowledging the input that they had received from other participants:

> I posted something and then I think X corrected me on something, and then I went through it and I was like 'oh yeah you're right' so I just corrected it, but I didn't correct it like, you know, wipe what I had written, I just put 'Oh well I was wrong on this point', so just a correction on that, so it's not like I was wiping it and making it look nicer but I just responded to what was she said and I said I was wrong you were right or something like that. (Pakistani female student)

However, participants pointed to one significant shortcoming in the design of the unguided research task which related to the absence of feedback on individual contributions to the research process and learning outcomes, which students felt would have enhanced their overall learning:

> Well I would prefer actually to get proper feedback, not only like we get on the problem in the class, but also proper feedback every time on our blog or wiki, or at least every some time. You know, we need to know. (Pakistani female student)

> I prefer if we can get individual feedback; that would be very helpful to me. (Chinese female student)

They were also not presented at the end of the cycle with an approved set of solutions for the problems under discussion, which the PBL tutor felt might have undermined their sense of 'learning through doing'—a core feature of the open discovery PBL approach embedded within the LLM programme design:

> There is a fear that if the students knew they were going to get the … electronic answers every week, that they might have less incentive to use the PBL process to achieve active learning. The idea of the PBL process is meant to encourage the students to learning through doing, active learning. (PBL tutor)

This left students feeling frustrated, without a sense of closure at the end of the PBL cycle that their solutions approximated to the 'right' set of answers that they should arrive at. Given the loose association between the PBL sessions and the formal learning conducted through the seminars and lectures, there was little opportunity within the programme to review the group's solutions and reach a view on their accuracy:

> I think that's the one thing that everyone kind of agrees with. We've all kind of said that throughout … because you put a lot of work into getting the answers but we're not always a hundred per cent sure that they are the answers, so that would be one thing that we would maybe like to improve. (Pakistani female student)

Discussion

Reception of the Study Methods and Tools

The results are striking given the cross-cultural make-up of the cohort and the different learning philosophies which students brought to the programme. The cohort's lack of familiarity with PBL and the open discovery approach, combined with a limited exposure to online learning methods at the outset of the programme, may be contrasted with the positive way in which participants embraced this learning culture as the modules progressed. This runs counter to what we may have anticipated taking place, with students' previous educational experiences and the novelty of the study context representing potential obstacles to the acceptance of the online study methods. Indeed, as Spaulding (1991) has found for face-to-face PBL sessions in medical education, difficulties can arise 'when a group of people of diverse personalities, backgrounds, and ages mix in an intense learning situation'— where students are expected to be 'considerate of each other's learning needs and altruistic enough to help each other find approaches and solutions to the topics under discussion' (p. 42). We might reasonably expect the networked learning approach to further complicate the adoption of PBL study methods for students new to this type of study approach, with computer-based communication offering an additional barrier to participation.

The evidence from the observed modules suggests a different picture, with students gradually embracing the study methods and online learning as they became more familiar with them, viewing the collaborative tools as enablers rather than barriers to group work in supporting the development of critical discourse. It is interesting to consider the extent to which this behaviour was stimulated by a well-devised assessment model. Slavin (1990) has argued that extrinsic rewards are instrumental in motivating students to work in cooperative learning groups and the assessment model for the LLM programme was certainly devised to recognise and reward online participation, albeit for a collaborative study model. Whilst the course instructor anticipated that the assessment rules governing the conduct of the research tasks would act as a driver for participation and the asynchronous textual exchange serve as an effective way in which international students could share information and overcome language barriers, it was less certain how group members would adapt their style of learning to the online space and use this medium to engage in critical discourse. Focus group feedback suggests that the assessment criteria were not decisive and that the online study methods in themselves complemented the sensemaking and reflection processes that students engaged with in tackling the case problems. On one level the evidence confirms that a strong alignment existed between the targeted study methods and choice of technology, with students using the blog tool in particular as it was intended to be used—to share knowledge and negotiate an agreed response to each of the targeted learning outcomes. On another level, we may detect through the comments of participants a strong intrinsic motivation to participate online. The pattern of asynchronous postings and evolution of a textual record of contributions within the group blog assisted students in reflecting on the problem under review, helping them to keep track of the complex argumentation process, and this was viewed as a more effective way of learning than engaging in face-to-face or synchronous discussion by telephone or web conferencing tools.

Role and Responsibilities of the PBL Tutor

The results are less clear when assessing the effectiveness of the PBL tutor's role in supporting the unguided group work. At face value, the separation of the PBL cycle into face-to-face (guided) and online learning (unguided) components appeared to work well: the evidence reflects how students successfully self-regulated disagreements and opened up their personal contributions for critical comments without recourse to the PBL tutor for support. This finding reflects a key characteristic of networked learning theory in relation to participant control, where the inversion of student and tutor roles is associated with students taking on greater responsibility to manage their online dialogue and collaboration. The PBL tutor's activity consequently remained focused on helping students to define learning outcomes in the face-to-face sessions and overseeing progress updates on the research activities in the midpoint sessions, without recourse to intervention in the online learning space. However, tensions arose over the level of feedback that individuals received on their contributions to the cases, with participants expecting the PBL tutor to offer individual and collective feedback in support of the unguided research task, both during and at the end of the PBL cycle. This perhaps highlights the limitations of the blended design approach for unguided PBL in addressing learner anxiety over progress and performance—a weakness which has been identified in other studies (Nicolajsen, 2014)—and indeed flags an inherent contradiction in the pedagogic methods employed for the LLM programme as a whole, with the unguided online component located within an otherwise traditional programme format of lectures and seminars and examination-based assessment. With this context in mind, it seems less strange that students would express a need for formal feedback from the programme team on the performance of a participant-controlled learning activity.

There is an emerging body of research focusing on tutorial responsibilities in supporting online PBL activity—specifically strategies for mitigating student anxiety in tackling collaborative group work. Danielsen and Nielsen (2010) have reported on the different dimensions of instructional support for PBL and how they may transfer over to the networked learning environment, highlighting the varied roles which tutors may adopt in managing student learning as 'expert', 'process oriented supervisor' and 'therapist'. Aside from facilitation and group-management skills in supporting student learning and ensuring that they remain on task as autonomous and critical thinkers, the experiences of the LLM students in this study shed light on another challenge, namely, how to recognise and validate individual contributions within participant-controlled activities, providing reassurance that students are on the right track in their research activities. This highlights a dilemma regarding the role of the tutor in supporting students, specifically the boundaries of the tutor's role in providing feedback to the group whilst at the same time stepping back and ensuring that the hallmarks of an unguided learning process are being respected. Danielsen and Nielsen (2010) argue that for a group to be functioning effectively, it should be constantly reflecting on action through a heightened sense of awareness regarding its study and work style. The tutor's task as a 'process supervisor' is to ensure that students remain aware of their working practices, enabling group members to reflect on their progress and become more self-assured in terms of their learning trajectory. For a purely self-guided design such as the LLM model, this is more challenging to realise, as the group processes should already be firmly embedded as part of the working practice of the group before individuals go online, with the tutor's role peripheral to the online collaborative activity once it is underway. Corrective action, if it is needed, must be prompted from within the group in regulating its own working practices, with students unable to rely on interventions from the tutor to keep on track.

A related challenge also focuses on closure at the end of the PBL cycle—selecting assessment and feedback methods which are consistent with a participant-controlled study approach, enabling students to review the progress of their learning without entering into the territory of more directive pedagogic practice through the communication of 'right' or 'wrong' answers. In this respect, peer review and peer assessment methods may have much to offer participant controlled inquiry, implicating students in the evaluation of their individual and collective learning, giving them the space to draw conclusions on their progress in addressing the learning outcomes identified at the outset of the PBL process.

Conclusion

The research reflects a preliminary step in the evaluation of the online delivery of an unguided PBL research activity for a small cohort of students over two modules of a study programme. Whilst acknowledging the limitations of this study, the results nonetheless indicate the potential for online tools to support reflective thinking and the elaboration of knowledge through self-managed learning, contributing to the emerging evidence base of blended design approaches for PBL (Donnelly, 2010; Savin-Baden & Wilkie, 2006) and networked learning research studies (Ryberg et al., 2006). In particular, the findings reveal how a group blog space may serve as an effective forum for evidence gathering and presentation of solutions in relation to the targeted learning outcomes, reflecting situated cognition—i.e. learning based on the 'thinking through of real-life problems' (Wheeler et al., 2005, p. 127). As students became more familiar with the learning methods, they displayed a greater willingness to engage in critical discussion and negotiation towards an agreed solution, reflecting the higher-order learning that was targeted in the PBL activities.

The findings suggest that a blended design approach based on networked learning principles for the online component of a course can offer the conditions for unguided group research to flourish, but that success is contingent on a number of factors being addressed. The study confirms the findings of other studies (e.g. Portimojärvi, 2006) that the alignment between the targeted study methods and the technology made available to learners is critical to their acceptance of the study methods: the chosen technology should be 'fit for purpose' and perceived by participants as enabling for student-directed learning to take place. The positioning of PBL within the overall programme culture is also important—specifically the relationship between the study, assessment and feedback methods for the PBL activity and the overall programme culture: the extent to which they complement and reinforce each other will shape the reception of the learning methods and the accompanying expectations over the level of feedback and pedagogic support that students should receive.

However, as Goodyear (2001) has observed, there is no actual determinism between course design for networked learning and the nature of the learning that may ensue—much will depend on the human dynamics in making use of the virtual space to support interaction and collaborative learning. For an unguided PBL design approach, this places the burden of responsibility on the PBL group itself to regulate and maintain effective group-intensive interaction, maximising opportunities for shared and interdependent learning online to take place. This requires learners to find their own intrinsic motivation to engage in collaborative and interdependent learning and develop the competencies to navigate the virtual space effectively. For novice learners this is a challenging undertaking to face, particularly the adjustment to self-directed learning strategies within an unstructured learning environment.

To address this challenge for novice learners, the key perhaps lies in managing the transition from structured to unstructured study through the simulation of problem-oriented learning methods in a controlled and formative way first, in this way allowing opportunities for the PBL tutor to provide feedback on individual and group performance in tackling the problem—focusing on process and outcomes. By simulating learning methods, students may be given the space and time to adapt to the new ways of working, developing their awareness of PBL methods and the skills and confidence to work effectively as a group online. Following this approach the induction phase assumes a critical role in helping to reduce the distance that students need to travel in acquiring the skills and mind-set to engage in problem-based inquiry. As we have observed in this study, with a cursory induction based on the undergraduate-guided PBL model, the adjustment can take time, with mature postgraduate students gradually adopting the study methods and use of the collaborative tools to build their knowledge and understanding as they became familiar with the networked learning approach, whilst still exhibiting signs of anxiety over their performance and the value of individual and collective learning in addressing the learning outcomes. With a scaffolded introduction, we may anticipate a speedier embrace of the learning methods, with participants more attuned to student-directed inquiry through online collaboration, with greater willingness and capabilities to engage in self-regulated learning inquiry.

References

Barrows, H. S., & Tamblyn, R. M. (1980). *Problem-based learning: An approach to medical education: Vol. 1. Springer series on medical education.* New York: Springer

Bromby, M. (2009). Virtual seminars: Problem-based learning in healthcare law and ethics. *Journal of Information, Law & Technology (JILT)* (3), Retrieved November 25, 2011, from http://go.warwick.ac.uk/jilt/2009_3/bromby

Costello, M. L., Brunner, P. W., & Hasty, K. (2002). Preparing students for the empowered workplace: The risks and rewards in a management classroom. *Active Learning in Higher Education, 3*(2), 117–127.

Cunningham, C. E., Deal, K., Neville, A., Rimas, H., & Lohfeld, L. (2006). Modeling the problem-based learning preferences of McMaster University Undergraduate Medical Students using a discrete choice conjoint experiment. *Advances in Health Sciences Education, 11*, 245–266.

Dalsgaard, C., & Godsk, M. (2007). Transforming traditional lectures into problem-based blended learning: Challenges and experiences. *Open Learning: The Journal of Open and Distance Learning, 22*(1), 29–42.

Danielsen, O., & Nielsen, J. L. (2010). Problem-oriented project studies—The role of the teacher as supervising/facilitating the study group in its learning processes. In: L. Dirckinck-Holmfeld, V. Hodgson, C. Jones, M. de Laat, D. McConnell, & T. Ryberg (Eds.), *Proceedings of the 7th International Conference on Networked Learning* (pp. 558–565). Retrieved January 14, 2012, from http://www.lancs.ac.uk/fss/organisations/netlc/past/nlc2010/abstracts/PDFs/Danielsen.pdf

de Leng, B. A., Dolmans, D., Muijtjens, A., & van der Vleuten, C. (2006). Student perceptions of a virtual learning environment for a problem-based learning undergraduate medical curriculum. *Medical Education, 40*(6), 568–575.

Donnelly, R. (2006). Blended problem-based learning for teacher education: Lessons learnt. *Learning, Media and Technology, 31*(2), 92–116.

Donnelly, R. (2009). The nexus of problem-based learning and learning technology: Does it enable transformative practice? *European Journal of Open, Distance and E-Learning.* Retrieved January 14, 2012, from http://www.eurodl.org/?p = archives&year = 2009&halfyear = 2& article = 371

Donnelly, R. (2010). Harmonizing technology with interaction in blended problem-based learning. *Computers & Education, 54*, 350–359.

Fox, S., & MacKeogh, K. (2003). Can elearning promote higher-order learning without tutor overload? *Open Learning, 18*(2), 121–134.

Goodyear, P. (2001). *Effective networked learning in higher education: Notes and guidelines.* Lancaster, UK: Centre for Studies in Advanced Learning Technology (CSALT).

Goodyear, P., Banks, S., Hodgson, V., & McConnell, D. (2004). Research on networked learning: An overview. In P. Goodyear, S. Banks, V. Hodgson, & D. McConnell (Eds.), *Advances in research on networked learning* (pp. 1–11). Dordrecht, The Netherlands: Kluwer.

Hmelo-Silver, C. E. (2004). Problem-based learning: What and how do students learn? *Educational Psychology Review, 16*(3), 235–266.

Hodgson, V., McConnell, D., & Dirckinck-Holmfeld, L. (2012). The theory, practice and pedagogy of networked learning. In L. Dirckinck-Holmfeld, V. Hodgson, & D. McConnell (Eds.), *Exploring the theory, pedagogy and practice of networked learning.* New York: Springer.

McCall, I. (2010). Online enhanced problem-based learning: Assessing a blended learning framework. *The Law Teacher, 44*(1), 42–58.

McConnell, D., Hodgson, V., & Dirckinck-Holmfeld, L. (2012). Networked learning: A brief history and new trends. In L. Dirckinck-Holmfeld, V. Hodgson, & D. McConnell (Eds.), *Exploring the theory, pedagogy and practice of networked learning.* New York: Springer.

Nicolajsen, H. W. (2014). Changing the rules of the game—Using blogs for online discussions in higher education. In V. Hodgson, M. de Laat, D. McConnell, & T. Ryberg (Eds.), *The design, experience and practice of networked learning.* New York: Springer.

Portimojärvi, T. (2006). Synchronous and asynchronous communication in online PBL. In E. Poikela & A. R. Nummenmaa (Eds.), *Understanding problem-based learning.* Tampere, Finland: Tampere University Press.

Ryberg, T., Koottatep, S., Pengchai, P., & Dirckinck-Holmfeld, L. (2006). Conditions for productive learning in networked learning environments: A case study from the VO@ NET project. *Studies in Continuing Education, 28*(2), 151–170.

Salmon, G. (1998). Developing learning through effective online moderation. *Active Learning, 9*, 3–8.

Savin-Baden, M., & Wilkie, K. (Eds.). (2006). *Problem-based learning online.* Maidenhead, England: Open University Press.

Schmidt, H. G. (1983). Problem-based learning: Rationale and description. *Medical Education, 17*, 11–16.

Schmidt, H. G. (1994). Problem-based learning: An introduction. *Instructional Science, 22*(4), 247–250.

Slavin, R. E. (1990). *Cooperative learning: Theory, research and practice.* Englewood Cliffs, NJ: Prentice Hall.

Spaulding, W. B. (1991). *Revitalising medical education. McMaster Medical School. The early years 1965–1974.* Hamilton, ON: B.C. Becker.

Walton, H. J., & Matthews, M. B. (1989). Essentials of problem-based learning. *Medical Education, 23*, 542–558.

Wheeler, S., Kelly, P., & Gale, K. (2005). The influence of online problem-based learning on teachers' professional practice and identity. *ALT-J: Research in Learning Technology, 13*(2), 125–137.

Woltering, V., Herrler, A., & Spitzer, K. (2009). Blended learning positively affects students' satisfaction and the role of the tutor in the problem-based learning process: Results of a mixed method evaluation. *Advances in Health Sciences Education, 14*, 725–738.

York Law School. (2009). *Guide to problem-based learning.* York, UK: University of York. Retrieved October 14, 2012, from http://www.york.ac.uk/media/law/documents/pbl_guide.pdf

Part III
The Practice of Informal Networked Learning

Chapter 10
Online Learning Communities for Teachers' Continuous Professional Development: An Action Research Study of eTwinning Learning Events

Brian Holmes and Julie-Ann Sime

Introduction

Online communities are increasingly being used in formal education to augment collaboration between students, and between students and tutors, in networked learning (Luppicini, 2007; McConnell, 2006). Whereas a reasonable body of research exists on the use of networked learning and learning communities in higher education, especially in postgraduate studies, less is known about their use in other sectors of education, such as continuous vocational education and training.

In the area of teachers' continuous professional development (CPD), learning communities are seen as offering valuable opportunities for authentic and personalised learning (Duncan-Howell, 2010), and informal exchange of good practice and peer learning (Avalos, 2011). Rather than separating the formal knowledge and theory for teaching from the practical knowledge gained from applying ideas in action, learning communities can help teachers to take a more systemic view through critical inquiry with peers (Cochran-Smith & Lytle, 1999; Vescio, Ross, & Adams, 2008). Guskey (2002, p. 382) posits that teachers prefer CPD that offers 'specific, concrete and practical ideas that directly relate to the day-to-day operation of their classrooms' and studies suggest that change happens when teachers believe in the pedagogical value of what they are learning, after seeing for themselves the positive effect on their pupils' learning (Ertmer, 2005; Ottenbreit-Leftwich, Glazewski, Newby, & Ertmer, 2010). Yet Boyle, While, and

B. Holmes (✉)
European Commission's Executive Agency for Education, Audiovisual and Culture (EACEA), Brussels, Belgium
e-mail: Brian.Holmes@ec.europa.eu

J.-A. Sime
Department of Educational Research, Centre for Technology Enhanced Learning, Lancaster University, Lancashire, UK
e-mail: j.sime@lancaster.ac.uk

V. Hodgson et al. (eds.), *The Design, Experience and Practice of Networked Learning*, Research in Networked Learning, DOI 10.1007/978-3-319-01940-6_10, © Springer International Publishing Switzerland 2014

Boyle (2004) note that attending an out-of-school training course is still the predominant mechanism for teachers' CPD.

This action research study looks at an example of teachers' CPD that offers teachers the opportunity to undertake inquiry-based learning informally with peers, in an online learning community and in the context of their everyday teaching practice—an eTwinning Learning Event (Holmes, 2012). Using the Community of Inquiry (CoI) Framework to examine the online learning community, it particularly investigates how the online community supports the development of teachers' competence in online collaboration and how social aspects contribute to this discourse. Moreover, the research looks at the impact of facilitation and how it influences critical thinking and meta-cognition.

The research addresses, specifically, online learning communities rather than other types of community such as Communities of Practice or Communities of Interest. Whereas these communities all share some common characteristics and can each contribute to teachers' CPD, the focus of online learning communities on individual learning in the context of a group has important consequences for the nature of the community, cognitive development and learner orchestration (Eraut, 2002; McConnell, 2006; Riel & Polin, 2004). The development of critical thinking and meta-cognition is seen as essential for deep and meaningful understanding (Garrison, Anderson, & Archer, 2001), knowledge development (Garrison, 1991) and the improvement of professional practice (Eraut, 1994).

This chapter begins with a discussion of different types of online communities and the educational experience they offer to participants. This is important to clarify and to take into account when considering the outcomes of this research. This is followed by a discussion of existing research on the CoI framework as it reflects the theoretical assumptions and concepts used in this research and the interrelations between them (Garrison, Anderson, & Archer, 2000). The context of eTwinning Learning Events is described and the methodology of action research explained before the findings of two action research cycles are presented. Finally, there is a discussion and a conclusion that offers an emerging model for designers and facilitators to use to enhance future educational experiences in online learning communities.

Online Learning Communities

A social revolution is taking place in the way information is shared and knowledge is constructed over the Internet (Castells, 2000). Social networking technologies are encouraging interaction, online collaboration and the development of relationships. They are facilitating the use of more social constructivist approaches in distance learning (Anderson & Dron, 2011) and there is a renewed interest by educationalists in the social concept of a 'community' to support groups of learners to collaborate, critically reflect and develop shared meaning with peers online (Ala-Mutka, 2010; OECD, 2008).

A community is more than simply a group of participants with a common interest. Rather, a community involves social interdependence, sustained by relationships and strong emotional ties developed over time (Barab, MaKinster, & Scheckler, 2003). It involves shared experience and knowledge building with a clear focus on practice and collaboration. Moreover, a community offers sufficient shared interest and value that the participants are motivated to interact and return (Leask & Younie, 1999).

The concept of an online community for learning is not without its critics. Grossman, Wineburg, and Woolworth (2000, p. 6) argue that the term *community* is 'an obligatory appendage to every educational innovation' and McConnell (2006, p. 21) cautions that it is 'currently being applied in too many educational contexts with little apparent understanding of what it might, or should, mean'. Fox (2005) wonders whether it is simply a prevailing feeling of nostalgia for the strong, tight communities of the past. Whereas Hodgson and Reynolds (2005) suggest that we are seeing a reaction to a previously exaggerated emphasis on individual autonomy and the social fragmentation that this may bring. Ryberg and Larsen (2008, p. 105) criticise research for distinguishing between the 'real' and the 'virtual' worlds and for treating communities as 'exotic islands and bounded social spaces'; instead they propose the *network* as a better metaphor for social forms of online learning.

Networked learning is seen by some scholars as an alternative approach to learning with technology that embraces network individualism and the multitude of learning resources, opportunities and relationships available via the Internet (Goodyear, Banks, Hodgson, & McConnell, 2004). It 'incorporates insights and assumptions from a number of theoretical perspectives' (Dirckinck-Holmfeld et al., 2004, p. 5) and, unlike Computer Supported Collaborative Learning (CSCL), does not privilege 'collaboration over other kinds of relationships' (2004, p. 12), emphasising instead the value of weak as well as strong ties (Ryberg & Larsen, 2008).

Despite the rhetoric, the vision put forward in networked learning is not at odds with that of online learning communities. On the contrary, networked learning embraces both individual and group learning in the context of multiple communities that embrace and value difference. Communities are thus part of a bigger picture; 'they are special cases of more general network phenomena that rely on a particular form of individualisation' (Jones, 2004, p. 86). The important point raised by the proponents of networked learning is that attention must be paid to issues of democracy, power and culture in an online learning community if we are to avoid an overemphasis on collaboration and consensus (Ferreday & Hodgson, 2009). This in turn implies careful design, organisation and facilitation of the educational experience.

Having discussed the concept of an online learning community, the next section discusses the CoI framework (Garrison et al., 2000) that is used to explore the online learning community.

Community of Inquiry Framework

The CoI framework offers a holistic approach to analysing the use of computer-mediated communication for educational purposes (Garrison et al., 2000). Originally devised for higher education, it has 'been adopted and adapted by hundreds of scholars working throughout the world' (Garrison, Anderson, & Archer, 2010, p. 5), cited in more than 1,500 scholarly papers (Google Scholar as of November 2012) and validated in a number of studies (Arbaugh et al., 2008; Garrison & Arbaugh, 2007). The model's strength lies in the way in which it considers the elements of learning, social interaction, tutoring and facilitation as being interrelated and mutually dependent. They are portrayed as three overlapping elements at the core of the educational experience: cognitive presence, social presence and teaching presence (see Fig. 10.1).

Cognitive presence is defined as 'the extent to which the participants in any particular configuration of a CoI are able to construct meaning through sustained communication' (Garrison & Arbaugh, 2007, p. 89) and is seen as vital to critical thinking and meta-cognition (Akyol & Garrison, 2011). It is at the heart of the learning process and is perhaps the most difficult presence to achieve (Arbaugh, 2007). Indeed, interaction within an online community may be good for group cohesion, but it is no guarantee of purposeful and systemic discourse (Garrison & Cleveland-Innes, 2005).

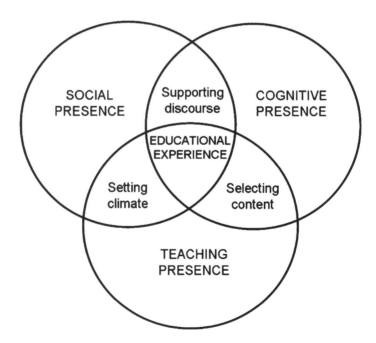

Fig. 10.1 The Community of Inquiry framework (Garrison et al., 2000, p. 88)

Teaching presence relates to the design of the educational setting and the facilitation offered during the learning process. Whereas the former is often the remit of the teacher or tutor, the latter may be shared with the participants as they collaborate and offer each other mutual support (Garrison et al., 2000). Referring to the work of Laurillard, Stratfold, Luckin, Plowman, and Taylor (2000), Anderson, Rourke, Garrison, and Archer (2001) suggest that the design should create a narrative path for learners through the material and activities, with clear learning goals. Moreover, a study by Shea, Sau Li, and Pickett (2006) suggests that teaching presence can reinforce the sense of community perceived by learners.

Social presence is defined as 'the ability of participants in a CoI to project themselves socially and emotionally, as "real" people (i.e. their full personality), through the medium of communication being used' (Garrison et al., 2000, p. 94). It both supports cognitive presence and is itself reinforced by online collaboration and discourse, which, in turn, is facilitated by teaching presence (Bangert, 2008). Social presence has been identified as an important factor for the establishment of trust, the development of a community and the building of social capital (Chen, 2007; Daniel, Schwier, & McCalla, 2003; Gannon-Leary & Fontainha, 2007; Gray, 2004a; Levy, 2003; McConnell, 2006; Moisey, Neu, & Cleveland-Innes, 2008; Tu & Corry, 2001).

Whereas most of the research conducted thus far using this framework has focused on one particular presence 'rather than on the nature of the relationship between the types of presence' (Garrison & Arbaugh, 2007, p. 167) and mainly with the use of quantitative data analysis, the research discussed here addresses all three elements in equal measure and applies both quantitative and qualitative analysis to a study of CPD.

Research Context and Methodology

The research is conducted in the context of the European Commission's eTwinning initiative, funded under the Comenius sub-programme of the Lifelong Learning Programme (LLP).[1] eTwinning started in 2004 to encourage school teachers to work together informally across Europe in joint pedagogical projects using the Internet (Gilleran, 2007). So far, there have been approximately 98,000 schools and 184,000 users (mainly teachers) registered in eTwinning, with 26,000 registered projects.[2] Teachers involved in eTwinning teach a range of subjects at primary and secondary school level in both general and vocational education to pupils between the ages of 4 and 19. A Central Support Service maintains the multilingual eTwinning portal,[3] provides a helpdesk for school teachers and periodically organises events, both

---

[1] http://eacea.ec.europa.eu/llp/comenius/comenius_etwinning_en.php.

[2] As of November 2012: http://www.etwinning.net/en/pub/news/press_corner/statistics.cfm.

[3] http://www.etwinning.net.

online and face-to-face. It is maintained under a public procurement contract by the European Schoolnet (EUN) which, in itself, is a thriving community for school teachers involving the Ministries of Education from across Europe (Leask & Younie, 2001).

Within the eTwinning initiative, Learning Events (LEs) are short-duration, non-formal learning opportunities for teachers to work together on a particular theme supported by a domain expert or tutor, typically a fellow eTwinning teacher. Satisfaction surveys conducted on the LEs and the eTwinning groups (eTwinning, 2009, p. 56) clearly indicated the success of the initiatives and provided a taste of what school teachers felt: 'Providing online training at a central level this school year through the LEs has responded perfectly to the need for further professional development opportunities'. However, they did not reveal details of what had happened and why. Hence, it was decided that more research was needed to understand practical aspects of design and facilitation, such as the role of the tutor, the influence of the LEs' duration on the development of the community and the extent to which the LEs are supporting competence development.

Action research was chosen as the most appropriate methodology, as it involves close collaboration between researcher and practitioners, with an emphasis on promoting change during the research process (Budd, Thorp, and Donohue, 1967, cited in Gray, 2004b) rather than as an afterthought in the research conclusions (Denscombe, 2007). The research was conducted with the tutor, Tiina, a school teacher from Finland, who organised and led the events. Staff of the eTwinning CSS (EUN) was also closely involved and helped to decide on the direction of the research. Action research was used to follow and influence the development of an online LE entitled 'Exploiting Web 2.0: eTwinning and Collaboration'.

An important feature of action research is that it involves cycles, or iterations towards a solution, that involve planning, action, observation and reflection leading to outcomes that transform both theory and practice. This chapter discusses the findings of two LEs, or cycles of action research.

Details of participants and methods used to gather data are described within each LE, below, as they are not the same in each cycle. Online questionnaires, interviews, forum participation logs and forum posts were used to collect data. Analysis of data involved both qualitative and quantitative methods. Qualitative analysis used the concepts and coding schemes of the CoI framework that have been widely used and validated in a number of previous studies (Arbaugh et al., 2008; Garrison & Arbaugh, 2007).

As is appropriate in an action research study, the research questions developed over time, with the support of the EUN staff and the tutor, into the following.

In an eTwinning Learning Event (LE) for school teachers' CPD:

- How does the online learning community influence the development of teachers' cognition, practice and competence?
- How do teaching presence and social presence influence the collaboration, the cognitive presence and the development of the community?

The First Learning Event

The first LE took place over a period of 11 days. Participants were 91 % female, representing 25 nationalities, and while only 3 % were native English speakers using English was not considered a problem (77 %). Fifty-three percent considered themselves experienced participants of eTwinning LEs. Data were collected through a final online questionnaire and analysed manually using the CoI framework as a theoretical lens. The response rate was high, with 82 % of the 156 teachers offering their opinion. Analysis of the questionnaire data revealed a high level of satisfaction with the event (98 %). Here, we briefly discuss the findings focusing on those that led to changes in the second LE; full details of the findings can be read in Holmes (2012).

The first research question considers how the online learning community influences the development of teachers' cognition, practice and competence. The feeling of connectedness was reported to be the same or higher than elsewhere in eTwinning (76 %), with 61 % indicating that the profile pages helped increase immediacy and intimacy (Gunawardena & Zittle, 1997) between participants. There was evidence that the teachers started to see the benefits of collaboration, with 47 % indicating a preference for collaboration and 17 % for learning alone. Several commented on the advantages of combining individual learning with group reflection and sense-making (Stahl, 2003). The teachers also had initial exposure to the challenges of online group dynamics, reciprocation and the role of moderators. While collaboration was seen to be beneficial, when successful some groups faced challenges in self-organising.

Most teachers reported increased confidence and competence in the use of Web 2.0 tools for collaboration (87 %); however, few participants expressed confidence in their ability to manage online groups of students. The results suggested that more personal experience was needed before the teachers would be comfortable in changing their own teaching practice; 'I wish I had more time to experiment more with the tools and communicate and collaborate in online groups' (anonymous, final questionnaire). As Guskey (2002) suggests, activities that are not grounded in everyday teaching practice may be less successful in changing teachers' practice.

Although there was a stronger sense of connectedness, only 27 % reported seeing the community develop as opposed to seeing relationships develop between individuals (43 %). Participants' attention appeared to be focused on the cognitive activities (67 %) with little time for the socio-emotional issues (11 %) that studies suggest can encourage collaboration and foster a community (Kreijns, Kirschner, & Jochems, 2003; Volet & Wosnitza, 2004; Zenios & Holmes, 2010). As a result there was not enough data to answer the second research question on how teaching presence and social presence influence the collaboration, the cognitive presence and the development of community.

The findings were discussed with both the LE tutor and the organisers of the LE activities, in order to agree changes that could enhance critical-thinking and

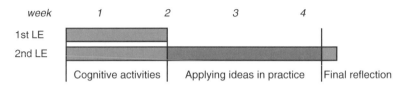

Fig. 10.2 Timing of the second LE compared with the first LE

competence development, increase socialisation and foster the community in the second LE. Three suggestions were made, and subsequently implemented in the second LE. It was suggested that cognitive presence could be reinforced by including explicit time for the teachers to try out the tools in their school and by adding a final activity for sharing stories and reflection amongst peers (see Fig. 10.2). Collaboration and critical thinking could be fostered through an increased teaching presence, with the tutor and the researcher orchestrating activities at key points (Dillenbourg, 2008) and encouraging mutual support. Social presence could be strengthened through the creation of a permanent, specific space for informal discussion in small groups—a virtual staff room.

The Second Learning Event

The second LE took place over 34 days with 142 teachers of 18 nationalities, including 4 % native English speakers. Forty-three percent considered themselves experienced participants of eTwinning and one teacher had also participated in the first LE. Data were once more collected using a final questionnaire with a 58 % response rate. Further data were collected via interviews of selected participants and from the messages in the discussions forums. The coding schemes of the CoI framework were used to analyse the latter, from the point of view of cognitive presence (Garrison et al., 2001), social presence (Rourke, Anderson, Garrison, & Archer, 2001) and teaching presence (Anderson et al., 2001). The results from the three sources were compared and analysed in order to reach conclusions as to the effect of the changes implemented.

The analysis of the results suggests that changes made to the event, specifically the addition of an opportunity to try out ideas in practice and then share reflections with others, had a positive effect on cognitive presence. Participants' comments in the final questionnaire and interviews indicate that those who had been able to apply what they had learned in their teaching practice had benefited from the experience. Several participants indicated that they felt more confident and competent about the use of Web 2.0 tools in their teaching practice (89 %) and for online collaboration with pupils (83 %):

> I was able to apply what I learned in the classroom and my pupils are very excited and they want to learn more (Roberta, female primary school teacher from Rumania).

Table 10.1 Phases of critical inquiry for cognitive presence (Garrison et al., 2001)

Phases of critical inquiry	Description	Example indicators	Socio-cognitive processes
Triggering event	Initial phase, issues and problems emerge	Sense of puzzlement	Asking questions
Exploration	Linking private thoughts to real world, as ideas are explored	Leaps to conclusions	Adds to established points but does not systematically defend/justify/develop addition
Integration	Constructing meaning, moving between reflection and discourse	Connecting ideas, synthesis	Integrating information from various sources—textbook, articles, personal experience
Resolution	Direct or vicarious action as solutions are implemented and assessed	Testing solutions	Evaluating results

In the final reflection activity, the participants had been asked to give an example of what they had done, what impact it had on their teaching practice and what recommendations they would pass to their colleagues. The analysis suggests that this was beneficial for critical thinking and meta-cognition, see Table 10.1. The CoI framework codes cognitive presence into four phases of critical inquiry (Garrison et al., 2001) and associates critical thinking with two of the four phases: integration and resolution. Most of the messages coded at these two levels were in the final reflection activity.

Participants who identified themselves as experienced 'eTwinners' (43 %) were compared with those with little or no experience. The progression from lower levels of cognition to higher levels was evident in the coded messages for participants with little or no previous experience of online collaboration. Figure 10.3 illustrates a typical example, with all posted messages against time for Lenuta, a female teacher of English from Romania. Lenuta stayed at the lower levels of cognition for most of the initial activities, with many messages showing no cognitive presence at all (56 %) or at the triggering event level (28 %). However, she demonstrated critical thinking during the final reflection activity (messages 30–32) with messages at the integration and resolution levels.

Data from interviews revealed that some participants did not feel confident or experienced enough to contribute to the final reflection activity; however, they mentioned how they had learned from having read the contributions of others (lurking). Overall, the reflection activity was useful for reflecting on experience, sharing knowledge and thinking about the wider consequences (meta-cognition).

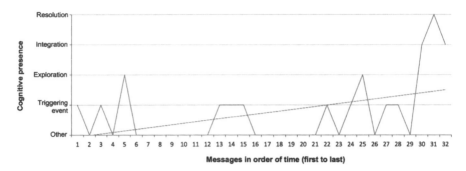

Fig. 10.3 Results of coding cognitive presence for the participant Lenuta

The analysis of the staff room forum suggests that the intervention of the tutors at key points had a positive impact on the discourse. Figure 10.4 shows the number of messages posted each day in the staff room over time. It shows that the messages posted by the participants in the early stages of the LE closely followed those posted by the tutors; however, this was not the case in the later stages when participants exhibited greater self-organisation and autonomy. At this stage the teaching presence was largely derived from the participants themselves supporting one another indicating that it is possible for tutors to step back and allow participants to take more control.

The staff room, where 48 % messages were posted, was seen as a valuable, stable place for reflection, for sharing emotions and for checking on the team's progress:

> I think that the Staff room was a good idea, intended as a really useful tool for the different groups, as a meeting point for members, where they could discuss topics, share proposals and take decisions in team (Annalisa, female teacher of German, from Italy).

Participants indicated that there was a community feeling in the staff room and that it helped to foster social interaction which they perceived as beneficial to their learning. This is in line with Shea and Bidjerano (2009) who found a positive influence of social presence on cognitive presence. These relationships became stronger over time, as the community developed:

> I believe that in some groups closer contacts were built as the course unfolded. It seems to me that people became more open and eager to help when they got hold of how things worked in such events (Beata, female teacher of English, from Poland).

When collaboration was not successful, participants perceived the staff room and the need to interact with others as an additional burden that had little value. Analysis of the messages suggested that when collaboration was less successful it was often associated with a lack of teaching presence or a more directive and formal style of communication as one participant showed.

The social activities in the staff room were initiated by cognitive activities organised by tutors. In other words, the teaching presence was instrumental in

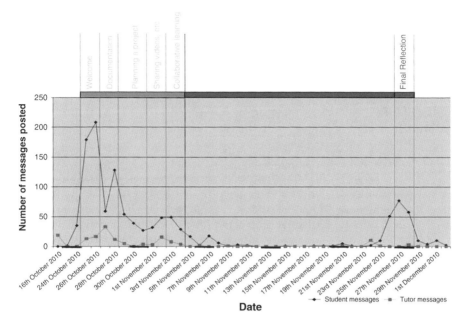

Fig. 10.4   Number of messages posted each day in the staff room over time

fostering effective social and cognitive presence (Rourke et al., 2001; Swan & Shih, 2005). Although interaction contained a strong social element it remained purposeful and primarily focused on learning, as Fig. 10.4 illustrates, there were very few messages posted during the period allotted for practice and interaction died off quickly once the final reflection activity was completed.

Discussion

Overall the research illustrates how an online learning community can support the development of school teachers' competence by providing opportunities for CPD that support critical inquiry with peers in the context of everyday teaching practice. The LE activities encourage an epistemology of practice (Eraut, 1994) with teachers expressing their understanding of what they are learning, and developing that understanding over time.

The findings from both LEs suggest that the cognitive activities provided an opportunity for school teachers to develop their technical skills and knowledge-*for*-practice (Cochran-Smith & Lytle, 1999). Evidence from the second LE supports the argument that it is also important for school teachers to have the opportunity to apply what they are learning in their own teaching practice in order to see the impact on their pupils' learning and develop knowledge-*in*-practice.

The combination of cognitive activities in the LE and the application of ideas in practice encouraged reflection-in-practice (Eraut, 1995) in the online discourse with peers. Moreover, the results from the final reflection activity of the second LE suggest that school teachers who are unable to try out ideas directly for themselves may still learn vicariously (Ertmer, 2005; Lave & Wenger, 1991) by collaborating and reflecting with others in the community. By allowing school teachers to see the impact of what they are learning on their teaching practice and reflect on the implications with other school teachers, the research suggests that they gained belief in the value of the changes being applied and were motivated to continue learning (Boyle et al., 2004; Guskey, 2002; Vescio et al., 2008).

The research highlights the importance of strengthening cognitive presence within the online community through cognitive activities and collaboration that encourages practitioner inquiry and critical thinking (Akyol & Garrison, 2011; Garrison et al., 2001; Garrison & Cleveland-Innes, 2005; Groundwater-Smith & Dadds, 2004). It offers empirical evidence as to the value for school teachers of reflecting on their practice (Akbari, 2007) with peers, fostering meta-cognition and connections to the wider social, cultural and political issues associated with teaching, thereby developing the meta knowledge-*of*-practice (Cochran-Smith & Lytle, 1999) that is essential for long-term teacher change and competence development.

The research suggests that cognitive development, reflection of 'a more deliberative character' (Eraut, 1995, p. 14) and the creation of an online community take time (Vratulis & Dobson, 2008)—the second LE was extended from 11 to 34 days to accommodate the additional practice and reflection activities. This requires considerable commitment from busy school teachers which must not be underestimated. Yet, the research also suggests that school teachers are often prepared to invest additional time in such CPD and in a professional community if it provides them with immediate benefit for their teaching (Bolam et al., 2005; Duncan-Howell, 2010). The LE appeared to be most beneficial for those participants who have little or no experience in the subject being learnt (in this case Web 2.0 tools). In undertaking the activities, they benefitted from collaborating with peers who were more experienced and who shared their knowledge. In return, the experienced participants supported and guided their peers.

The research supports the view that online collaboration and discourse, cognitive development and sense of community are significantly influenced by the teaching presence (Garrison et al., 2000; Shea et al., 2006; Shea & Bidjerano, 2009; Swan & Shih, 2005). This may be initially provided by the tutor in the design of the activities and in online moderation, framing discussion within the learning context, encouraging critical thinking and offering feedback (Anderson et al., 2001; Boud & Walker, 1998; Garrison et al., 2001; Kanuka, Rourke, & Laflamme, 2007; McConnell, 2006), as demonstrated by the final reflection activity in the second LE. However, the results show that it is possible for the tutor to step back as the community develops and teaching presence emerges from the participants themselves offering mutual support and guidance (Hlapanis & Dimitracopoulou, 2007; Salmon, 2000). The tutor needs to find an appropriate balance between structure and guidance on the one hand, and flexibility and autonomy on the other (Vlachopoulos & Cowan, 2010). Thomas, Jones, Packham, and Miller (2004) suggest that finding an appropriate level of teaching presence requires competence in online moderation, and an ability to organise, understand and encourage learning, rather than a deep knowledge of the subject matter. Moreover, without appropriate teaching presence, the results confirm that participants tend to stay at the lower levels of critical thinking as seen in the coding of cognitive presence (Angeli, Valanides, & Bonk, 2003; Pawan, Paulus, Yalcin, & Chang, 2003).

The research suggests that social presence is essential for effective collaboration, for engendering the trust and confidence needed for online reflection and for fostering the development of the community. Social presence was engendered in the LE by the social affordances of the environment (Conole & Dyke, 2004; Kreijns, Kirschner, & Jochems, 2002), such as the online discussion forums and participant profile pages. However, as the results of the second LE suggest, just as important was the inclusion of time, space and activities specifically dedicated to social interaction and building social presence (Kreijns et al., 2003; Swan & Shih, 2005). The addition of a virtual staff room, with small groups at round tables and activities to support informal reflection, helped to increase group cohesion (Seddon & Postlethwaite, 2007), to provide the necessary 'grounding' for group work (Stahl, 2005) and to foster a sense of community (McMillan & Chavis, 1986).

The research supports the view that cognitive presence, teaching presence and social presence are interrelated and interdependent in an online learning community (Garrison, Cleveland-Innes, & Fung, 2010), and a careful balance of all three is required to ensure a purposeful and effective educational experience for its participants. Social interaction was important; however, the community was primarily focused on achieving the learning activities (Lockhorst, Admiraal, & Pilot, 2010) and was therefore ephemeral, being active only for as long as it served the purpose of learning (Garrison & Arbaugh, 2007; Riel & Polin, 2004).

The reliability and validity of these findings should be considered. The reliability of qualitative interviews can be criticised as potentially offering inaccurate accounts of experience that can be biased by the researcher's interpretation. However, interviews do allow participants to offer their own reflections and allow researchers to gain insight into their perceptions, attitudes and values (Silverman, 2006). In this study, the participants clearly appreciated the opportunity to do so. Reliability in the questionnaires was ensured by pilot testing and in the interviews was ensured by having a common structure with predetermined questions. The qualitative analysis was carried out by a single researcher, and then the findings were checked against the notes made by the tutor Tiina. There were no issues with inter-rater reliability.

Validity was ensured by several means. A mixed methods approach was used to triangulate, or cross reference the data. The interview data was supplemented by analysis of questionnaire data and observational data in the form of forum posts and activity logs. The action research methodology enabled a flexible and reflexive approach whereby emerging findings influenced future actions.

The tutor Tiina acted as a critical friend and regular reflexive discussions were held. For example, when it was realised that there was confusion with the term 'competence', a supplementary questionnaire was issued. Finally, the qualitative data was analysed using the previously validated coding schemes of the CoI framework. Their validation and use in many publications provides some confidence in their reliability (Garrison et al., 2010) and facilitates comparison and generalisation of results.

The CoI model helped to ensure that the results were analysed both holistically and from the point of view of cognitive, social and teaching aspects. Applying the CoI coding schemes was straightforward for the coding of cognitive presence, revealing interesting insights into the change in critical thinking over time. It was less so for the coding of social presence, where the indicators proposed (Rourke et al., 2001) needed to be interpreted in the context of the social affordances (Kreijns et al., 2002) offered by Web 2.0 environments, with their automated support for threaded discussions, replying and profiling. Similarly for the coding of teaching presence, it was felt that the proposed indicators (Anderson et al., 2001) suggested instruction and 'teacher as subject expert', rather than being more neutral with a stance that equally embraces peer learning and 'tutor as facilitator'. The CoI framework would benefit from an update to the indicators proposed for coding messages, based upon recent research such as discussed here.

A model for conducting teachers' CPD in an online learning community, with tutor moderation, emerges from the research and may support future eTwinning LEs to be effective educational experiences. The model presented in Figs. 10.5 and 10.6 may also inspire useful reflections on other forms of online professional learning community; note that aspects concerning online moderation are presented separately as they may be a useful reference for tutors and online moderators (eModerators) in general. The model includes suggestions, based upon practical experience from the two LEs, concerning the pre-allocation of participants to small groups for project work; the establishment of basic rules for online interaction in forums; and the provision of opportunities for creative expression as well as structured discourse. For a full description of the research and model see Holmes (2012).

Conclusions

There is a renewed interest in the social concept of community to support groups of learners to collaborate online, critically reflect and develop shared meaning with peers. Teachers' CPD is one area where online learning communities are seen as offering valuable opportunities for authentic and personalised learning, informal exchange of good practice and peer learning. This research offers a contribution to the literature on practice in teachers' CPD and to the CoI framework.

Action research conducted in the context of an eTwinning Learning Event (LE) and discussed in this chapter offers useful insights into how an online learning

Aspects relevant to design of school teachers' continuous professional development (CPD) in an eTwinning Learning Event (LE):

✓   **Online learning community.** An eTwinning LE is effectively a community of teachers that can provide a supportive, trusted environment to exchange experience and share good practice during CPD activities at a distance. However, it takes time to establish a community and LEs need to be sufficiently long for relationships and trust to develop through social interaction (e.g. three to four weeks).

✓   **Social space.** To support social interaction, it is useful to have a dedicated space for informal discussion to take place between participants at any time during the course of the activities (e.g. a virtual 'staff room').

✓   **Social Interaction.** The teachers should be supported to get to know one another via the functionalities offered in the online learning environment for social interaction (e.g. profile pages, an informal 'staff room', etc.).

✓   **Critical reflection.** Teachers may benefit from discussions with their peers, as part of the CPD activities, on what they are learning and their practical experience. This reflection is both intellectual and emotional. It helps them to understand the wider consequences for their own teaching practice and their professional competence development.

✓   **Active 'lurking'.** Less experienced teachers who are unable to try things out for themselves or do not contribute fully to the discussions are still likely to benefit from participating in a community that includes more experienced teachers.

✓   **Teaching practice.** Teachers are more likely to be motivated to participate if the community and the CPD activities are clearly focused on improving teaching practice and the learning outcomes of pupils. Moreover, they are more likely to be convinced of new ideas if they have the time and opportunity to try them out in their everyday teaching practice as part of the CPD activities.

✓   **Collaboration.** The community is fostered by activities that encourage participants to get to know one another and to collaborate (e.g. welcome activities and joint projects). Teachers may prefer to collaborate in small groups and pre-allocating the participants according to some common interest may help them to get started (e.g. in groups of up to 10 participants who teach pupils of similar ages).

✓   **Creative expression.** The structured discussions may be usefully balanced by opportunities for the teachers to express themselves freely and creatively using text, pictures, diagrams and videos (using online blogs, Google docs®, YouTube®, etc.).

✓   **Competence in online moderation.** In order to support the development of teachers' competence in online collaboration and moderation, in addition to the main subject of the LE, the CPD activities could usefully finish with a final reflection on whether teachers' expectations for collaboration had been met, the lessons they had learnt from their experience and how their own competence in online moderation had developed.

Fig. 10.5 Emerging model of an online learning community for school teachers' CPD

Aspects relevant to online moderation of an eTwinning Learning Event (LE) by a tutor:

✓ **Key role of the tutor**. The tutor has an essential role to play in designing activities and orchestrating learning, and therefore should be experienced in online moderation. It is preferable that the tutor is also knowledgeable about the subject(s) being addressed in the activities or that the expertise exists with some of the participant teachers.

✓ **Tutor presence**. The availability of a tutor gives the teachers confidence that there is someone there to support them if needed and can help to engender a sense of community. The tutor should guide the LE according to the experience of the teachers and their development over time. It may be appropriate to offer feedback and support at the start of the activities, but then to step back as the teachers become more autonomous and offer each other support.

✓ **Social presence**. Social and emotional aspects are important and should form an integral part of the activities (e.g. sharing feelings during discussions). The tutor should encourage sharing of experiences and feelings.

✓ **Social practice**. It may be useful for the tutor to establish basic rules of good practice for social interaction in the discussion forums and social space. These rules could be usefully developed with the LE participants before the CPD activities by asking them what they expect from one another, from the tutor and from the community as a whole.

✓ **Reflection-in-practice**. Wherever possible, teachers should be encouraged and supported to act upon their reflections. This includes, for example, giving them the possibility to change groups if they find that collaboration is not working.

✓ **Cognitive presence**. During the course of the LE, the design of the activities and the guidance of the tutor should encourage teachers to try out in their teaching practice what they are learning and to discuss their experience with their peers. The tutor should encourage critical thinking in the discussions by, for example, initially prompting reflection around key questions. Teachers are likely to need encouragement to further explain their answers so that peers may better understand and build upon their contribution.

✓ **Closing the community**. Finally, the tutor should close the community down once the CPD activities have finished in order to avoid disappointment due to the reduction in interaction that typically follows the end of learning activities.

Fig. 10.6 Emerging model for online moderation (eModeration) of an online learning community for school teachers' CPD

community can support the CPD of school teachers. The research illustrates, and supports, Guskey's (2002) claim that there are positive benefits for teachers of trying-out what they are learning in the context of their everyday teaching practice as part of CPD activities rather than afterwards when the training has finished.

It supports the view that teachers' motivation, attitudes and propensity for change may be positively influenced by seeing for themselves the impact on their students' learning (Ertmer, 2005; Ottenbreit-Leftwich et al., 2010). The research highlights the importance of online moderation and the essential role that a tutor or teacher has in designing activities that engender collaboration, encourage critical thinking and foster mutual support amongst peers. It shows how tutors may effectively provide different levels of support and guidance at different stages of the community's development in order to help participants to build their confidence, develop their autonomy and become self-organising. These aspects are important as they help learning to go beyond the simple acquisition of skills and prepare learners for the ill-defined problems of the future—an essential feature of effective CPD.

The results suggest that social presence is essential for effective collaboration and that sufficient time, space and activities should be included for social interaction, e.g. virtual staff room. The use of the CoI framework was valuable in analysing the online learning community as it allowed a holistic view as well as examining the cognitive, social and teaching presence. The use of action research enabled further consideration of how the design of the learning environment and the role of the tutor influence the educational experience. A model emerges from the research that may be useful for designing and moderating future eTwinning LEs. It may also inspire other, similar, examples of using online learning communities for CPD, for teachers or other related professional groups.

Acknowledgments Many thanks to Tiina Sarisalmi and to Anne Gilleran, Riina Vuorikari and other colleagues at the European Schoolnet (EUN) for their invaluable support.

References

Akbari, R. (2007). Reflections on reflection: A critical appraisal of reflective practices in L2 teacher education. *System, 35*(2), 192–207.

Akyol, Z., & Garrison, D. R. (2011). Assessing metacognition in an online community of inquiry. *The Internet and Higher Education, 14*(3), 183–190.

Ala-Mutka, K. (2010). *Learning in informal online networks and communities.* Seville, Spain: Institute for Prospective Technological Studies (IPTS), JRC, European Commission.

Anderson, T., & Dron, J. (2011). Three generations of distance education pedagogy. *The International Review of Research in Open and Distance Learning, 12*(3), 80–97. Retrieved April 9, 2012, from http://www.irrodl.org/index.php/irrodl/article/view/890/1663

Anderson, T., Rourke, L., Garrison, D., & Archer, W. (2001). Assessing teaching presence in a computer conferencing context. *Journal of Asynchronous Learning Networks, 5*(2), 1–17.

Angeli, C., Valanides, N., & Bonk, C. J. (2003). Communication in a web-based conferencing system: the quality of computer-mediated interactions. *British Journal of Educational Technology, 34*(1), 31–43.

Arbaugh, J. B. (2007). An empirical verification of the Community of Inquiry framework. *Journal of Asynchronous Learning Networks, 11*(1), 73–85.

Arbaugh, J. B., Cleveland-Innes, M., Diaz, S. R., Garrison, D. R., Ice, P., Richardson, J. C., et al. (2008). Developing a community of inquiry instrument: Testing a measure of the

Community of Inquiry framework using a multi-institutional sample. *The Internet and Higher Education, 11*(3–4), 133–136.

Avalos, B. (2011). Teacher professional development in teaching and teacher education over ten years. *Teaching and Teacher Education, 27*(1), 10–20.

Bangert, A. W. (2008). The influence of social presence and teaching presence on the quality of online critical inquiry. *Journal of Computing in Higher Education, 20*(1), 34–61.

Barab, S. A., MaKinster, J. G., & Scheckler, R. (2003). Designing system dualities: Characterizing a web-supported professional development community. In S. A. Barab, R. Kling, & J. Gray (Eds.), *Designing for virtual communities in the service of learning* (pp. 53–119). Cambridge, England: Cambridge University Press.

Bolam, R., McMahon, A., Stoll, L., Thomas, S., Wallace, M., Greenwood, A., et al. (2005). *Creating and sustaining effective professional learning communities.* Nottingham, England: DfES Publications.

Boud, D., & Walker, D. (1998). Promoting reflection in professional courses: The challenge of context. *Studies in Higher Education, 23*(2), 191–206.

Boyle, B., While, D., & Boyle, T. (2004). A longitudinal study of teacher change: What makes professional development effective? *Curriculum Journal, 15*(1), 45–68.

Castells, M. (2000). *The rise of the network society* (2nd ed., Vol. 1). Oxford, England: Blackwell Publishing.

Chen, I. Y. L. (2007). The factors influencing members' continuance intentions in professional virtual communities a longitudinal study. *Journal of Information Science, 33*(4), 451–467.

Cochran-Smith, M., & Lytle, S. L. (1999). Relationships of knowledge and practice: teacher learning in communities. *Review of Research in Education, 24,* 249–305.

Conole, G., & Dyke, M. (2004). Discussion understanding and using technological affordances: A response to Boyle and Cook. *ALT-J: Research in Learning Technology, 12*(3), 301–308.

Daniel, B., Schwier, R., & McCalla, G. (2003). Social capital in virtual learning communities and distributed communities of practice. *Canadian Journal of Learning and Technology, 29*(3), 113–139.

Denscombe, M. (2007). *The good research guide: For small-scale social research projects.* Maidenhead, England: Open University Press.

Dillenbourg, P. (2008). Integrating technologies into educational ecosystems. *Distance Education, 29*(2), 127–140.

Dirckinck-Holmfeld, L., Esnault, L., Gustafson, J., Hodgson, V., Lindström, B., Jones, C., et al. (2004). EQUEL position paper—Special interest group 6: The theory and practice of computer supported collaborative learning. Coordinated by Lancaster University, EU Commission e-learning initiative.

Duncan-Howell, J. (2010). Teachers making connections: Online communities as a source of professional learning. *British Journal of Educational Technology, 41*(2), 324–340.

Eraut, M. (1994). *Developing professional knowledge and competence.* Abingdon, England: Routledge.

Eraut, M. (1995). Schon shock: a case for refraining reflection-in-action? *Teachers and Teaching: Theory and Practice, 1*(1), 9–22.

Eraut, M. (2002). *Conceptual analysis and research questions: Do the concepts of "Learning Community" and "Community of Practice" provide added value?* Paper presented at the Annual Meeting of the American Educational Research Association. Retrieved December 26, 2011, from http://eric.ed.gov/ERICWebPortal/contentdelivery/servlet/ERICServlet?accno=ED466030

Ertmer, P. (2005). Teacher pedagogical beliefs: The final frontier in our quest for technology integration? *Educational Technology Research and Development, 53*(4), 25–39.

eTwinning. (2009). *Beyond school projects—A report on eTwinning 2008-2009.* Brussels, Belgium: eTwinning Central Support Service.

Ferreday, D., & Hodgson, V. (2009). *The tyranny of participation and collaboration in networked learning.* Paper presented at the 6th International Conference on Networked Learning.

Retrieved April 26, 2009, from http://www.networkedlearningconference.org.uk/past/nlc2008/abstracts/PDFs/Hodgson_640-647.pdf

Fox, S. (2005). An actor-network critique of community in higher education: implications for networked learning. *Studies in Higher Education, 30*(1), 95–110.

Gannon-Leary, P. M., & Fontainha, E. (2007). Communities of Practice and virtual learning communities: Benefits, barriers and success factors. *eLearning Papers, 5*. Retrieved December 26, 2008, from http://www.elearningpapers.eu/index.php?page=doc&doc_id=10219&doclng=6

Garrison, D. R. (1991). Critical thinking and adult education: A conceptual model for developing critical thinking in adult learners. *International Journal of Lifelong Education, 10*(4), 287–303.

Garrison, D. R., Anderson, T., & Archer, W. (2000). Critical inquiry in a text-based environment: Computer conferencing in higher education. *The Internet and Higher Education, 2*(2–3), 87–105.

Garrison, D. R., Anderson, T., & Archer, W. (2001). Critical thinking, cognitive presence, and computer conferencing in distance education. *American Journal of Distance Education, 15*(1), 7–23.

Garrison, D. R., Anderson, T., & Archer, W. (2010). The first decade of the community of inquiry framework: A retrospective. *The Internet and Higher Education, 13*(1–2), 5–9.

Garrison, D. R., & Arbaugh, J. B. (2007). Researching the community of inquiry framework: Review, issues, and future directions. *The Internet and Higher Education, 10*(3), 157–172.

Garrison, D. R., & Cleveland-Innes, M. (2005). Facilitating cognitive presence in online learning: Interaction is not enough. *American Journal of Distance Education, 19*(3), 133–148.

Garrison, D. R., Cleveland-Innes, M., & Fung, T. S. (2010). Exploring causal relationships among teaching, cognitive and social presence: Student perceptions of the community of inquiry framework. *The Internet and Higher Education, 13*(1–2), 31–36.

Gilleran, A. (2007). eTwinning—A new path for European schools. *eLearning Papers, 5*. Retrieved December 26, 2008, from http://www.elearningpapers.eu/index.php?page=doc&doc_id=10218&doclng=6

Goodyear, P., Banks, S., Hodgson, V., & McConnell, D. (2004). *Advances in research on networked learning*. Dordrecht, The Netherlands: Springer.

Gray, B. (2004a). Informal learning in an online community of practice. *Journal of Distance Education, 19*(1), 20–35.

Gray, D. E. (2004b). *Doing research in the real world*. London: Sage Publications Ltd.

Grossman, P., Wineburg, S., & Woolworth, S. (2000). *What makes teacher community different from a gathering of teachers?* Seattle, WA: Center for the Study of Teaching and Policy, University of Washington.

Groundwater-Smith, S., & Dadds, M. (2004). Critical practitioner inquiry: Towards responsible professional communities of practice. In C. Day & J. Sachs (Eds.), *International handbook on the continuing professional development of teachers* (pp. 238–263). Maidenhead, England: Open University Press.

Gunawardena, C., & Zittle, F. (1997). Social presence as a predictor of satisfaction within a computer-mediated conferencing environment. *American Journal of Distance Education, 11*(3), 8–26.

Guskey, T. R. (2002). Professional development and teacher change. *Teachers and Teaching: Theory and Practice, 8*(3), 381–391.

Hlapanis, G., & Dimitracopoulou, A. (2007). The school-teacher's learning community: Matters of communication analysis. *Technology, Pedagogy and Education, 16*(2), 133–151.

Hodgson, V., & Reynolds, M. (2005). Consensus, difference and 'multiple communities' in networked learning. *Studies in Higher Education, 30*(1), 11–24.

Holmes, B. (2012). *Online learning communities for school teachers' continuous professional development: The cognitive, social and teaching aspects of an eTwinning Learning Event*. Unpublished doctoral thesis, Lancaster University. Retrieved from http://dl.dropbox.com/u/73078359/Holmes%20PhD%20Online%20Learning%20Communities%20CC.pdf

Jones, C. (2004). Networks and learning: communities, practices and the metaphor of networks. *ALT-J: Research in Learning Technology, 12*(1), 81–93.

Kanuka, H., Rourke, L., & Laflamme, E. (2007). The influence of instructional methods on the quality of online discussion. *British Journal of Educational Technology, 38*(2), 260–271.

Kreijns, K., Kirschner, P. A., & Jochems, W. (2002). The sociability of computer-supported collaborative learning environments. *Journal of Education Technology & Society, 5*(1), 822.

Kreijns, K., Kirschner, P. A., & Jochems, W. (2003). Identifying the pitfalls for social interaction in computer-supported collaborative learning environments: a review of the research. *Computers in Human Behavior, 19*(3), 335–353.

Laurillard, D., Stratfold, M., Luckin, R., Plowman, L., & Taylor, J. (2000). Affordances for learning in a non-linear narrative medium. *Journal of Interactive Media in Education (JIME), 2*. Retrieved December 30, 2011, from http://jime.open.ac.uk/jime/issue/view/18

Lave, J., & Wenger, E. (1991). *Situated learning: Legitimate peripheral participation.* Cambridge, England: Cambridge University Press.

Leask, M., & Younie, S. (1999). *Characteristics of effective on-line communities for teachers: issues arising from research.* Paper presented at the EDEN 1999 Open Classrooms Conference.

Leask, M., & Younie, S. (2001). The European schoolnet. an online. European community for teachers: a valuable professional resource? *Teacher Development, 5*(2), 157–175.

Levy, P. (2003). A methodological framework for practice-based research in networked learning. *Instructional Science, 31*(1), 87–109.

Lockhorst, D., Admiraal, W., & Pilot, A. (2010). CSCL in teacher training: what learning tasks lead to collaboration? *Technology, Pedagogy and Education, 19*(1), 63–78.

Luppicini, R. (2007). *Online learning communities.* Charlotte, NC: Information Age Publishing.

McConnell, D. (2006). *E-learning groups and communities.* Maidenhead, England: Open University Press.

McMillan, D. W., & Chavis, D. M. (1986). Sense of community: A definition and theory. *Journal of Community Psychology, 14*(1), 6–23.

Moisey, S., Neu, C., & Cleveland-Innes, M. (2008). Community building and computer-mediated conferencing. *Journal of Distance Education, 22*(2), 15–42.

OECD (2008). Innovating to learn, learning to innovate: Paris, OECD.

Ottenbreit-Leftwich, A. T., Glazewski, K. D., Newby, T. J., & Ertmer, P. A. (2010). Teacher value beliefs associated with using technology: Addressing professional and student needs. *Computers & Education, 55*(3), 1321–1335.

Pawan, F., Paulus, T., Yalcin, S., & Chang, C. (2003). Online learning: Patterns of engagement and interaction among in-service teachers. *Language, Learning & Technology, 7*(3), 119–140.

Riel, M., & Polin, L. (2004). Online learning communities: Common ground and critical differences in designing technical environments. In S. Barab, R. Kling, & B. Gray (Eds.), *Designing for virtual communities in the service of learning* (pp. 16–50). Cambridge, England: Cambridge University Press.

Rourke, L., Anderson, T., Garrison, D., & Archer, W. (2001). Assessing social presence in asynchronous text-based computer conferencing. *Journal of Distance Education, 14*(2), 50–71.

Ryberg, T., & Larsen, M. (2008). Networked identities—Understanding relations between strong and weak ties in networked environments. *Journal of Computer Assisted Learning, 24*(2), 103–115.

Salmon, G. (2000). *E-moderating: The key to teaching and learning online.* London: Kogan Page.

Seddon, K., & Postlethwaite, K. (2007). Creating and testing a model for tutors and participants to support the collaborative construction of knowledge online. *Technology, Pedagogy and Education, 16*(2), 177–198.

Shea, P., & Bidjerano, T. (2009). Community of inquiry as a theoretical framework to foster "epistemic engagement" and "cognitive presence" in online education. *Computers & Education, 52*, 543–553.

Shea, P., Sau Li, C., & Pickett, A. (2006). A study of teaching presence and student sense of learning community in fully online and web-enhanced college courses. *The Internet and Higher Education, 9*(3), 175–190.

Silverman, D. (2006). *Interpreting qualitative data: Methods for analyzing talk, text, and interaction* (3rd ed.). London: Sage Publications Ltd.

Stahl, G. (2003). *Meaning and interpretation in collaboration.* Paper presented at the Proceedings of the International Conference on Computer Support for Collaborative Learning (CSCL'03). Retrieved November 30, 2008, from http://www.cs.colorado.edu/~gerry/cscl/papers/ch20.pdf

Stahl, G. (2005). Group cognition in computer-assisted collaborative learning. *Journal of Computer Assisted Learning, 21*(2), 79–90.

Swan, K., & Shih, L. F. (2005). On the nature and development of social presence in online course discussions. *Journal of Asynchronous Learning Networks, 9*(3), 115–136.

Thomas, B., Jones, P., Packham, G., & Miller, C. (2004). *Student perceptions of effective E-moderation: a qualitative investigation of E-College Wales.* Paper presented at the Networked Learning 2004. Retrieved April 5, 2012, from http://www.networkedlearningconference.org.uk/past/nlc2004/proceedings/Individual_Papers/Thomas_et_al.htm

Tu, C.-H., & Corry, M. (2001). A paradigm shift for online community research. *Distance Education, 22*(2), 245–263.

Vescio, V., Ross, D., & Adams, A. (2008). A review of research on the impact of professional learning communities on teaching practice and student learning. *Teaching and Teacher Education, 24*(1), 80–91.

Vlachopoulos, P., & Cowan, J. (2010). Reconceptualising moderation in asynchronous online discussions using grounded theory. *Distance Education, 31*(1), 23–36.

Volet, S., & Wosnitza, M. (2004). Social affordances and students' engagement in cross-national online learning: An exploratory study. *Journal of Research in International Education, 3*(1), 5–29.

Vratulis, V., & Dobson, T. M. (2008). Social negotiations in a wiki environment: A case study with pre-service teachers. *Educational Media International, 45*(4), 285–294.

Zenios, M., & Holmes, B. (2010). Knowledge creation in networked learning: combined tools and affordances. Paper presented at the Proceedings of the 7th International Conference on Networked Learning 2010. Retrieved June 24, 2010, from http://www.lancs.ac.uk/fss/organisations/netlc/past/nlc2010/abstracts/Zenios.html

Chapter 11
Analysing Learning Ties to Stimulate Continuous Professional Development in the Workplace

Bieke Schreurs

Introduction

In this chapter we look at Networked Learning in the context of continuous professional development of teachers in the workplace. Networked learning involves the use of information and communication technology (ICT) to promote collaborative connections between learners, their tutors/instructors and learning resources (Goodyear, Banks, Hodgson, & McConnell, 2004). As ICT drives increasingly varied forms of mediated collaboration and contact, the field of Networked Learning seeks to provide accounts of how learners appropriate these new tools to learn on and through the Internet. The field's focus is on how learners (or learning designers) can build and cultivate social networks, seeing technology as just one (albeit critical) enabler, rather than ICT-innovation as an end in itself (Schreurs, Teplovs, Furgeson, Buckingham-Shum, & De Laat, 2013).

To know how to support Networked Learning in the workplace, it is important to get insight in how professionals learn from each other by building up connections to support their continuous professional development. Networked Learning Theory provides a lens to look at continuous professional development from this social perspective. We believe that greater awareness of how professionals are connected, and how these connections are driven by their work-related problems, may help to raise awareness about the presence of learning spaces, populated by the networks/communities, in which professionals participate (De Laat, 2012). This awareness facilitates learning between professionals as they can (independently, or with the help of a facilitator) jointly utilise the architecture of these professional development networks (Schreurs & De Laat, 2012). To do so, professionals first need to get insights into their own learning relationships and the networks that exist around them. Therefore we will represent a methodology to capture continuous professional development

B. Schreurs (✉)
LOOK, Open Universiteit, Heerlen, The Netherlands
e-mail: bieke.schreurs@ou.nl

V. Hodgson et al. (eds.), *The Design, Experience and Practice of Networked Learning*, 207
Research in Networked Learning, DOI 10.1007/978-3-319-01940-6_11,
© Springer International Publishing Switzerland 2014

activities in the workplace. The description of the methodology will show how the insights gained by the teachers in their own social learning activities as part of their continuous professional development can help them to organise their learning space to support their own professional development. This methodology to capture continuous professional development in the workplace resulted in the development of a web 2.0 tool, The Network Awareness Tool (De Laat & Schreurs, 2011). We will describe how the tool can be applied in the field of Networked Learning and can be designed as a plugin in online learning environments visualising data to understand and stimulate networked learning activities both online as in the workplace.

A Networked Learning Perspective on Continuous Professional Development

Organisations, when thinking of continuous professional development, often rely on refreshment courses given by experts, in-service training, or personalised learning trajectories. But formal learning activities like training and workshops are often seen as less effective due to the fact trainings are to 'far' away from the daily practice and teachers find it difficult to transform the insights gained in formal trainings to concrete expertise usable in their daily teaching. Therefore both research literature and educational institutions are moving beyond the restriction of traditional activities such as workshops and short trainings to encompass a more complex and broader view on continuous professional development. At the same time there is a large body of research that convincingly shows that forms of informal work-related learning are important drivers for professional development (Berings, 2006; De Laat, 2011; Eraut, 2000; Marsick & Watkins, 1990; Smith, 2008). Also teachers themselves place a high value on learning informally (yet strategically) with and from each other (Armour & Yelling, 2007). But until now, there is no common agreement on what informal learning characterises or how it can be measured. Recently a shared notion is that the social aspect of informal learning is often overlooked and that we need to pay attention to the cultural and social relations that characterise informal learning in the workplace (Eraut, 2004; Smith, 2008).

In our view the pedagogical framework for Networked Learning, based on the work of McConnell (1994, 2006), provides us the lens through which we look at the social learning component of continuous professional development. The learning component here is seen as a form of informal learning situated in practice, where people rely strongly on their social contacts for assistance and development (De Laat & Coenders, 2011). In schools, continuous professional development involves opportunities for teachers to share their expertise, learn from peers, and collaborate on real-world projects (Vrasidas & Glass, 2004). Continuous professional development can be regarded as a form of bottom-up knowledge creation, because teachers themselves learn from and with each other and develop learning outcomes through their interactions.

Networked learning focuses on the *diversity of social relationships* that people develop, the *strategies* they use to maintain them and the *value* this creates for learning (De Laat, 2012). Networked learning stresses the importance of an evaluation of the ongoing learning process and the creation of a supportive (online) learning environment (McConnell, 2006). But continuous professional development in the workplace is difficult to evaluate because it is often invisible to others and even the learners themselves may not be aware of the learning that occurs. The knowledge acquired can be tacit and the learning activities are not corresponding to the traditional idea of learning as codified propositional knowledge (Eraut, 2004). As a consequence continuous professional development activities in organisations go undetected, remain off the radar of HR departments and management staff and are therefore hard to assess, manage and support (De Laat & Schreurs, 2013) and for that reason there is little practical evidence how continuous professional development in the workplace can be supported by the use of ICT. Therefore a great need is recognised in research, policy and practice for tools that can visualise continuous professional development activities in the workplace. By so implementing these tools, we can make the bottom-up learning more visible and create insights into how we can support the learning networks to become more efficient and embedded within an organisation.

This leads to the following main research question in this chapter: How can Networked Learning Theory help to visualise teachers' professional development?

A Methodology to Investigate Continuous Professional Development in the Workplace

The methodology we present is designed to allow professionals to visualise their continuous professional development networks in the workplace and assess it collaboratively to optimise their learning environment. The type of continuous professional development we investigate is open, self-determined and based on collaborative learning activities. The methodology is based on former work in the field of Networked Learning (De Laat, Lally, & Lipponen, 2007; Haythornthwaite & De Laat, 2010; Toikkanen & Lipponen, 2011) and is closely linked to and uses methodologies of Social Network Theory and Sociometric, Social Capital Theory and Communities of Practice. The methodology makes use of a mixed methods approach to triangulate several data sources (De Laat, 2006). The aim of the multi-method approach is to paint a more complete picture of social processes teacher in professional development networks are engaged in.

First we will present the methodology and the philosophy behind it. Secondly we will present the results of the paper-based method that has been applied with over 150 teachers and management staff in 5 different projects. The method is designed to triangulate, validate and contextualise our findings and to stay close or be connected to the first-hand experiences of the participants themselves.

This multi-method research framework combines data collection methods based on social network analysis (SNA) to find out 'who is talking to whom', content analysis (CA) to find out 'what they are talking about', and contextual analysis (CxA) focusing on the experiences and settings of the participants to find out 'why they are talking as they do' (De Laat, 2006).

Step 1. Social Network Theory: Who Is Talking to Whom

According to Moreno (1947), Sociometric tests show 'in a dramatic and precise fashion that every group has beneath its superficial, tangible, visible, readable structure an underlying intangible, invisible, unofficial structure, but one which is more alive, real and dynamic than the other' (Moreno, 1947, p. 268). To investigate continuous professional development, it is exactly this invisible and informal structure this study wants to bring to light. Social Network Theory asserts that the constitution of a network may influence the accessibility of information and resources and that the social structure may offer potential for the exchange of resources (Borgatti, Mehra, Brass, & Labianca, 2009; Granovetter, 1973). Understanding the network constitution can reveal important evidence on the information flow and shared knowledge within an organisation (Daly, 2010). Constitutions of networks exist when people interact with each other by communicating, sharing resources, working, learning or playing together, supported through face-to-face interaction as well as through the use of ICT (Haythornthwaite & De Laat, 2010). Each interaction defines a connection between people, known as a social network tie. These ties vary in strength from weak to strong according to the range and types of activities that people engage in. In other words, networked relationships—ties— connect the dots between otherwise isolated people. The total of all the dots (people) and ties is the constitution of the overall network. Social Network Theory tries to explain both the antecedents and the consequences of social networks. Following Social Network Theory, we can investigate, for example, if teachers with a central role in a network learn more from their colleagues (consequence) or investigate if teachers who learn a lot, get a central position in a network (antecedent) (Moolenaar, Daly, & Sleegers, 2011). The structure of a network can be investigated by using SNA. The impact of the structure of social networks can be studied on three levels: first the positions people have in a network (individual level), the type of ties people have (ties level), and finally the overall network structure (network level). In this study we only study one type of tie, i.e. the learning tie. Frequently used network concepts are: actor centrality; network brokers, structural holes and isolates; strong and weak ties; network density; network centralisation; and network density. But there is little evidence on which SNA measures are applicable in the field of learning (Toikkanen & Lipponen, 2011). To give value to the results of the SNA outcomes, it is important to know more about the content and the context in which the learning takes place.

Step 2. Social Capital Theory: What They Are Talking About

While social network theory highlights the structural dimensions of learning networks, we also use social capital theory to frame social network studies from the perspective of content. Networks are always about something (Coburn & Russell, 2008; Jones, Asensio, & Goodyear, 2000). Social capital theory provides a lens through which we can examine the relational resources embedded in social ties and the ways in which actors interact to gain access to these resources (Moolenaar, 2010; Nahapiet & Ghoshal, 1998). The first systematic analysis of social capital was produced by Bourdieu (1985) who defined the concept as the aggregate of the actual or potential resources existing within the relationships of a durable network. According to Lin (2001), the common denominator of all major social capital theories can be summarised as: The resources embedded in social relations and social structure which can be mobilised when an actor wishes to increase the likelihood of success in purposive action.

For this step, we conduct an interview to find out what these learning relationships are about. During this step, a lot of attention is paid to the questions referring to the content of a learning tie, how they are created and maintained, what learning strategies and competencies are used.

Step 3. Communities of Practice: Why They Are Talking as They Do

The third step of the methodology is based on the idea that learning relationships (in our context of continuous professional development in the workplace) are emergent. This explicitly assumes continuous professional development to be already present, in the form of everyday social relationships (De Laat, 2012). This bottom-up approach is different from the top-down approach that, for instance, Sloep et al. (2012) employ. They view a learning network as a tool that supports the professional, for example, by facilitating peer support in a virtual learning environment (e.g. Sie et al., 2012). Contrary to this view, we see learning networks as existing social phenomena. From this perspective, learning cannot be designed: it can only be designed for—that is, it can be facilitated or frustrated (Wenger, 1998, p. 229). In the theory of Communities of Practice Wenger (1998) believes that communities enable the learners to develop a space for a shared activity in which their learning is situated. Here they connect ideas, share problems and insights in a constructive way, and connect with concepts with which they are already familiar, using new knowledge that is collaboratively constructed through their dialogues and social interactions. This means that tools and spaces can be designed to facilitate learning and indeed here is a place for learning architecture and we are in need of:

> Those who can understand the informal yet structured, experiential yet social, character of learning—and can translate their insights into designs to service learning—[as they] will be the architects of tomorrow (Wenger, 1998, p. 225).

In our (bottom-up) view, professionals and their managers ideally need to become the architects of their own professional learning spaces. For example, to design for learning the architect can make sure that (1) the desired artefacts are in place, like curricula, expert advice, procedures, tasks ICT Tools, etc. and (2) the right people are at the right place, in the right kind of relation to enable learning to happen (Wenger, 1998). To support the creation of a fruitful learning environment for the professionals, we organise a focus group discussion with all stakeholders involved.

Research Method

Participants and Procedure

We investigated the continuous professional development activities within a team of 24 teachers from a secondary vocational school in the Netherlands. The school participated in the study as part of a school improvement plan focused on teacher professional development in the use of ICT in their teaching practices. Twenty-two teachers participated in the study. The members of the team work in two different locations (9 versus 13 teachers).

Step 1 Method: Who Is Learning from Whom

Based on the methodology described in the previous paragraph, we developed a method to collect the data on learning ties formed between the teachers as a form of continuous professional development. The aim of this method is to visualise teacher professional development networks using a paper-based version for drawing network connectivity on the so-called contact cards. To fill in the contact cards, we ask participants to draw a graphical presentation of the people they engage and learn from around a particular topic and how frequent (1–5) they meet (see Fig. 11.1 for an example of a contact card).

This task is done with one or maximum two teachers at a time, preceded by an elaborated instruction, both oral- and paper-based. We asked participants to start from the individual perspective (ego-network), by putting him or her name at the centre of his own social learning space, and asked them to draw all social connections (as lines between themselves and their fellow teachers as learning sources)

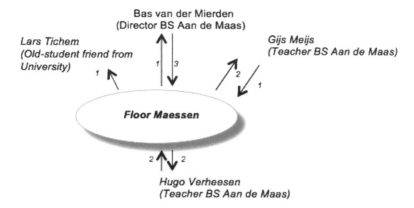

Fig. 11.1 Example of a paper-based contact card. The informal network of Floor Maessen on using white a board

they rely upon for one particular learning challenge or work-related problem. This method has been applied with over 150 teachers and management staff in 5 different projects to study their networks for informal learning.

By connecting the contact cards of personal networks into organisational networks, we traverse between ego- and whole network perspectives and shed a light on the information flow between informal learning networks within the organisation and the expertise the organisation taps into related to particular learning topics.

In our research 22 of 24 team members filled in the contact cards. Based on the drawings in the contact cards, we build a case-by-case matrices for the team we investigated.

Step 1 Results: Who Is Learning from Whom

We used UCINET (Borgatti, Everett, & Freeman, 2002) to conduct SNA. The network data is used to measure the density of a network, the centrality of persons within a network, detect key persons and to visualise overall the structure of the network (Borgatti et al., 2002; Scott, 1991).

Individual Level: Who Are the Key Persons? Indegree and Outdegree

First we looked at the individual level. We started with calculating the outdegree centrality (number of ties that an actor directs to others) which indicates the extent to which an individual interacts with other members in the network (Wasserman &

		Outdegree	Indegree
16	Govinda	6	3
18	Grady	5	1
8	Gordon	5	0
4	Gomer	5	2
6	Gonzalo	3	1
11	Gorman	3	0
2	Golding	3	1
22	Grandpro	3	7
20	Graham	3	5
3	Goliath	2	0
17	Gower	2	0
15	Gough	2	1
19	Graeme	2	1
5	Gomez	1	1
13	Gorran	1	0
1	Godwin	0	5
10	Gore	0	5
7	Gopal	0	4
14	Gottfried	0	2
9	Gordy	0	1
21	Gram	0	6
12	Goronwy	0	0

Faust, 1994). To investigate continuous professional development activities, we also gathered data about the reciprocity of the relations. In this respect we cannot only see if a person reaches out to colleagues to learn with, we can also measure if an individual is approached by others to learn from. To indicate the number of ties going to a person, we calculated the indegree centrality. In Table 11.1 you can see the indegree and outdegree of the individuals involved in the network. Two teachers have an outdegree of 0 because they did not fill in the contact card (12 Goronwy and 7 Gopal) the other teachers with an outdegree of 0 did not indicate any form of learning relation with one of their team members. However from a learning perspective, for example, it is interesting to see that Gopal, although he did not fill in the contact cards, has an indegree of 4. This means that four teachers indicated Gopal as a person they learn from. Therefore it is important we keep Gopal in our dataset, even though he did not fill in the contact cards. Teacher 16, 18, 8 and 4 are the ones that reach out the most to others to learn from about the use of ICT in education. On the other hand teacher 22, 20, 1, 10 and 7 are the ones who are most approached by other teachers to learn from. Based on this information, we could say that teacher 16, 18, 8 and 4 are the most active building learning ties around the topic of ICT. Teachers 22, 20, 1, 10 and 7 are the most important sources to learn from about the topic of ICT. We could assume that these persons are experts in the field of ICT. However at this point this is pure speculation. Content analysis conducted in step 2 could help explain why these persons are considered as important learning sources by their colleagues.

The Overall Network Structure Level

In Table 11.2 we can see an overview of the data. Within this population of 24 teachers, the teachers indicated a total of 46 learning ties amongst peers. The average number of learning ties formed is 2.09. We can see that the standard deviation for outdegree (1.88) and indegree differ (2.17) so we can say that teachers differ more in the amount of learning ties they receive then they form themselves. So teachers are on average similar in seeking out to colleagues to learn from, but they differ in the amount of peers who approach them as learning sources. This result is also explained by the overall network centralisation of indegree and outdegree.

Centralisation represents the percentage how much the networked learning ties are centred around one person. Our results indicate that the distribution of learning ties of people reaching out to other colleagues to learn from is not so much centralised (19.50 %) around the same persons. This could mean that all team members are equally active in learning ICT from their colleagues. The indegree centralisation is a bit higher. So people reach out more to the same central persons, although the indegree centrality is also only 24.49 %. If all colleagues would reach out to one person, the indegree centrality would be 100 %. This could be the case, for example, if this school had only one teacher everyone turned to learn to use ICT in the classroom.

By calculating the density of the network, this is the proportion of ties within the network, we know how well the networked learning activities is distributed within the team. If all the team members indicate they learn from each team member, the density would be 100 %. If no one would learn from each other, there would be no ties and the density would be 0 %. In our research the density of the learning network is 11 %, see Table 11.3. This means there are 46 learning ties out of the 399 (N of Obs) possible learning ties, see Table 11.3. The density of the learning network is dependent on the total number of respondents. Smaller populations tend to have denser networks than larger populations. There is no common agreement of network measures make a learning network effective. Is high density or low density for a learning network effective? To make a statement on solid ground, we need more data to triangulate the results. This data is collected in step 2 and step 3 of our methodology.

Table 11.2 Descriptive statistics of Freeman's degree centrality

		Outdegree	Indegree
1	Mean	2.09	2.09
2	SD	1.88	2.17
3	Sum	46	46
4	Variance	3.54	4.72
8	Minimum	0	0
9	Maximum	6	7
10	N of Obs	22	22

Network centralisation (Outdegree) = 19.501 %
Network centralisation (Indegree) = 24.490 %

Table 11.3 Density statistics of the informal network of project 2 based on a whole network perspective

Density	SD	No. of Ties	Variance
0.11	0.31	46	0.10

The Visualisation of the Network Structure

To move to step 2 and 3, we need a concrete artefact for the teachers to understand and reflect how they develop their continuous professional development around the topic of ICT in the workplace. We believe that an important first step to analyse continuous professional development is to make the learning activities visual as represented in Fig. 11.2. By visualising the learning ties teachers develop, teachers can see who is involved, assess what they produce, participate and value it. As such these learning tie visualisations serve as a kind of mediating artefact boot strapping conversations about continuous professional development activities in organisations and strengthen their learning relationships. This we feel is needed in order for bottom-up continuous professional development to become recognised, supported and legitimised as a powerful form of bottom-up learning alongside formal learning initiatives. We also use these visualisations as a reflection tool for the teachers and a working instrument to get more in depth data for step 2, the content analysis and step 3 the context analysis.

Based on the data gathered with the contact cards and represented in Tables 11.1, 11.2 and 11.3, we created, with the use of Netdraw (Borgatti et al., 2002), a graphical representation of the ICT informal learning network present within the school (see Fig. 11.2). The team members are represented as nodes and the learning ties between the colleagues as ties. Next to the nodes and ties, you can also visualise attribute data of the nodes. These attributes can show additional properties embedded within the network. For example, you can use different colours, different node sizes or different shapes. In our research project we received additional data about the two different locations where these teachers are working.

In the visualisation you can easily see the results represented in the tables. The network is not so dense, you see four central people in the network, getting the most ties in their direction (direction of the arrow). Including the additional information in different shapes, you can also see in Fig. 11.2, teachers indicate proportionally more to have a learning tie with teachers working at the same location (location 1 is indicated with a bullet, location 2 with a square).

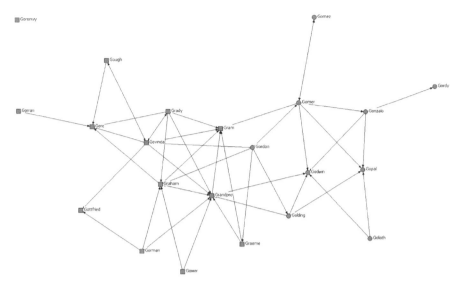

Fig. 11.2 A multidimensional graph of informal professional development networks

Step 2 Method. Content Analysis: What Are They Learning About

For step 2, we conducted an interview to find out what these learning relationships are about. During this step, a lot of attention is paid to the questions referring to the content of a learning tie, how they are created and maintained, what learning strategies and competencies are used. To stimulate the bottom-up approach, we decided to organise a group interview with all 24 team members. The visualisation of the first step was used as a mediating artefact to guide the discussion. The visualisation helped to identify certain positions people hold in the network and during the group interview these positions were explained by identifying the reasons why. The following questions were asked to get more insights into the individual level:

1. Who do you go to, to learn from and is this reflected in the visualisation?
2. Is it surprising that certain people are more in the centre of the visualisation?
3. Why would that be, what do they have to offer?

   Because we only investigate one type of learning tie the following question was asked:

4. What kind of expertise and experiences around the topic of ICT do you share in these learning relations?

And last the following question was asked to get more insights into the overall structure of the network:

5. Do you have the feeling this is a dense network? Do you learn about ICT from many colleagues? Why? Why not?

Step 2 Results. Content Analysis: What Are They Learning About

The centrality of the key persons (individual level) was explained during this group interview by the content of the learning ties (tie level). In the bullet team Gopal was identified by the teachers as the overall informal ICT expert, in the square team Grandpro had the highest indegree because she has the knowledge about integrating videos into PowerPoint, an ICT application most teachers need in their classroom teaching. Graham (highest indegree) was responsible for the support of the online environment of the square team. In general they did not perceive the learning network as dense. Only four main subjects were mentioned as learning topics in the overall learning network: the use of PowerPoint in the classroom, the use of video in the classroom, the import of video material in PowerPoint and the use of the new online Learning environment for teachers. The limited amount of ICT use and related learning questions around ICT could be an explanation for the perceived low network density of 0.11.

Step 3 Method. Context Analysis: Why They Are Learning as They Do

To get an insight into the context, the following questions were asked during the same team meeting, again using the visualisation as a tool to guide the conversation:

1. Do you think the network visualisation represents the real setting?
2. What strikes you in this visualisation?
3. What is your explanation for this?
4. What can be done to optimise the workplace for learning?

On top of the group interview, we held an interview with the team manager to reflect on the results of the team session.

Step 3 Results. Context Analysis: Why They Are Learning as They Do

During the team discussion, all team members agreed that the visualisation represented the real setting, except for the two team members who did not fill in the contact cards. The first thing that striked the team members the most was that the network structure represented their physical division. They also pointed out that they saw in the visualisation that the density of the network in location square is much higher than in location bullet. They mentioned two reasons for this distinction: The teachers in the square location, the one with a higher density, use an online learning environment to support their teaching. The teachers assumed that the use of this learning environment triggers more learning questions about the use of this online environment in their teaching and therefore stimulate teachers to create more learning ties around the use of ICT. Secondly the bullet location team said that Gopal, the most central person in the bullet team network, is really the informal ICT expert in the team and everybody goes to him for questions, rather than asking and sharing expertise amongst the whole team.

To further stimulate the bottom-up approach, we asked the team to formulate solutions to stimulate the uptake of ICT in the classroom and therefore stimulate the knowledge exchange and relation building around the topic within the team. To stimulate the exchange amongst the overall network and to stimulate the knowledge sharing between the two locations, the team suggested to implement the use of the online learning environment in both locations. At the same time, the teachers suggested to use this environment to share information across the two locations. Secondly they proposed to use team meetings to share information about the use of ICT, to stimulate the informal learning around this topic. The key persons (with highest indegree), the central informal ICT experts, were asked to share their knowledge and distribute their expertise throughout the overall learning network through information sessions during the team meetings. In this respect the team members proposed to use formal meetings to initially spread information about the topic of ICT. This new information can then create new insights amongst all team members to stimulate the informal learning around the topic of ICT.

To end, we also wanted to investigate what value these learning ties create for the continuous professional development of the teachers. Therefore we included three questions at the bottom of the contact cards to collect data on how teachers value bottom-up continuous professional development activities. Therefore we asked the participants to fill in a question about the importance of the learning ties they develop for their personal development (1 = not important at all; 2 = not important; 3 = neutral; 4 = important; 5 = very important). As you can see in Table 11.4, the mean is very high. Most respondents find their learning ties very important revenues for their own professional development.

The interview with the team manager confirmed the results of the context analysis we did together with the team members. He added that the density of the learning network 11 % was indeed low. Not only because of the lack of physical

Table 11.4 Descriptive statistics importance of learning network for own professional development

N	Minimum	Maximum	Mean	SD
18	2	5	4.05	0.80

proximity between the teams, but also because some colleagues are still reluctant to integrate ICT in their practice. He was surprised by the creative solutions suggested by his team. Agreements were made to create the necessary arrangements to start up the use of the online learning environment in both locations. Finding out about peoples position in this learning network was also perceived as an interesting insight in the informal learning network. In the beginning of the key district project, three key persons were approached to promote the use of ICT in their team. The SNA showed that instead of only three key persons we see that five actors who are being frequently approached. This finding is supported by an indegree centralisation of 24.5 % (see Table 11.2). This helped the manager to set up a bigger core team of ICT experts, identify different roles and strategies of the actors within the network that could influence networked learning activities.

The Network Awareness Tool

The paper-based version of the contact cards is a good starting point for visualising and studying continuous professional development activities in the workplace. The use of the contact cards indicates the added value of such a practice for the teachers in schools (De Laat, 2011). But the paper version also has some shortcomings. With the paper version, the overall network data is collected in a semi-structured interview. This has the downside that the data is dependent on the memory and reflection capacity of the actor: actors often forget names, persons and/or conversations. The collected data we gathered using the paper version of contact cards is only a snapshot of an existing dynamic practice taken at a certain point in time. To understand the reasons behind informal learning network developments and how they evolve over time, we need to gather data on the dynamics of networked learning. Therefore we found it necessary to improve our research practice for finding ways to collect more realistic and accurate solutions to collect data over time to represent continuous professional development activities in all its dimensions and simultaneously finding ways to provide the participants with instant feedback (Schreurs & De Laat, 2012). To do so we designed an online tool, the Network Awareness Tool (De Laat & Schreurs, 2011), with web 2.0 features which could address the shortcomings of a paper-based research method for visualising informal networked learning activities (Schreurs & De Laat, 2013).

On the other hand, online learning environments or online networking sites to support learning automatically record a digital path of users' social behaviour within the online community. The data provide information on users interactions, are abundant, time-stamped and free of human memory biases (Glasgow, 2013). This methodology heals the potential to be adopted and plugged into the virtual world (Schreurs & De Laat, 2012) and investigates online teacher or student professional environments (Schreurs et al., 2013). Semantic analysis can be conducted for creating tag clouds dealing with the content of the networks. Social networks analysis can be applied to datasets who interacts with whom and who downloads resources, etc. If we use this set-up, a more holistic and full story can be created about the online informal learning activities of people and organisations can therefore analyse their users and see how to support and encourage online communities to share and learn from each other. Tools like these can extend the discussion on the application of Networked Learning.

Conclusion and Discussion

This chapter is an attempt to stimulate a discussion amongst researchers within the area of Networked Learning to think about technological solutions and methodologies to gather and analyse relational data on learning to create a holistic view of peoples off-line and online informal lifelong learning activities in education, work and society. In our research on social professional development networks amongst teachers in and between schools, we presented a methodology to be used as a reflection tool, to give professionals opportunities to gain insights into their own social learning activities and that of others in and beyond their organisation. The methodology also holds the potential to stimulate new networked learning ties and give insights into the social learning content and social capital of an entire organisation. In addition, the methodology design aims at assisting continuous professional development in the workplace at three distinct levels of the organisation's network. Firstly, on the individual level, it allows a professional to identify her ego-network. The visualisation of the ego-network promotes professionals' *self-reflection* by making them aware of the people that they learn from and what knowledge they hold. Secondly, on the group level, the methodology can detect and visualise relationships that revolve around a specific topic. The visualisations can also be used to identify key persons within a network based on the number of ties (incoming and outgoing). Teachers become aware that they are not alone in their classroom and that professional development is a social activity; one that is spontaneous and deeply connected to day-to-day challenges in the workplace. Another advantage of these visualisations is that they serve as very concrete artefacts for the teachers to help them reflect on how they act as networkers building a social space for informal learning. This research shows that the presented methodology is a useful research-driven intervention tool to detect, connect and facilitate informal networked learning. With this methodology, we can detect multiple (isolated) networks in the organisation and connect ideas and stimulate participants to think of solutions to support their own professional development in certain domains. Using this approach, organisations can link in with existing informal networks of practice and unlock their potential for organisational learning by giving them a voice and make their results more explicit within the organisation. With this approach, we create the possibility to evaluate how the continuous professional development could benefit the teachers and therefore the quality of the school. Having insights into the learning ties formed in the workplace gives the possibility to create or optimise the space professionals need to learn from each other (De Laat, 2012). This perspective gives rise to a more bottom-up—self-governing—understanding of learning where workers with their colleagues interact about their work experiences through sharing their experiences, knowledge and contacts providing access to new or alternative resources.

Acknowledgement This book chapter is directly and indirectly the result of a continuous collaboration amongst researchers (and their networks) of LOOK Scientific Research Center for Teachers Development of the Open University of the Netherlands. To acknowledge this collaboration, this chapter is written in the 'we' form.

References

Armour, K. M., & Yelling, M. (2007). Effective professional development for physical education teachers: The role of informal, collaborative learning. *Journal of Teaching in Physical Education, 26*(2), 177–200.

Berings, M. (2006). *On-the-job learning styles: Conceptualization and instrument development for the nursing profession.* Unpublished PhD dissertation, Universiteit van Tilburg, Tilburg, The Netherlands.

Borgatti, S. P., Everett, M. G., & Freeman, L. C. (2002). *Ucinet for Windows: Software for social network analysis.* Harvard, MA: Analatic Technologies.

Borgatti, S. P., Mehra, A., Brass, D. J., & Labianca, G. (2009). Network analysis in the social sciences. *Science, 323*(5916), 892–895.

Bourdieu, P. (1985). The social space and the genesis of groups. *Theory and Society, 14*(6), 723–744.

Coburn, C. E., & Russell, J. L. (2008). District policy and teachers' social networks. *Education Evaluation and Policy Analysis, 30*, 203–235.

Daly, A. J. (2010). Relationships in reform: The role of teachers' social networks. *Journal of Educational Administration, 48*(3), 359–391.

De Laat, M. F. (2006). *Networked learning.* Apeldoorn, The Netherlands: Politieacademie.

De Laat, M. F. (2011, January). *Bridging the knowledge gap: Using social network methodology for detecting, connecting and facilitating informal networked learning in organizations.* Paper presented at the 44th IEEE Annual Hawaii International Conference on System Sciences, Kuaui, HI.

De Laat, M. (2012). *Enabling professional development networks: How connected are you?* Heerlen: Open Universiteit in the Netherlands.

De Laat, M. F., & Coenders, M. (2011). Communities of practice en netwerkenleren. In J. Kessels & R. Poell (Eds.), *Handboek human resource development: Organiseren van het leren* (pp. 417–428). Houten, The Netherlands: Bohn Stafleu van Logum.

De Laat, M., Lally, V., & Lipponen, L. (2007). Investigating patterns of interaction in networked learning and computer-supported collaborative learning: A role for social network analysis. *International Journal of Computer-Supported Collaborative Learning, 2*, 87–103.

De Laat, M. F., & Schreurs, B. (2011). *Network Awareness Tool: Social software for visualizing, analysing and managing social networks*. Heerlen: Ruud de Moor Centrum, Open Universiteit Nederland.

De Laat, M. F., & Schreurs, B. (2013). Visualizing informal professional development networks: Building a case for learning analytics. *American Behavioral Scientist, 20*(10), 1–18.

Eraut, M. (2000). Non-formal learning and tacit knowledge in professional work. *British Journal of Educational Psychology, 70*, 113–136.

Eraut, M. (2004). Informal learning in the workplace. *Studies in Continuing Education, 26*(2), 247–273.

Glasgow, K. (2013, February). *Hand in glove, or square peg, round hole: An exploration of social network analysis applied to online community trace data*. Paper presented at iConference, Fort Worth, TX. doi:10.9776/13166

Goodyear, P., Banks, S., Hodgson, V., & McConnell, D. (2004). *Advances in research on networked learning*. Norwell, MA: Kluwer.

Granovetter, M. (1973). The strength of weak ties. *American Journal of Sociology, 78*, 1360–1380.

Haythornthwaite, C., & De Laat, M. F. (2010). Social networks and learning networks: Using social network perspectives to understand social learning. In L. Dirckinck-Holmfeld, V. Hodgson, C. Jones, M. De Laat, D. McConnell, & T. Ryberg (Eds.), *7th International Conference on Networked Learning*. Lancaster, England: Lancaster University.

Jones, C., Asensio, M., & Goodyear, P. (2000). Networked learning in higher education: Practitioners' perspectives. *Journal of the Association for Learning Technology, 8*(2), 18–28.

Lin, N. (2001). *Social capital: A theory of social structure and action*. New York: Cambridge University Press.

Marsick, V. J., & Watkins, K. E. (1990). *Informal and incidental learning in the workplace*. London: Routledge.

McConnell, D. (1994). *Implementing computer supported cooperative learning*. London: Kogan Page.

McConnell, D. (2006). *E-learning groups and communities*. Maidenhead, England: SRHE/OU Press.

Moolenaar, N. M. (2010). *Ties with potential: Nature, antecedents and consequences of social networks in school teams*. Unpublished doctoral dissertation, University of Amsterdam, The Netherlands.

Moolenaar, N. M., Daly, A. J., & Sleegers, P. J. C. (2011). Ties with potential: Social network structure and innovative climate in Dutch schools. *Teachers College Record, 113*(9), 1983–2017.

Moreno, J. L. (1947). Progress and pitfalls in sociometric theory. *Sociometry, 10*(3), 268–272.

Nahapiet, J., & Ghoshal, S. (1998). Social capital, intellectual capital, and the organizational advantage. *Academy of Management Review, 23*(2), 242–266.

Schreurs, B., & De Laat, M. (2012, April). *Network Awareness Tool—Learning analytics in the workplace: Detecting and analyzing informal workplace learning*. Paper presented at LAK12: 2nd International Conference on Learning Analytics and Knowledge, Vancouver, British Columbia, Canada.

Schreurs, B., & De Laat, M. (2013). *The Network Awareness Tool: A web 2.0 Tool to visualise informal learning in organisations*. Manuscript submitted for publication.

Schreurs, B., Teplovs, C., Furgeson, R., Buckingham-Shum, B., & De Laat, M. (2013, April). *Visualizing social learning ties by type and topic: Rationale and concept demonstrator*. Paper presented at LAK13: 3th International Conference on Learning Analytics and Knowledge, Leuven, Belgium.

Scott, J. (1991). *Social network analysis: A handbook*. London: Sage.

Sie, R. L. L., Berlanga, A. J., Sloep, P. B., Rajagopal, K., Drachsler, H., & Fazeli, S. (2012). *Social tools for networked learning: Current and future research directions*. Networked Learning Conference 2012.

Sloep, P. B., Berlanga, A. J., Greller, W., Stoyanov, S., Van der Klink, M., Retalis, S., et al. (2012). Educational innovation with learning networks: Tools and developments. *Journal of Universal Computer Science, 18*, 44–61.

Smith, M. K. (2008). *Informal learning*. Retrieved from http://www.infed.org/biblio/inf-lrn.htm

Toikkanen, T., & Lipponen, L. (2011). The applicability of social network analysis to the study of networked learning. *Interactive Learning Environments, 19*(4), 365–379.

Vrasidas, C., & Glass, G. V. (Eds.). (2004). *Current perspectives in applied information technologies. Online professional development for teachers*. Greenwich, CT: Information Age Publishing.

Wasserman, S., & Faust, K. (1994). *Social network analysis*. Cambridge, England: Cambridge University Press.

Wenger, E. (1998). *Communities of practice: Learning, meaning, and identity*. Cambridge, MA: Cambridge University Press.

Chapter 12
Learning Through Network Interaction: The Potential of Ego-Networks

Asli Ünlüsoy, Mariette de Haan, and Kevin Leander

Our communication and interactions with others are increasingly more mediated and facilitated by web-based platforms and mobile tools. Social networking sites are good examples of such mediated communication. These sites are web-based platforms that allow users to send private and/or public messages, post comments, build web content, and/or take part in live chats. While some networking sites highlight making social connections as a central characteristic (e.g., Facebook, Twitter, LinkedIn, Google+), others prioritize content sharing based on user participation and user-generated content (e.g., Instagram, Reddit, YouTube). What these platforms have in common is that they facilitate flows of, for instance, news, updates, comments, invitations, and messages. There are millions of users of these sites, many of whom have adopted the habits of posting information, public and private messages, checking various networking sites for updates as part of their daily routine. Mobile access to social networks consolidated the place of these sites in our lives even more, and the related social practices (e.g., using applications like WhatsApp, foursquare, or Twitter) became increasingly more embedded in everyday life.

Networking platforms are not specifically designed for education or learning purposes. Yet these sites are potentially valuable for learning. These are information-rich environments with many opportunities to discover, explore, enhance knowledge, and share experiences (Ito et al., 2010). The quality and novelty of the shared information may be debatable. In some forums and collective knowledge platforms (such as Wiki's), false and poor quality content can (and mostly do) get corrected and be improved by input of others. On other platforms the

A. Ünlüsoy (✉) • M. de Haan
Faculty of Social and Behavioral Sciences, Utrecht University, Langeveld Building,
Heidelberglaan 1, 3584 CS Utrecht, The Netherlands
e-mail: a.unlusoy@uu.nl; m.dehaan@uu.nl

K. Leander
Department of Teaching & Learning, Vanderbilt University, Nashville, TN, USA
e-mail: kevin.leander@vanderbilt.edu

V. Hodgson et al. (eds.), *The Design, Experience and Practice of Networked Learning*,
Research in Networked Learning, DOI 10.1007/978-3-319-01940-6_12,
© Springer International Publishing Switzerland 2014

content is open for debate, discussion, and commentary (e.g., Reddit). These platforms provide seemingly endless opportunities for exploring and navigation (Cousin, 2005). Levy (2000) summarizes the process of accessing knowledge in networks as "everyone knows something, nobody knows everything, and what any one person knows can be tapped" (in Jenkins, 2009, p.72). In this manner individuals are presented with multiple perspectives, from multiple resources including people with varied levels of expertise. These experiences are relevant for learning, because they enable individuals to examine various viewpoints, to enrich knowledge, and to form opinions.

In this chapter, following this line of reasoning, we claim that social networks mediated by networked technologies provide ongoing opportunities to engage in activities and conversations that could potentially lead to learning. The kinds of social relationships and interactions that occur online heavily define the learning potential in networks, an issue that will be the center of this contribution.

Social networking platforms remain largely unexplored regarding the learning possibilities they create. There are several important bodies of work that can guide our expectations regarding learning in informal, social networks. First, sociocultural approaches to learning provide the groundwork for understanding learning as a situated, social, distributed phenomenon that is inseparable from the social context in which it occurs (Rogoff & Lave, 1999; Wertsch, 1998). Second, networked learning studies, built upon the principles of sociocultural approaches, provide the necessary "update" for understanding and conceptualizing learning in a world where people are challenged with new and emerging technologies and new social practices and where technology-infused forms of communication and collaboration are the standard (Hodgson, McConnell, & Dirckinck-Holmfeld, 2012).

In the following sections, we address the sociocultural and networked learning frameworks. We will then present a network analytic approach in relation to learning, explaining in particular the advantages ego-network (henceforth egonet) analysis and discuss the contribution of this method to networked learning research. We will finish with presenting our study conducted within networked learning framework, using ego-network methods.

Sociocultural and Network Perspectives of Learning

Sociocultural approaches have argued for the distributed and interactional characteristics of learning prior to the rise of network technologies. Human development is seen as both constituting and constituted by social, cultural, and historical activities and practices, as such cognition and culture function together in a mutually defining process (Rogoff, 2003). In this approach, learning is a process that results from interacting and participating in cultural practices (Lave & Wenger, 1991). A key aspect of learning is mediation. Mediation refers to the way that human mind and culture interact, namely, through available psychological, cultural, and material tools (i.e., language, signs, symbols, and items of the physical surrounding)

(Cole & Wertsch, 2004). In order to understand these interactive learning processes, "mediated activities" are seen as natural units of observation in sociocultural approaches (Wertsch, 1998).

Current digital practices seen from sociocultural perspectives mediate our self-representation, communication, understanding of the world, and learning (Gee, 2004; Wertsch, 2002). Our encounters with networked technologies in hardware and software forms (e.g., respectively phones, laptops, online sites, apps) as well as our participation in the networked communities enable new ways of accessing and processing information (Erstad, 2012). The social character of our learning became more visible with the rise of network technologies, for it is now possible to trace resources distributed over a network and see a person's connections within a larger social network (Gee, 2008). These developments ask for a rethinking of how we should understand "mediated activity" taking into account that "activity is distributed in increasingly dispersed ways; it is often engaged in by loose and shifting communities of people; it has fuzzy and flexible system boundaries, and is mediated by tools and signs that are highly mobile and hybridized" (Leander, & De Haan, 2011). Learning activities mediated through networked technologies are systematically explored and explained with networked learning (NL) studies.

In NL studies, learning is understood as "learning in which information and communication technology [...] is used to promote connections: between one learner and other learners, between learners and tutors; between a learning community and its learning resources" (Goodyear, Banks, Hodgson, & McConnell, 2004, p.1). The underlying ideas of NL align with sociocultural approaches. Knowledge is understood as emergent and social in nature; interaction and collaboration with others are considered as key activities for constructing knowledge (Hodgson et al., 2012). Also, the facilitating role of tools (specifically networked technologies) in the processes of learning and teaching is strongly emphasized and thoroughly studied (McConnell, Hodgson, & Dirckinck-Holmfeld, 2012).

A large proportion of NL studies are devoted to matters of formal learning. Institutional, online, and (semi-)structured learning platforms (such as Massive Open Online Courses (MOOCs) offered by universities) are thoroughly studied (e.g., Kop, Fournier, & Mak, 2011), and how certain characteristics of these online platforms (e.g., asynchronous communication) influence the experiences of learners and teachers is often questioned (e.g., De Laat & Lally, 2004). Attention to informal learning practices in social networking platforms is still largely lacking, although it is acknowledged that at school, children learn with and from each other besides the formal school curriculum and networked technologies have a significant place in facilitating and improving these informal learning practices (Sørensen, Danielsen, & Nielsen, 2007). Similarly, in NL studies work place or professional learning practices have shown how informal learning experiences account for a great deal of knowledge creation (e.g., De Laat, 2006; Haythornthwaite, 2006).

However, not much attention is given to informal learning that happens in and through the social networking sites described earlier in this text. As argued earlier in the text, social networking sites are not merely for pastime; they occupy a significant place in the contemporary culture. As such, they should be acknowledged as sites of participation, sharing, inquiring, and discovering where peer cultures can flourish, interests can develop, and expertise can be shared (Ito et al., 2010). The significance of networks for learning is discussed in the following section.

Network Characteristics and Learning Potential

Personal motivations and goals largely define why and how people participate in social networks and what they do when they are online. In their research on youth and social media, Ito and colleagues identified two motivation factors to participate in online social networks: friendship-driven and interest-driven ones (2010). In the former, friendships are carried to online platforms, while in the latter, a particular interest (e.g., politics, drawing, and gaming) precedes friendship ties and exceeds local, social, and cultural boundaries. These two motives serve different purposes, but they are not mutually exclusive forms of networking. In the same study they have also identified different levels of commitment in network participation, depending on what the main reason for participating in the network was. They labeled these aims as follows: "hanging-out" with friends was the most common reason why youths participated in networks, and "messing around" was a more experimental use of social media directed at exploring new technologies and new ways of self-expression which required a deeper level of commitment in network activities. Finally, they identified young people who "geek out" that were considered the most committed group; they were developing games, creating novel digital artifacts, and sharing expertise in gaming, fandom, or another specialized interest.

The motivations and varying levels of social media engagement of youth cannot be understood as an isolated and solely individual practice; it is also important to consider the kinds of relational ties they have in their networks that shape these motivations. A general distinction regarding the types of ties in networks is between weak and strong ones (e.g., Granovetter, 1973; Haythornthwaite, 2000). Relations that are marked by emotional bonding, a shared history, and multiple common others like family and friendships are called strong whereas ties with casual acquaintances are called weak (Granovetter, 1973). There are various ways to operationalize this distinction. For instance, Granovetter (1973) differentiated ties by frequency of being contact; Krackhardt (1992) made a distinction based on the content of interactions and studied "friendship" versus "professional advice" ties in a workplace network.

The information flows and knowledge activity with weak and strong ties tend to be different from each other (Haythornthwaite, 2009). Strong ties promote an increased social interaction and support, frequent collaboration, commitment to common activities, and sharing of resources, but some argue that they also lack novelty of experience and knowledge and limit autonomy (e.g., Burt, 2001). Weak ties deliver new information, but they are more effortful relationships to maintain (Haythornthwaite, 2009). Studies suggest that information exchange and support for learning can come from both kinds of ties. For instance, Ito and colleagues (2010) indicate that specific interest groups that are formed to improve their skills and knowledge generally consist of weak ties. However, there is also evidence that strong network ties foster community members' intentions to share knowledge and their willingness to adopt new ideas (Krackhardt, 1992). Besides, there is a vast amount of literature that discusses how homogeneity, geographical dispersion, and density of network contacts impact on the probability of fostering the innovative quality of networked communities, which does point to the complex relationship between network characteristics and their learning potential (e.g., Coe & Bunell, 2003).

Significance of Egonet Methods for the Study of Networked Learning

Egonet research is a social network analysis method that considers personal social networks from a "bottom-up" perspective; starting with the individual actor and accounting for the individual's direct relationships (Alexander, 2009). It is a method that maps an individual actor's dyadic relations to other people and the connections between them (Wellman, 1983). The actor in the center is called *ego*, and "others" related to ego are called with their Latin name *alters*. The mapping generally consists of two steps. First, a "name generator" is used to evoke and list alters. The criteria to prompt names can vary greatly (e.g., from listing frequently contacted people to people with whom one shares secrets) depending on the research goals (Alexander, 2009). Second, "name interpreter" questions generate information about the alters' characteristics (e.g., age, gender, level of education) and about the relationship characteristics (e.g., kinship or friendship, frequency of meetings with ego, geographical distance to ego).

Network information can be collected by means of a survey or interview, but in either case the focus is not on the traditional individual's attitudes or motivations, but on the respondent's social context and relationships. This method enables the researcher to see the respondent within his/her immediate social context and provides qualitative and/or quantitative data that can be used for rich descriptions, explorations, as well as testing hypotheses and explaining phenomena (Chamberlain, 2006).

The quantitative data collected by means of egonet methods provides not only descriptive information about the respondents and their networks but is also well suited for advanced statistical analyses. This type of data is frequently analyzed with multilevel regression analyses (MLA) (e.g., Flap & Völker, 2001; van Duijn, van Busschbach, & Snijders, 1999) as these analyses are typically done to separate several spheres of influence. As Hox says: "individual persons are influenced by the social groups or contexts to which they belong, and the properties of those groups are in turn influenced by the individuals who make up that group" (2010, p.1).

These mutual influences between individual and social structure are considered in MLA a "nested" social structure, with individuals embedded in social groups. MLA makes it possible to separately estimate the influence of individuals' characteristics and the influence of the social structures' characteristics on the outcome (Hox, 2010). A typical example of a two-level data structure occurs frequently in educational research where pupils are "nested" within schools. With MLA the pupil's characteristics and the school characteristics can separately be assessed for their impact on an outcome variable (for instance, success in the standardized tests). Likewise, in the data from egonet methods, the personal network contacts are nested under the ego (van Duijn et al., 1999). Therefore, MLA is seen as a method to "separate" network factors from individual factors.

This methodology is well suited to apply in networked learning studies as it enables to see an individual, "a learner," as a connected person and to map flows of interaction, collaboration, and knowledge creation between the learner and his/her learning resources. Our study in the next section is an example for mapping young people's connections "in the wild."

Current Study: The Dutch Context, Concepts, and Research Questions

The research presented in this section represents some issues relevant to NL studies and an applied example of egonet method. This research is a part of the Wired Up project (www.uu.nl/wiredup) which is a multidisciplinary project that studies identity formation and learning in the modern digital world, both for Dutch youth and youth from different ethnic minorities living in the Netherlands. It is a multi-method project in which survey and network interview methods were combined. Here, only the analyses and results of the network part of the survey study are presented.

Young people in the Netherlands are avid visitors of social networking sites with 91 % of youths actively using their social network accounts in 2010 (Central Bureau of Statistics, 2011). Our aim with this study was to explore the online ego-networks of youth, particularly to map out with whom these young people kept in touch frequently, to understand the characteristics of these contacts, and to see the kinds of activities that they did together. As argued earlier in the chapter, social network platforms are not specifically designed as learning environments, but they potentially support learning. We have focused on activities such as "asking advice and giving feedback"; "editing/creating web content together"; "sharing links, texts, and digital artifacts"; and "discovering new information." Questions related to asking, sharing, and editing indicate activities that required interaction with network contacts and that were potentially building up knowledge. However, the question regarding discovery was about understanding the awareness of novel experiences happening as related to active involvement in social networks.

We focused on "discovery of new information" as a measure of awareness of learning, although all other network activities we addressed with our survey are in themselves relevant learning activities as well. Our rationale was that often when people are doing something enjoyable or are busy with daily routine activities, they do not realize that they learn (Gee, 2008). Learning is a complex phenomenon with many facets, and discovering new information and the "light-bulb moments" constitutes only one facet of this complexity. Discovery of new information was used in the current study as we had reasons to believe that according to the youth we studied, this was a recognizable concept that could be associated with "learning" for them.

In this chapter, while we are showing how certain network characteristics such as network density, geographical dispersion, and homogeneity of network members' characteristics relate to the possibilities for learning, it is not our intention to generate "fixed" network typologies. Following Coe and Bunell (2003), we suggest that one should make no general presumptions as to how configurations of network relations in terms of, for instance, their spatial organization, density, and heterogeneity foster innovation and generate knowledge. From these premises, we answered the following research questions (for detailed explanation of the analyses and results, please refer to Ünlüsoy, Haan, Leander, and Volker, submitted):

1. What are the compositional features of youths' online networks?

   - Who are the most frequently contacted alters in terms of their relation to the respondents, gender, age, and ethnicity?
   - Where are alters located? Do they meet each other regularly online and offline?
   - To what extent are relationships between respondents and alters perceived as "personal" (i.e., emotionally close)?
   - What topics do they talk about online?

2. What characterizes their networks' structure in terms of density?
3. What is the frequency of their networked interactions?

   - How often do they keep in touch via an online platform (e.g., check each other's profile pages)?
   - How often do they share online links, photos, and videos?
   - How often do they create, edit, and upload digital artifact, texts, and visual materials?
   - How often do they ask for advice and receive feedback from each other?

4. Can certain characteristics of these networks predict the (self-perceived) discovery of new information?

Method

Sample

The survey was carried out in the course of 2010 among 1,408 students in 7 secondary schools in the Netherlands. The results below come from 1,227 respondents (87 %) of the total survey population. We have excluded 181 cases in total, because 29 cases (2 %) reported no network activity and 152 (11 %) did not finish answering the survey or failed to provide reliable and consistent information on their network contacts and activities. Of the 1,227 respondents over half (56 %) were female. The sample age was 12–18 on average 14.4. The respondents were from different levels of secondary schools in the Netherlands and from different ethnic backgrounds (Dutch 33 %, from Moroccan background 24.4 %, from Turkish background 12.6 %, and other ethnicities 30 %). We applied a stratified sampling procedure that yielded data distributions largely congruent with census data with respect to age, gender, and education level and was representative for urban youth population.

Instrument and Procedure

The network section of the questionnaire captured data regarding the *five most frequently contacted alters* in online network platforms. While asking for the frequently contacted people, we have not set a criterion of minimum or maximum frequency of meeting, nor did we specify the kind of networking platform or kind of relationship. The respondents were free to choose any contact they had regular contact with. The likelihood that the frequently contacted people represent strong ties is high, but we did not aim to obtain data particularly on strong ties.

In order to explore who these alters were, we asked about age, gender, and ethnicity of each alter. Furthermore, we asked the relation between each alter and respondent (i.e., family, friend, and acquaintance), emotional closeness, location, frequency of online/offline meetings, and topics of conversations. Topics in the networks were captured with a dichotomous (yes–no) 17-item list. As stated above we also asked about the frequency of common network interactions: sharing links, texts, and digital artifacts; asking for advice; giving feedback; editing/creating digital artifact(s); and keeping in touch. The frequency measure to these questions was from 1 = "almost never," 2 = "monthly," 3 = "2 or 3 times per month," 4 = "2 or 3 times per week" to 5 = "daily." Finally, we asked how frequently they discovered new information and new things (artifacts, gadgets, platforms) as a result of dialogue with each one of their contacts. The frequency of "discovery" was measured with the same scale as above. Finally, we asked if the alters knew each other and used this information to compute network density.

Respondents took the survey in their classrooms or a computer room in their school through a template that was facilitated online. Before the survey sessions, instructors explained the general aims of the survey. During the survey, the instructors remained present to supervise the survey process and answer any questions. Most survey rounds took 30–40 min.

Data Analysis

The first three research questions were answered with descriptive statistical analyses (e.g., frequencies, averages) using SPSS software. The fourth research question was analyzed with multilevel regression analyses to identify significant predictors of discovery using MLwin2.02 software (Rasbash, Charlton, Browne, Healy, & Cameron, 2005). The design was such that the network contacts were nested in each ego-network. Data requirements were met. A nested structure of our data was confirmed after comparing a simple regression model to the nested model. We observed that the network interaction variables (e.g., asking advice, feedback) were correlated. It is known as multicollinearity and causes inflation of the regression coefficient estimates, overestimating the impact of independent variables on the dependent (Hox, 2010). However, due to the large sample size and the acceptable variance inflation factors (VIF) which were all below 5 and tolerance levels above 0.20 (Williams, 2011), the network interaction items remained intact. We were able to test the impact of each network interaction on the dependent variable (i.e., discovery).

Results

Ego-Network Composition

We obtained information regarding 6,135 alters in total. The relationship between the respondents and alters was as follows: the vast majority (77 %) were friends, 15 % were family members, and 8 % were acquaintances. Other sociodemographic variables of alters are presented in Table 12.1.

Table 12.1 Sociodemographic characteristics of alters

	Percentages
Gender	
Female	55.8
Male	44.2
Age	
Younger than 12	2.1
Between 12 and 18	88.2
Older than 18	9.7
Ethnicity	
Dutch	44.7
Moroccan	12.5
Turkish	14.1
Other ethnicities	28.7

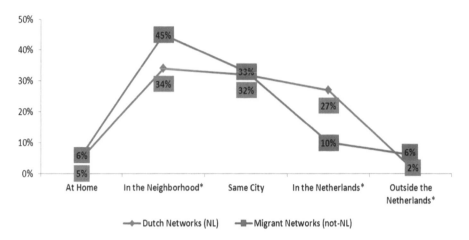

Fig. 12.1 Geographical distribution of alters

The networks were *homogeneous* in the sense that there was a large overlap in all demographic characteristics between the respondents and alters. Regarding gender, 73.7 % of alters were the same gender as the respondents. Girls had more gender overlap in their networks than boys. Regarding age, 88.2 % of the alters were in the same age group as respondents. Regarding ethnicity, 62.4 % of the total network contacts were from the same ethnic background as the respondents.

The *location* of the majority of the alters (77.6 %) was in close proximities of the respondents. Figure 12.1 shows the geographical distribution of alters in migrant and Dutch networks. Migrants had significantly more alters living in the neighborhood ($F(1) = 12.6$; $p < 0.001$) and outside the Netherlands ($F(1) = 18.29$; $p < 0.001$), whereas in Dutch networks more alters were living in the Netherlands ($F(1) = 83.57$; $p < 0.001$). As was to be expected, the proximity between respondents and alters with regard to geographical location resulted in a strong and significant correlation between meeting alters "online" and meeting them "offline" ($r = 0.44$; $p < 0.001$). A small number of alters (2.4 %) were only met in online platforms and never in person.

Ego–alter relations were mostly characterized as emotionally close ties. Most of the online relationships (53.1 %) were reported as "very close" and "close," 25.5 % of relations were "somewhat close", 10.2 % were perceived "not close," and the remaining 11.2 % were "not close at all." Dutch and migrant youths' networks had no significant differences regarding the closeness of ties.

Respondents talked about a wider range of socially oriented topics in comparison to interest-driven topics. Among the 9-item list of *socially* oriented and 8-item interest-driven topics, the average amount of items egos talked with alters was, respectively, ($M = 3.6$; $SD = 2$) ($M = 1.5$; $SD = 1.6$). Socially oriented topics are thus more popular in these online relationships. We have observed that Dutch youths were talking significantly more about *socially* oriented topics than their migrant peers ($F(1) = 9.49$; $p < 0.05$). For interest-driven topics there were no significant differences between these groups.

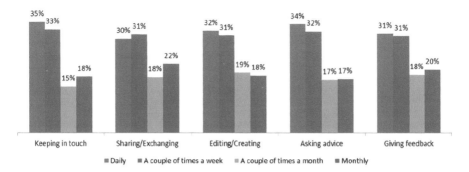

Fig. 12.2 Frequency of network interactions

Ego-Network Structure

The density of relationships in ego-networks was high. The majority of alters (69.3 %) knew each other. The average density in the sample was $M = 0.64$ (SD = 0.32) indicating that most ego-networks consisted of dense relations. An ANOVA showed significant difference in network density scores of Dutch and migrant youths' networks, with migrant youth having denser connected networks ($F(1) = 9.03$; $p < 0.01$).

The Frequency of Network Interactions

We observed that on average 58.2 % of the respondents reported that they were engaging in network activities regularly on varying frequencies. The most regularly participated activities were "asking for advice" with 87.4 %, followed by "sharing/ exchanging" 81.8 %, "keeping in touch" 79.1 %, "editing/creating" 78.6 %, and finally "giving feedback" 67.6 %. The percentages indicating the frequency per network activity (excluding the responses that reported "not active") are shown in Fig. 12.2.

Predicting Discovery in Networks

Question four about predicting the (perceived) discovery of new information was answered by means of multilevel regression analysis (MLA). The structure is such that the network characteristics (i.e., level one, henceforth mentioned as "network level") are nested under egos (i.e., level two, henceforth mentioned as "ego level"). This structure enables to study the variance parameters *within* ego-networks (i.e., differences per alter) and *between* ego-networks (i.e., differences per ego-network) (for further details refer to van Duijn et al., 1999). For the statistical procedure of the analysis, please refer to Ünlüsoy et al., (submitted).

The total variance of "discovery" was divided between network and ego levels (46 %–54 %, respectively). In other words, 54 % of "discovery" was attributed to the differences between egos' and 46 % to networks' characteristics, which points to the importance of relational or network aspects for explaining "discovery." The main effect of an ego's gender was the only significant variable on ego level, indicating that girls experience slightly less discovery in their networks than boys ($\beta = -.03, p < 0.05$).[1] On the network level we found that the amount of "interest-driven topics" significantly and positively ($\beta = 0.02, p < 0.05$) predicted "discovery," which means that shared interests lead to more new information. Regarding each network activity item, we also found a positive and significant influence on "discovery." From the highest influence to lowest, the effects were as follows: "sharing/exchanging" ($\beta = 0.32$, $p < 0.001$), "giving feedback" ($\beta = 0.24$, $p < 0.001$), "asking advice" ($\beta = 0.22, p < 0.001$), "editing/creating" ($\beta = 0.13$, $p < 0.001$), and "keeping in touch" ($\beta = 0.04, p < 0.01$). In other words, the more these activities are performed, the more youths perceive these online relationships as leading to discovering new information. The final model explained 71 % of the variance in total, with 45 % on the ego level and 26 % on the network level.

Discussion

The aim of this study was to describe characteristics of youths' online networks in detail and to study learning possibilities as a result of network participation. The results make evident that the main motivation to be in networks is socially driven, the majority of contacts are friends, and a proportion of interactions, however small, are about specific interests. These results are parallel to earlier studies that research the relationships between (informal) learning, new media, and online social networks (Ito et al., 2010).

Learning in online networks seemed a likely result of meddling with network technologies. We inquired whether popular social network activities, representing broad categories of participation, like sharing links, giving feedback, and editing/creating artifacts, would be related to the discovery of new information. We found that these network activities strongly and positively predicted the discovery of new information. However, we cannot know exactly how our subjects interpreted the "discovery of new information" and thus what exactly is learned from the activity according to the respondents, nor we can claim that "discovering new information" solely represents learning in all its complexity. Yet we can say that youths'

---

[1] β Scores are standardized regression coefficients or beta coefficients; they indicate the amount of change on the dependent variable ('discovery') at 1 standard deviation change on the predictor variables.

encounters with network technologies (phones, laptops, online sites) as well as their participation in these networked communities enable new ways of accessing and processing information. Based on our results we can also say that a more frequent participation in network interactions led our respondents to discover new information.

Whether or not youth also expand their lifeworlds with online communities still remains to be seen. Building bridges beyond one's own community is an important characteristic of learning in the digital age. A widely accepted hypothesis in this regard is that "diversity in one's network provides access to unique learning resources" (Burt, 2001; Granovetter, 1973). However, we have observed scarcity of diversity in youth networks. Similarities between respondents and alters prevailed (i.e., girls befriend girls; ethnic groups befriend people from same ethnic backgrounds). A likely explanation for this result is that people tend to befriend similar others and the groups based on similar characteristics also tend to be densely connected (McPherson, Smith-Lovin, & Cook, 2001).

The high scores in emotional closeness between our respondents and alters indicated that the majority of network relationships were "strong tie" relationships. The online groups that these youths built were based on emotionally close ties which are locally based and largely homogeneous. Another possible explanation for the lack of heterogeneity may be that in this age group, youth are still fostering the ties to their immediate community and that being accepted and being similar may allow for a safer exploring of the world.

Our results showed that youth frequently encounter new information even though their networks mostly consist of strong ties. This argument is somewhat in contrast to the ideas of Granovetter (1973) that it is the "weak ties" that bring new information to networks. However, this finding supports our initial stance that we should simply not talk in a priori and universal typologies when describing how networks and their particular ties relate to a potential to be innovative, gain knowledge, or form learning communities but that these relations always need to be contextualized and understood from their local, specific settings and social dynamics.

Regarding egonet methods, as a means to study networked learning, our study shows the possibilities with survey data. Using this method for designing the data collection (i.e., egonet survey) as well as for the analyses had significant advantages. Our survey design guided by an egonet framework enabled us to study various aspects of network composition and network structure. With our analysis we were able to show how personal and network characteristics predicted (perceived) discovery of information in social networks. Other more qualitative research designs could provide insight into interpretations of relationships, the evaluation of network activities or narratives that describe learning experience in online networks. Whether qualitatively or quantitatively used, egonet methodologies enable the researcher to study learning as a social phenomenon and study the learner in the midst of a web of social relationships.

In the literature the focus is shifting towards studying learning experiences across learning environments (school and elsewhere) and over longer periods of time (e.g., lifelong learning) (e.g., Erstad, 2012; Leander, Phillips, & Taylor, 2010). There is an increased emphasis on studying meaningful learning experiences throughout life, accounting for multiple spaces and places as "learning sites" and for "bridging the binary opposition between formal and informal learning" (Erstad, Gilje, Sefton-Green, & Vasbø, 2009, p.100). One way forward in this line of research is to include online networking platforms as a learning context. Here again, an egonet approach can have an added value because it provides insights into the individual in context and produces information about opportunities to learn in complementary, interrelated contexts, including the relations between online and offline contexts (see Leander, De Haan, Prinsen, & Ünlüsoy, in preparation).

Concluding Remarks

In this chapter we explored the value of egocentric network methodologies to study informal learning activities for networked learning research. We have shown the relevance and value of this methodology, even with a limited amount of survey questions as in the study presented. We believe that networked learning as a theoretical and practical framework has successfully guided the research to explore and explain different aspects and affordances of technologies while highlighting the importance of the social context and the communities in which people learn, and it will continue to do so. We suggest that the "uncharted" area of online social networks and the possible learning experiences that occur in these networks are yet other areas that deserve attention in this line of research.

References

Alexander, M. L. (2009). Qualitative social network research for relational sociology. In *Proceedings of The Australian Sociological Association Conference 2009: The future of sociology*. Retrieved October 29, 2011 from http://www.tasaconference2009.com/

Burt, R. S. (2001). Structural holes versus network closure as social capital. In N. Lin, K. Cook, & R. S. Burt (Eds.), *Social capital: Theory and research* (Controversy and integration series, pp. 31–56). New York: Aldine de Gruyter.

Central Bureau of Statistics. (2011). *Dutch youth very active on social networks*. Retrieved September 2, 2011 from http://www.cbs.nl/en-GB/menu/themas/vrije-tijd-cultuur/publicaties/default.htm

Chamberlain, D. (2006). Social network building: Combining qualitative interviews with egonet analysis. *Proceedings of The Australian Sociological Association Conference 2006*. Retrieved October 29, 2011 from http://www.tasa.org.au/conferences/conferencepapers06/

Coe, N. M., & Bunell, T. G. (2003). 'Spatializing' knowledge communities: towards a conceptualization of transnational innovation networks. *Global Networks, 3*(4), 437–456.

Cole, M., & Wertsch, J. V. (2004). *Beyond the individual-social antinomy in discussions of Piaget and Vygotsky*. Retrieved March 25, 2013 from http://www.massey.ac.nz/~alock/virtual/colevyg.htm

Cousin, G. (2005). Learning from cyberspace. In R. Land & S. Bayne (Eds.), *Education in cyberspace*. London, England: Routledge Falmer.

De Laat, M. F. (2006). *Networked learning*. Apeldoorn, The Netherlands: Politieacademie.

De Laat, M., & Lally, V. (2004). It's not so easy: Researching the complexity of emergent participant roles and awareness in asynchronous networked learning discussions. *Journal of Computer Assisted Learning, 20*(3), 165–171.

Erstad, O. (2012). The learning lives of digital youth—Beyond the formal and informal. *Oxford Review of Education, 38*(1), 25–43.

Erstad, O., Gilje, Ø., Sefton-Green, J., & Vasbø, K. (2009). Exploring 'learning lives': Community, identity, literacy and meaning. *Literacy, 43*(2), 100–106.

Flap, H., & Völker, B. (2001). Goal specific social capital and job satisfaction: Effects of different types of networks on instrumental and social aspects of work. *Social Networks, 23*(4), 297–320.

Gee, J. P. (2004). *Situated language and learning: A critique of traditional schooling*. London, England: Routledge.

Gee, J. P. (2008). *Social linguistics and literacies: Ideology in discourses*. London, England: Taylor & Francis.

Goodyear, P., Banks, S., Hodgson, V., & McConnell, D. (2004). Research on networked learning: An overview. In P. Goodyear, S. Banks, V. Hodgson, & D. McConnell (Eds.), *Advances in research on networked learning*. Dordrecht, The Netherlands: Kluwer.

Granovetter, M. S. (1973). The strength of weak ties. *American Journal of Sociology, 78*(6), 1360–1380.

Haythornthwaite, C. (2000). Online personal networks: size, composition and media use among distance learners. *New Media Society, 2*(2), 195–226.

Haythornthwaite, C. (2006). Learning and knowledge networks in interdisciplinary collaborations. *Journal of the American Society for Information Science and Technology, 57*(8), 1079–1092.

Haythornthwaite, C. (2009, January). Crowds and communities: Light and heavyweight models of peer production. In *System Sciences, 2009. HICSS'09. 42nd Hawaii International Conference on System Sciences* (pp. 1–10).

Hodgson, V., McConnell, D., & Dirckinck-Holmfeld, L. (2012). The theory, practice and pedagogy of networked learning. In L. Dirckinck-Holmfeld, V. Hodgson, & D. McConnell (Eds.), *Exploring the theory, pedagogy and practice of networked learning* (pp. 291–305). London, England: Springer.

Hox, J. J. (2010). *Multilevel analysis: Techniques and applications*. London, England: Taylor & Francis.

Ito, M., Baumer, S., Bittanti, M., Cody, R., Herr-Stephenson, B., Horst, H. A., et al. (2010). *Hanging out, messing around, and geeking out: Kids living and learning with new media*. Cambridge, MA: MIT Press.

Jenkins, H. (2009). *Confronting the challenges of participatory culture: Media education for the 21st century*. Cambridge, MA: MIT Press.

Kop, R., Fournier, H., & Mak, J. S. F. (2011). A pedagogy of abundance or a pedagogy to support human beings? Respondent support on massive open online courses. *International Review of Research in Open and Distance Learning, 12*(7), 74–93.

Krackhardt, D. (1992). The strength of strong ties: The importance of philos in organizations. In N. Nohria & R. G. Eccles (Eds.), *Networks and organizations: Structure, form, and action* (pp. 216–239). Boston, MA: Harvard Business School Press.

Lave, J., & Wenger, E. (1991). *Situated learning: Legitimate peripheral participation*. Cambridge, MA: Cambridge University Press.

Leander, K., & De Haan, M. (2011). Networking expansive forms of identity and learning: Examining the new media practices of immigrant youth in the Netherlands. In *The American Educational Research Association (AERA), 2011 Annual Meeting*. SIG-Cultural Historical Research, New Orleans, LO.

Leander, K. M., Phillips, N. C., & Taylor, K. H. (2010). The changing social spaces of learning: Mapping new mobilities. *Review of Research in Education, 34*(1), 329–394.

McConnell, D., Hodgson, V., & Dirckinck-Holmfeld, L. (2012). Networked learning: A brief history and new trends. (pp. 3–23). In L. Dirckinck-Holmfeld, V. Hodgson, & D. McConnell (Eds.), *Exploring the theory, pedagogy and practice of networked learning*. London, England: Springer.

McPherson, M., Smith-Lovin, L., & Cook, J. M. (2001). Birds of a feather: Homophily in social networks. *Annual Review of Sociology, 415–444*.

Rasbash, J., Charlton, C., Browne, W. J., Healy, M., & Cameron, B. (2005). *MLwiN version 2.02*. Bristol, England: Centre for Multilevel Modeling, University of Bristol.

Rogoff, B. (2003). *The cultural nature of human development*. New York: Oxford University Press.

Rogoff, B., & Lave, J. (Eds.). (1999). *Everyday cognition: Its development in social context*. Cambridge, MA: Harvard University Press.

Sørensen, B. H., Danielsen, O., & Nielsen, J. (2007). Children's informal learning in the context of schools of the knowledge society. *Education and Information Technologies, 12*(1), 17–27.

van Duijn, M. A., van Busschbach, J. T., & Snijders, T. A. (1999). Multilevel analysis of personal networks as dependent variables. *Social Networks, 21*(2), 187–210.

Wellman, B. (1983). Network analysis: Some basic principles. *Sociological Theory, 1*(1), 155–200.

Wertsch, J. V. (1998). *Mind as action*. New York: Oxford University Press.

Wertsch, J. V. (2002). *Voices of collective remembering*. Cambridge, MA: Cambridge University Press.

Williams, R. A. (2011). *Multicollinearity* [pdf document]. Retrieved May 5, 2012 from http://www.nd.edu/~rwilliam/stats2/l11.pdf

Chapter 13
Mobile Learning and Immutable Mobiles: Using iPhones to Support Informal Learning in Craft Brewing

Steve Wright and Gale Parchoma

Introduction

This chapter is a case study of the use of iPhones in informal learning processes and practices in two craft breweries. The authors suggest that actor-network theory (ANT) has a significant contribution to make in researching networked learning, particularly in *informal* contexts where the boundaries of any network are not predefined by a course, curriculum or institution but are assembled by the participants. How these networks are assembled and held together must be traced and grounded in empirical observation.

We draw on the "surprisingly enduring" (McConnell, Hodgson, & Dirckinck-Holmfeld, 2012, p. 6) definition of networked learning as:

> learning in which information and communications technology (ICT) is used to promote connections: between one learner and other learners, between learners and tutors; between a learning community and its learning resources. (Goodyear, Banks, Hodgson, & McConnell, 2004, pp.1)

ANT however emphasises a symmetrical consideration of all elements: learners, ICT and resources rather than privileging any one as the object of attention. Like one of its methodological antecedents, ethnomethodology, ANT rejects the use of predefined social categories as both topic of study *and* resource for explanation. In ANT an a priori social aggregate such as "community" can only be asserted by showing how it is formed and how it is assembled and held together through tracing

S. Wright (✉)
Faculty of Health and Medicine, Furness College, Lancaster University,
Lancaster LA1 4YG, UK
e-mail: s.t.wright@lancaster.ac.uk

G. Parchoma
University of Calgary, Education Tower 602B, 2500 University Drive N.W., Calgary,
AB, Canada T2N 1N4
e-mail: gale.parchoma@ucalgary.ca

V. Hodgson et al. (eds.), *The Design, Experience and Practice of Networked Learning*, 241
Research in Networked Learning, DOI 10.1007/978-3-319-01940-6_13,
© Springer International Publishing Switzerland 2014

the associations between its actants. Only through demonstrating and describing how such a formation emerges and the work required to maintain its existence can an aggregate such as "community" be invoked, conceptualised as an emergent networked effect. As such ANT is *not a theory of learning*. As an approach it seeks to iconoclastically pull down traditional dualisms such as agency/structure and contemporary ones such as real/virtual or digital/non-digital in order to "reassemble the social" (Latour, 2005). Rather than considering interpersonal "social processes" in given institutions such as "classroom learning", an ANT approach undertakes symmetrical consideration of how both human and non-human agencies perform realities.

The metaphor of a network is intentionally used as one which is flexible and nonhierarchical–standing in contrast to traditional sociological metaphors of "social structures" or bounded institutions. These networks are always provisional and contingent–the sociologist's job is to describe the work involved in the formation, maintenance and subsequent reinforcement or collapse of such networks through assembling case studies from empirical observation and description (Latour, 2005; Law, 2009).

In this opening commentary, we have sought to establish the relationship of an ANT-informed approach to networked learning with the broader concerns of this book. We have outlined relationships to other literature: transporting and enrolling texts from other authors in order to set out how this case study relates to the theory, design and practice of networked learning. ANT-derived terms can helpfully describe this requirement as an "obligatory point of passage" (Callon, 1986) through which our account must pass.

Defining Terms: Entangling Networked, Informal and Mobile Learning Through ANT

Engagement with ANT as an approach in educational research "has been sporadic rather than sustained" (Fenwick & Edwards, 2010, p. 1). While there is much written within ANT about knowledge and knowing, it is *not* a theory of learning. However it poses a substantial challenge to many established models, methodologies and concepts used to consider and research learning.

In an early collection of papers on networked learning edited by Steeples and Jones (2001), the variety of theoretical frameworks used to research NL are drawn together. Among these is a work by Fox (2001) that considers how ANT challenges conventional conceptions of what learning is and where and how it happens. He argues that:

> One of the first ways in which traditional learning theory should be revised concerns the hallowed notion of "the learner" and the associated notion of "the learning process"... learning at some point in a network can transform the network.... Learning is one of the processes which builds up and breaks down networks, although there may be other processes which achieve similar effects. (Fox, 2001, pp. 84–85)

In moving the focus of attention of learning away from the *individual* learner within the symmetrical analysis of human and non-human actants and agency, Fox took an ambitious step into attempting to consider how learning could be engaged with or accounted for using ANT. However Fox did not extend this line of reasoning to consider *how* learning could assemble or transform an actor-network or how different actor-networks may change as learning builds them up or breaks them down. Through our case study we seek to draw on, explore and theorise these notions.

Fox also suggests where we could productively look for such cases arguing that:

> If NL were simply to focus on educationalised learning processes through cyberspace, it would miss all the natural, informal and situated learning which occurs, through the internet as well as through other social networks and spaces, outside of deliberately designed educational activities. . .The possibility exists that the study of learning, even networked learning, which occurs 'naturally', 'incidentally', 'situatedly' and 'pervasively' in everyday life and workplaces in particular, will repay educational designers, just as clothes designers frequently benefit from the close observation of street fashion. (Fox, 2001, p. 78)

Learning that occurs naturally, incidentally, situatedly and pervasively is often classified as informal. Tusting (2003) evokes the criteria of accreditation, place, planning and power as distinguishing characteristics among formal, designed-to-happen (planned, assessed and accredited by educational institutions); non-formal, but intended-to-happen (pre-planned, organised workplace learning); and informal, learner-led efforts where learning just happens (in the absence of externally imposed criteria or authority). While these distinctions are useful, Colley, Hodkinson and Malcolm (2002) contend that such distinctions are only partial, in that "attributes of formality and informality are interrelated in different ways in different situations" (p. 9).

An influential model of "informal and incidental learning", developed by Marsick and Watkins (2001), further distinguishes interrelationships between informal and incidental learning within a range of situated practices. Informal learning is defined as contextual, intentional, "triggered" by an internal or external stimulus, "integrated into daily activities", "haphazard and influenced by chance", marked by involvement in "an inductive process of reflection and action" and importantly, "linked to the learning of others" (p. 28). Drawing on their earlier, widely cited work, "incidental learning" is further defined as a *by-product* of intentional activity that frequently occurs even though people are seldom aware of it (Marsick & Watkins, 1990). We will return to and problematise terms throughout our chapter. The intersection of informal learning with networked communication technologies which Fox considered has seen rapid expansion since the publication of his chapter. One area of particular attention in contemporary research has been the development, diffusion and widespread adoption of Internet-connected mobile devices and "smartphones" such as the iPhone. However, informal learning and smartphone use remains under-represented in the literature (Frohberg, 2006). Furthermore investigations in this field are marked by particular practices and discourses. A literature review by the authors looked at how researchers extolled the use of mobile devices but typically controlled both the devices in use and the tasks to be completed, frequently in quasi-experimental studies within formal educational settings.

We contrasted this with the self-selected use of mobile devices without such controls in informal learning (Wright & Parchoma, 2011). This chapter seeks to contribute towards increasing the representation of informal mobile learning by presenting detailed observation of the use of iPhones in the situated practices of craft brewing.

Setting the Scene: The Participants and Practices of Craft Brewing

The following post on an Internet forum was the instigator of this study:

> I just love the brew pal software. Its help [sic] me learn quite a lot about brewing, even to the point that it's helping me get ready for my first all grain, I do think if it wasn't for the app I would be months behind where I am now in terms of understanding the stuff that's going on. (Participant 1)

This unsolicited account was posted in response to a discussion thread on "iPhone and iPad brewing software". As a forum participant, the account quoted above drew our attention in its explicit linkage of a mobile smartphone application to *learning* and *understanding* and to the *practice* of craft brewing. It also implies a framing by the participant of learning as "understanding the stuff that's going on"— evoking an information acquisition view of learning. We explore the tensions of such a view with broader formulations of learning as negotiating situated actions. We seek to unpack and explore this tension further in this paper and expand the latter view through the symmetrical analysis of ANT.

The ten forum participants who posted to the thread were the purposive sample for this research project, all of whom were emailed. After receiving replies from the majority, two were selected for participant observation—one novice and one experienced brewer—based on pragmatic considerations of time and proximity to the researcher in the north of England.

In order to understand the function of a computer app in brewing, we give a brief overview of the processes and practices involved. There are three main approaches to home brewing: (1) using a premade kit where just water and yeast are added, (2) starting with malt extract and (3) starting with the raw materials of malted grain. The latter process of all-grain brewing involves steeping malted grains in water within a narrow temperature range that enables enzymes in the malt to break down starches into fermentable sugars—a process called mashing. This mixture of sugar and water, called "wort", is then boiled with hops which contribute bitterness, flavour and aroma. The wort is then rapidly cooled before yeast is added. The yeast ferments the sugars, transforming the sweet wort into the carbonated alcoholic liquid we know as beer.

In order to predict and try to control the outcomes of each stage of this process, a lot of relatively complex and highly interdependent calculations of temperature, time, volume and density of dissolved sugars are required. An example below is a formula (Tinseth, 1995) for calculating bitterness from a hop addition:

$$\text{Utilisation} = (1.65 \times 0.000125^{\wedge}(OG - 1))$$
$$\times ((1 - 2.72^{\wedge}(-0.04 \times \text{Hop Boil Time}))/4.14)$$

$$\text{IBU} = \text{Utilisation}^{*}(oz \times (AA\%/100)^{*}7,490)/\text{Volume of batch in gallons}$$

Definitions: OG = "original gravity", a measure of sugars dissolved in a liquid as a measure of specific gravity.

IBU = International Bittering Units, one of the standard measures of bitterness. AA = Alpha Acids, a measure of bittering potential of a hop based on α acids as percentage of total hop weight.

Rather than undertaking all these calculations laboriously by hand, craft brewers use a variety of tools to support them. Reference tables, worksheets and software packages have recently been joined by apps for a range of mobile devices, including iPhones. However, it is not *only* calculations that inform brewing but also qualitative sensory judgements of taste, colour and aroma. Apps also provide support for these assessments, including predicting colour from recipe ingredients and providing standardised reference colour charts. There is little hard data on the number of home brewers using such software; however one of the apps considered here, BrewPal, has an active user base of over 20,000 users as indicated by upgrades to new versions (BrewPal, 2013, personal communication).

Methods Assemblage: Multimodal and Focussed Ethnography

ANT has its origins in ethnographic studies of scientific practices where it was "developed to analyse situations in which it is difficult to separate humans and non-humans, and in which the actors have variable forms and competencies" (Callon, 1998, p. 183). We have already sought to introduce some ANT terms such as "obligatory points of passage" and "translation" following Law's suggestion that ANT "is not abstract but is grounded in empirical case studies. We can only understand the approach if we have a sense of those case studies and how these work in practice" (Law, 2009, p. 141). We seek to continue this approach in our exposition of the two cases—introducing concepts and terminology through empirical examples rather than abstractions, via illustrating what ANT can contribute to understanding informal learning networks.

In seeking to describe how mobile devices are *used* in the informal situated learning practices of craft brewing, we frame this investigation through Humphreys' (2006) analysis of visual ethnographic methods for examining mobile phone uses. Humphreys argues that well-considered analyses of photographic artefacts from field studies can "add significantly to our understanding of how mobile devices are contextually defined and used" (p.55).

Marcus (1998) proposes that ethnographic studies should adopt a multi-sited methodological approach to investigating field sites which are interconnected with other locations wherein:

> Research is designed around chains, paths, threads, conjunctions, or juxtapositions of locations in which the ethnographer establishes some sort of literal, physical presence, with an explicit logic of association or connection among sites that in fact defines the argument of the ethnography. (Marcus, 1998, p. 90)

This concept of following connections aligns to the ANT sensibility to *follow the actors* (Latour, 1987) by tracing their chains, paths and threads which assemble a network and can include materials, participants' accounts, images and media files. These chains and paths are traced outward from the site of observation, which is bounded by a "brew day" of around 7 h duration in the participants' home breweries. In observing time- and location-bound intensive activity, we draw on methods associated with "focussed ethnography" "a form of short-term ethnographies [sic] by which information relevant to the development or change of technological systems are collected in an intensive and rapid way" (Knoblauch, 2005: 8), making extensive use of audio, video and photographic records to supplement traditional field notes.

By following chains and connections and using a network metaphor, an ANT approach rejects and seeks to "bypass" (Latour, 2005, p. 22) the binary divisions and a priori categories of much of social theory such as natural/social, micro/macro, structure/agency and subject/object, which are instead seen as *effects* of the process of assembly and collapse of the networks of relations between heterogeneous actants. This, together with its principle of symmetrical consideration of all elements—both human and non-human—has practical effects on the method of participant observation. A praxiographic orientation is required which "allows and requires one to take objects and events of all kinds into consideration when trying to understand the world. No phenomenon can be ignored on the grounds that it belongs to another discipline" (Mol, 2003, p. 158).

Within a praxiographic approach, objects, materials, yeast, grains, gas, burners, welding, iPhone apps, videos, conversations, accounts and actions all require attention. The observer should not pre-select one single human actor alone as object of attention and interest nor preconceive that they alone are where "learning" is to be found, thereby excluding other processes and practices as belonging to "science" or "nature". Attention is directed to neither "the social" nor "the natural" but the material-semiotic relationships among these networks of elements that *perform* such dualisms (Law, 2009). This approach gives "an unfamiliar take on many familiar issues" (Fenwick & Edwards, 2010, p. 2) and may involve following or starting with an unlikely actor as a research subject. An exemplary example within networked learning theory is by Thompson (2012) who starts from the delete button and uncovers issues, tensions, politics and dangers as people and professional practices are enmeshed with Web 2.0 technologies.

In the two cases described in this paper, we follow non-human actors, tracing the movements of recipes through two different breweries, enmeshing and assembling a network of actants including a brewer, brewery equipment, an iPhone, apps, podcasts, YouTube videos, grains, yeast, hops and more. First we describe each case in detail, giving an account of the practices supported by illustrative photos, screenshots and other images collected from the fieldwork. The images show the arrangements and juxtapositions of materials, technologies and practices and are organised sequentially. Our focus on sequence and temporality is an intentional response to the current paucity of studies of the use of mobile devices in informal learning practices. Furthermore, a thick description and detailed illustrations can travel to, be enrolled in and translated into other accounts and conceptualisations where a gloss would lose the richness of relevance. Detailed description also allows us to anchor and illustrate terms and concepts we use.

Fieldwork Site 1: Novice Brewery, Mobile Device and Immutable Mobile Recipe

We use the term "novice brewery" intentionally to consider symmetrically *all* of the elements, human and non-human alike, as novices in a newly assembled brewery rather than to isolate the brewer as the singular repository of "experience" or location of "learning" (a theoretical consideration we return to in our discussion).

One of the authors observed this site during the brewery's second ever all-grain brew day. Participant 1 (P1) had previously been brewing for "9 years on and off" using premade canned extract kits to which only water was added. In the construction of the brewery, his iPhone was used to take photos of aspects of assembly and welding and to post these images along with text descriptions and requests for advice and solutions to issues on the Internet discussion board previously mentioned.

Following Latour (2005, pp. 224–225) we present a series of images in Fig. 13.1 to illustrate actants and sequences. We then describe the images introducing terms from actor-network to explicate the socio-material practices observed. We emphasise that the diagram shows a sequence of actions and practices which can be explained through concepts of "moments of translation" or the "assembly of a network" but the diagram is not a visualisation of those ideas per se, for which we would direct the reader to the diagrams in Callon (1986).

The diagram is a closed loop with the start and end of a commercially produced beer (1a) called Cocker Hoop, made by Jennings Brewery in the UK. Participant 1 had purchased two bottles of this beer to compare with both the unfermented wort and with his finished product once packaged and matured.

A recipe for making a copy of this beer was published in the book "Brew Your Own British Real Ale at Home" (1b). This book has outline instructions on brewing methods, along with a collection of recipes for reproducing commercial beers. The recipes list quantities of malts and hops together with calculated measurements including bitterness and gravity. Participant 1 owned a copy of this book but had not

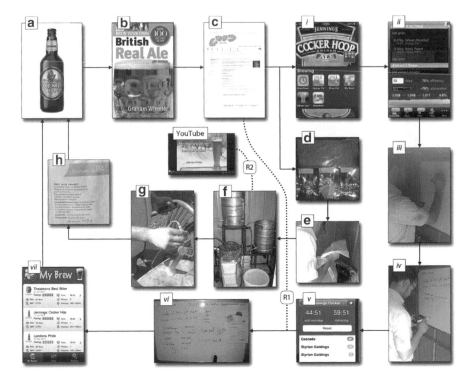

Fig. 13.1 Translations of an immutable recipe in a novice brewery

read it in detail and did not refer to it while brewing. He preferred to use apps as they were "more interactive" describing how with "a book you've got to sit through it and read it and if you don't absorb it yeah you've lost it by the time you've flicked the page over; whereas with an app, you flick back to it and all the information's just there for you". He had previously entered recipes from the book into the BrewPal app and then varied quantities and added, subtracted or substituted ingredients and looked at the calculated outcomes of these simulated variations. The role of simulation in this setting and its relationship to creativity and the transition towards mastery is explored further in Wright, Short and Parchoma (in press).

Some of the recipes from the book had been selected by a web-based home-brew merchant, "Worcester Hop Shop", who had partially reproduced the recipes on the company website (1c). The recipe has now moved through intermediaries from book to web page to printout but it is not "translated". In ANT terminology the recipe is here an example of an "immutable mobile". Despite moving from book to web, it has retained its form and fidelity.

The company offers a service to assemble and send out the recipe as a weighed and packaged kit of ingredients accompanied by a printed copy of the recipe. Here the transformation of the recipe and its dispatch enacts the ANT concept of "translation". Translation is set out as a four-stage process by Callon (1986) and is taken from the French word *traduction*, which carries different implications than those associated English word "translation" with its focus on language (a point we shall return to). In step 1 of the translation process, the home-brew supply company has "problematised" an issue: how to get the right quantities and ratios of ingredients to transform a recipe from words into a beer. Through their website they act to interesse (step 2) home breweries by providing a solution to this problem: they transform the written recipe into measured and packaged materials. By ordering the kit P1 is "enrolled" (step 3) into their actor-network as a "customer". Their construction and transformation of the recipe becomes authoritative. Their interpretation now acts as a "spokesperson" for the recipe-as-materials. We again encounter an "obligatory point of passage"—the web ordering system—for making *this* version, *their* version, of the recipe. They then engage in step 4, "mobilisation of allies" (couriers, customers, etc.), to complete the translation and send the materials to the home brewery. Through this process, they are, in turn, enrolled into other actor-networks of transportation: deliveries, vans, drivers and a distribution network of a courier company that transports the materials to the brewery. Once at the brewery, the materials will be further translated as the assembled equipment enrols them into its actor-network. The concept of translation thus involves much more than mere changes of state or movements of materials or ideas. The materialisation of an authoritative account (here a pre-packaged recipe) reinforces its power, which is where the material-semiotic approach of ANT builds on and extends Foucaultian notions of discourses and knowledge as power. It does this through the symmetrical analysis of the agency of humans *and non*-humans that we use here to consider how materials reinforce and make durable structures of knowledge and power.

We return to the diagram where the sequential paths now split and run in parallel. On the "inner circuit" are the material transformations and processes of brewing. On the outer circuit are the inscriptions and accounts of these transformations. The two are related in our case studies and the iPhone is entangled in both. As we shall see, at times the iPhone acts as an *intermediary*: merely moving information without alteration. However, at other stages, it becomes a *mediator*, transforming and changing relationships.

On the inside track, the recipe-as-materials (1d) comprises preweighted and mixed grain, preweighed and separately packaged hops and a packet of dried yeast. Water is heated to the temperature prescribed by the recipe and the grain is mixed into the water (1e). Brewing processes (mashing, boiling with hops and cooling) are all carried out. Each stage involves measurement and is recorded on the outer circuit. Finally the beer is run off and cooled (1f) and the gravity of the liquid is measured (1 g). Here the brewer holds a thermometer in his right hand, recording the temperature, while a hydrometer gives a reading of the specific gravity; however, this reading is affected by temperature. In his left hand the participant holds the iPhone using his thumb on the touch screen to enter the gravity and temperature readings which are then corrected by the app. Afterwards he writes this information down on the whiteboard. Cooling completed, the packet of yeast (1 h) is pitched into the wort. The yeast ferments the wort into beer which is then bottled, matured and eventually drunk and compared for taste, aroma and colour with the originating beer (1a).

Participant 1 described how the equipment in use (1f) was constructed with reference to videos on YouTube, which he accessed on his iPhone (R2). He had supplemented this by posting images taken with his iPhone and descriptions of the equipment to the Internet forum along with questions when he encountered problems. Messages from other forum members identified methods and materials he could use to construct equipment such as the cooling coil from garden hose, copper pipe and plumbing fittings.

Alongside and enmeshed with these practices are inscriptions of their progress: recorded actions, measurement and outcomes of calculations. These form the outer circuit of images and illustrate how the iPhone does not stand alone as a device but is entangled with other practices and materials—supporting the documentation of processes.

The brewer has several apps installed and has changed his phone background to an image of the bottle label of the commercial beer he is copying (1i). He opens up the BrewPal app (1ii) and the screen displays the ingredients to be used along with calculated gravities, volumes and alcohol, as well as a predicted colour. Other screen displays show volumes of liquids required and calculations for hop bitterness.

The recipe has been input into this device by reading from the printout of the recipe (1c, 1d) and selecting menu items using finger or thumb on the touch screen to select items displayed in menus. However through this process the immutability of the recipe falls apart. While it has been held together as it moved through intermediaries, from book to website to reproduction on printed page, here it is mediated—becoming transformed as it moves. The iPhone app can be understood as having agency enrolling both the brewer and the recipe through problematising the complex calculations and offering a solution. It has also enrolled the brewery and become a spokesperson for the performance of the equipment. However, through interaction with the brewer and the problematic touch-screen selection interface, this translation from page to electronic version and now to whiteboard has encountered a betrayal. A slip of a finger on the iPhone screen has resulted in a different hop being unintentionally selected from the menu.

The term "translation" has been identified as encompassing an ever-present potential for breakdown; thus it is a difficult term to translate from its origins in Callon's work in French to an English discourse. Both French words used by Callon, *translation* (meaning movement) and *traduction* (meaning linguistic transformation from one language to another), are translated into English as "translation". Implicated within both is the idea that when something—a word, a "fact" or an object—moves from one setting to another, there is always the risk of "*trahison* [treason and difference]" (Law, 2003, p. 10). This may happen through a new context and assemblage of relations serving to change the associated status, implication or meaning of the object. It can also result from a breakdown when a translation is left incomplete or disrupted. We see the results of just such a breakdown enacted here at the interface of human and screen.

Despite the much-vaunted functionality of the touch screen and app to enable updating information during the brewing process, this is not enrolled in the process observed. The participant takes time to re-inscribe the recipe from the iPhone onto a whiteboard (2iii) accounting for this change as

> "with the mobile problem you got is you got to get it in and out of your pocket all . . . time if you want to look at it".

This is not only difficult to do but risky too: a dropped phone will break while a dropped marker pen will bounce. On the whiteboard the recipe is easily visible, accessible but also mutable. Erasing and rewriting can break down what was previously held together as immutable: recognising this P1 also attaches a copy of the recipe printed out from BrewPal to the whiteboard as a reference.

Having written information from screen to board, the brewer then re-inscribes the information copied to the whiteboard into a different app "BrewTimer" on the iPhone (1iv, 1v) because moving the information digitally is not prevented. This app is used to measure times and sound alarms to start a new practice or process, such as adding hops to the boil or turning the gas off to end the boil.

The process of comparing the inscription on the packaged hops as containing "41 g Challenger" to the inscription in BrewPal now reproduced on the whiteboard and being input into the BrewTimer App of "Cascade" leads to a major disruption. Once this discrepancy is identified, the participant described his confusion as:

> I should have some centennial hops, why have they sent me challenger? . . . I think it must be the recipe. . . I'll have to go have a look at recipe on't website.

This observation leads to the only use during the brewing process of connection to the Internet (R1) as the phone's mobile data connection and browser app are used to view the recipe on the supplier's website and check this against the versions of the recipe on the phone apps and whiteboard. This requires work and effort and the assembly of a new network of technologies and connections to retrace a route and the previous translations, to undo them and return the mobile recipe to its prior form.

We see here shifts in the configuration of the network. The whiteboard becomes the spokesperson for the recipe: it becomes the authoritative source and is updated and revised from information retrieved from the supplier's website through the phone browser. The status of the other accounts (those in the two apps) was left uncorrected as evidenced by screen shots from the device emailed at the end of the observation. However, the coexistence of differing accounts is glossed over as the pressure of time required action and a single corrected account on the whiteboard was sufficient—the iPhone's role as spokesperson now supplanted by a different medium.

This pressure of time is also measured and compartmentalised through the mobile device. The Brewtimer app is started, translating the problem of time measurement and reminders of action into a countdown clock and sequence of alarms and onscreen messages. As these sound they prompt action in the brewery as taps are opened, liquid pumped and new timers started.

At the end of the brew, the whiteboard (1vi) is a composite record of the physical transformations: a checked-off list of completed actions and a record of the outcomes of calculations, times and measurements. These results of situated actions are entered into the app and juxtaposed and contrasted with the plans and predictions of the recipe and apps. A smaller volume of wort at a lower gravity (density of sugars) was produced, indicating inefficiency in equipment and processes.

Some records of volumes and gravities from the white board are also entered into another app which is used to track fermentation activity and outcomes over the next week, as well as sensory evaluation and assessment of the finished product (1vii).

The final calculations indicated substantially lower outcomes than predicted. An explanation of lower than expected outcomes was developed through subsequent equipment checking and cleaning. P1 found several areas where unused liquid remained latent in different parts of the brewing process. This "dead space" affected the overall efficiency of the brewery and thus impacted on the calculations made from an assumed "typical" iPhone app representation of an effective brewery. In response to this mismatch of prototypical calculated brewery and the brewery assembled in use, multiple changes were enacted to equipment through subsequent re-engineering, realignment and other adaptations and reconfigurations of brewery equipment. These changes to material configurations also brought changes to human/machine practices with accounts of these changes shared through images taken using the iPhone and posted to the online forum and via twitter. We return to consider the relationship of these changes to learning from an ANT viewpoint after exploring continuities and differences of equipment and practices in an experienced brewery.

Fieldwork Site 2: Experienced Brewery and the Fluid Object of a Recipe

Fieldwork location 2 was in a more experienced brewery. Participant 2 (P2) "started kit brewing 4 years ago . . . all grain for 2 years and 3 months" and had been brewing approximately 2–3 times per month. He estimated that about half of his brewing was based on published recipes and the other half his own formulations.

Figure 13.2 follows a similar pattern to the one used for P1, once again illustrating the temporal and sequential ordering of practices and arrangement of materials. The simpler construction of the diagram is not intended to evoke simpler processes nor more sophisticated practices but rather reflects development in fieldwork methodology and a more coherent and explicitly sequential capturing of the images used here

The original beer (2a) is an American Ale which the brewer knows well and likes. A recipe for "cloning" the brew is published in a book (2b) which P2 is using for the first time. He reports that he wants to take a beer that he knows quite well to "see how it matches up [but] if it's miles apart [I] probably won't brew anything else out of it". Unlike P1, for P2 the published recipe is not just a resource to follow and guide practice but is itself a topic of investigation. This evaluation is informed

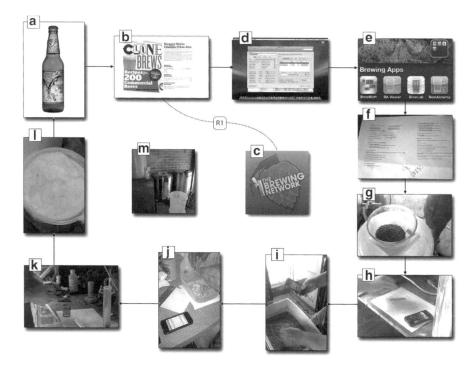

Fig. 13.2 Translations of a fluid recipe in an experienced brewery

by P2's regular listening to podcasts on brewing different beer styles and recipes from "The Brewing Network" he downloads to his iPhone (R1) and listens to while commuting to work or during breaks on a night shift.

The recipe is entered into "BeerAlchemy" on P2's computer (2d) as he "prefers to use a keyboard" (helping to avoid the errors in translation when using a touch screen, as witnessed with P1). The recipe is then transferred via intermediaries: a printer to render a printed version on an A4 sheet of paper (2f) and via a Wi-Fi connection to sync with the BeerAlchemy app on P2's iPhone (2e). P2 describes the use of the app on a brew day as being "for the calculations really ...you can do all the adjustments on here, the amounts and everything". The recipe has changed form and location but merely passed through these intermediaries—retaining its fidelity, remaining immutable.

The next moment of movement requires change as the recipe is translated from words and figures on screen and printed page through calculations and measurements into materials: grains, hops and yeast (2 g) which are weighed and combined. The brewery has an inventory of grains stored in sealed containers and hops in a freezer drawer. However, in the process of weighing out, it becomes evident that there is insufficient pale ale malt available and substitution is required. Here the recipe is changed.

The calculations for this change are written down on the printout: the quantity of pale ale malt available and used is recorded first. Then other potential substitute ingredients in stock (lager malt and wheat malt) are identified and weighed then recorded using pencil, paper and an iPhone calculator app (1 h). The calculator app is closed and the BeerAlchemy app reopened. The figures from the paper-and-pencil inventory audit are input into the onscreen recipe which calculates new predictions from the change in ingredients. Adjustments are made in the app so that the predicted outcomes match the guidelines of the original recipe. The substitute grains are then weighed out using the amounts from the new recipe version displayed on screen and the grains are mixed together for mashing.

In this complex process, the more structural four-step sequence of translation drawn on in P1 becomes inadequate: the recipe emerges at the end translated into grains but in a new though recognisable configuration. Rather than working to maintain immutability, the work is to enable and adapt to changed circumstance. The recipe is no longer something "immutable" but instead has shifted its boundaries. This shift from immutability to fluidity is reflected in later work derived from and responding to early ANT. de Laet and Mol (2000) studied the diffusion, spread and variation of a bush pump for delivering clean groundwater in Zimbabwe. They note how its spread, adoption and installation required it to be adaptable to local situations and that it enrols other technologies in its network but these are variable by situation rather than fixed in advance. However these are not vague or random. "The Bush Pump's various boundaries define a limited set of configurations. They each, one might say, enact a different Bush Pump. But these different Bush Pumps have in common that they are indeed a pump" (p.237–8). De Laet and Mol argue that "the Zimbabwe Bush Pump is a fluid actor. It brings a lot about, but its boundaries and constitution vary and its success and failure, instead of being clear-cut, are a matter of degree". This *fluid technology* reinforces its mobility not through immutability but through adaptation and change. In the adaptation of this recipe in the experienced brewery, where it maintains its overall form but becomes fluid through the substitution of some ingredients, we suggest that this concept is a useful one—and will return to consider the possible implications with regard to learning.

Once the recipe is adapted, water is added to the grains and the temperature measured. The temperature attained is too low so the mobile app is used to make a rapid calculation of how much boiling water will need to be added to bring the temperature up appropriately (2i). The kettle is boiled, the measured amount added and the temperature achieved with a thermometer used to check the outcome against the app's prediction—they match.

Hop additions are measured and separated out with the iPhone placed next to the scales and the recipe displayed on the app screen (2 k). At the end of the boil, P2 uses the same methods and materials as P1 to measure and temperature-correct the specific gravity the specific gravity reading of the wort using a hydrometer of the app (2 l). Finally yeast is pitched and fermentation starts rapidly and ferments fully.

On the other side of the brewery was a set of new equipment (2 m) which was being customised—including a household hot water tank, a steel tank and an insulated catering pot to create a new larger capacity and more flexible brewery enabling greater volumes and variations of beers to be made from one mash.

The final assessment was that the beer was "very good!", though *not* a very close approximation of the original beer. However, P2's account did not specifically attribute the non-approximation to any particular factor such as the situated adaptation of the grains used. As noted at the start of this case, another aspect of the practice was evaluation of the recipe book. P2 reported subsequently brewing another recipe from this book, a "Lagunitas IPA". However that was *also* adapted from the published version, though not in response to resource limitations but with reference to "expert information" from a podcasted interview with the Lagunitas head brewer who gave a different formulation of the hop blend used compared to that written in the book.

Drawing Together

We have focussed in particular on the methods used by actants in particular actions and sequences of events. The iPhone strengthens the localised brewery networks through its provision of timely calculation and measurement recording, segmenting and combining units of time, volumes and weight. Its apps support refinements to brewery practices through predicting and assessing outcomes of brewer, brewery and material actions. In the novice brewery, once the mobile *has* become part of the network, it becomes an obligatory point of passage for the recipe as a centre of calculation for prediction and assessment. Across the broader actor-network of the craft brewing community, it distributes comparable evidence (e.g. images and measurements) that influences changes in socio-material practices.

In both breweries the iPhone is used around this situated practice of a brew day. Constant Internet connectivity is peripheral to the primary uses of the iPhone. The apps stand alone and other functions are self-contained. The Internet connection is used at moments of breakdown for reference to online text. The online connection is also used before and after practice—both to retrieve information and post accounts of development and equipment construction and adaptation. Both participants use it to access expert knowledge delivered in didactic form. P1 makes reference to videos from YouTube which he watched and which informed the construction of his brewery and methods of brewing. These he watched on his mobile device when he had time: mobility and flexibility to access a demonstration lecture are key parts of his account. P2 referred to downloading and listening to podcasts by master brewers on particular styles on his commute to and from work. Both brewers post regular accounts of their broader practices using the Internet to post images of ingredients, equipment and processes and exchange text accounts of recipes and evaluations of processes and products such as tasting evaluations on Twitter and the brewing forum.

The iPhone's touch-screen interface leads to problems and resulting disruption and confusion for P1. Its account becomes authoritative despite a betrayal in translation as the app becomes a mediator rather than intermediary. Other problems with ingredients also became evident from the screenshots. However work and effort are expended trying to make the instructions from the BrewPal app fit the ingredients in hand and to maintain the immutability of the recipe. In contrast P2 acknowledged this issue and bypassed it by using a keyboard instead, then synced the data with the mobile device. However, making notes and recording actions and calculations primarily remain the prerogative of simpler assemblages of inscription devices: pencil-and-paper or pen-and-whiteboard.

Without the iPhone the calculations would be delegated to computer spreadsheet or software. If these were not available, then the worksheets and reference tables in books along with calculator or pencil-and-paper would support the processes of calculation. These would be *far* slower and more laborious making the rapid fluidity of P2's adaptation of the recipe a more complex process requiring movement away from the assemblage and arrangement of the other materials required for these calculations: the scales, pencil, paper and grains. Mobility of calculation device is important. In P1's brewery the possibility of simulation for recipe variations when time is available—on the bus to work was given as an example—would also be excluded by more fixed arrangements.

By contrast in the experienced brewery, the iPhone is used to support change and substitution. All the elements are configured to enable and support fluid changes, recipes become fluid as they enter the brewery and the brewery is configured to perform such fluid objects. The app supports and undertakes the complex procedure of calculating extract potentials and colour changes resulting from ingredient substitutions. P2's experience with the ingredients suggests likely minimal effects on flavour. These practices starkly contrast with the constraint and work to maintain immutability in the novice brewery. The concept of a fluid object provides a useful vocabulary to describe not only how the recipe here changes as it is transformed, its ingredients shift a little but its overall configuration remains recognisable, but also as a point of contrast to rigid immutable objects in a novice actor-network. Such a vocabulary also evokes metaphors used specifically to learning such as the rigidity of scaffolding for a novice compared to a fluidity of an accomplished master. However it also brings with it the sophisticated nuances of exploring interaction and agency of technologies which we suggest has a particular perspicacity for researching *networked* learning.

Extending Out: Some Implications

From this fieldwork we draw three implications relating to the three domains of concern: the design of mobile learning apps, theorising informal networked learning and the challenge ANT makes to the epistemology of networked learning.

Implications for Mobile Learning Application Design

As we have shown by drawing together the two accounts, the iPhone is central to practice and the assembly of a network of resources, tools, peers, devices and the accounts of practice in both breweries. A dedicated app or suite of apps are used to plan, support, record and create persistent records of situated practices. These apps are designed for this purpose and enable simulation (used extensively by P1 in varying materials in recipes to see outcomes). Echoing Fox's suggestions that observations like this of informal educational practices could "repay educational designers, just as clothes designers frequently benefit from the close observation of street fashion" (2011, p.78), we suggest that the development of mobile learning in formal education could draw useful inferences from our fieldwork which demonstrates the effectiveness of developing specific tools for supporting simulation, calculation and recording of situated practices (e.g. fieldwork, research data gathering).

Recording and sharing of situated observation, measurement and calculation has commonalities with many learning and teaching practices in further and higher education—especially in the many disciplines which use fieldwork and data gathering. We suggest that these observations of how such practices unfold in informal learning have productive application in the selection or development of apps to support mobile learning in formal education. Such a move would stand in contrast to the current vogue for the development of information-aggregation apps to disseminate and "push" official institutional information to students such as timetables and notifications rather than development of apps to support practice, and through that enabling situated learning.

Assembling and Differentiating Informal Networked Learning

In tracing practices in two home breweries, attending to participants' accounts and following the paths left by their practices, we see an informal learning network being constructed. Both access didactic content as podcasts or videos, choosing to access them when they can and when they are useful. Both also submit ideas and experiences as text and images and engage in discussion with peers in an online forum and via microblogging. Both also met with peers in person through a local home-brewing club. Additionally they submitted beers for informal peer assessment at these meetings subsequently posting accounts of the responses to forums, as well as more formal assessment by recognised experts (beer writers, brewing industry professionals and accredited judges) in competitions. These acts of seeking out expert assessment in informal learning contexts are explored further in Wright et al. (in press).

This assembled informal network has clear continuities and similarities with networked learning practices and structures in formal educational settings such as those surveyed in McConnell et al. (2012). Participants' informal learning practices include sharing resources, undertaking self-directed study and engaging in collaborative knowledge construction supported by expert direction and peer review.

If *informal* networked learning is assembled in such a similar way to *formal* networked learning, can, or should, we meaningfully differentiate the two? Marsick and Watkins (2001) claim that informal learning can be differentiated from formal learning by context, intention and how it is "triggered" by an internal or external stimulus. They further suggest that informal learning is marked by involvement in "an inductive process of reflection and action;" and importantly, that informal learning is "linked to the learning of others" (p. 28) which reflects findings from this study. However, other aspects of the model are more problematic: in particular, the suggestion that informal learning is somehow different by virtue of its being "integrated into daily activities", and "haphazard and influenced by chance", (p.28) while incidental learning is defined as a by-product of intentional activity that frequently occurs even though people are seldom aware of it (Marsick & Watkins, 1990).

As we have shown, drawing such *clear* distinctions between occurrences of formal and informal learning is problematic and posits that a more nuanced view wherein "attributes of formality and informality are interrelated in different ways in different situations" (Colley et al., 2002, p. 9) is more appropriate. Recognising such heterogeneity and situational specificity seems a more productive way of differentiating these areas of learning rather than attempting to differentiate the learning processes themselves. Furthermore, and also in contrast with Marsick and Watkin's (2001) claim that informal learning "generally takes place without much external facilitation or structure (p. 30), our participants activity sought out didactic learning experiences and incorporated these externally structured experiences into their learning processes. Participants' purposeful inclusions of instances of learning as knowledge acquisition within their broader range of self-directed, empirical, experimental and peer-to-peer learning choices provide evidence of contextualised attributes of formality and informality.

Through considering situated mobile app use in practice as an example of mobile-supported situated practice and noting some of the developments participants made to their equipment configurations in response to differences between app predictions and outcomes of practice, which in turn influenced calculation and assessment activities, we identify distributed learning occurrences. Whereas the agency of the iPhone in providing flexible access to apps is valued in both breweries, P1 and P2 enrol supplemental technologies to avoid iPhone interface problems during the brewing process. Where BrewPal, BrewTimer and BeerAlchemy apps each play specialised roles in supporting brewery effectiveness, their effectiveness as translators and mediators is negotiated both within brewing practices and via participants' engagements with peer learners in Internet forums. Thus mobile technologies in relation to evolving practices are at once active subjects in mediating learning processes and objects of reconfiguration. It is to these reconfigurations of assembled socio-material networks we now turn.

Speaking Back to Theory: Extending NL with ANT

In setting out an ontology and epistemology of networked learning, Hodgson, McConnell, and Dirckinck-Holmfeld (2012) argue that networked learning theory "attempts to transcend the dualism between abstract mind and concrete material social practice"; however, the role of technology is reduced to mediating "connections within and between a learning community and its different actors" (p. 293). Mediation in this construction appears closer to what ANT considers an *intermediary* devoid of agency or merely a transporter of meaning rather than a conceptualisation of mediation as active agency within a process of translation. We argue that it is this sophisticated vocabulary and set of understandings specifically developed to analyse complex networks of humans and technologies and how they are assembled that ANT brings to researching networked learning. It addresses many of the concerns of the epistemology of networked learning Hodgson et al. (2012) set out—in particular resisting technological determinism and seeking to transcend dualisms. By adopting ANT's view of mediation as agency, rather than reducing it to a vehicle for the transportation of an agency that is "a fundamentally human characteristic" (Hodgson et al., p. 302), we gain a more nuanced view of how the agencies of technologies can disrupt or support, interfere or make durable processes such as learning.

This is the argument that Latour (1991) makes in proposing that "technology is society made durable" wherein ostensibly interpersonal actions are delegated to technologies which both reinforce and substitute for them. He gives the example of signs asking hotel guests not to take keys away and how these are reinforced by the simple technology of attaching a weighty fob, persuading guests not to carry heavy keys but instead to check them in at reception. By following this line of argument and its extension to networked learning through Fox's (2001) suggestion that we abandon a singular focus on the individual learner, we become free to explore the practical outcomes of adopting a symmetrical praxiographic approach to fieldwork. Rather than beginning with a priori categories such as "a community" or "an institution", we become free to trace heterogeneous associations and to look at the ways translation and mediation work to enrol and distribute agency and change. We can then consider learning as it is occurring and how it is reconfiguring *all* of a socio-material network rather than restricting ourselves to just considering or evaluating changes only in its human elements.

References

Callon, M. (1986). Some elements of a sociology of translation: Domestication of the scallops and the fishermen of St Brieuc Bay. In J. Law (Ed.), *Power, action and belief: a new sociology of knowledge?* (pp. 196–223). London, England: Routledge.

Callon, M. (1998). Actor-network theory—The market test. *Sociological Review, 46*, 181–195. doi:10.1111/1467-954X.46.s.10.

Colley, H., Hodkinson, R., & Malcolm, J. (2002). *Non-formal learning: Mapping the conceptual terrain.* A consultation report to the Learning Skills Development Agency. Retrieved 19 April, 2013, from the in-formal education archives: http://www.infed.org/archives/e-texts/colley_informal_learning.htm

de Laet, M., & Mol, A. (2000). The Zimbabwe bush pump: Mechanics of a fluid technology. *Soc Stud Sci, 30*, 225–263. doi:10.1177/030631200030002002.

Fenwick, T., & Edwards, R. (2010). *Actor-network theory in education.* London, England: Routledge.

Fox, S. (2001). Studying networked learning: Some implications from socially situated learning theory and actor-network theory. In C. Steeples & C. Jones (Eds.), *Networked learning: Perspectives and issues* (pp. 77–92). London, England: Springer.

Frohberg, D. (2006, September 11–14). *Mobile learning is coming of age—What we have and what we still miss.* Paper presented at the the 4th DELFI Conference, Darmstadt, Germany.

Goodyear, P., Banks, S., Hodgson, V., & McConnell, D. (Eds.). (2004). *Advances in research on networked learning.* Boston, MA: Kluwer.

Hodgson, V., McConnell, D., & Dirckinck-Holmfeld, L. (2012). The theory, pedagogy and practice of networked learning. In L. Dirckinck-Holmfeld, V. Hodgson, & D. McConnell (Eds.), *Exploring the theory, pedagogy and practice of networked learning* (pp. 291–305). New York: Springer.

Humphreys, L. (2006). Photos and fieldwork: Capturing norms for mobile phone use in the US. In J. R. Höflich & M. Hartmann (Eds.), *Mobile communication in everyday life: ethnographic views, observations and reflections* (pp. 55–78). Berlin: Frank & Timme GmbH.

Knoblauch, H. (2005). Focused ethnography. *Forum: Qualitative Social Research, 6*, 44.

Latour, B. (1987). *Science in action: How to follow scientists and engineers through society.* Harvard, MA: Harvard University Press.

Latour, B. (1991). Technology is society made durable. In J. Law (Ed.), *A sociology of monsters: Essays on power, technology, and domination* (pp. 103–131). London, England: Routledge.

Latour, B. (2005). *Reassembling the social: An introduction to actor-network theory.* Oxford, England: Oxford University Press.

Law, J. (2003). *Traduction/Trahison: Notes on ANT.* Lancaster. Retrieved from http://www.lancs.ac.uk/fass/sociology/papers/law-traduction-trahison.pdf

Law, J. (2009). Actor network theory and material semiotics. In B. S. Turner (Ed.), *The new Blackwell companion to social theory* (pp. 141–158). Chichester, England: Wiley-Blackwell.

Marcus, G. E. (1998). *Ethnography through thick and thin.* Princeton, NJ: Princeton University Press.

Marsick, V. J., & Watkins, K. E. (1990). *Informal and incidental learning in the workplace.* London, England: Routledge.

Marsick, V. J., & Watkins, K. E. (2001). Informal and incidental learning. *New Directions for Adult and Continuing Education, 2001*(89), 25–34. doi:10.1002/ace.5.

McConnell, D., Hodgson, V., & Dirckinck-Holmfeld, L. (2012). Networked learning: A brief history and new trends. In L. Dirckinck-Holmfeld, V. Hodgson, & D. McConnell (Eds.), *Exploring the theory, pedagogy and practice of networked learning* (pp. 3–24). New York: Springer.

Mol, A. (2003). *The body multiple: ontology in medical practice.* Durham, NC: Duke University Press.

Thompson, T. L. (2012). I'm deleting as fast as I can: Negotiating learning practices in cyberspace. *Pedagogy, Culture & Society, 20*(1), 93–112. doi:10.1080/14681366.2012.649417.

Tinseth, G. (1995). Glenn's hop utilization numbers. Retrieved 19 April, 2013, from http://realbeer.com/hops/research.html

Tusting, K. (2003). A review of theories of informal learning. *Working Paper No. 2*, from http://www.nrdc.org.uk/uploads/documents/doc_636.pdf

Wright, S., & Parchoma, G. (2011). Technologies for learning? An actor-network theory critique of 'affordances' in research on mobile learning. *Research in Learning Technology, 19*(3), 247–258. doi:10.1080/21567069.2011.624168.

Wright, S., Short, B., & Parchoma, G. (2013). Supporting creativity in craft brewing—A case study of iPhone use in the transition from novice towards mastery. *International Journal of Mobile and Blended Learning, 5*(3), 52–67.

Editor Bios

Vivien Hodgson is Professor of Networked Management Learning in the Department of Management Learning and Leadership at Lancaster University Management School, UK and visiting Chair at E-Learning Lab, Aalborg University, Denmark. Vivien has coordinated and participated in many 'e-learning' research projects in both Europe and Latin America. She has written extensively in international journals on open and collaborative approaches to learning and the importance of dialogue and critical reflection in the design and process of networked learning.

She is the co-editor of the new Springer book series on networked learning and recently stood down as one of the founding co-chairs of the international biannual conference series 'Networked Learning'. She is on the editorial board of several journals and on the Steering Committee of SoLAR (Society for Learning Analytics Research). From 1995 and 1998 she was seconded to the Socrates programme of the European Commission in Brussels where she was responsible for the Open and Distance Learning (Minerva) Action.

Maarten de Laat is full Professor at the Open Universiteit of the Netherlands. He is director of the Social and Networked Learning research programme, which concentrates on exploring social learning strategies and networked learning relationships that facilitate professional development in the workplace. His research is focused on informal learning in the workplace, lifelong learning, professional development and knowledge creation through (online) social networks and communities and the impact technology, learning analytics and social design has on the way these networks and communities work, learn and create value. He has published and presented his work extensively in research journals, books and conferences. He is co-chair of the international Networked Learning Conference as well as co-chair of the Minitrack Social Media & Learning at the HICSS conference. Maarten is also a member of the steering committee of SoLAR.

David McConnell is a researcher and practitioner in networked learning. He has written extensively on teaching, learning and assessment in higher education and has published over 80 papers in refereed journals and co-authored several books.

V. Hodgson et al. (eds.), *The Design, Experience and Practice of Networked Learning*,
Research in Networked Learning, DOI 10.1007/978-3-319-01940-6,
© Springer International Publishing Switzerland 2014

His monographs *Implementing Computer Supported Cooperative Learning* (Kogan Page, 2nd edition, 2000), and *E-Learning Groups and Communities* (Maidenhead, SRHE/OU Press, 2006) received enthusiastic acclaim. David has participated in a wide variety of internationally funded research projects concerned with e-community developments, intercultural Sino-UK pedagogy and networked collaborative learning. He was the founder and co-chair of the Networked Learning Conference series and is the co-editor of the Springer Book Series on Researching Networked Learning. He was the founder and Director of the Doctoral Programme in E-Research and Technology Enhanced Learning, Lancaster University (worldwide delivery via the Internet), and has held chairs in Higher Education at the Universities of Sheffield, Open University (UK), Lancaster, Glasgow Caledonian.

Thomas Ryberg is Professor mso in the Department of Communication and Psychology at Aalborg University (AAU), Denmark. He is part of the research centre: 'e-Learning Lab—Center for User Driven Innovation, Learning and Design' (www.ell.aau.dk). His primary research interests are within the fields of Networked Learning, Problem-Based Learning (PBL), Computer-Supported Collaborative Learning (CSCL) and Technology-Enhanced Learning (TEL). He is co-chair of the International Networked Learning Conference and member of the Aalborg PBL Academy Management Board. He has participated in European and international research projects and networks (EQUEL, Kaledioscope, COMBLE, PlaceMe, EATrain2), and in development projects in South East Asia and Latin America (VISCA, VO@NET, ELAC). In particular, he is interested in Problem-Based Learning, and how new media and technologies transform our ways of thinking about and designing for Networked and Hybrid Learning.

Author Bios

Nina Bonderup Dohn is an associate professor in Humanistic Information Science at the Department of Design and Communication, University of Southern Denmark. She holds an M.A. in philosophy and physics and a Ph.D. in learning theory. She was a Visiting Scholar for 7 months at the Department of Philosophy, University of California, Berkeley, in 2000–2001 and again in 2009–2010. In 2013 she is a Visiting Scholar for 6 months at the Centre for Research on Computer Supported Learning and Cognition, University of Sydney. Her main research areas integrate epistemology, learning sciences, web communication and technology-mediated learning. She has published extensively in Danish and English on philosophical and pedagogical issues within knowledge theory, web 2.0, ICT-mediated learning, and teaching and learning in higher education. Nina's webpage is found here: http://www.sdu.dk/staff/nina

Mariëtte de Haan's research focuses on diversity and learning. She has studied learning in a Native American community, in multi-ethnic classrooms, in migrant (parent) communities, and currently studies the informal learning of immigrant teens online. A recurring theme in her research is how education and learning are shaped by the conditions of the socio-cultural communities they are part of, such as those associated with the knowledge society or with globalization and migration dynamics.

You will find her other publications here http://www.uu.nl/staff/mdehaan

Janne Gleerup is a researcher at the Institute of Psychology and Educational Studies, Roskilde University. Her current field of research and teaching activities focus on Work Life Studies oriented especially towards the conditions of adult learning. In various Research Projects she explores the potentials and barriers concerning the production and introduction of new digital designs for learning and work organization at the workplace level. She is currently participating in the creation of a new Research Center of Action Research, located at Roskilde University, among other things focusing on development of new methods of participatory research.

V. Hodgson et al. (eds.), *The Design, Experience and Practice of Networked Learning*,
Research in Networked Learning, DOI 10.1007/978-3-319-01940-6,

John Hannon is a lecturer in academic development at La Trobe University who specializes in the integration of learning technologies into higher education curriculum. His research and curriculum work focus on transitions in teaching and learning practice and academic work that are associated with the use of digital technologies in higher education. He received a Ph.D. from La Trobe University that investigated the transformative effects of emerging technologies on sociality and higher education learning. He publishes about practices with educational technologies, academic development, professional practice and intercultural communication, and has received two awards for his publications.

Simon Heilesen is an associate professor of net-based communication at Roskilde University, Denmark. His teaching and research focus partly on designing for net-based communication and learning, and partly on stimulating digital literacy in various social and professional groups. He initiated the Academic-IT initiative at Roskilde University, which advocates the use of new media in research, professional communication and teaching. He is an editor of the periodical Læring og Medier (Learning and Media), and a member of various national and international associations for e-learning and e-science.

You will find other publications and more details on Simon at: http://forskning. ruc.dk/site/person/simonhei

Niels Henrik Helms is an associate professor and head of innovation at University College Zealand. He has a longstanding track record of research and development work in ICT innovation and learning. His main focus is on the relationship between media, learning and innovation.

Research Areas: Relationship between technology, knowledge and learning; Sociology of artefacts; UX for citizens with special needs, Relations between learning and creativity, Processes in innovation—technology, organization and competence.

You will find publications and more details at: https://www.ucviden.dk/portal/en/ persons/niels-henrik-helms%28a23d1301-4a7a-4155-8e2f-6b0f000f9ceb%29.html

Dr. Núria Hernández Nanclares is Associate Professor at the Applied Economics Department of University of Oviedo (Spain). She specializes in innovative teaching for Higher Education and Economics, both fields in which she focuses her research currently. The main working areas are forms of assessment and alternative assessment methods, active methodologies in Higher Education and Social and learning Networks.

Currently, she is involved in bilingual teaching in Economics with a CLIL approach. Her main area of expertise is International Economics and most of her teaching is related to this area.

Dr. Brian Holmes recently obtained his Ph.D. in e-Research & Technology-Enhanced Learning from Lancaster University. His thesis examines the influence of online learning communities on teachers' professional development under the EU's eTwinning initiative, as discussed in the chapter. Dr. Holmes is Interim Director of the European Commission's Executive Agency for Education, Audiovisual and Culture (EACEA) in Brussels which, inter alia, supports European co-operation projects in education and training. He is a chartered software engineer and holds an MBA from the Paris business school ESCP Europe. For further information on EACEA, see http://eacea.ec.europa.eu

Juliette Hommes, M.D. and Ph.D. student focused on effective collaboration in medical education. Main interests are: social networks, group processes, problem-based learning and cohort studies.

Kevin Leander's work focuses on literacy and math learning 'on the move'. His work tries to (1) provide clearer understandings of how people assemble learning pathways and trajectories and (2) as not only learners are in constant movement across settings, but also media of different sorts (school texts, digital images, film), accompanying discourses, and literacy practices. His research tries to answer how we can understand the geographies of various forms of media and how learners on the move use them to construct space, place, culture, society and identity.

Kevin Mogensen is a researcher, Post.Doc., Ph.D., M.A. in Educational Studies, at Roskilde University. His current field of research is especially oriented towards the studies of young people's gendered educational practices, and the processes that make certain gender practices problematic among peers as well in relation to the teachers in vocational college and high school. In various Research Projects he explores the local educational practices of 'schooling', young people's resistance and young men and women's experiences of risk and vulnerability.

Gale Parchoma is an associate professor in the Faculty of Education at the University of Calgary, Canada. From 2007 to 2012 she contributed to the development of and was a lecturer in the e-Research and Technology-Enhanced Learning doctoral programme at Lancaster University in the UK. Her academic interests focus on the relationships among technologies and pedagogies in formal and informal learning environments. Gale has published a book on e-learning in higher education, as well as journal articles and book chapters on digital identity, technological affordances, teaching and technology philosophies-in-practice, leadership roles in learning design teams, human–computer interaction and e-learning policies in higher education. She was the lead investigator for a UK Research Council and Technology Strategy Board funded project on simulation-based medical education. Gale has been an invited speaker at workshops and conferences in the UK, Germany, and Singapore.

Linda Perriton was a practising HRD consultant before studying for an M.A. in Management Learning and Ph.D. at Lancaster University, and joining the University of York as a lecturer in HRD in 2000. Her main area of teaching and research interest is in learning and development, specifically critical approaches to reflective practice, workplace development interventions and management education. Linda's previous published work has dealt with issues of the historicity of management development practices, including a series of papers focusing on management development for British women managers in the twentieth century.

Michael Reynolds is Emeritus Professor of Management Learning at Lancaster University Management School. His main research interests encompass the design and application of experiential learning, with a particular focus on the differences between tutor intentions and the student experience. Michael has written widely on general groupwork issues but is perhaps best known for his work that highlights issues of control in self-directed learning designs, and the application of group dynamics and social theory to educational design.

Dr. Bart Rienties is senior lecturer at the Department of Higher Education at University of Surrey. As educational psychologist, he conducts multidisciplinary research on work-based and collaborative learning environments and focuses on the role of social interaction in learning. His primary research interests are focused on computer-supported collaborative learning, the role of motivation in learning, and the role of the teacher to design effective blended and online learning courses. More information at www.bartrienties.nl

Bieke Schreurs is a researcher at the Open University of the Netherlands since April 2010. She is involved in research projects to support primary and secondary schools to stimulate the professional development of teachers through workplace learning and networked learning activities. She does research on implementing measures to streamline (ICT) innovations in schools. In 2012 she started her Ph.D. 'The Capital of Networked Learning' to investigate how professionals build up learning ties to support their continuous professional development in the workplace. She received the M.A. degree in Communication Science at the K. U. Leuven in Belgium in 2003.

You will find more details and other publications on http://www.ou.nl/web/bss

Dr. Uzair Shah is a Lecturer in the Department of Management Learning & Leadership at Lancaster University Management School, UK. His higher education qualifications are from universities in Malaysia and the UK. He has also taught at undergraduate and postgraduate levels in British and Pakistani universities. His recent research project explored teachers' use of learning technology in pedagogical practices. He has an interest in cultural and contextual dimensions of learning. Uzair is particularly interested in exploring the pluralistic nature of professional practice. His research interests also include looking at how context influences and affects professional practice, and the opportunities it presents for professional learning and development.

Dr. Julie-Ann Sime researches into the design of technology-enhanced learning environments, and is particularly interested in the development of competence in professional learning. She has been involved in European collaborative research for over 20 years, working with partners to investigate complex training situations involving 3D environments, games and simulations. She is interested in how educational theory is put into practice, and how designers and educators can be supported in their use of new technologies. Dr. Sime is Director (Part 2) of a Doctoral Programme in e-Research & Technology-Enhanced Learning, Educational Research Department, Lancaster University, where around 100 students are researching into technology-enhanced learning in professional contexts. For further information, see http://www.lancs.ac.uk/fass/edres/profiles/Julie-Ann-Sime/

Asli Ünlüsoy is a Ph.D. candidate working in the 'Wired Up' project at the Utrecht University. She studies personal networks of immigrant youth in the Netherlands; specifically, how (informal) learning experiences take place in these networks and how social media and emerging mobile technologies mediate these experiences. She applies network analytical methods and both qualitative and quantitative approaches for her research. She has published on out-of-school learning practices and new literacies. She received two master's degrees on development and social-ization in childhood and adolescence (Utrecht University) and on early childhood education (Middle East Technical University).

Koen Veermans obtained his Ph.D. at the Instructional Technology at the University of Twente in the Netherlands. Currently he is working as a researcher at the Centre for Learning Research and the Department of Teacher Education at the University of Turku in Finland, where he is heading a project that investigates the effects of combining virtual and real laboratories in general education. Besides that he has an interest in applications of social network analysis in all levels of education.

Dr Richard Walker is VLE Service Group Leader and E-Learning Development Team Manager at the University of York. Richard moved to York in 2003 to oversee the implementation of the University's virtual learning environment. Previously, he held research and teaching posts at Nyenrode Business University (the Netherlands) and at the Euro-Arab Management School in Granada, Spain. He has published on instructional design frameworks for blended learning in a variety of journals, as well as approaches to the institutional adoption of learning technologies.

You will find his other publications and more details at https://richardmarkwalker.wikispaces.com/

Hanne Westh Nicolajsen holds a position as associate professor at the Department of Communication, Aalborg University in Copenhagen, Denmark. Her main research interest is organizational use of ICT focusing on the use of ICT in support of changed organizational practices with regard to innovation, knowledge manage-ment and learning. In the later years her focus has been divided between two areas. One area is user and employee-driven innovation with focus on idea competitions and crowdsourcing within knowledge-intensive organizations. Another stream of research—mainly driven by empirical experiments—is strengthening of PBL (problem-based learning) and social learning processes within higher education, in particular the use of ICT for Networked Learning.

Her research has been published in several international journals among which Journal of Business and Industrial Marketing, Library Management, International Journal of E-Services and Mobile Applications, Scandinavian Journal of Informa-tion Systems, IEEE Vehicular Technology Magazine, Telematics and Informatics as well as book chapters and international conferences.

You can find out about other publications and more details on http://www.latrobe.edu.au/ctlc/contacts/staff-profile

Steve Wright is a Learning Technologist in the Faculty of Health and Medicine and Ph.D. candidate in Educational Research at Lancaster University, UK. His research interests are around informal learning, mobile learning, sensory assessment and draw in particular on science and technology studies. He has published on mobile learning research and informal mobile learning and creativity. His Ph.D. research is focused on how tasting is learned, assessed and practiced. As a learning technology practitioner, he supports students and staff in developing networked learning courses. He has developed open educational resources for student and staff induction to networked learning which are made available under creative commons licenses from http://openlearning.lancs.ac.uk

Author Index

V. Hodgson et al. (eds.), *The Design, Experience and Practice of Networked Learning*,
Research in Networked Learning, DOI 10.1007/978-3-319-01940-6,
© Springer International Publishing Switzerland 2014

Subject Index

V. Hodgson et al. (eds.), *The Design, Experience and Practice of Networked Learning*, 279
Research in Networked Learning, DOI 10.1007/978-3-319-01940-6,
© Springer International Publishing Switzerland 2014